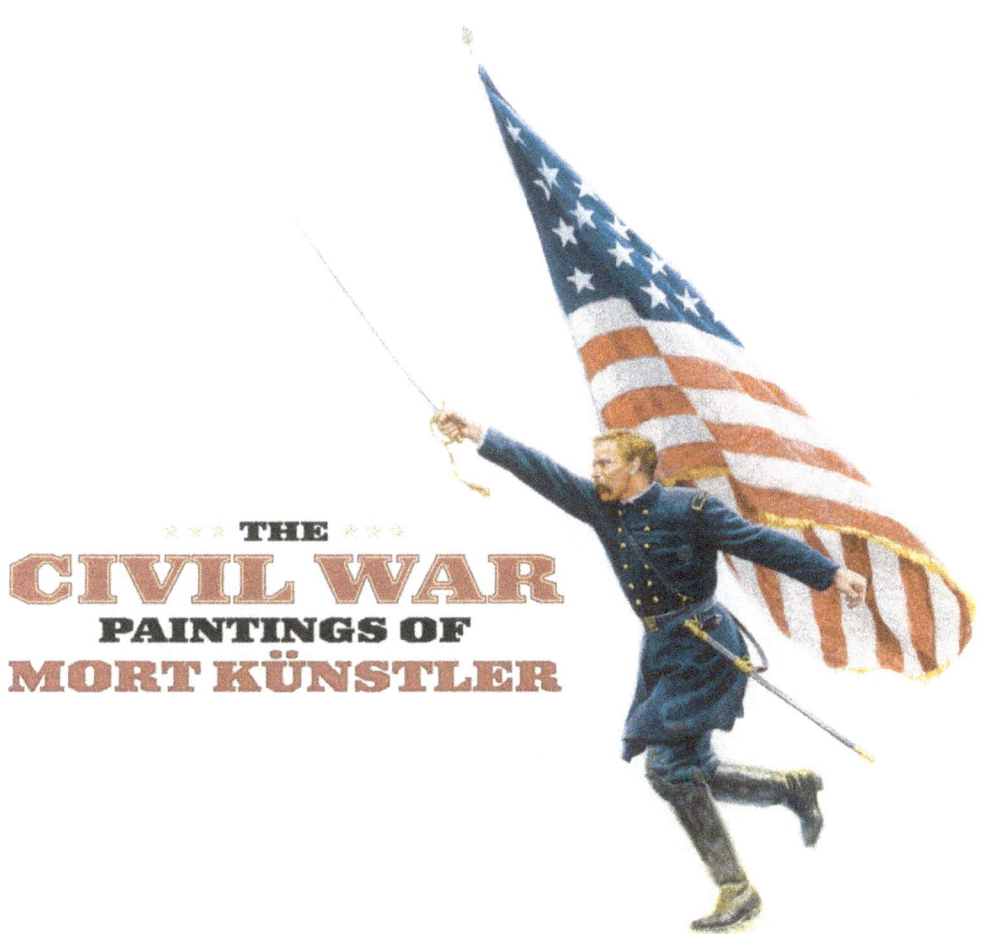

THE CIVIL WAR
PAINTINGS OF
MORT KÜNSTLER

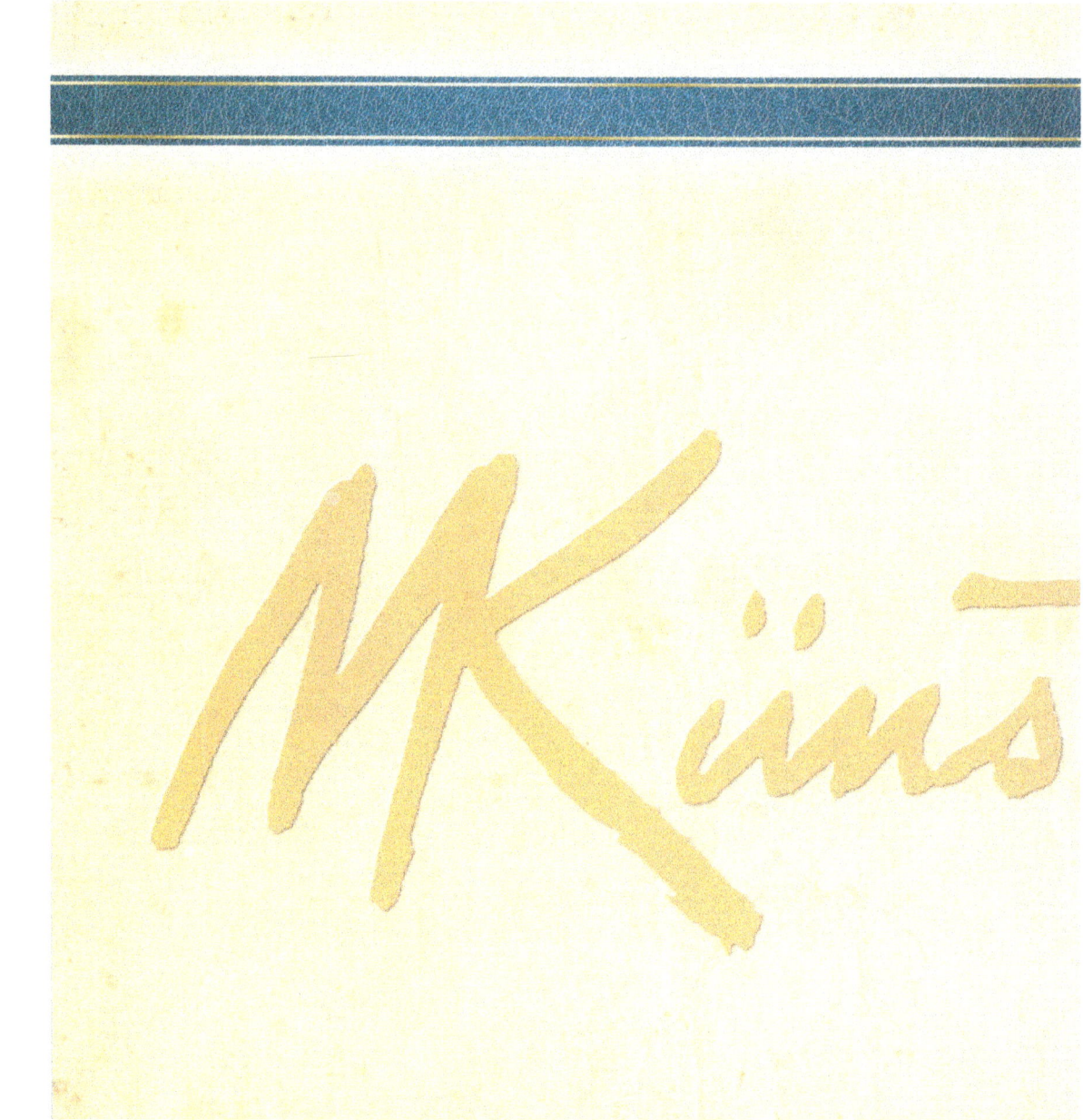

★★★★ THE ★★★ CIVIL WAR PAINTINGS OF MORT KÜNSTLER

CUMBERLAND HOUSE
NASHVILLE, TENNESSEE

The Civil War Paintings of Mort Künstler
Volume 3: The Gettysburg Campaign
Published by Cumberland House Publishing, Inc.
431 Harding Industrial Drive
Nashville, Tennessee 37211

Text based on the writings of Rod Gragg, Mort Künstler, James M. McPherson, and James I. Robertson Jr. All art dimensions are presented height x width in inches.

Cover design by Gore Studio, Inc., Nashville, Tennessee

Library of Congress Cataloging-in-Publication Data

Künstler, Mort.
  The Civil War paintings of Mort Künstler / Mort Künstler.
      v.   cm.
    Contents: v. 3. The Gettysburg campaign.
    ISBN-13: 978-1-58182-557-2 ; ISBN-10: 1-58182-557-9 **ISBN-13: 978-1-68442-842-7 (hc)**
    1. United States—History—Civil War, 1861–1865—Pictorial works—Catalogs. 2. United States—History—Civil War, 1861–1865—Art and the war—Catalogs. 3. Künstler, Mort—Catalogs. I. Title.
  E468.7.K844 2006
  759.13—dc22   2006015631

Especially for my dear sister, Rhoda

CONTENTS

FOREWORD

It is simply beyond questioning that no three days in American history have been as much studied as the first seventy-two hours of July 1863, when two massive armies—both composed of Americans—gave each other their undivided attention at Gettysburg, Pennsylvania. Neither army commander wanted to fight there. Gen. George G. Meade, commanding the Union's Army of the Potomac, had spotted better ground some miles to the south, where he hoped to be able to meet and defeat his foe. Robert E. Lee, leading his seemingly invincible Army of Northern Virginia, would have been happy to fight no battle at all. He did not leave Virginia and cross the Potomac River into the North to come as a conqueror. There was never any question of him winning territory to keep. He was on a grand raid to resupply his army from the fields of Maryland and Pennsylvania, keep Meade north of the Potomac, give Virginia a breather, and possibly to impress Northern civilians and foreign governments that the Union was vulnerable, could not win, and that it was time to make a peace.

Neither general got what he wanted, and the three-day battle that followed after their unanticipated encounter at Gettysburg all but crippled both armies for the rest of the year. Indeed, the losses would be such that

Lee's officer corps and command system would never be the same for the rest of the war, while Meade saw one of his army corps all but disappear. It started, as battles do, by accident rather than design. In south-central Pennsylvania, all roads converged at Gettysburg. On July 1, those roads turned into magnetic field forces. Skirmishing escalated to engagement, and the gravity of war quickly sucked more and more men from both armies toward the crossroads like a black hole. By the end of the day, the Confederates had possession of the town and drove the Yankees back to nearby Cemetery Hill and other elevations on the outskirts.

If Lee expected an easy victory, however, he found on the dawn of July 2 that Meade had rushed in sufficient force to bolster his dispirited advance forces, and throughout the rest of the day, more and more Federals would arrive, finally extending Meade's line almost three miles in a fishhook atop high ground south and east of town. Lee lined up his army along Seminary Ridge, facing the foe, and then launched ferocious assaults on Meade's right on Culp's and Cemetery Hills, and on his left on Little Round Top. Both ends of the Northern line held in spite of brutal fighting and more than one close call.

The result was July 3 and all that was left to Lee: an assault on the Union center. It came in the afternoon, after a thundering artillery bombardment, when nearly fifteen thousand Confederates advanced across three-quarters of a mile of fields and gullies and up the slopes of Cemetery Ridge. Half of them never returned. "Pickett's Charge," "Longstreet's Assault"—it came to have many names—ended on the bayonets of Meade's line, and with it died any hope of a Confederate victory on Northern soil. Lee's raid was at an end. It may have bought Virginia a season of respite from Yankee threats, but at the price of a third of Lee's men in casualties, while Meade paid a similar price and would not be back to strength until the next spring. The far-reaching impact of Gettysburg on the war—and whether or not it had any serious impact at all—is still being assessed more than a century later.

Mort Künstler's vast portfolio on Gettysburg covers the nascent beginnings of the battle in the shadow of the Lutheran seminary on the town's western fields, to the rain-rutted roads over which Lee's army dragged itself out of Pennsylvania, to a president's immortal words. Künstler has no less than sixteen paintings on the afternoon charge of July 3, depicting in detail the preparations for the greatest field artillery bombardment of the war and conveying the soul ache of the tattered and tortured survivors who stumbled back to Seminary Ridge from places whose simple names beguile the human cost paid at the Angle and under the shaded canopy of the Copse of Trees. Pondering these paintings offers precious insight into the Southern mind-set that William Faulkner later articulated with these words: "For every Southern boy fourteen years old, not once but whenever he wants it, there is the instant when it's still not yet two o'clock on that July afternoon in 1863."

Gettysburg has inspired Künstler to create breathtaking portals for our mystical connection with the soldiers who fought on this historic ground. He has walked the ground, studied the farms and fields, pored over period photographs, reviewed battle reports, and researched weather conditions for each painting with the care and commitment of a historian. We are the beneficiaries of these "lectures," which he has laid out carefully with his sketch pad and brush. He has placed all these elements on his palette and translated unimaginable events and incredible personalities to us through his marvelous canvases. His use of color, light, and shadow dramatically showcase Lee and Longstreet, Buford and Chamberlain, Pickett and Armistead, Hancock and Dilger in ways that underscore why Künstler is the premier artist of the Civil War.

William C. Davis

✦✦✦ THE ✦✦✦
CIVIL WAR
PAINTINGS OF
MORT KÜNSTLER

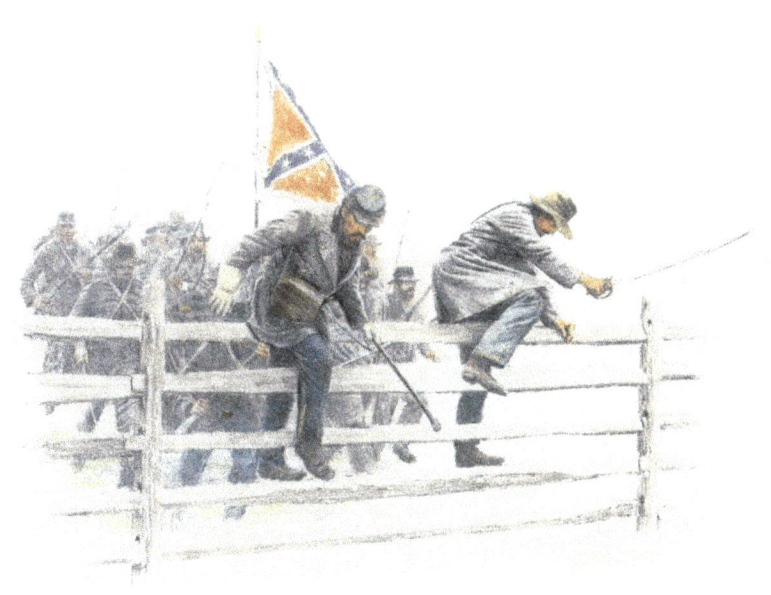

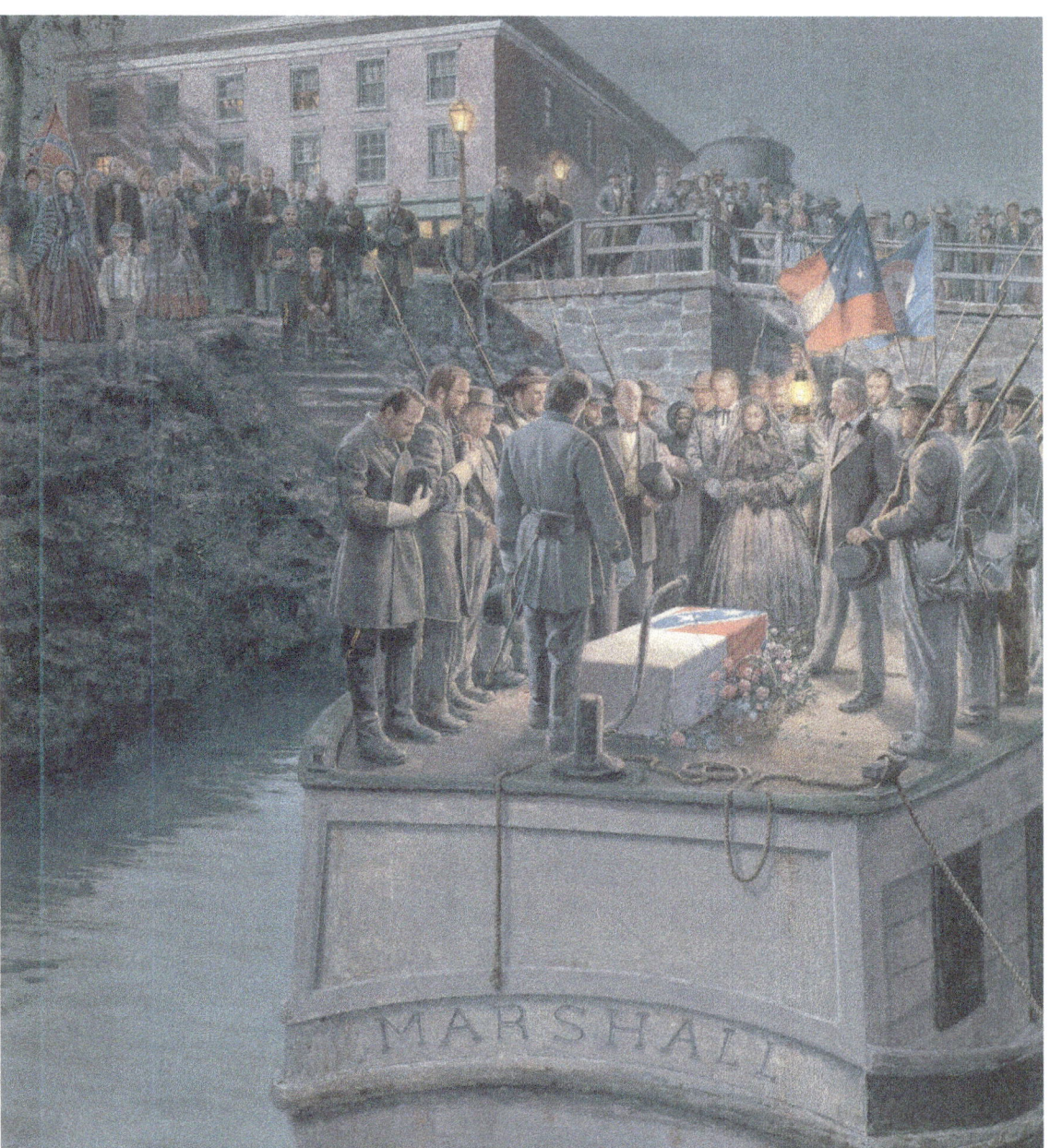

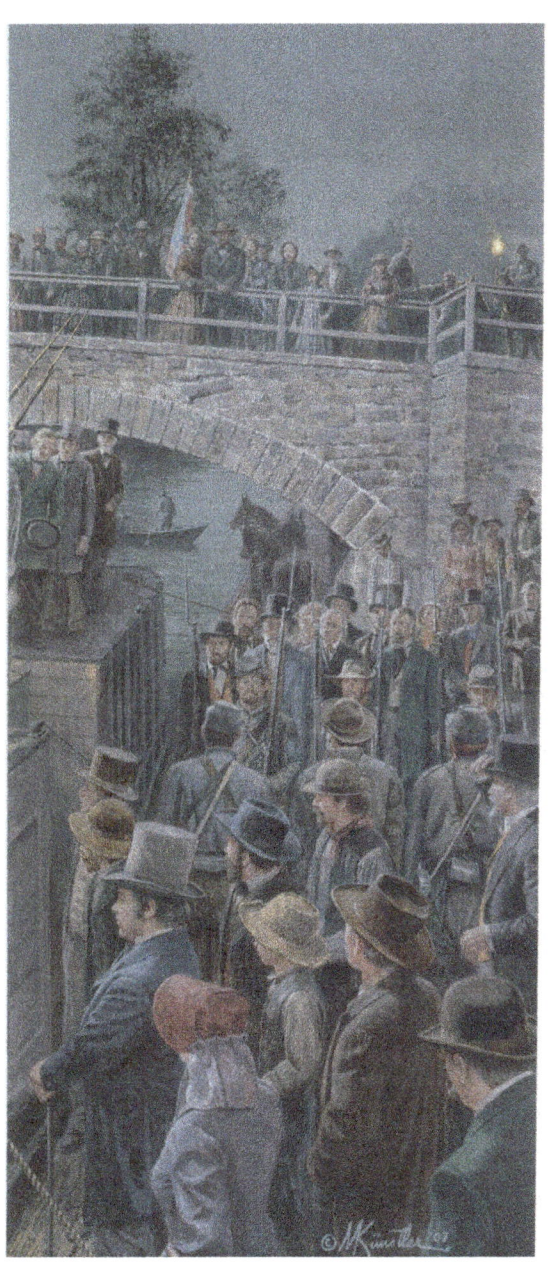

GOING HOME

STONEWALL JACKSON PROCESSION
LYNCHBURG, VA.
MAY 13, 1863

2007, oil, 32 x 42

AS THE ARMY OF Northern Virginia prepared for the invasion of Maryland and Pennsylvania, an absence cast a pall over the ranks. Missing was Thomas J. "Stonewall" Jackson. His final fight had ended a few weeks before on May 10, 1863. Robert E. Lee's irreplaceable "right arm" had been seriously wounded at the battle of Chancellorsville, but he died of pneumonia days after the battle had been won. After lying in state at the Virginia governor's mansion and the Capitol and following a private memorial service in Richmond, Jackson's body was transported back home to

15

Lexington, Virginia, for burial. The initial part of the journey was by train, first to Gordonsville and then to Lynchburg, where it arrived at 6:30 p.m. on May 13. There a memorial service was held at the First Presbyterian Church. Early on May 14, the body and funeral party proceeded through the city in a solemn procession, escorted by thousands of mourners. At the Kanawha Canal, the cortege was transferred to the canal boat *Marshall*. A familiar craft on the canal, the *Marshall* had the task of taking Jackson up the James River on the final leg of his journey home.

For a long and memorable while, the *Marshall* waited at its mooring below Lynchburg's Ninth Street Bridge, with Jackson's flag-draped casket aboard and surrounded by a group of mourners. Finally, the craft's lines were cast off, and the boat headed up the canal, while a huge crowd—including about fifteen hundred recovering Confederate soldiers from the city's hospitals—lined the bridge to pay their respects to the fallen leader. Like all canal vessels, the boat was towed upriver by a team of mules, advancing toward its destination no faster than three miles an hour.

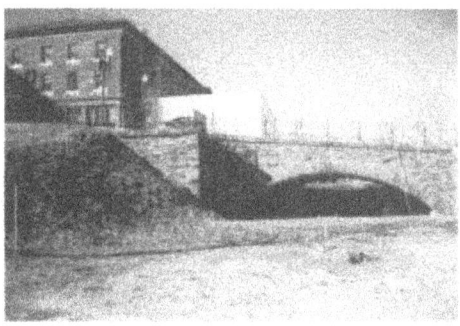

Lynchburg's Ninth Street Bridge today

As far as I could determine, Jackson's final journey home had never been portrayed on canvas before. Thus, one reason this painting is so meaningful to me is that it reconstructs a remarkable but little-known event. I was also attracted by

16

the artistic elements of this scene. We have a very extraordinary procession to honor a great fallen leader, and it's conducted with typical nineteenth-century American protocol and ceremony. This scene also includes a picturesque bridge that's still standing today—and is probably an unappreciated landmark even to many Lynchburg residents. Add to all this the canal boat *Marshall*—

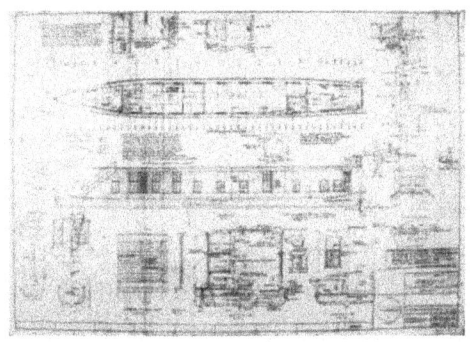

Blueprints of the canal boat *Marshall*

whose features are very well documented—and you have all the elements for a memorable painting.

Even the time of day made for good art. The procession set out up the canal at about ten o'clock that evening, and the scene was illuminated by lanterns and torches. To an artist, those facts suggest a historical scene with a wonderful blending

17

of light—the cool, soft moonlight and the warm, glowing light of lanterns. It was an artist's dream setting. So was all the wonderful cooperation I received from public officials, friendly citizens, and local historians in the Lynchburg area. Jerry Shores of The Framery and Arts in Lynchburg introduced me to Sally Ann Schneider, executive director of the Lynchburg Historical Foundation. Professor James I. Robertson Jr., the foremost authority on Stonewall Jackson, escorted me on a research trip to the city. There we were assisted by an outstanding group of citizens—Mayor Joan Foster, Dennis Beeton of Dixie Outfitters, Nancy Marion of The Design Group, Col. Keith Gibson of the Virginia Military Institute Museum in Lexington, and O. L. Raines, who is the builder of an authentically constructed model of the canal boat *Marshall*. While in Lynchburg, I examined the *Marshall*'s preserved iron hull and

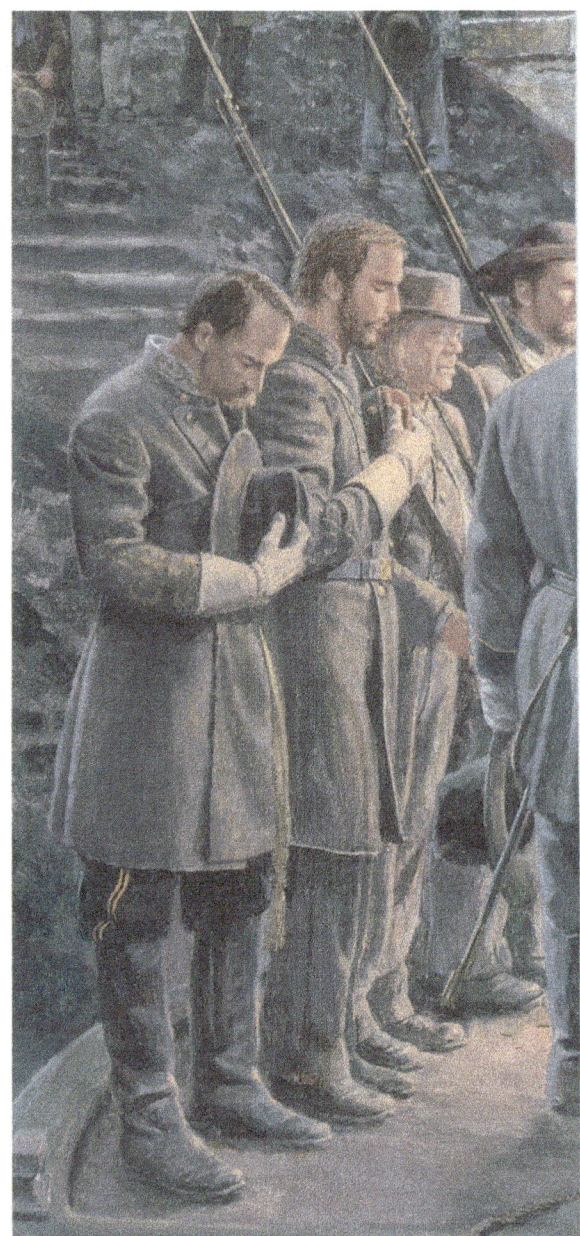

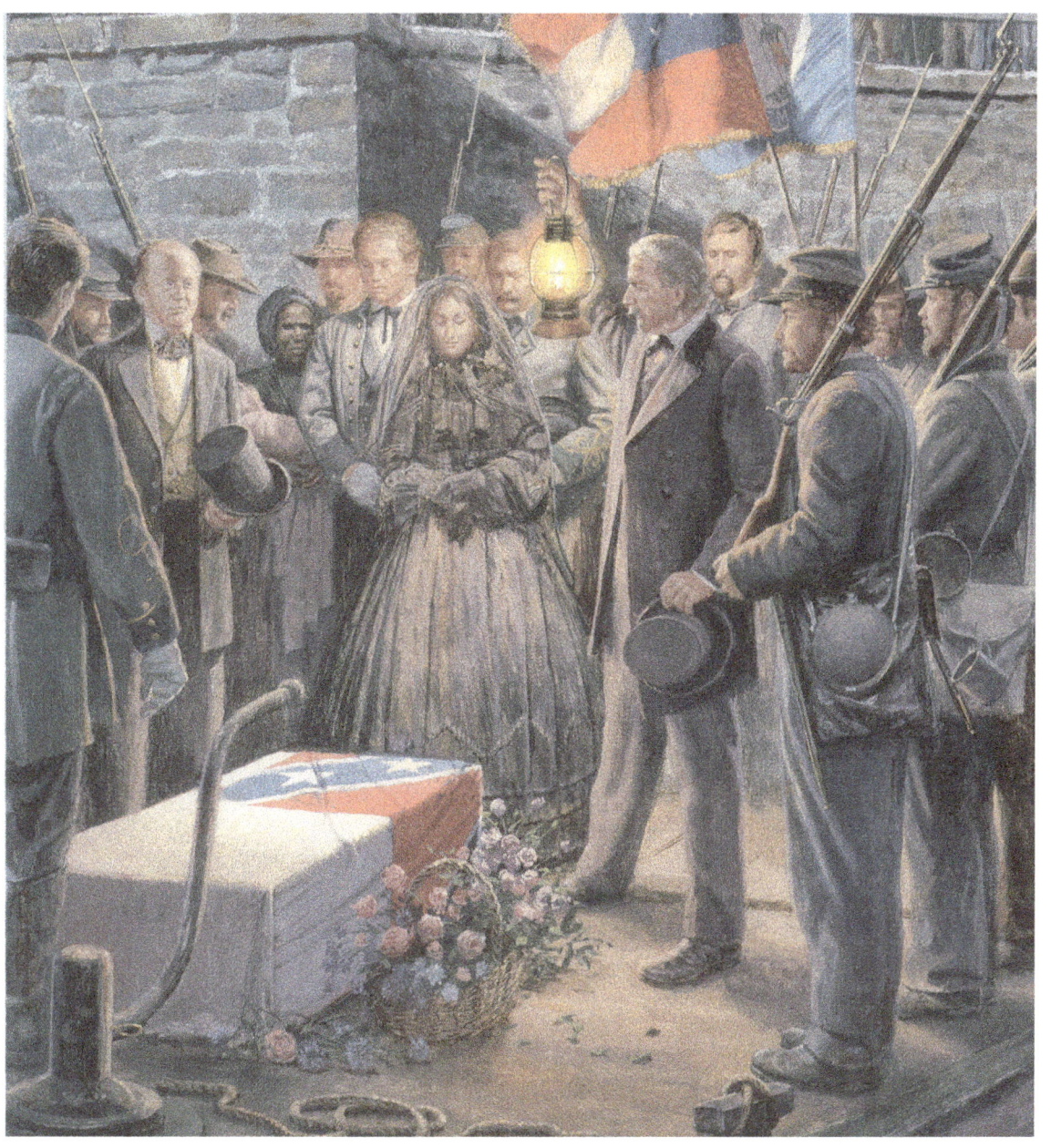

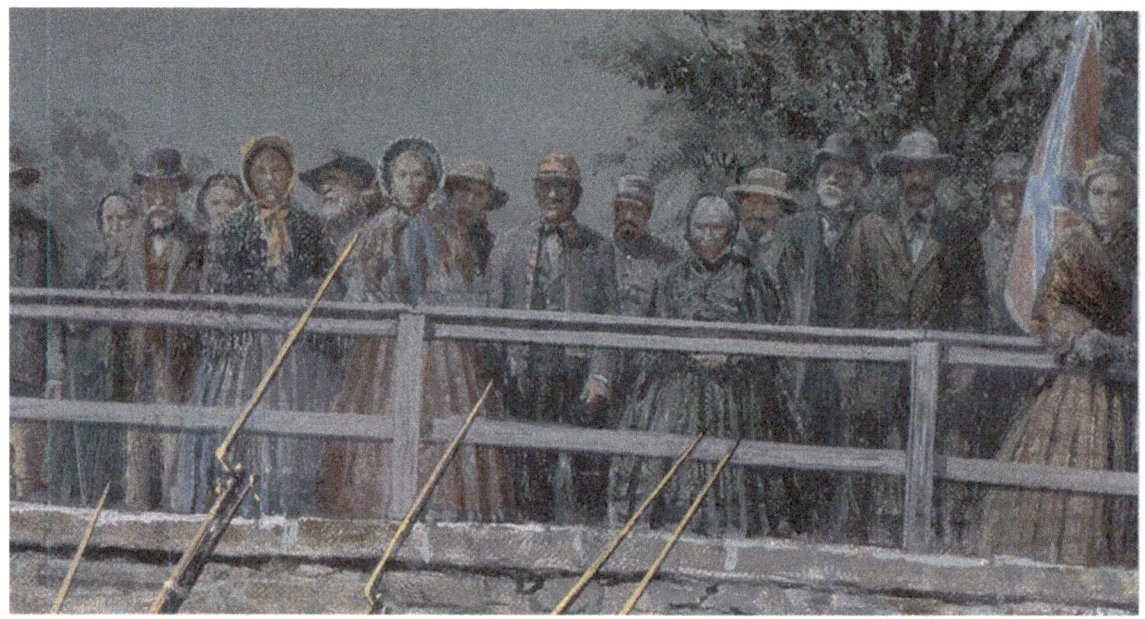

visited the site of the boat landing where the canal had been. It now is completely filled with sand and silt, but the stone Ninth Street Bridge still remains. There, too, is the neighborhood's landmark building, Amazement Square, which is a key feature in the painting.

The painting's composition is designed to lead the viewer's attention to the general's widow, Mary Anna Jackson. I used perspective, shadows, and even the mooring rope to achieve this, but the most important element is the lantern held by Mayor William Branch. Its warm, yellow orange light contrasts with the cool moonlight and brings the viewer's eye inexorably to the center of interest. The bright colors of the flag and flowers also serve that purpose. (I'm told this was the first time the Second National flag was used.

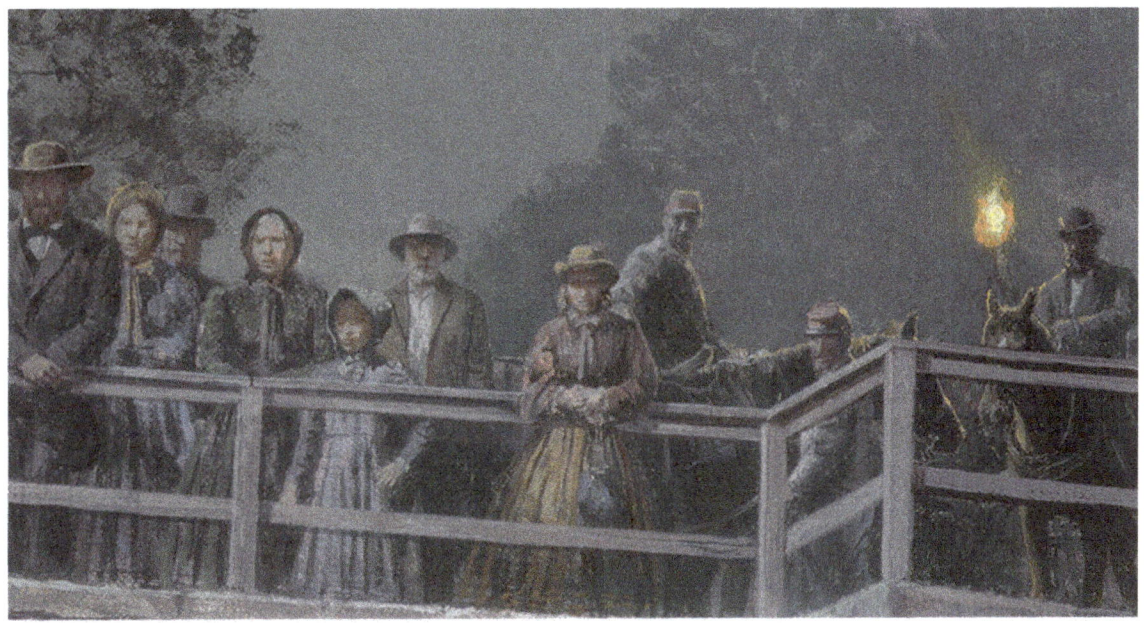

According to Professor Robertson, this was the first flag made according to the design of the Second National banner and was supposed to fly over the Confederate Capitol.)

The bald gentleman with glasses is Governor John Letcher, a good friend of Jackson's, who accompanied the body from Richmond to Lexington. Behind Mrs. Jackson and to her right is Maj. Sandie Pendleton, and to her left, behind the lantern, is Dr. Hunter McGuire. Beside Pendleton is Mary Anna's servant, who holds the Jackson's six-month-old daughter, Julia.

The title of the painting—*Going Home*—is also very special. It comes from a black spiritual of the same name.

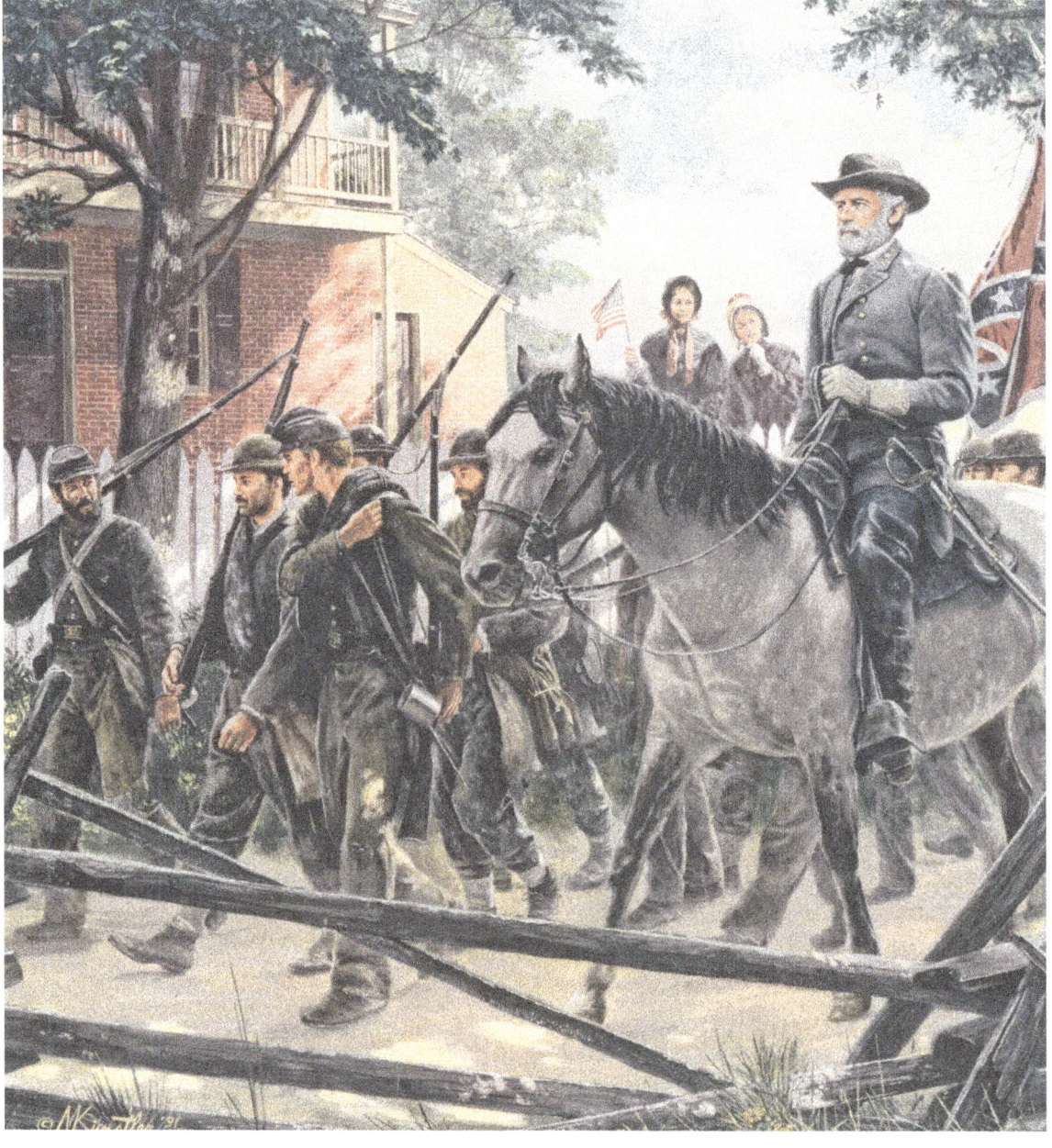

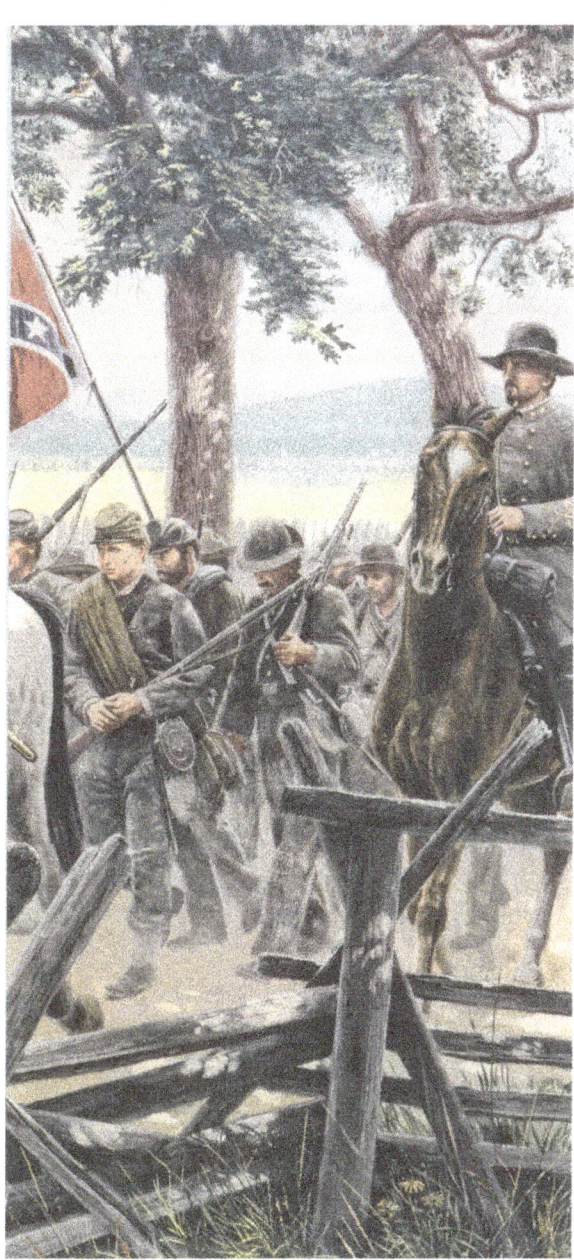

 ## "OH, I WISH HE WAS OURS"

HAGERSTOWN, MARYLAND
JUNE 26, 1863
1991, oil, 24 x 32

ROBERT E. LEE's Army of Northern Virginia marched into Maryland in mid-June 1863. Biographer Douglas Southall Freeman describes two interesting encounters between the general and Maryland women shortly after Lee himself crossed the Potomac.

The first occurred during a heavy rain on the morning of June 25 as soon as Traveller's hooves touched the Maryland bank. Lee was greeted by a group of ladies who wished him victory and offered flowers to him and James Longstreet and George E. Pickett. Then they produced a garland to

place on Traveller. Lee gallantly suggested that such decoration was not be-
fitting a commander of infantry, but he allowed a soldier to carry the wreath
for him.

The next day, Lee rode through Hagerstown toward Chambersburg. He
found himself welcomed by another group of ladies. This time one of them
asked for a lock of his hair. When he pled that he could not afford such a
loss, since his hair was thinning, others noted how much he had aged in the
ten months since they had last seen him.

Within this group was a woman who had ventured out amid her Southern
sympathizing friends to demonstrate her loyalty to the North by waving a
small Union flag. After observing Lee's rapport with his well-wishers, she
commented, "Oh, I wish he was ours!"

Such thoughts were likely borne of the frustration permeating the North
that no commander had yet emerged to counter Lee's battlefield prowess.
Even then, while the Confederates were marching on Northern soil, a suc-
cession of Union commanders was underway, and command of the Army of
the Potomac passed from Joseph Hooker to George Gordon Meade.

In this painting, I made Lee the center of interest as his column marches
along what is today Route 11; in 1863 it was a tree-shaded country lane. Following Lee on horseback is aide Lt. Col. Walter Taylor. It had rained earlier
in the day, accounting for the lack of dust stirred up by the troops.

I traveled between Hagerstown and Chambersburg, looking for an appropriate setting for this scene. However, I could not find the type of house I
was looking for on Route 11. Instead, the house in the background is based
on what was typical of mid-nineteenth-century houses in Maryland and

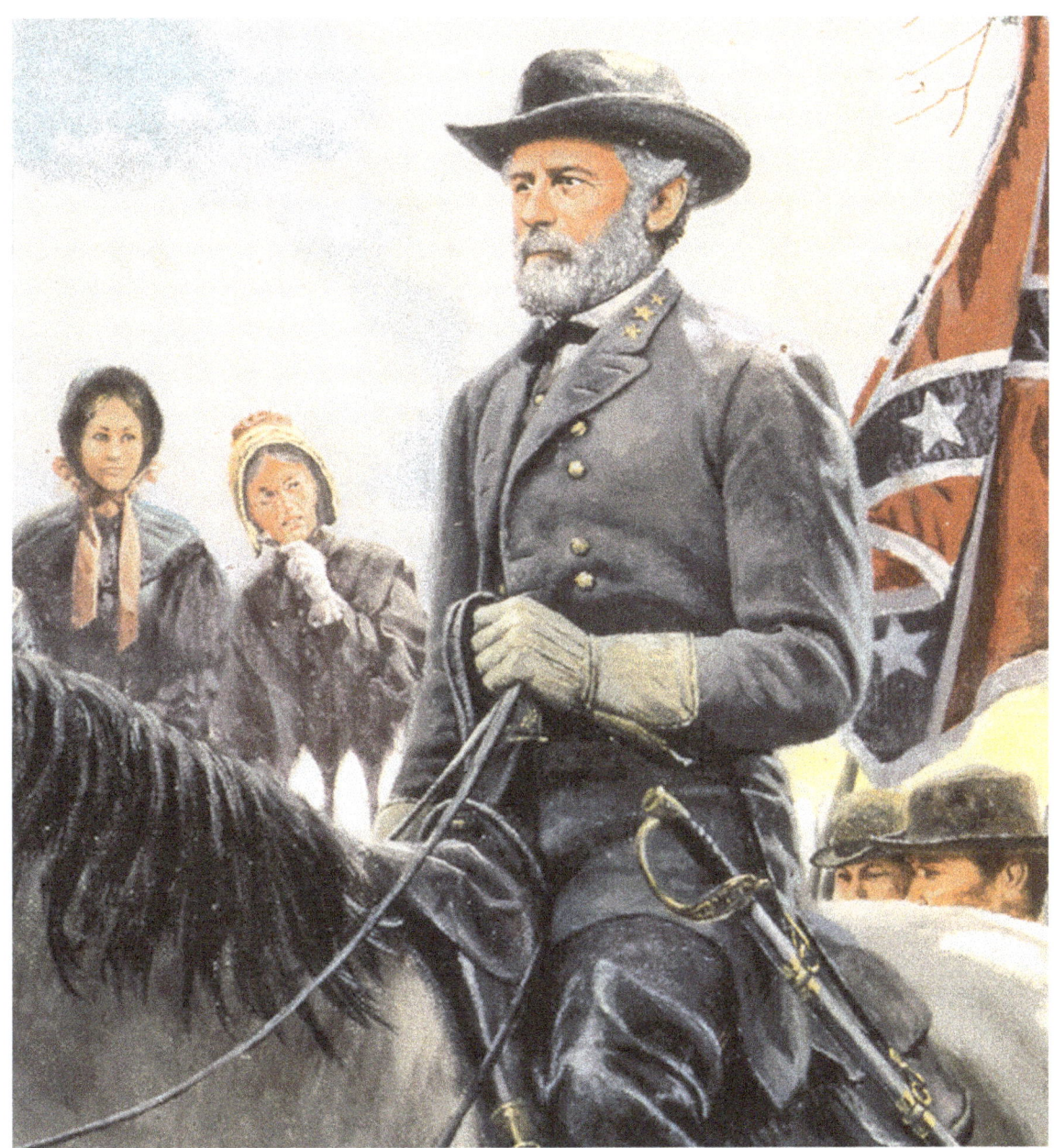

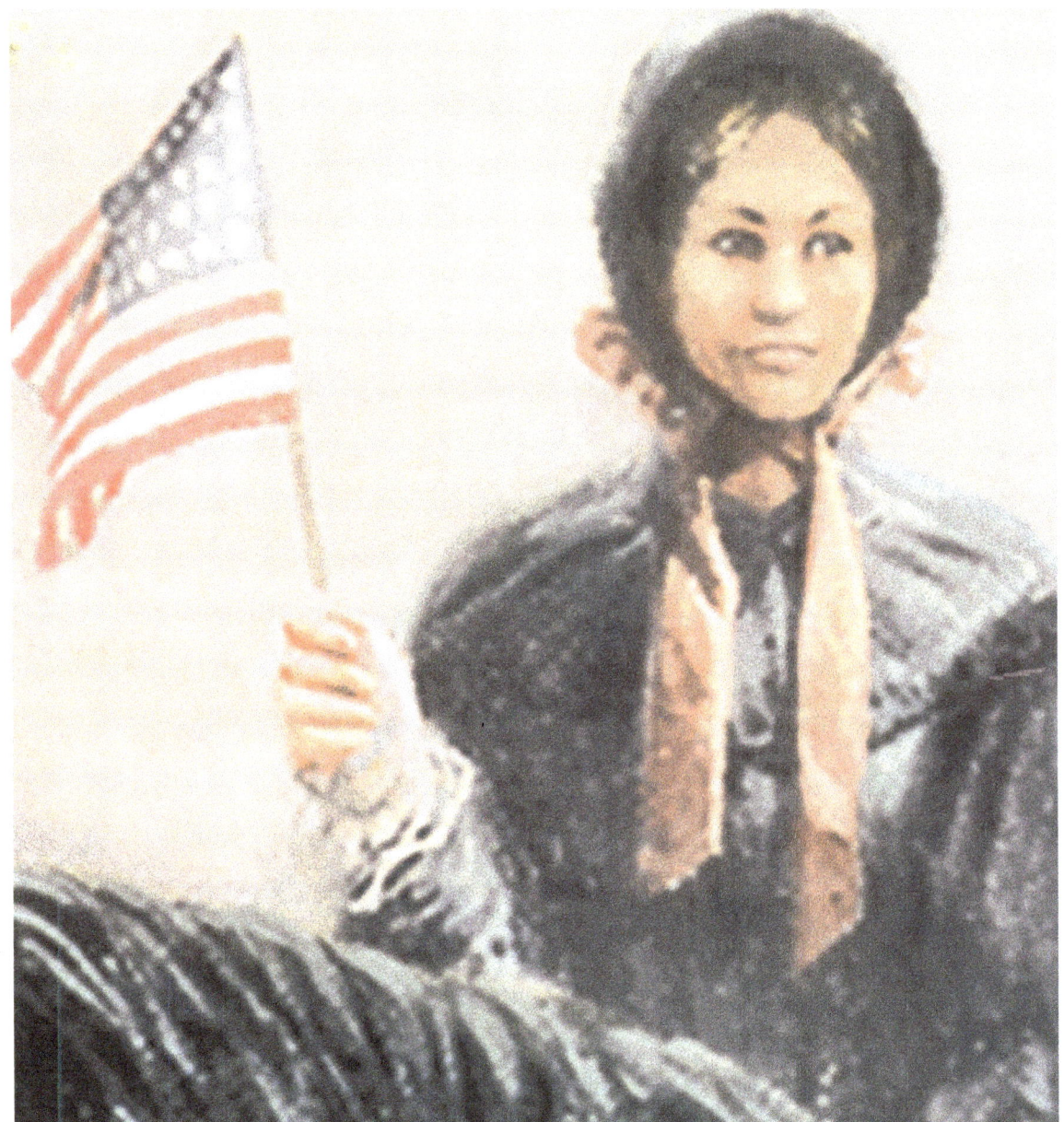

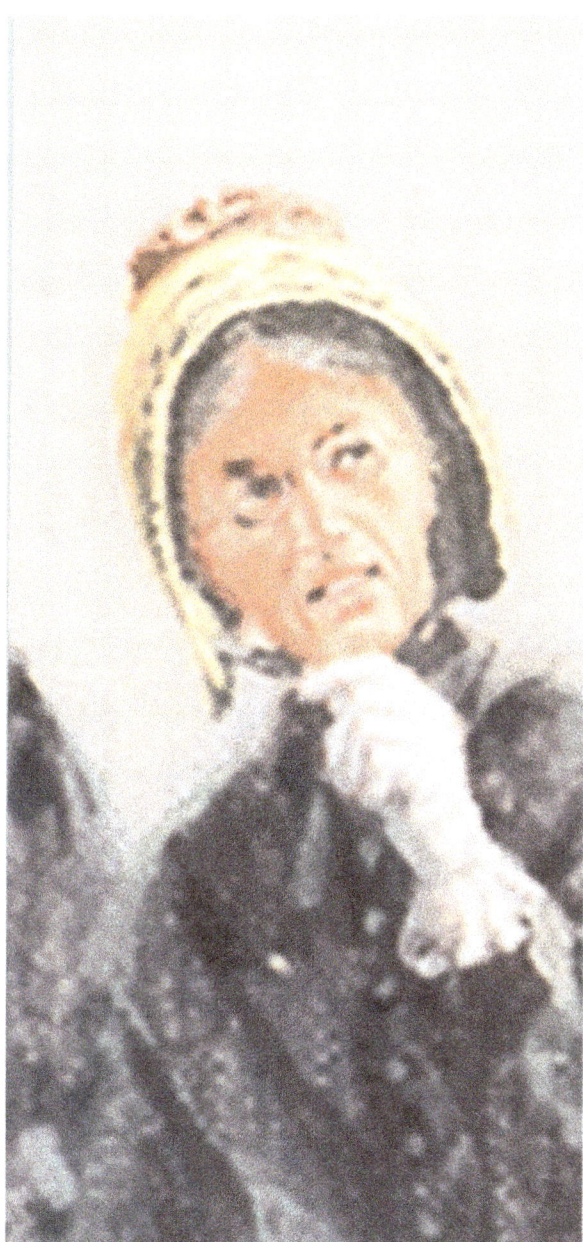

southern Pennsylvania. Many still exist in the area, so I had plenty of inspiration.

The Maryland countryside spreads out in the distance. Directly behind the Confederate battle flag is a white oak, the state tree of Maryland. An oriole (the state bird) can be seen perched on one of the branches, and black-eyed susans (the state wildflower) abound along the roadside.

The white picket fence was typical of the time and area, as was the "worm" fence in the foreground.

27

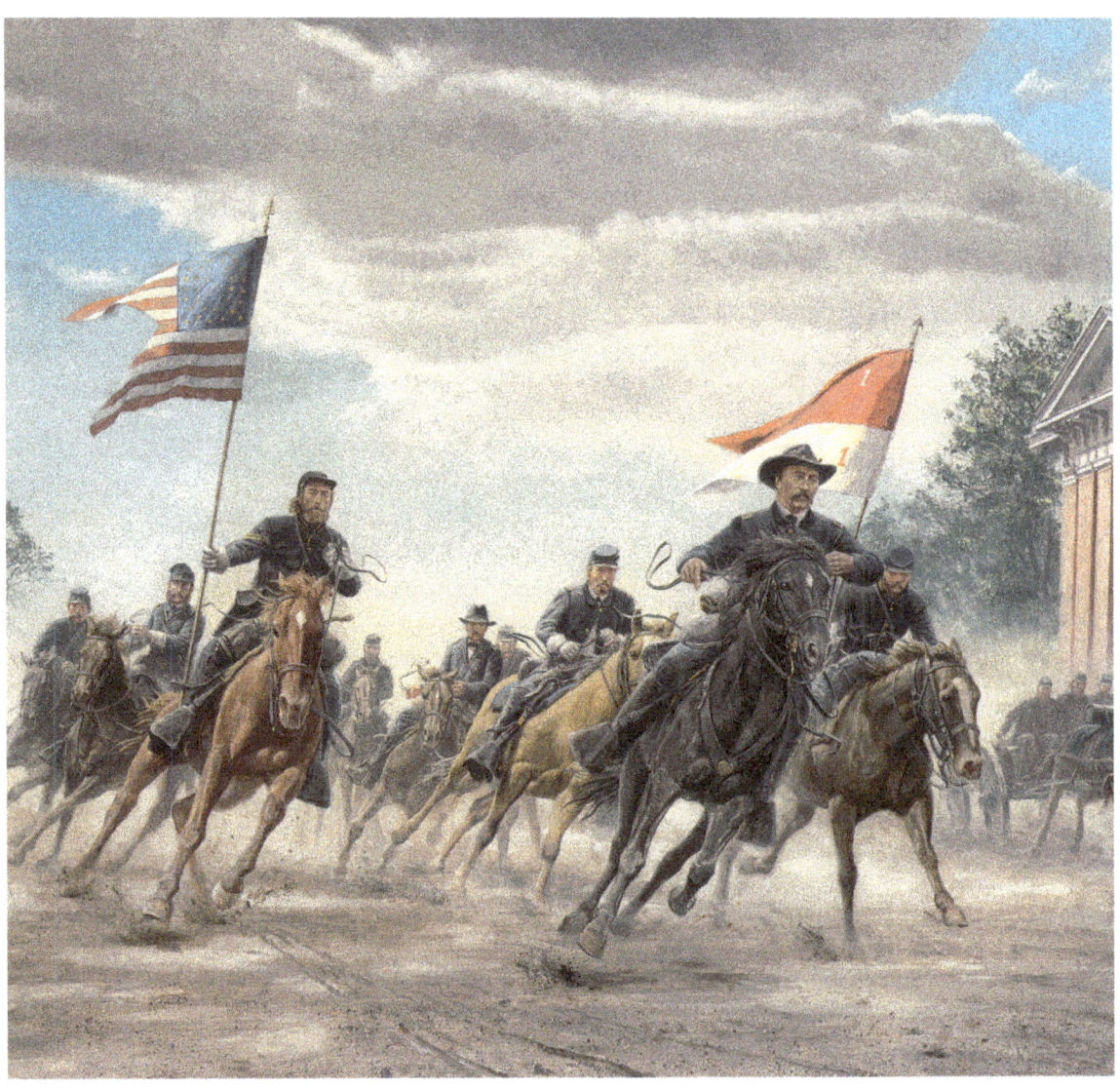

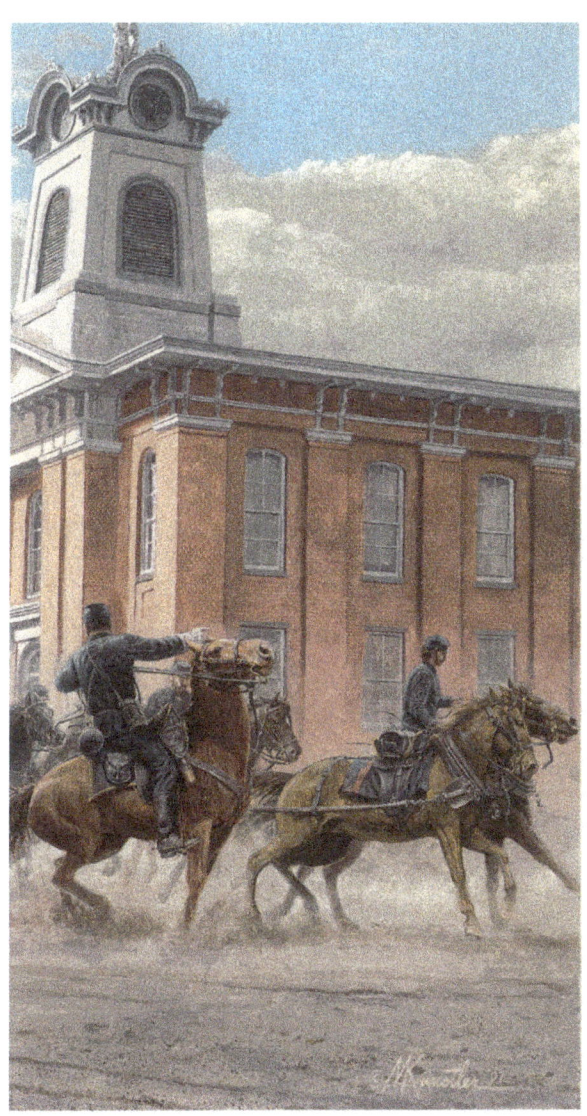

RENDEZVOUS WITH DESTINY

GEN. JOHN BUFORD AT GETTYSBURG
JUNE 30, 1863

2007, oil, 24 x 36

WHILE LEE'S ARMY WAS advancing toward Harrisburg, York (after passing through Gettysburg), and Carlisle, the Union army was in sluggish pursuit, concentrating around Frederick, Maryland, by June 27. On June 28, George Gordon Meade received official orders naming him as the new commander of the Army of the Potomac. Within twenty-four hours, he had the army on the march, informing the War Department that his primary goal was "keeping Washington and Baltimore well covered." His army was stretched across a twenty-mile front,

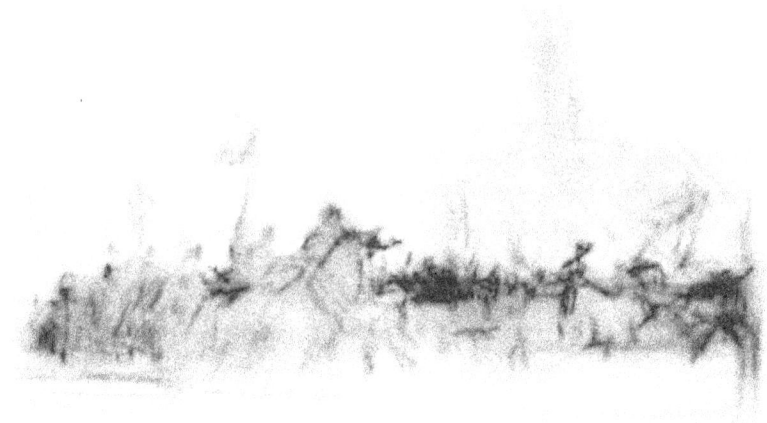

from Emmitsburg to Westminster, Maryland. When he learned that A. P. Hill and James Longstreet were east of Chambersburg, Pennsylvania, Meade shifted everything he had toward Emmitsburg. In the forefront of the Union forces closest to the Confederates was Brig. Gen. John Buford's First Cavalry.

Buford's horsemen had been probing the Emmitsburg area, seeking to make contact with the Confederates, and narrowly missing an encounter at the small town of Fairfield, about eight miles from Gettysburg. At 11:00 a.m. on June 30, he brought his division—two cavalry brigades and six pieces of field artillery—to Gettysburg. His orders were to "cover and protect the front, and communicate all information of the enemy rapidly and surely." Among his first reports was that the townspeople were "in a terrible state of excitement on account of the enemy's advance upon this place." This was not a reference to the town's first exposure to Confederate troops; Jubal Early's division had visited the town on June 26 and confiscated supplies and goods from merchants and farms prior to rushing off to York. But in the moments prior to Buford's arrival, Confederate patrols had been in the town. They rode west on the Cashtown Pike shortly before the Union troopers galloped in. Suspecting that Southern infantry were not far behind the Confederate horsemen, Buford deployed a heavy picket line along the ridges west of town and along the roads north of town.

Because Buford was the first commander from either side to occupy the town, he set the stage for the approaching battle. Known to his troops as

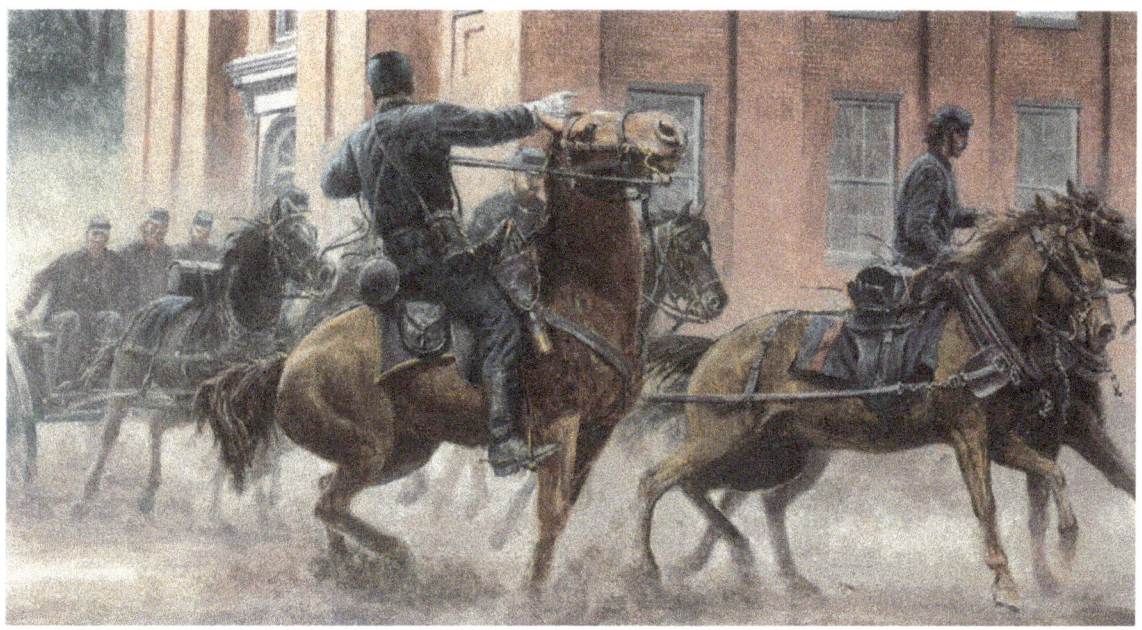

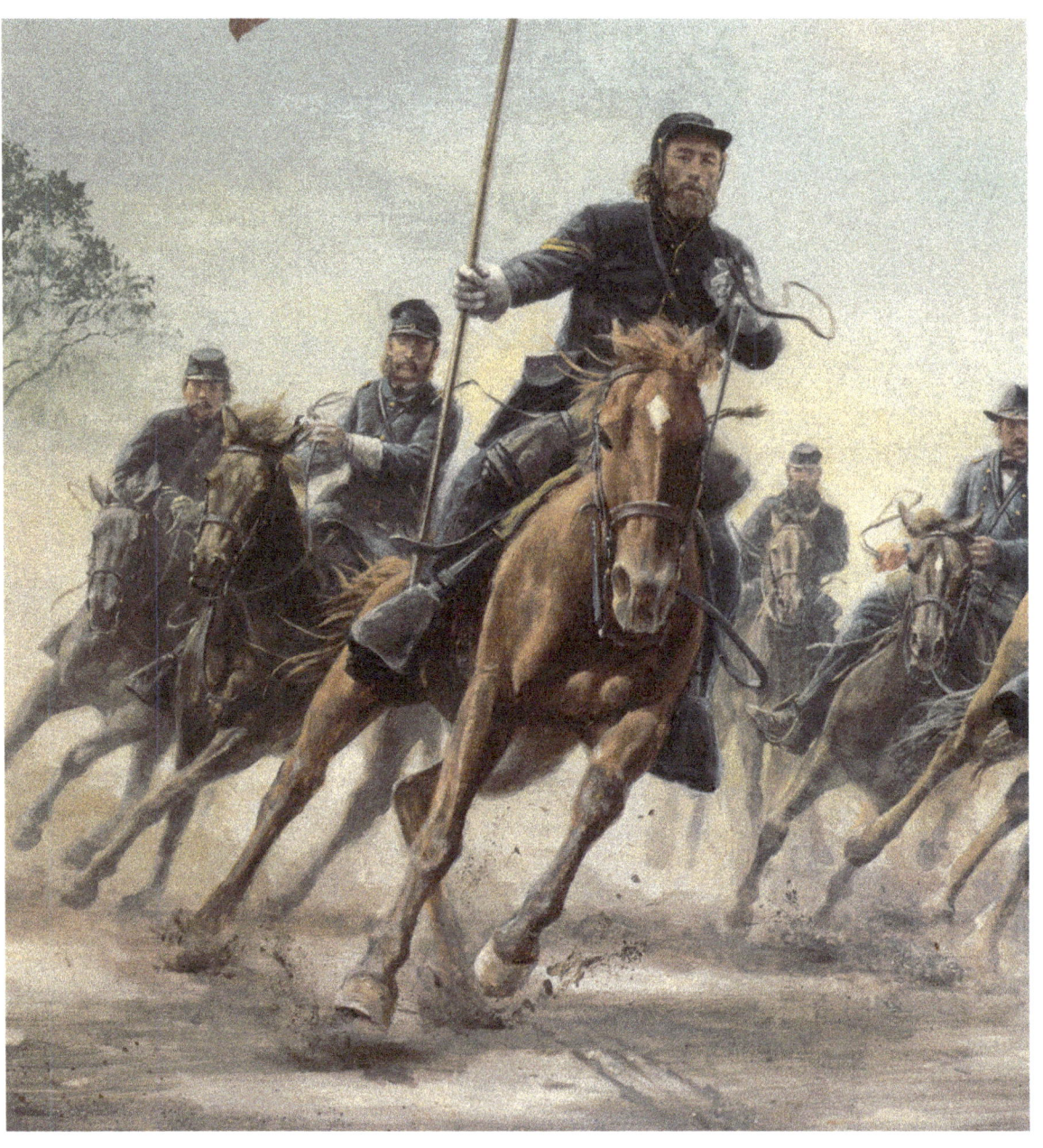

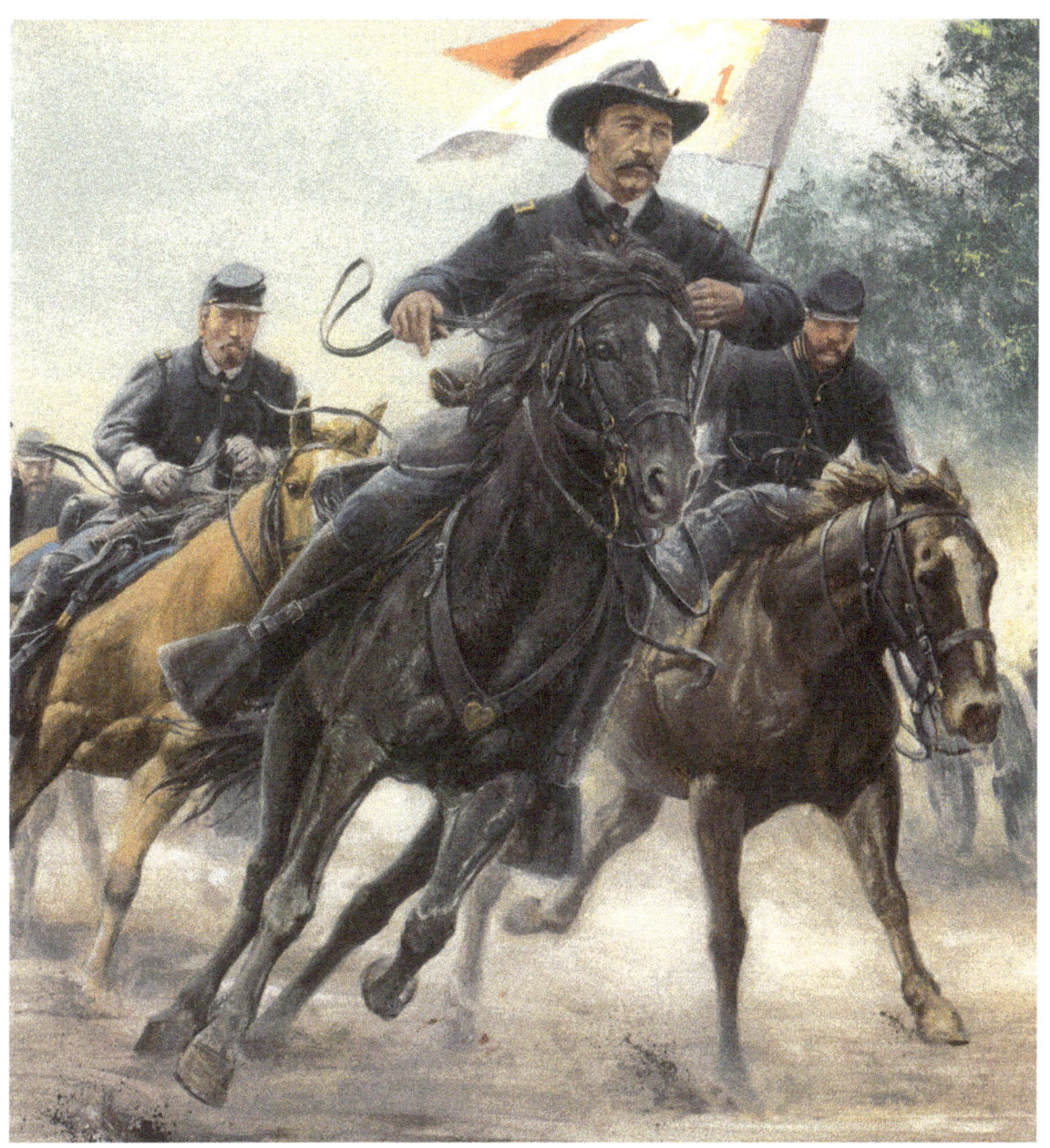

"Old Steadfast," the thirty-seven-year-old Buford was considered one of the best cavalry officers in the Army of the Potomac, and at Gettysburg he showed why that was true. In addition to setting up strong defensive lines on the ridges flanking the town's west side, he selected an excellent fall-back position on Cemetery Ridge to the rear.

In my estimation, John Buford was one of the great heroes to emerge from the battle of Gettysburg. When he entered the town that morning, he led his horse soldiers by the Adams County Courthouse and positioned his artillery on Seminary Ridge. Apparently no one had ever painted the courthouse in this setting. It's a handsome, distinctive Civil War–era building that has been

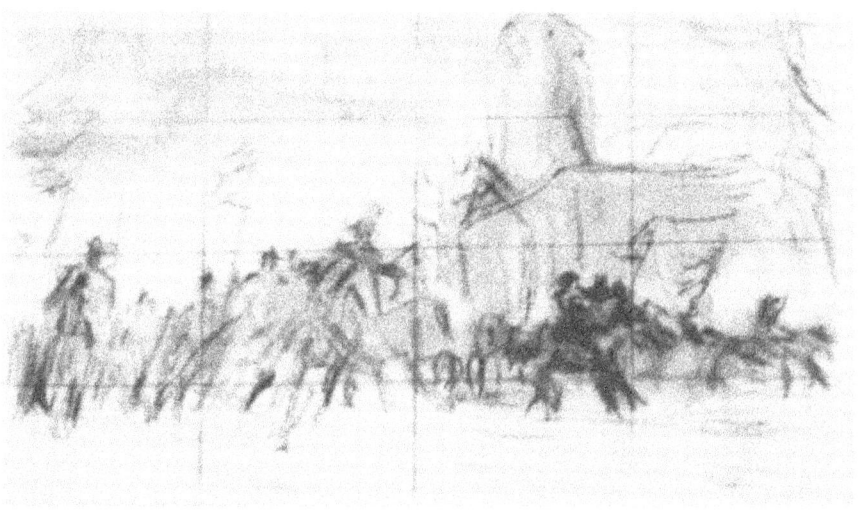

beautifully restored, and I felt it was the perfect setting for this painting of Buford. I love the excitement in this painting: the action, the bright morning, the horses, military tack, and Buford.

It had rained in the early morning, which gave me an opportunity to paint an interesting, clearing sky that radiated sunlight. The dark clouds at the top of the painting, based on weather reports of the day, lend much more drama to the scene than a blue sky would have done. I placed the white portion of the cavalry guidon directly behind Buford's black hat—the darkest dark against the lightest light—which draws the viewer's eye to the center of interest. I was also able to use the brightest color, the red portion of the guidon, to attract attention to Buford as the painting's center of interest.

In a painting like this one, the action has to appear authentic—not just the faces, the weapons, and the equipment, all of which have been thoroughly researched and carefully depicted—but the *feel* of the moment has to be genuine. To achieve that, I had to paint the horses in the midst of urgent movement. Thankfully, I've studied and painted horses for decades, so I was able to apply that experience, knowledge, and technique to this scene. The result conveys the sense of crisis felt by the Union army in the face of Lee's bold moves in Pennsylvania.

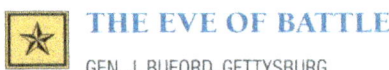

THE EVE OF BATTLE

GEN. J. BUFORD, GETTYSBURG

JUNE 30, 1863

1993, gouache, 13¼ x 11¼

During the evening of June 30, Gen. John Buford strolled the grounds of the Lutheran Seminary at Gettysburg, contemplating the enemy's next move and preparing for a fight. He had spoken earlier with brigade commander Col. Tom Devin, whose men were watching the roads to the north.

At one point in that conversation, Devin reflected on the fruitlessness of their searching thus far for Lee's army and commented that whatever Confederates he might encounter would be few in number and easily handled by his men.

Buford did not agree and warned Devin, "They will attack you in the morning and they will come booming—skirmishers three deep. You will have to fight like the devil until supports arrive."

His scouts had already identified the enemy as A. P. Hill's corps, and in a 10:30 p.m. dispatch to Gen. John F. Reynolds, he indicated that the Confederates were "massed just back of Cashtown, about nine miles from this place." To this he added information collected from a courier captured that

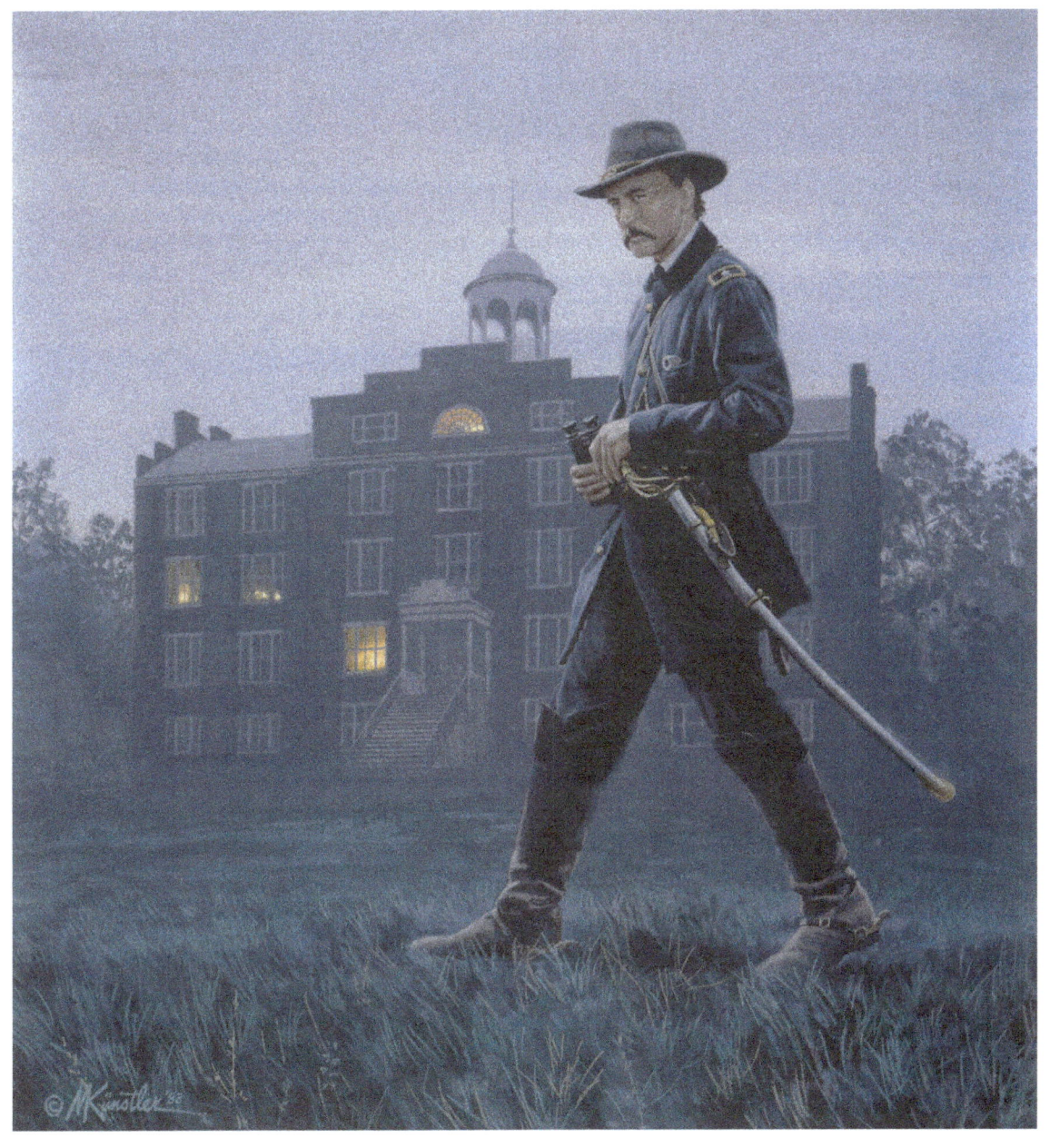

day who spoke of Richard S. Ewell's corps advancing from Carlisle, with Robert S. Rodes's division in the lead. Then Buford added, "Longstreet . . . is still behind Hill."

Buford was tense and anxious throughout the evening, more so than any of his men had ever seen him before. He kept his scouts in the field all night, moving north and west of the town, gathering more information on how many Confederates were in the area. "Look out for campfires during the night and for dust in the morning," he directed.

The seminary building known as the Old Dorm in 1863 (now known as Schmucker Hall) offered a distinctive perch from which to view the surround-

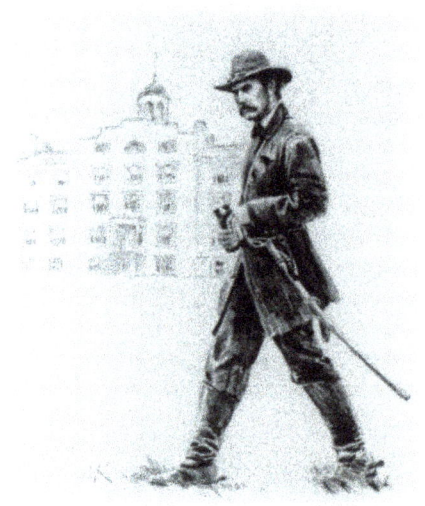

ing countryside. Buford took advantage of the platform to scan the western horizon for approaching Confederates and the southern approaches for Federal troops.

The moon was full that night, and so I used it to bathe the scene of the wary Buford prowling the seminary grounds, pondering what the morning would bring and how many Confederates his men would be facing.

FACING ➤

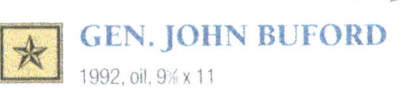

GEN. JOHN BUFORD

1992, oil, 9⅞ x 11

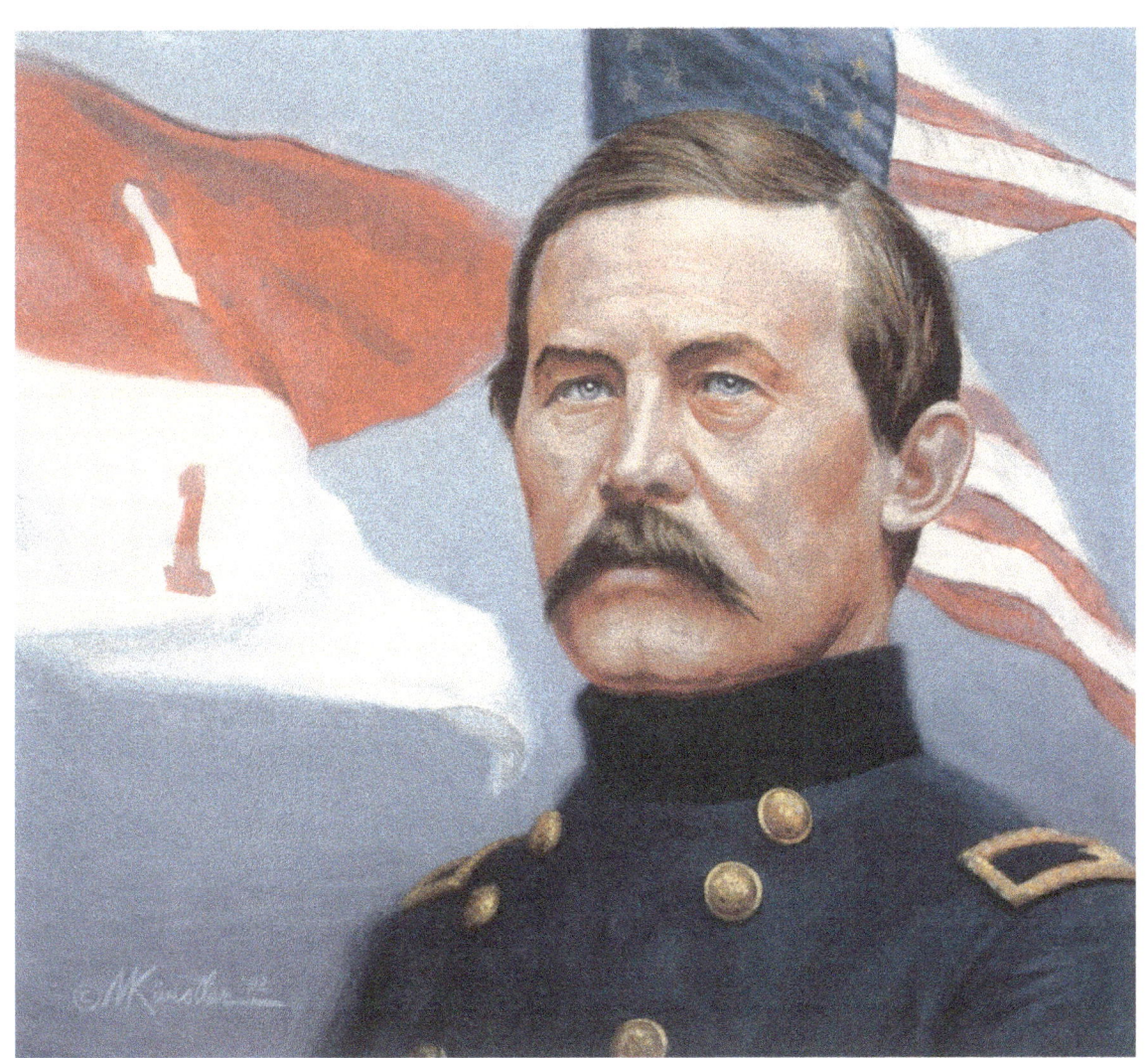

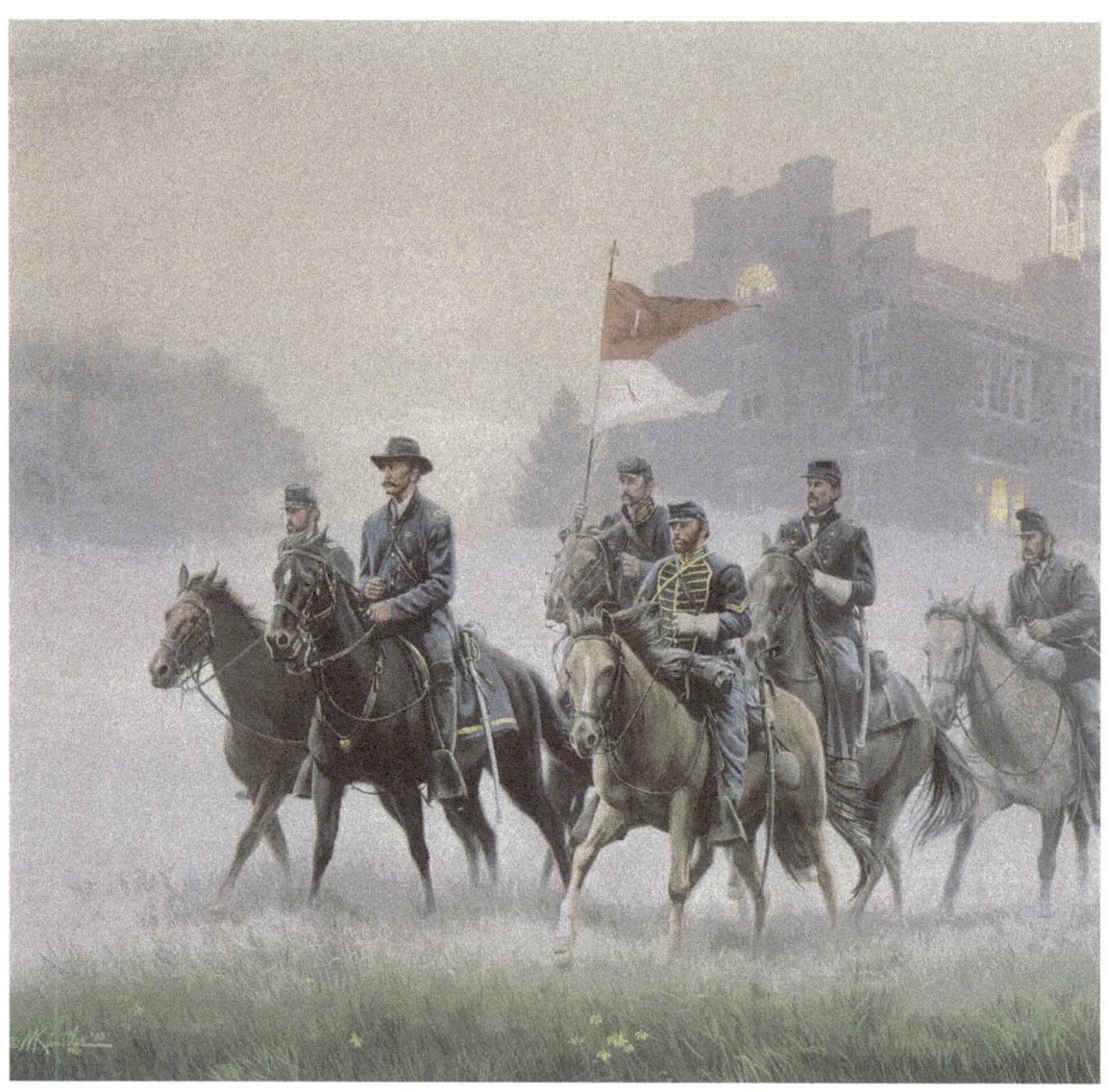

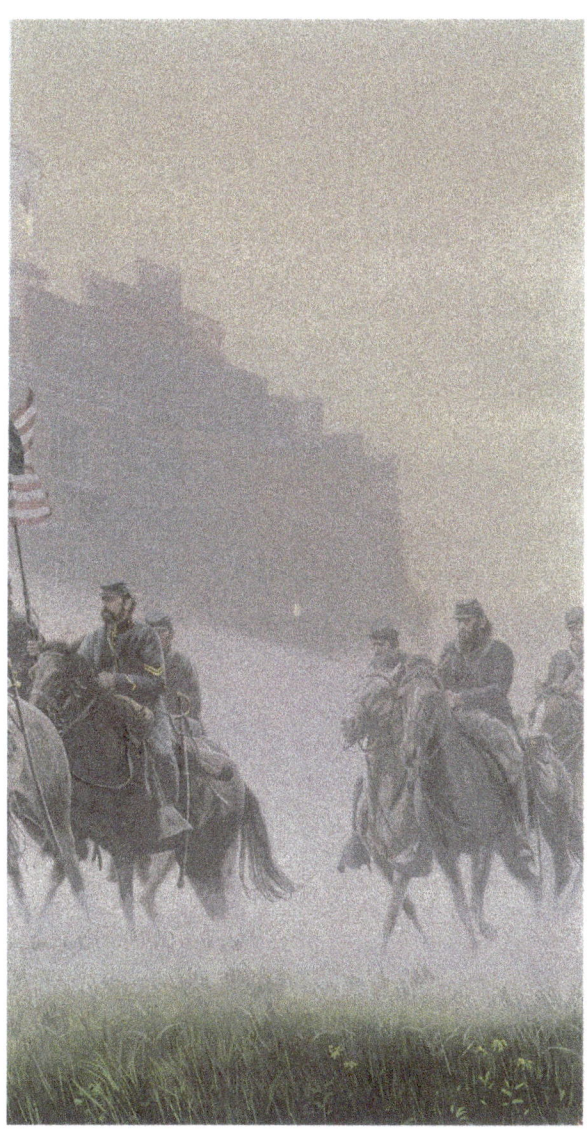

MORNING RIDERS

GEN. J. BUFORD, GETTYSBURG
JULY 1, 1863, 5:15 A.M.

1993, gouache, 18¾ x 29¼

BUFORD WAS A DRIVEN man in command of nearly three thousand cavalrymen and anticipating the imminent arrival of the full force of the Army of Northern Virginia and Robert E. Lee. Weighing against the Union troopers scattered across the ridges and roads was the tactical knowledge that unsupported horse soldiers could not hold off infantry indefinitely. Buford knew he could not expect support to arrive until midmorning.

Still, Buford had only vague orders in hand from Meade's headquarters. From his immediate superior, Alfred

41

Pleasonton, he was charged to "cover and protect the front" at Gettysburg, which he interpreted to mean that he was not to abandon the town without a fight. At the least, his men needed to delay the enemy's advance. If Union infantry should join him before his men were dislodged from the area, then a battle would follow. All of his experience told Buford that if it came to that, Gettysburg would not be a bad place to make a stand.

Shortly after sunrise, he received word that John F. Reynolds's First Corps was marching toward him that morning, and Reynolds would be followed by Oliver O. Howard's Eleventh Corps. That information meant that all Buford's preparations at Gettysburg had given Meade's army a strong position for the approaching battle.

"By daylight on July 1," Buford wrote, "I had gained positive information of the enemy's position and movements, and my arrangements were made for entertaining him until General Reynolds could reach the scene."

I always search for something that has never been done before when I contemplate a new painting. I knew I wanted to do a picture of Buford, so I focused my attention on the early morning after reading of the heavy mist that was encountered on that fateful day.

The Lutheran Seminary building still exists, so it was relatively easy to see the lighting effect on the structure's cupola at that hour. The sun comes up over Culp's Hill and hits the cupola first, providing me with an unusual lighting effect. Buford left his headquarters with his entourage and headed northwest to supervise the line he had set up on McPherson's Ridge.

We see Buford riding a black horse, followed by his headquarters flag. In the foreground is a bugler in a yellow-striped jacket followed by the rest of the general's staff coming out of the mist. The view is the west side of the seminary building. The facade has changed slightly over the years, but in 1863 the building looked pretty much the way it looks today.

This was a fascinating picture for me to work on. I thoroughly enjoyed painting the architecture and the lighting effect and once again had the opportunity to portray Buford, the man who selected the terrain on which the battle was fought.

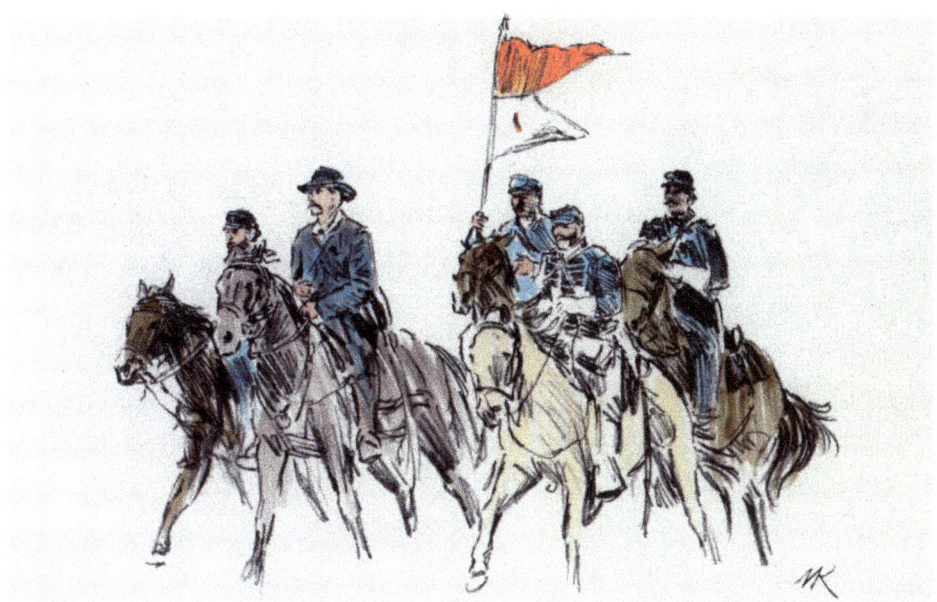

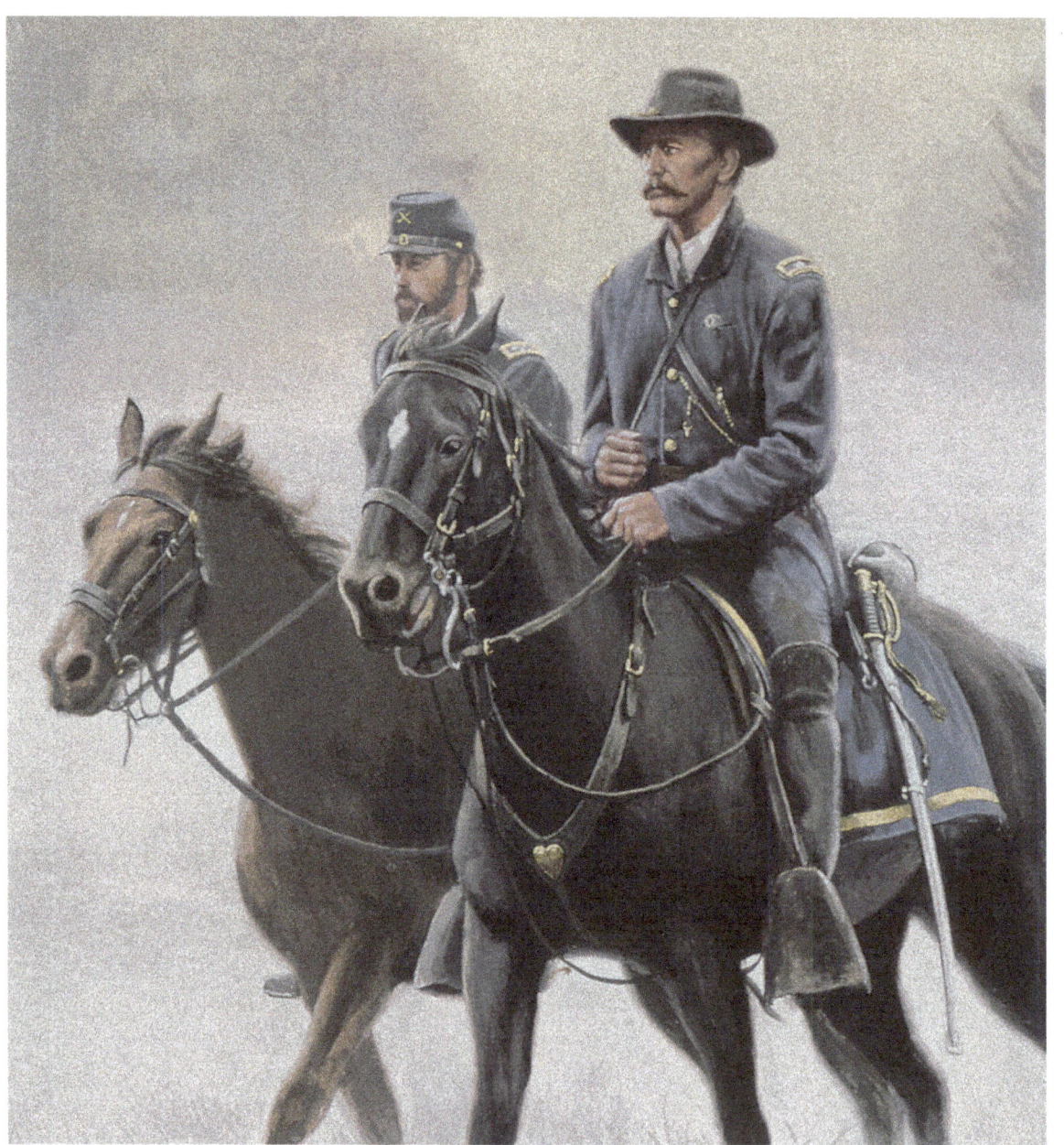

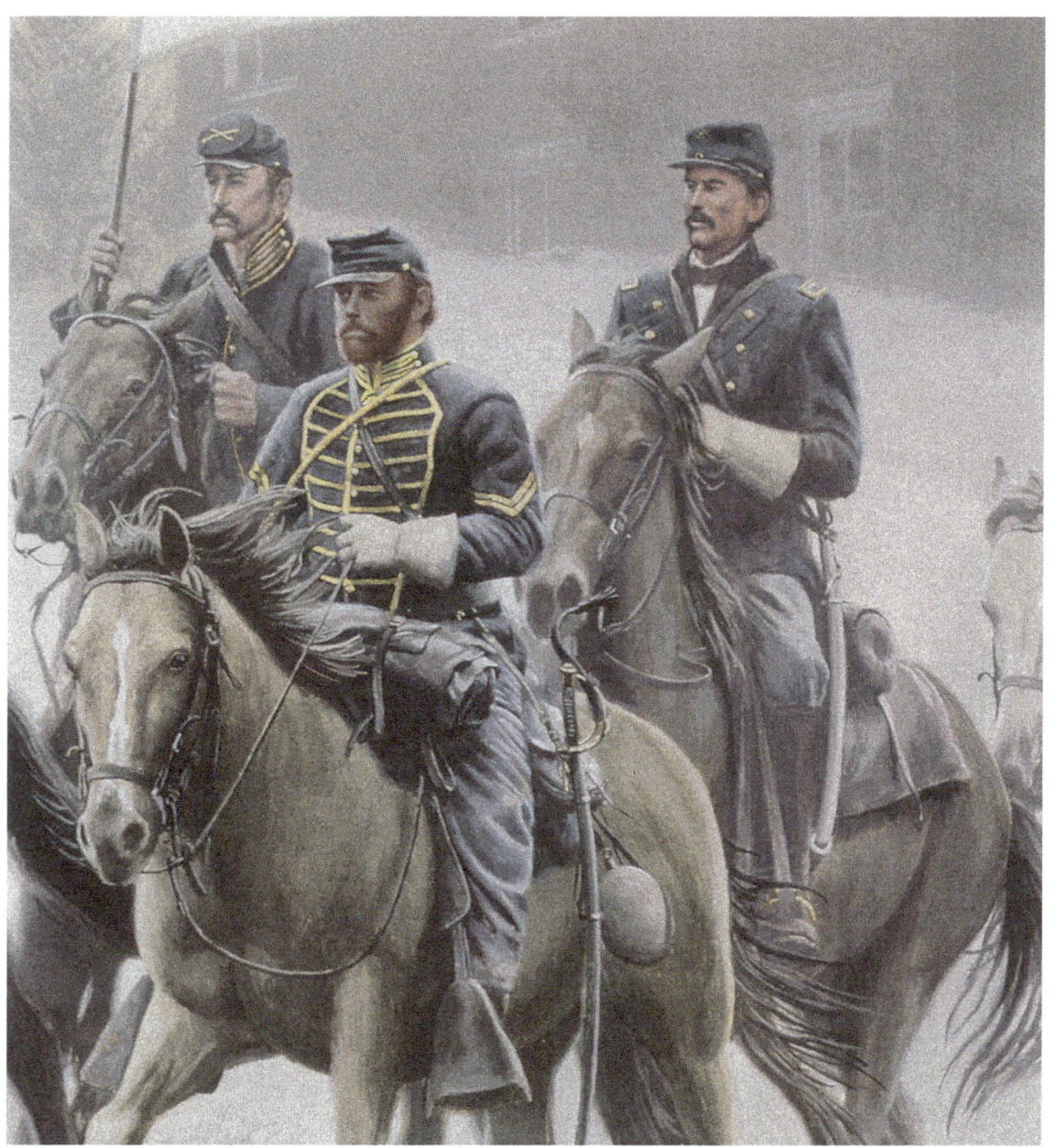

"HOLD AT ALL COST!"

GEN. J. BUFORD AT GETTYSBURG

JULY 1, 1863, 9:30 A.M.

1993, gouache, 12½ x 36⅛

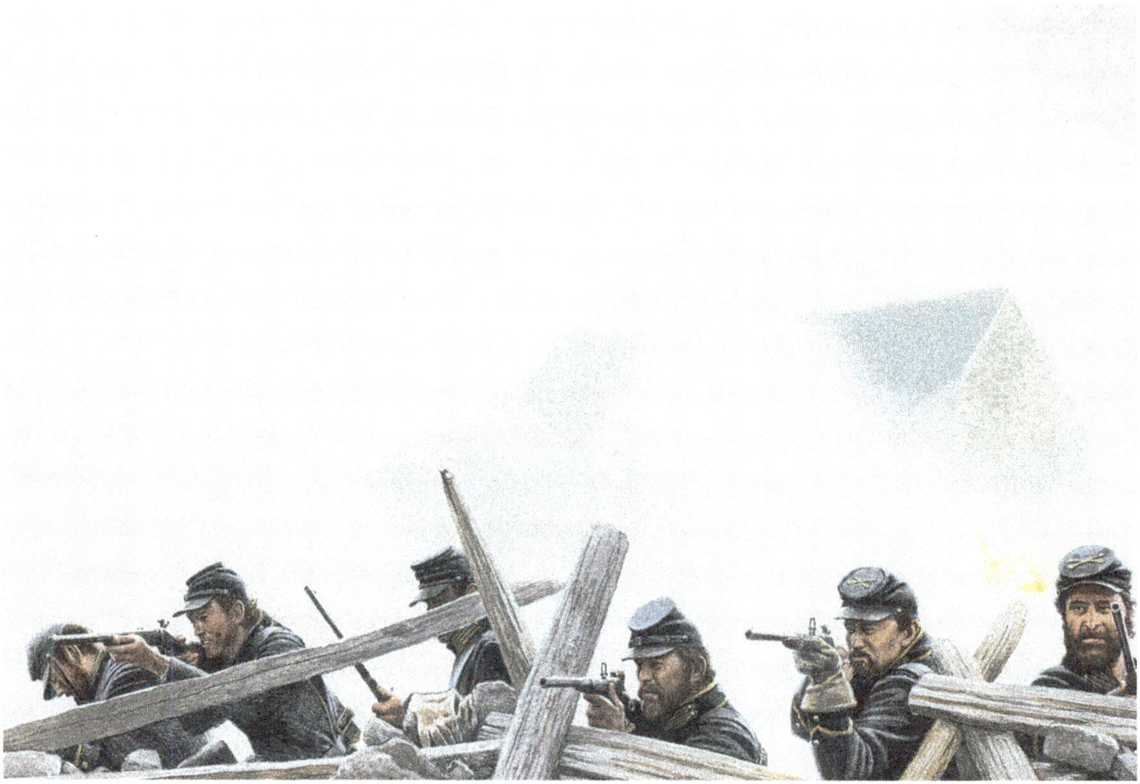

THE FIRST SHOT OF the battle of Gettysburg was fired around 7:30 a.m. on July 1 by Lt. Marcellus Jones of the Eighth Illinois Cavalry. In response, skirmishers from Col. Birkett D. Fry's Thirteenth Alabama returned fire and advanced, and Confederate gunners opened fire with a 3-inch gun, expecting that Federal militiamen were all that stood between them and Gettysburg. But the troops before them held their positions, and soon the

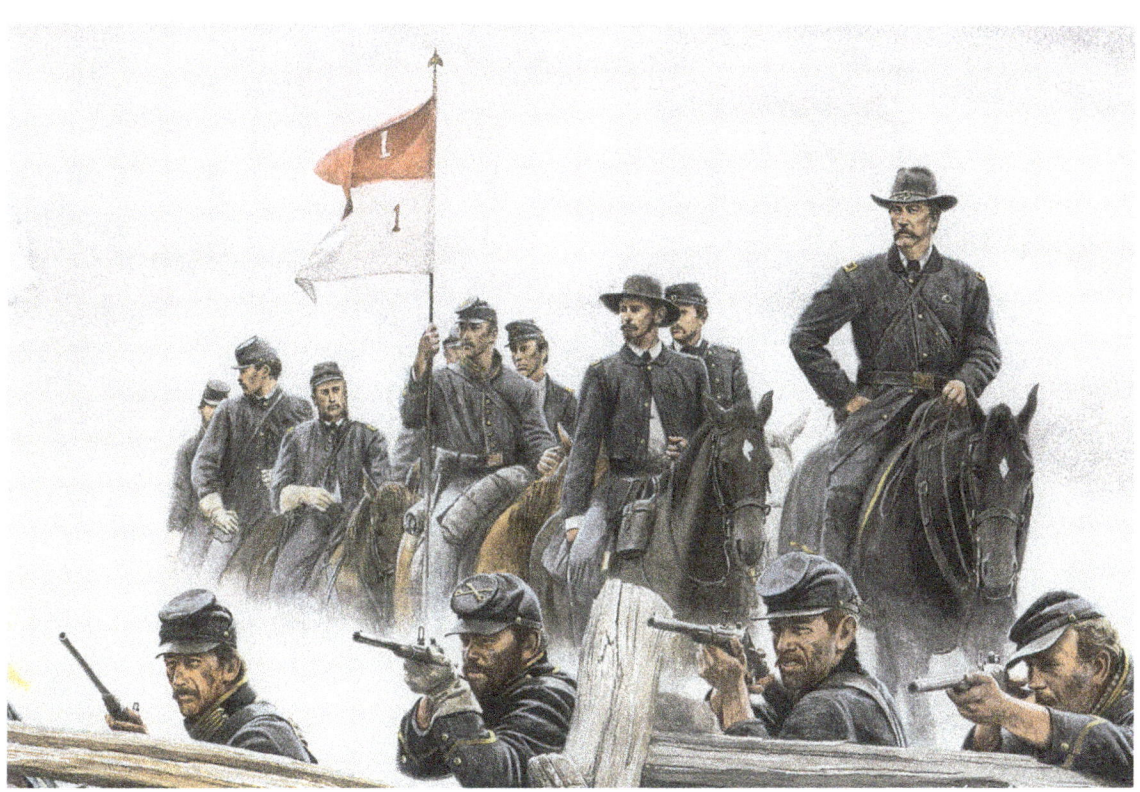

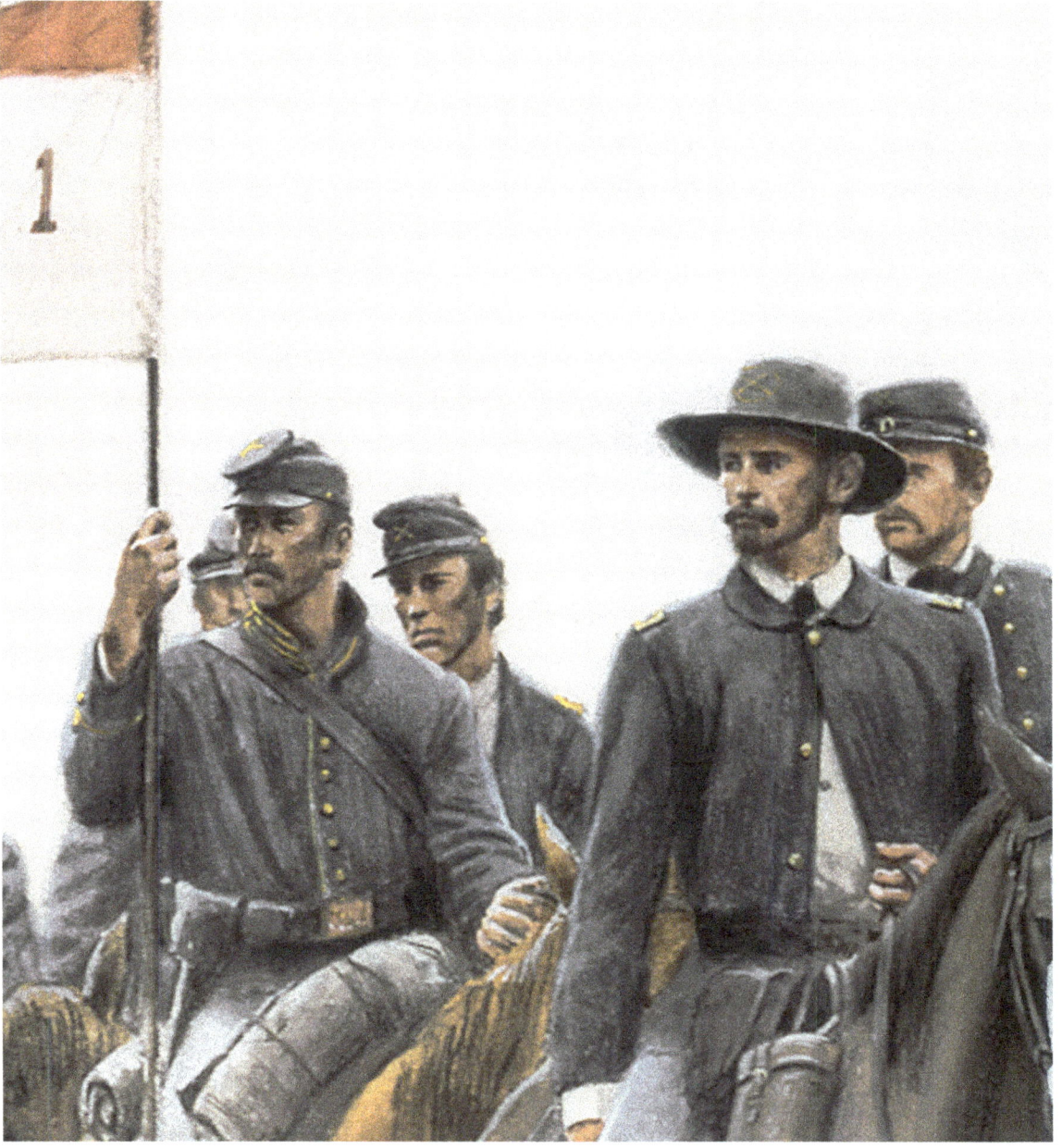

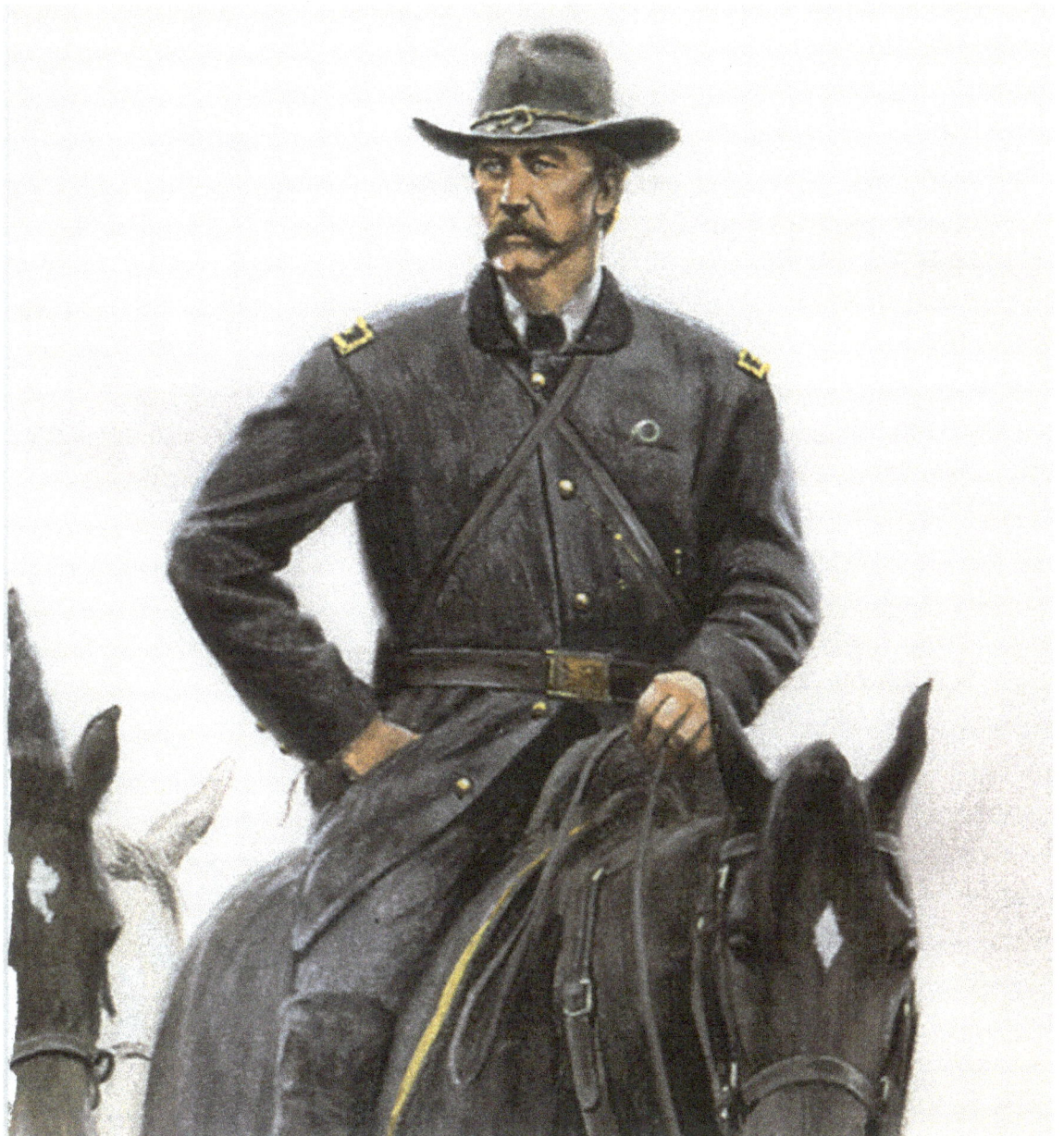

Confederate commanders grasped that they had encountered Union troops, although they did not yet perceive them to be dismounted cavalry. Instead, playing into Buford's hands, they took the time to deploy in a full line of battle rather than rush the picketed horsemen. Confederate Gen. Henry Heth had wanted to advance his division quickly up the Chambersburg Pike, clearing the way with just a skirmish line. But the hefty resistance induced his front-line brigades to halt and deploy, a movement that took ninety minutes.

It helped that the Union troopers were equipped with breech-loading carbines, which gave them a faster rate of fire than the Confederate infantry's rifles and also created the illusion of a greater force at hand than the 550 men of Buford's advanced skirmish line. At 9:00 a.m. the Confederates were arrayed in a mile-wide battle line and began to sweep toward the first Union-occupied ridge west of the town. Slowly, Buford's troopers withdrew from that ridge to the next, until they came to their main line at McPherson's Ridge, having given their general more than two hours in the fight for time, waiting for the arrival of Reynolds and the First Corps.

In the painting, Buford and his staff have taken position behind the dismounted cavalrymen on McPherson's Ridge, behind a small stone wall and some rail fencing. The firing has just begun at long range, as evidenced by the raised rear sights of the troopers' Sharps carbines. In portraying Buford's men, I wanted to show a defensive line in a long, narrow composition that would accommodate many cavalrymen.

With his men in a strong defensive position and the Confederate attack underway, Buford has done his job. He wears a sack coat with a black velvet collar, which enabled me to add some authentic and human touches, such as the watch chain and pipe.

I faced a challenge in showing several cavalrymen up close. The problem is that all the troopers are dressed more or less alike and use the same weapons, which tends to make the picture boring. To address this problem, I emphasized the differences in their faces and varied their poses and uniforms.

This scene shows almost every component of a Federal cavalry brigade: the commanding officer and staff, the horse soldiers on the front line, and the unit's guidon. The number ones on the red and white bars of the flag indicate that this detachment is part of the First Division of the First Corps.

I was fascinated with my subject while working on this painting. The architecture and the lighting were a challenge, and again I had an opportunity to portray Buford at one of the critical moments of the battle of Gettysburg. His foresight in choosing a strong defensive position came into play repeatedly throughout the next three days.

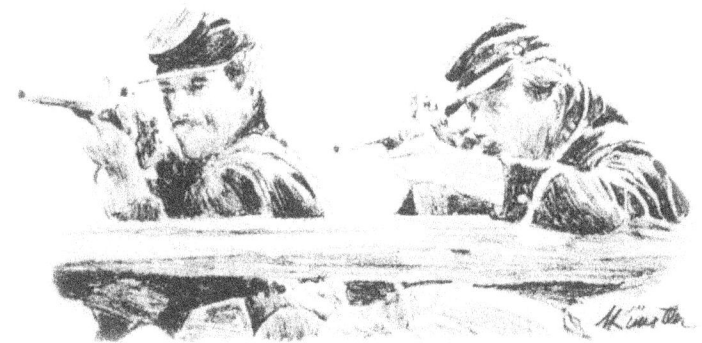

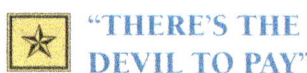

"THERE'S THE DEVIL TO PAY"

GEN. JOHN BUFORD AT GETTYSBURG

JULY 1, 1863

1990, oil, 30 x 54

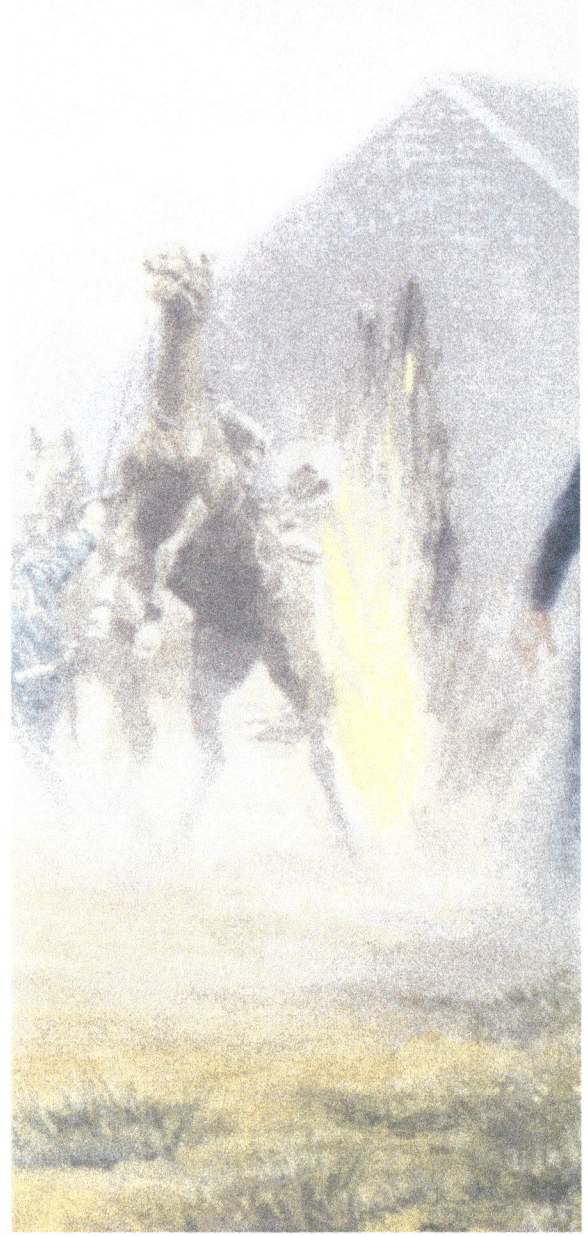

THE TITLE OF THE painting is based on John Buford's reply to John F. Reynolds when he announced the arrival of the First Corps at Gettysburg by asking, "What's the matter, John?"

We see Buford dismounted, holding field glasses and pointing to the Confederates on the other side of Willoughby's Run. Reynolds peers through his field glasses to see the enemy through the smoke and dust. The action takes place on McPherson's Ridge at the site of the present-day monuments to Buford and Reynolds. McPherson's barn, which still stands,

52

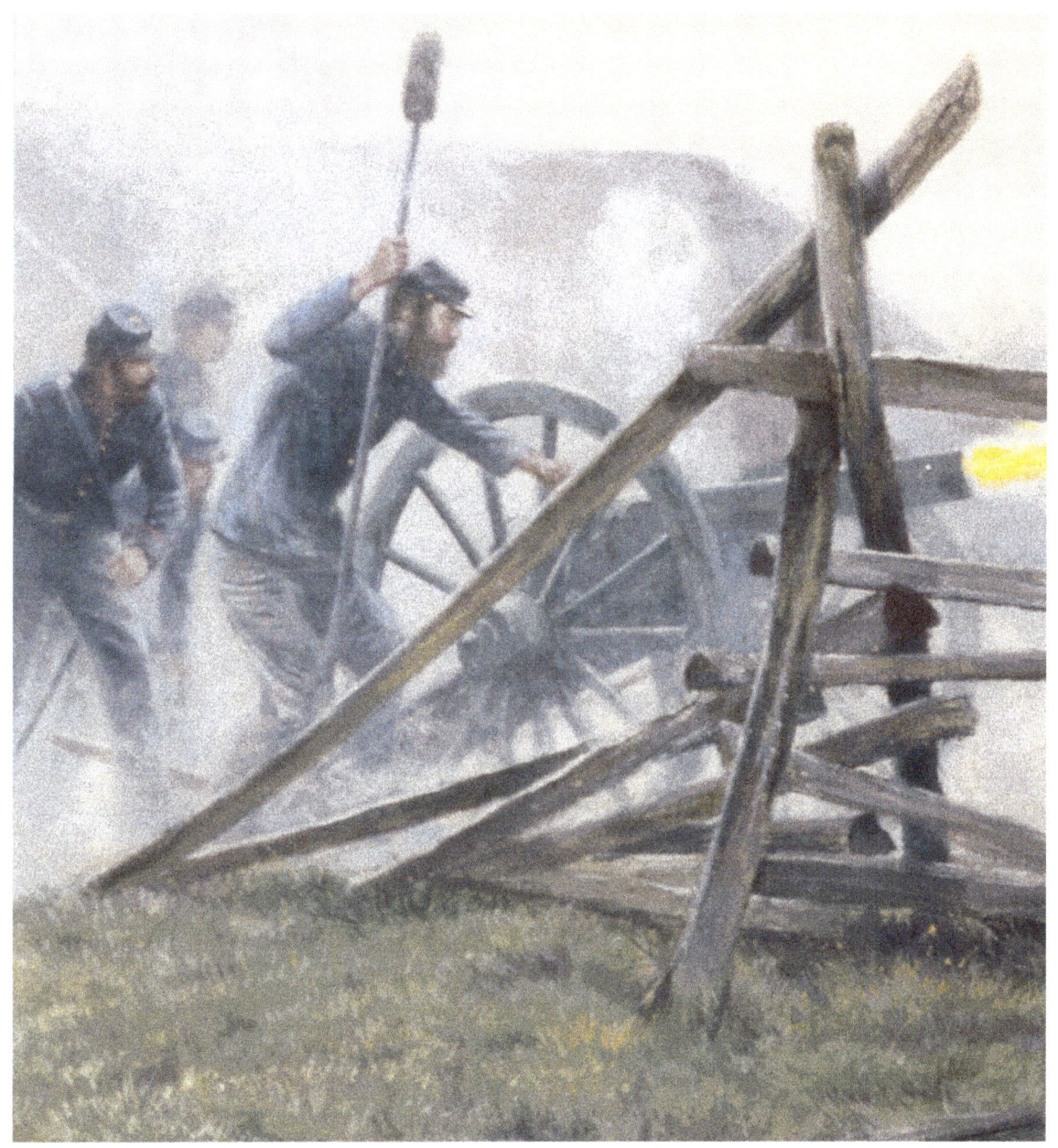

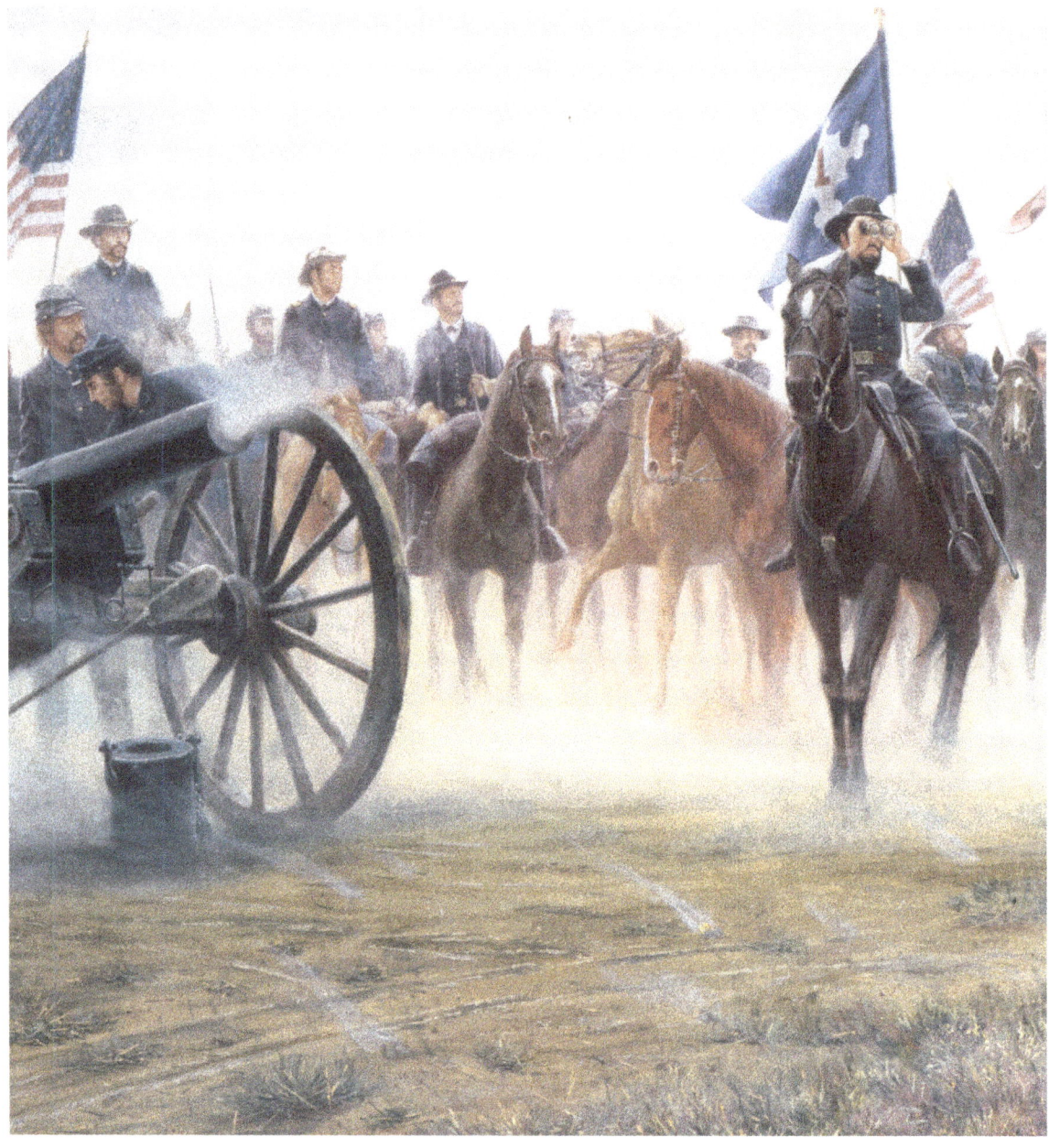

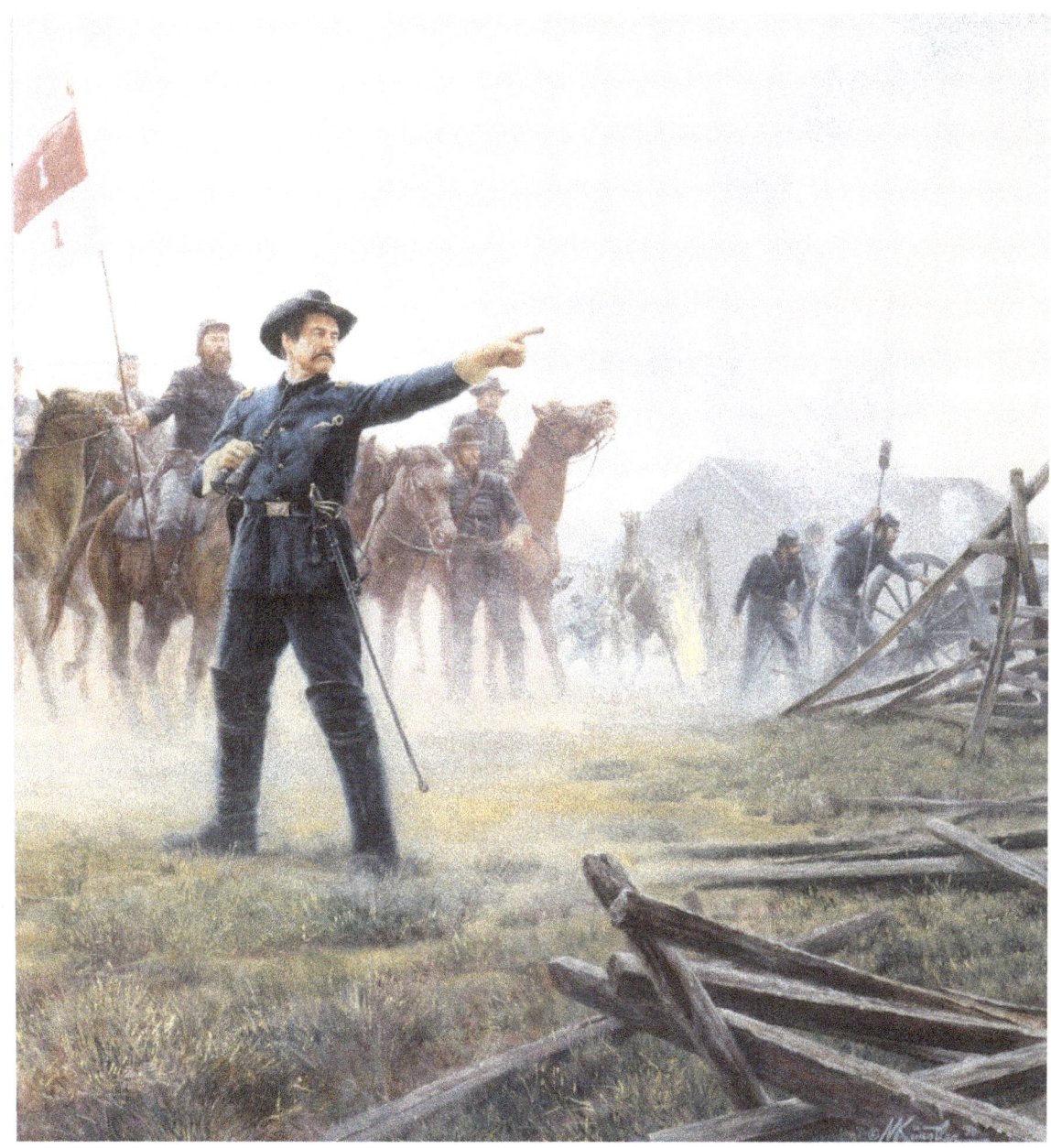

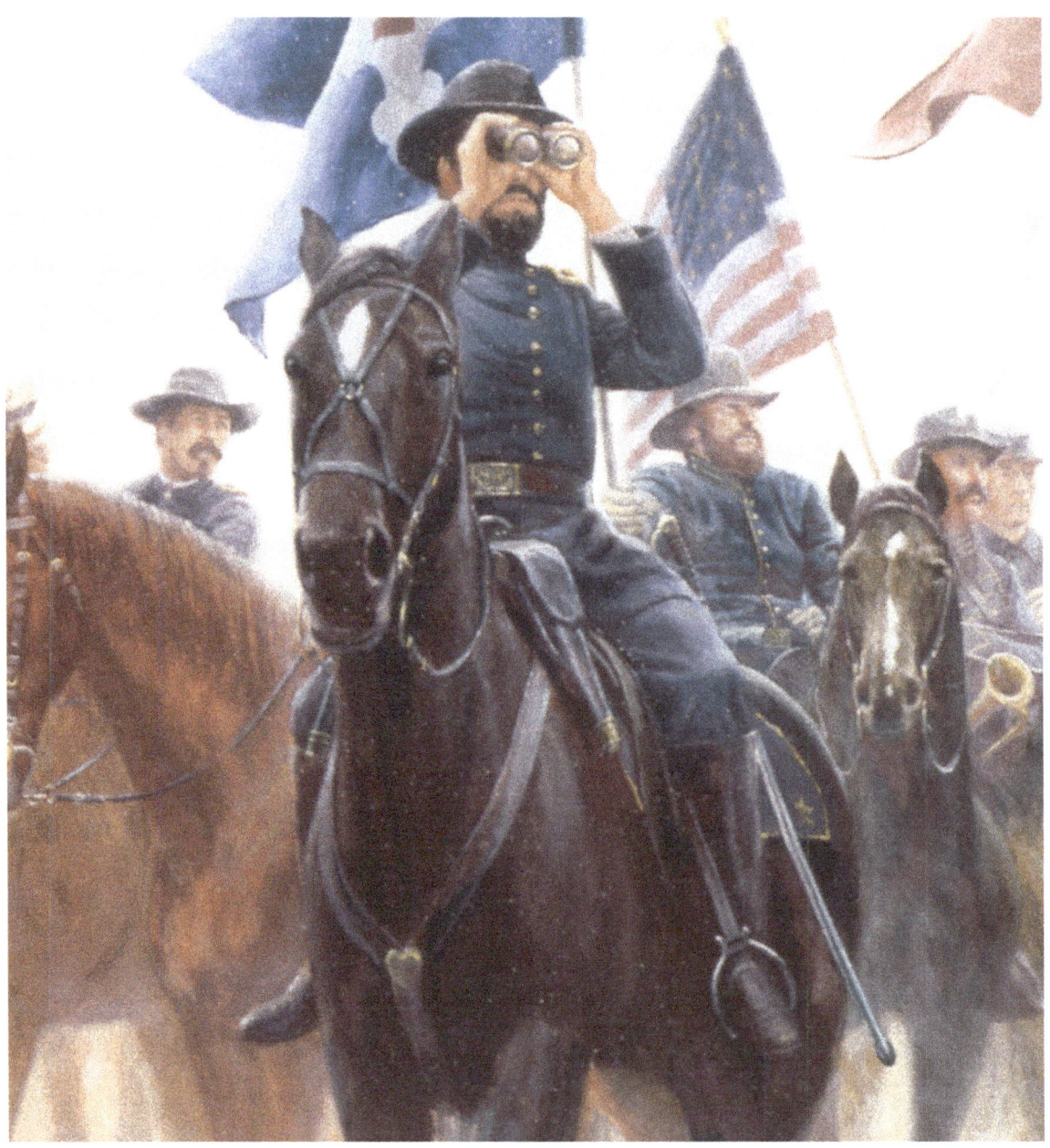

is seen in the right background. The two artillery pieces are both 3-inch ordnance rifles, part of Lt. John Calef's Battery A, Second U.S. Artillery. They were positioned at this site and are there to this day. The worm fence has been torn down at this point to prepare the ridge for defense. In the background, a shell bursts near one of the horse holders of the dismounted cavalry while the animals are being led to a safer area behind the ridge.

Buford's ever-present pipe protrudes from his chest pocket. His headquarters flag, carried by the corporal behind him, with the two number ones in block lettering (First Brigade, First Division), was the standard headquarters flag adopted for the Cavalry Corps in early 1863. His horse is held by a dismounted sergeant, immediately below the general's outstretched arm.

Reynolds, on a black charger, has a western-style saddle, which is preserved in the J. Norward Wirt Collection at the MOLLUS Museum in Philadelphia, and a brace of pistols in horse holsters attached to the saddle. His uniform is regulation dress for general officers, with the buttons grouped in threes and a velvet collar and cuffs. Directly behind him wafts his headquarters flag, as illustrated in the second volume of *Headquarters Flags, American Military Equipage*. A fragment of the actual flag is also on display at the MOLLUS Museum. The cavalry escort for Reynolds was Company L of the First Maine Cavalry. Their guidon flies between the two headquarters flags. The other flag in the painting is the artillery guidon of Calef's Battery, with Calef seen mounted to the immediate right of the guidon and directly behind the artillery piece in the left foreground. The officer directly to the left of Reynolds is Capt. Miles Keogh, one of Buford's aides, who would die in 1876 at the Little Big Horn, with George Armstrong Custer.

DISTANT THUNDER

GEN. ROBERT E. LEE AT CASHTOWN
JULY 1, 1863

1998, oil, 24 x 40

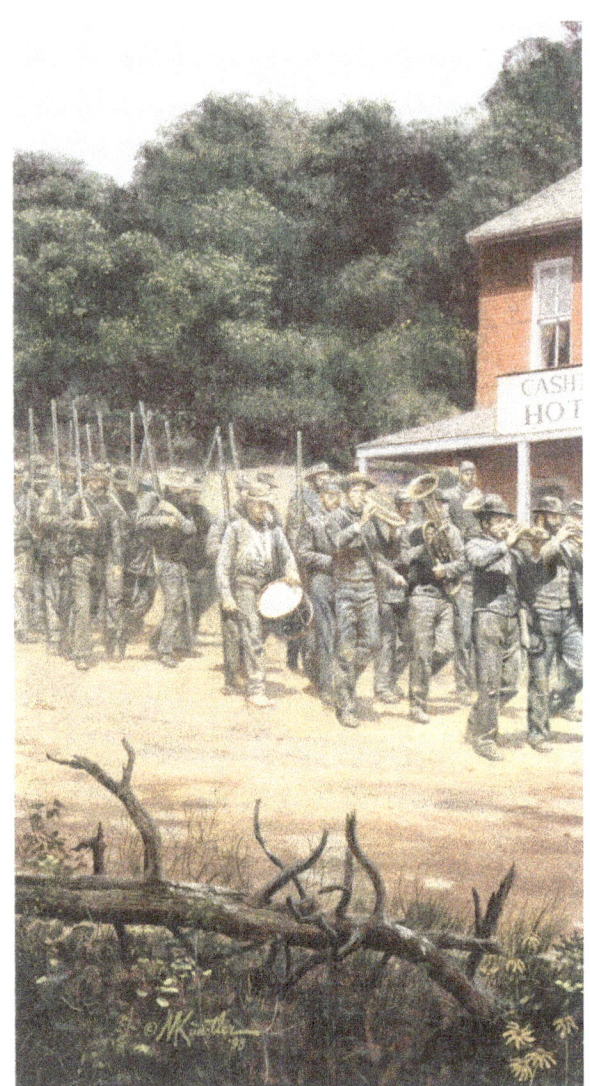

ROBERT E. LEE BEGAN July 1 with few expectations. The night before, he had camped with some of the rearmost elements of his army at Greenwood, west of the Cashtown Gap. He planned to spend this day consolidating his army near Cashtown or possibly Gettysburg. At midmorning, he and James Longstreet heard artillery fire in the east, but neither knew what was happening or what troops might be engaged.

When no answers were forthcoming, Lee left Longstreet and rode to A. P. Hill's headquarters at Cashtown.

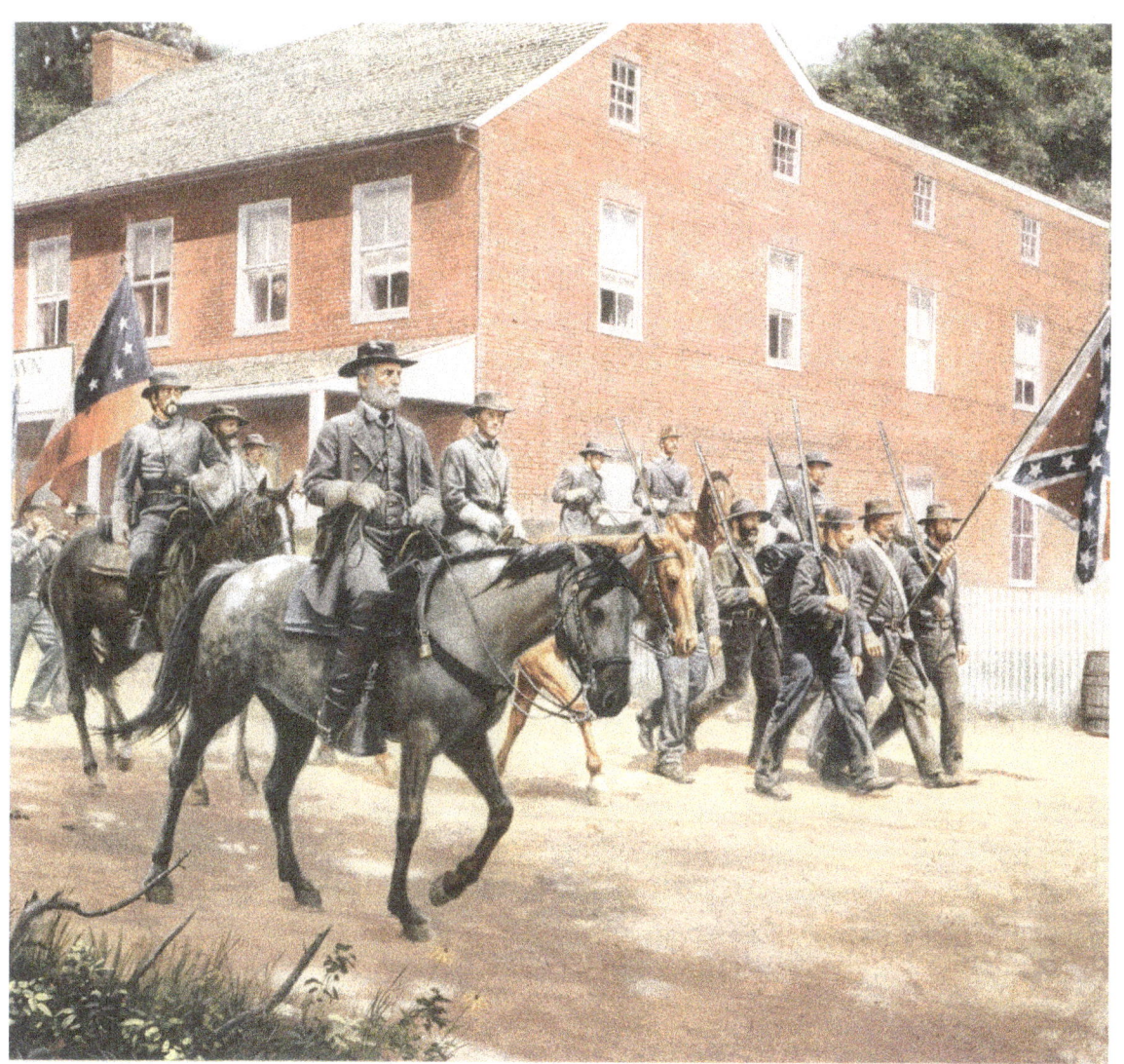

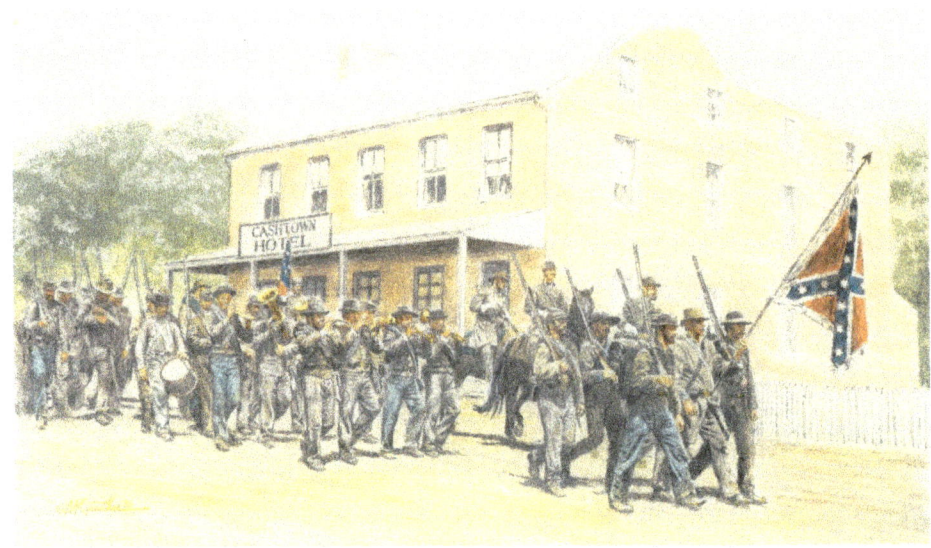

"STRIKE UP A LIVELY AIR . . ."

CASHTOWN, PENNSYLVANIA, JULY 1, 1863

1993, mixed media, 11¼ x 19½

There, Lee found Hill, who had been ailing, as concerned as he was. Hill reported that Henry Heth had been sent to Gettysburg with two divisions and two artillery battalions. Heth had since sent back word that he had encountered Union cavalry, and Hill confirmed that he had instructed Heth not to initiate a general engagement. Hill rode off to investigate the situation, and Lee waited at Cashtown until about noon. Then impatience got the better of him, and he rode toward the sounds of the guns in order to take control of what was beginning to sound like a large engagement. He ordered Richard H. Anderson to follow with his division.

After 135 years of Gettysburg-related artwork, there are still many scenes that beg to be painted—or painted as I believe they occurred. Prior to the 135th anniversary of the battle, I visited the Cashtown Inn and pondered the events that transpired on the road outside the inn's front door: the marching foot soldiers, their officers, and Robert E. Lee. I imagined the pageantry and drama of the particular moment when Lee would have passed the inn, and I decided this would make a powerful and memorable picture.

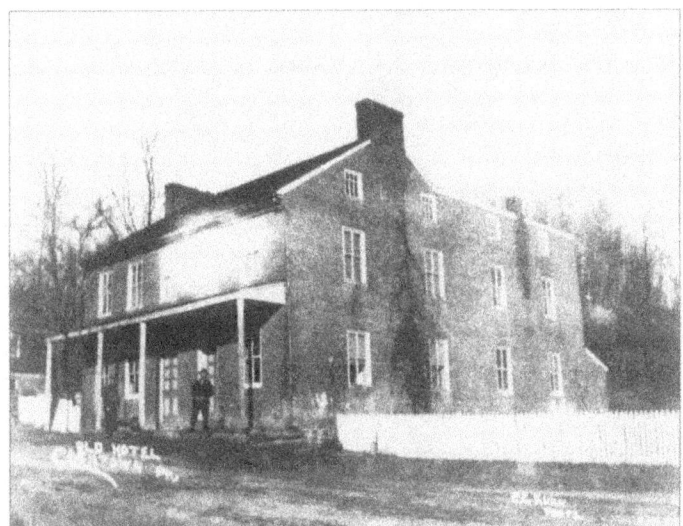

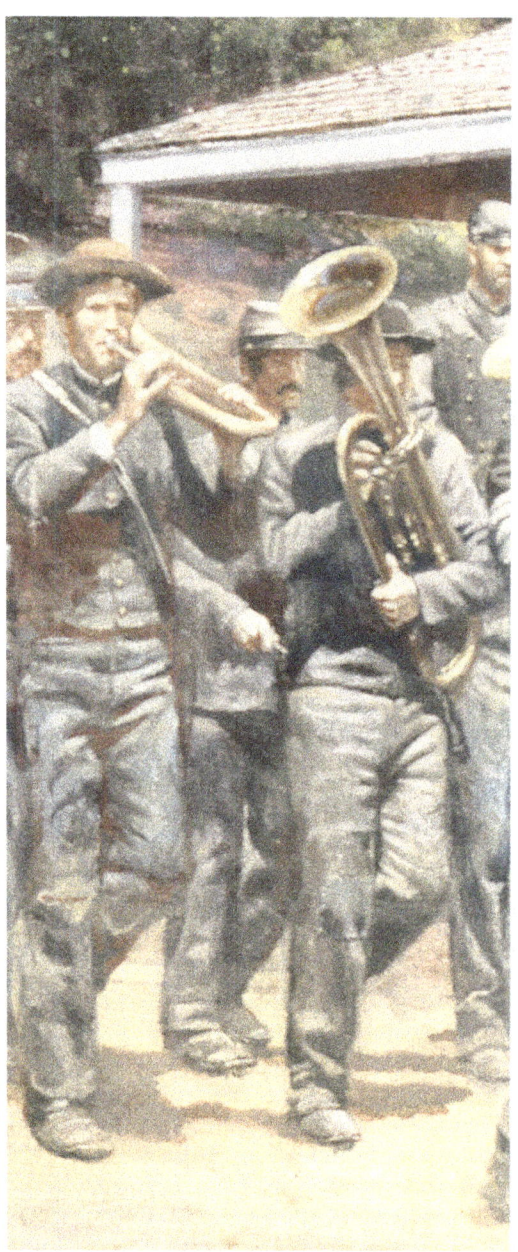

Lee and his staff passed the inn at Cashtown about midday on July 1, while Anderson's brigade was moving up the road. Several bands also went by the inn that day, and I thought of a scene similar to Thomas J. "Stonewall" Jackson's triumphant 1862 entry into Winchester, Virginia, which was the subject of my painting *Jackson Enters Winchester.*

In Cashtown, it had rained the night before, which kept the dust down, and the morning's mist had given way to a bright, sunny day. These weather conditions allowed me to use the contrasts of light and shade to create a dramatic effect. I deliberately placed Lee in shade to create the greatest contrast of light and dark between the black of the underside of Lee's hat against the white of the sunlight on the side of the porch. This brings the eye immediately to Lee, the center of interest.

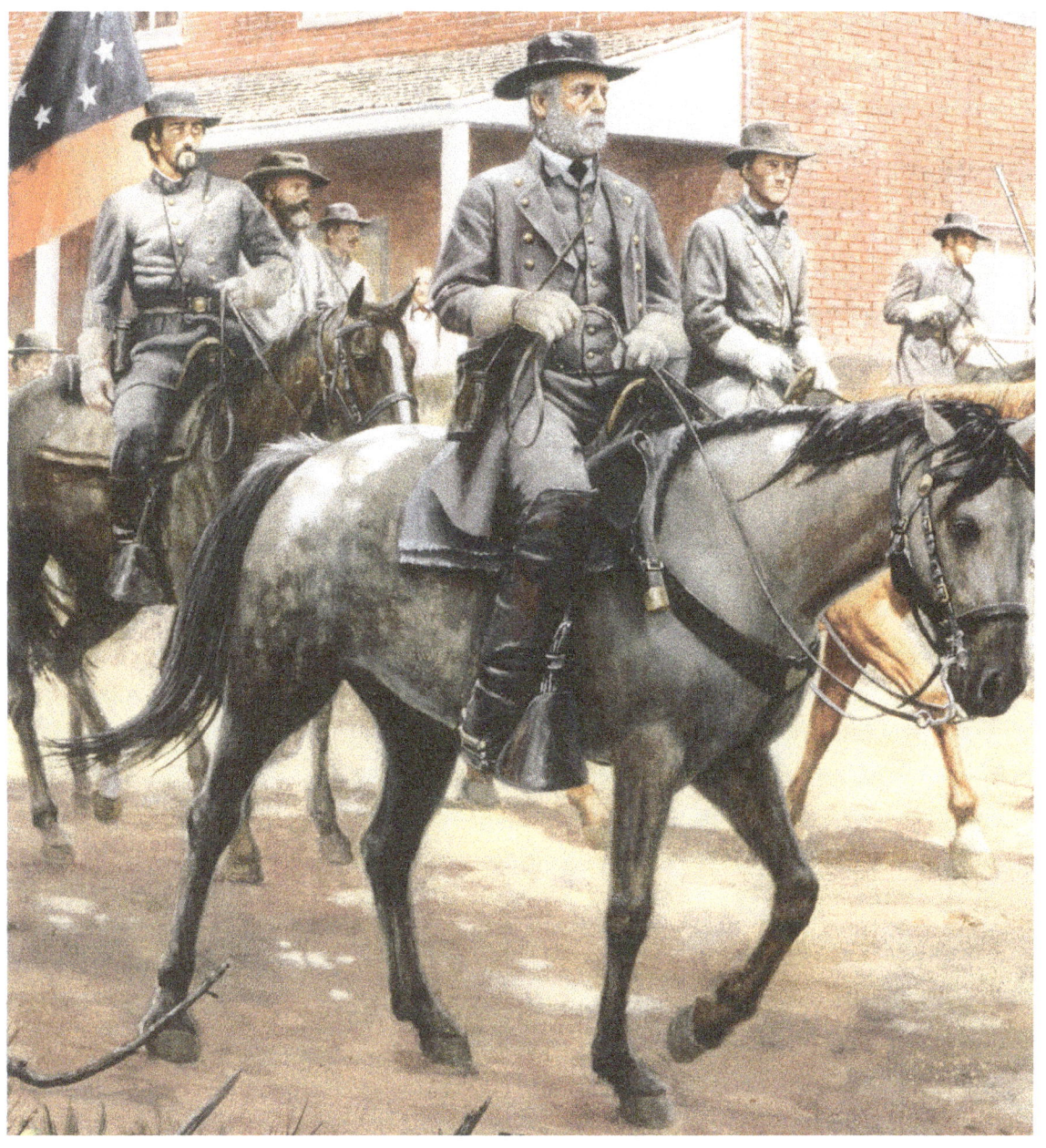

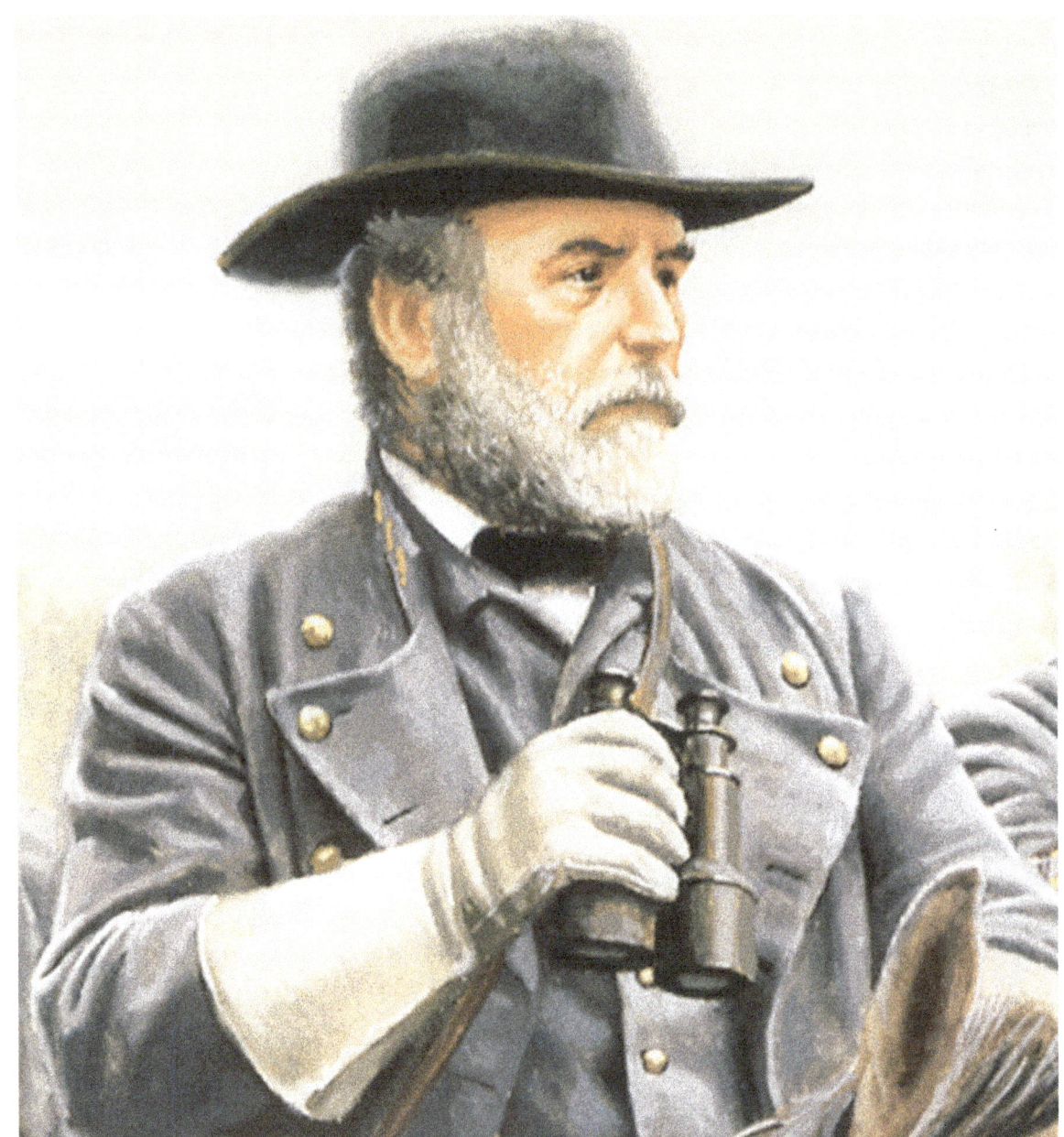

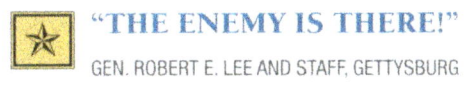

"THE ENEMY IS THERE!"

GEN. ROBERT E. LEE AND STAFF, GETTYSBURG

1993, gouache, 17 x 13¼

AROUND 1:30 P.M. LEE found Hill a little more than a mile southwest of Oak Hill, off the Chambersburg Pike, on a patch of ground known as Belmont Ridge. The fighting Lee witnessed seemed to be more an artillery duel than a battle, which suited him, since he did not want to engage the enemy until Longstreet's corps had come up. In the meantime, two of Richard S. Ewell's divisions appeared, giving the Confederates a numerical advantage over the two Union corps then at Gettysburg. Lee would have preferred to wait for Longstreet, but Ewell's men attacked as soon as they saw the enemy. Although he had no idea as to how much of Meade's army was closing in on the crossroads of Gettysburg, Lee had little choice but to order Hill into the fray. Random chance had given him an opportunity to attack the enemy's front and flank simultaneously. He could not ignore it, although he did not know where the other Union corps were.

Most of my paintings of Gettysburg were done as part of a companion book to Ron Maxwell's 1993 movie *Gettysburg*, which was based on Michael

Shaara's novel *The Killer Angels.* Shaara built his narrative around four central characters: Robert E. Lee and James Longstreet for the Confederates and John Buford and Joshua Lawrence Chamberlain for the Union. I wanted to include a portrait of each man in the book, as well as a painting of each individual in a specific situation. That is how this painting of Lee came about.

LEE ON TRAVELLER

1995, mixed media, 18⁄ x 25⁄

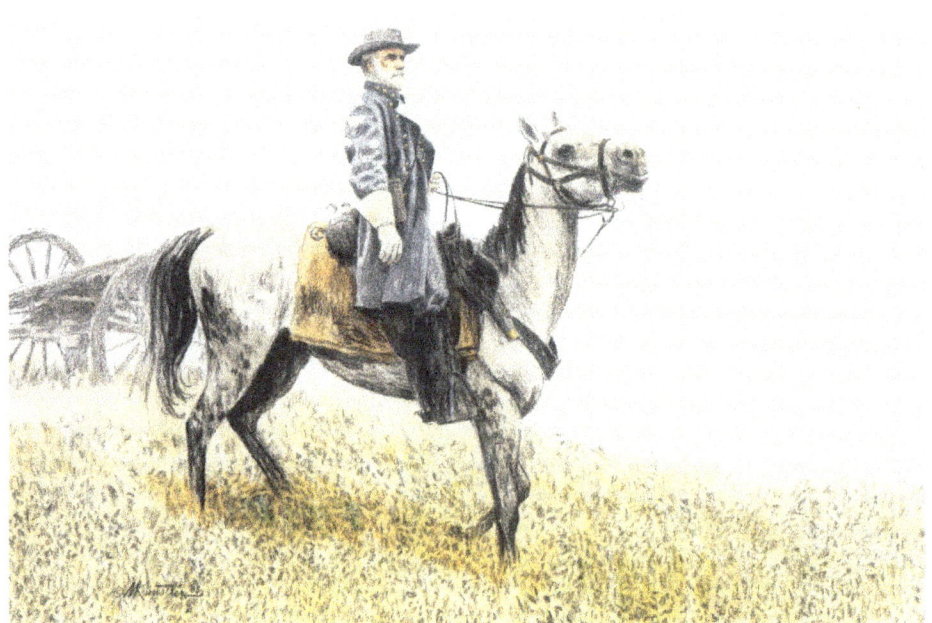

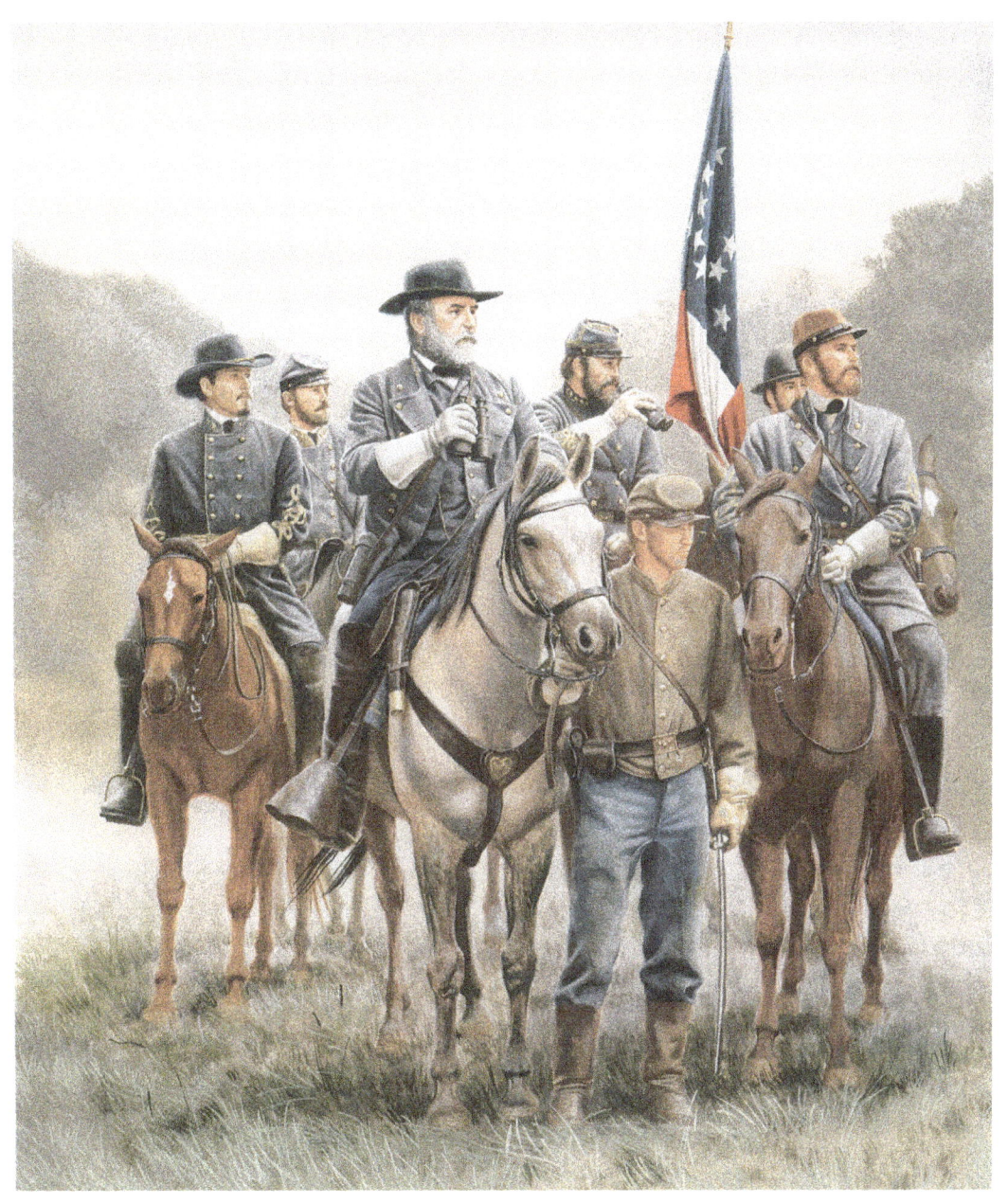

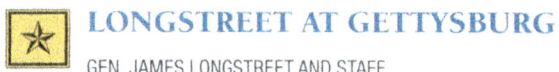

LONGSTREET AT GETTYSBURG

GEN. JAMES LONGSTREET AND STAFF

1993, gouache. 16¼ x 13

AFTER THE DEATH OF Stonewall Jackson, James Longstreet became not only Robert E. Lee's senior lieutenant but also his senior adviser. Occasionally, the fact that Longstreet, as well as his staff, was not from Virginia was a source of tension with other commands within the Army of Northern Virginia. Some historians have pointed out that Longstreet, as a non-Virginian, had a strategic vision that encompassed the whole Confederacy, while many Virginians (including Lee) focused their thinking primarily on their native state.

In the decades that followed the war, Lee and Longstreet's relationship was obscured by critics who could never find fault with Lee's generalship. But there is no doubt that in the weeks preceding the battle of Gettysburg and for the months after the battle and leading to Appomattox Court House, Lee and Longstreet were in accord. The great question of Gettysburg, though, is how the Lee-Longstreet partnership malfunctioned on this battlefield.

Longstreet joined Lee on the battlefield at midafternoon on July 1. The two commanders scanned the same landscape, and Longstreet allegedly said

68

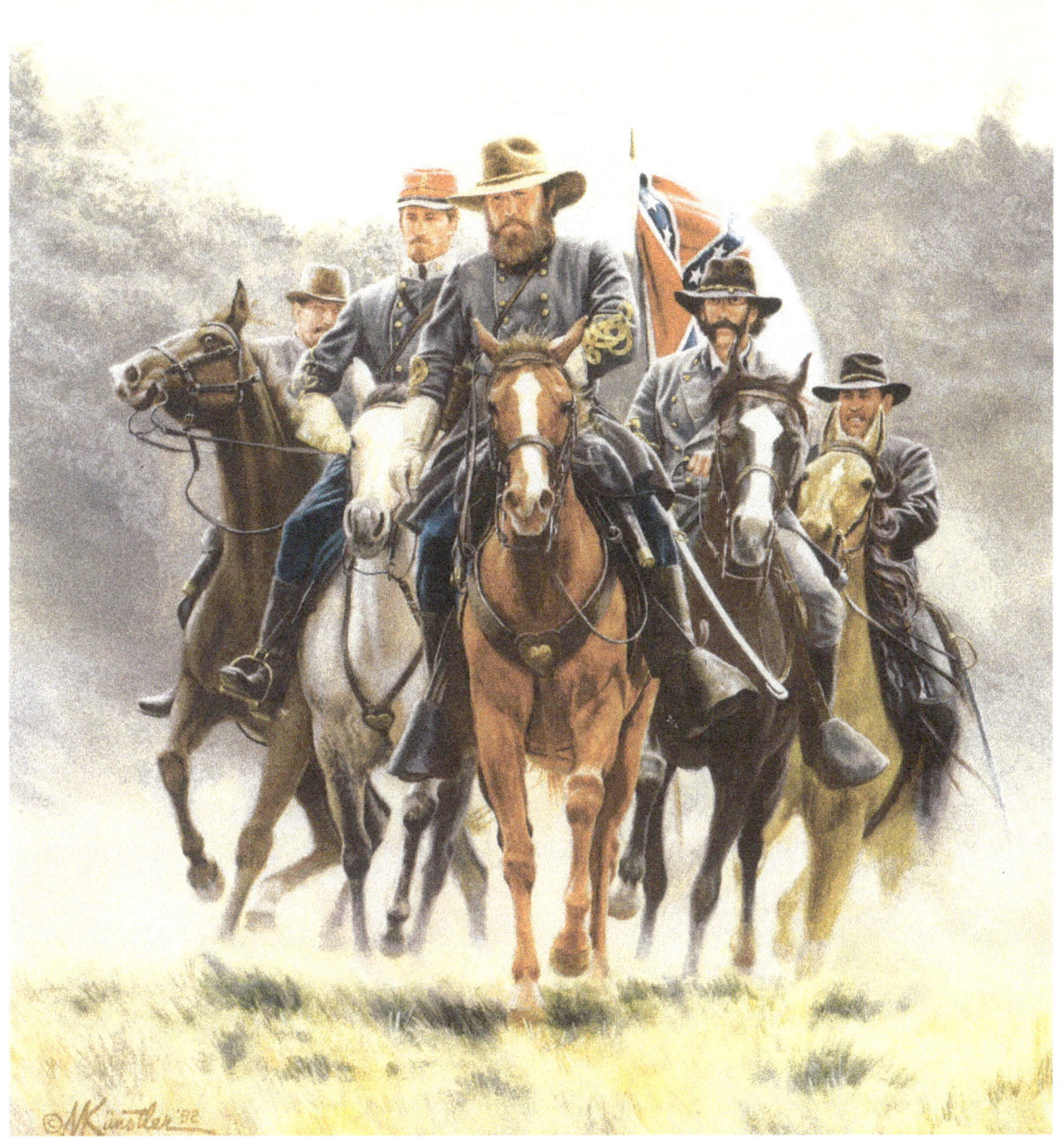

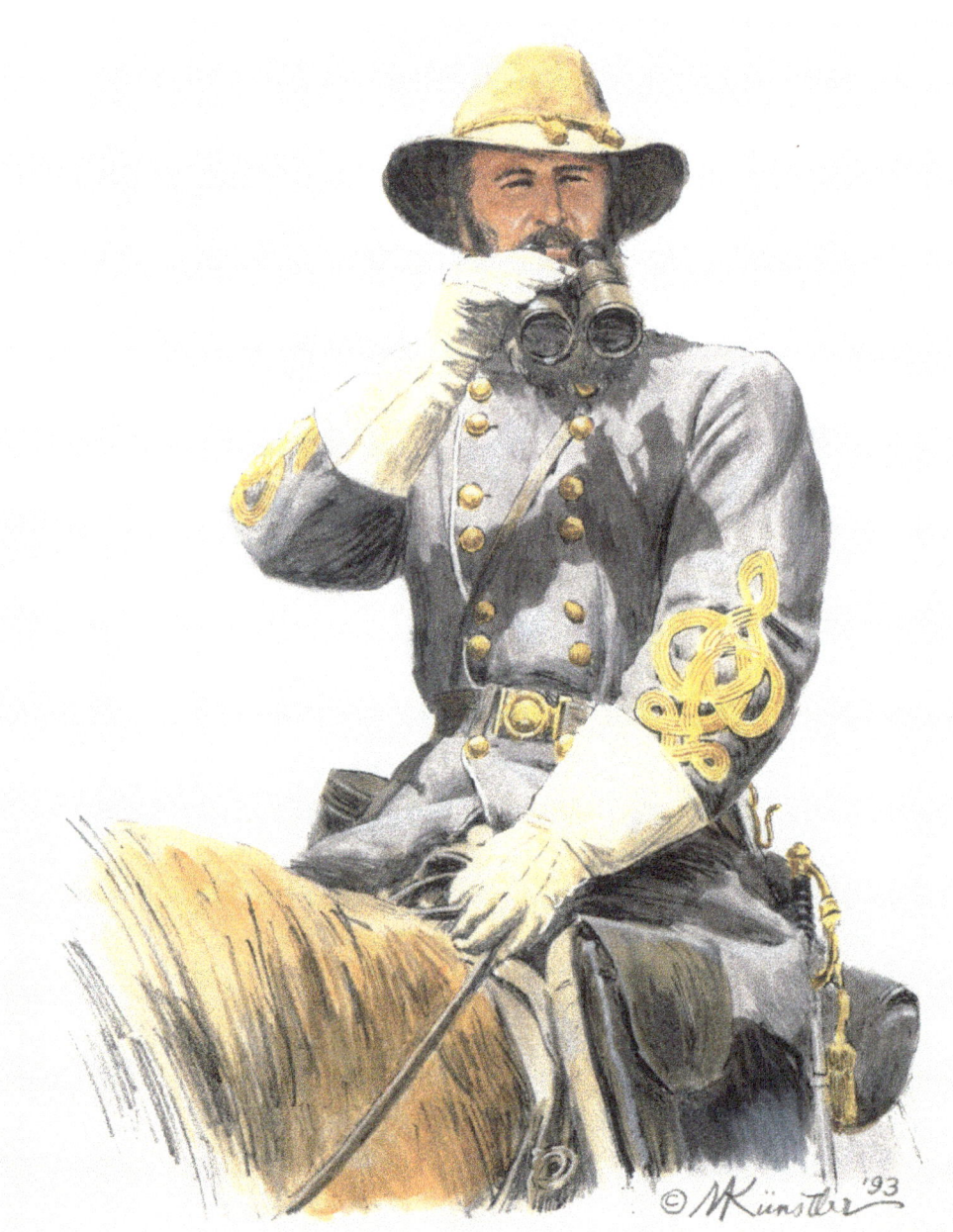

that the terrain was perfect for the kind of offensive-defensive campaign he imagined and proposed flanking and withdrawal tactics to engage Meade.

Lee, however, supposedly responded, "No," pointed forcefully toward Cemetery Ridge and said, "The enemy is there, and I am going to attack him there."

"If he is there," Longstreet replied, "it will be because he is anxious that we should attack him: a good reason, in my judgment, for not doing so."

"OLD PETE"

GEN. JAMES LONGSTREET

1993, mixed media, 14¼ x 9½

◄ FACING

"WE ALL DO OUR DUTY"

GEN. JAMES LONGSTREET

1993, mixed media, 11¼ x 9½

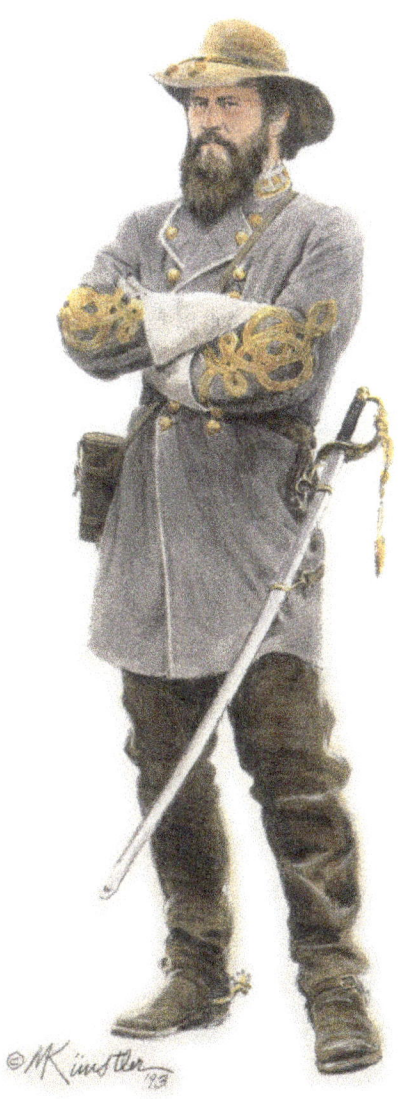

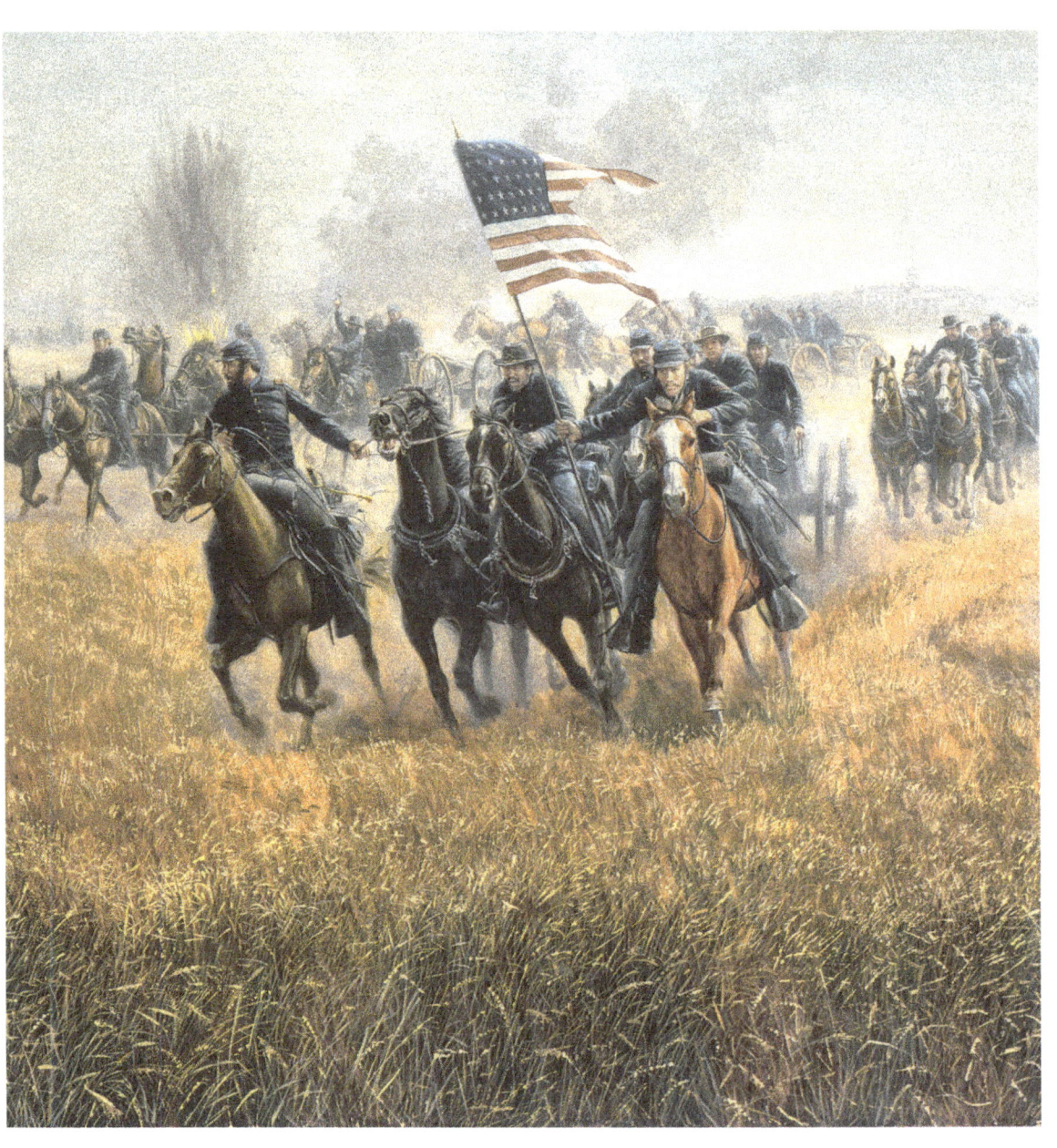

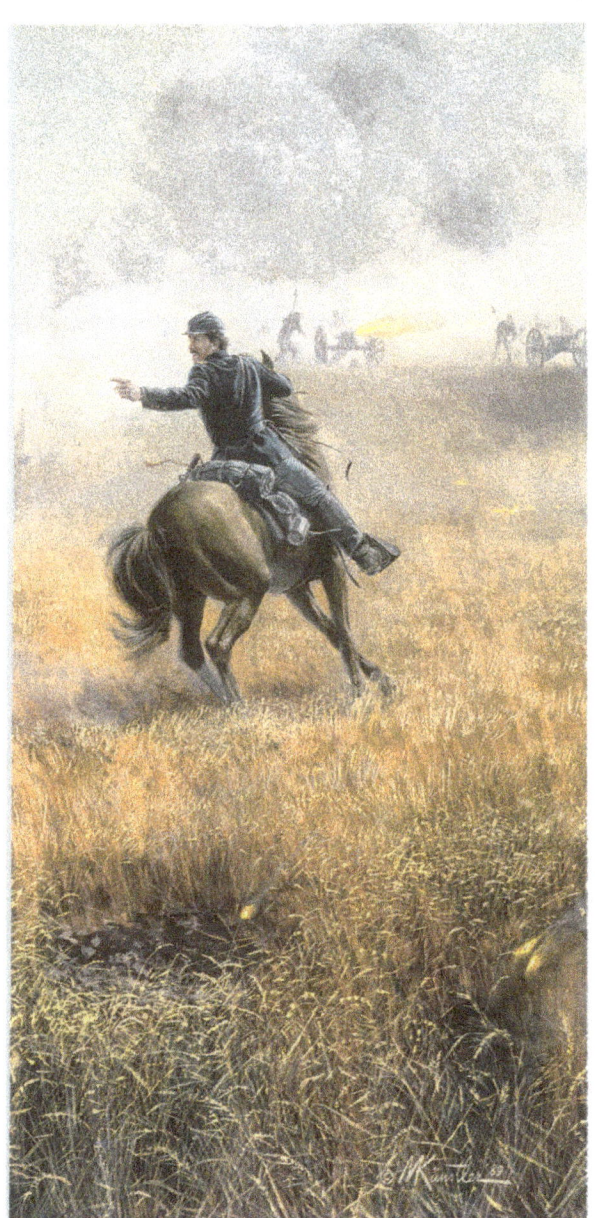

 ## DILGER AT GETTYSBURG

JULY 1, 1863

1989, oil, 28 x 42

BY MIDAFTERNOON, THE UNION line was beginning to buckle under the Confederate onslaught. In the action of that afternoon, Capt. Hubert Dilger, one of the foremost artillerists in the Union army, ordered two of his guns forward of the main battle line without infantry support. This type of bold action was unheard of at the time, and it is the moment depicted here.

Under fire, Dilger orders a section of two guns forward to a more advantageous position against the Confederate guns on Oak Hill. The section's lieutenant guides the off-lead horse, which is shying from the gunfire. A corporal with the battery guidon rides next to the lead driver. Six horses pull the limber that tows the cannon, and behind them is the caisson. Each gun usually had a crew of ten. Dilger's second gun follows on the right.

In laying out the painting, I studied various angles and researched harnesses, saddles, gun carriages, and artillery implements. Artillerymen faced tremendous danger during this maneuver; they were completely exposed as they directed the six-horse team.

Dilger's deployment occurred over open farmland that was mostly wheat field and pasture. In the lower right corner, shells have scorched the ground, and small fires have begun.

The section made its courageous move at about 4:00 p.m., and sunlight can be seen breaking through the heavy smoke to the right, or west, of the picture. The two artillery pieces to the far right are where the battery was posted originally, and the battery's monument stands there today.

In the background is the Old Dorm of Pennsylvania College (now known as Gettysburg College). The building stands today basically unchanged, but because of the town's growth, it is difficult to see the dormitory from where Dilger's men stood. The small field where his section charged, however, has been preserved.

Dilger's men were exceptional, and his battery performed well, but it had little effect against the Confederate attack that afternoon. Later his men heroically held off Southern infantry by themselves, giving retreating Union troops sufficient time to form a secondary line of defense on Cemetery Hill.

The special danger artillerymen faced during the war has often been overlooked. This is my tribute to these unsung heroes on this famed battlefield.

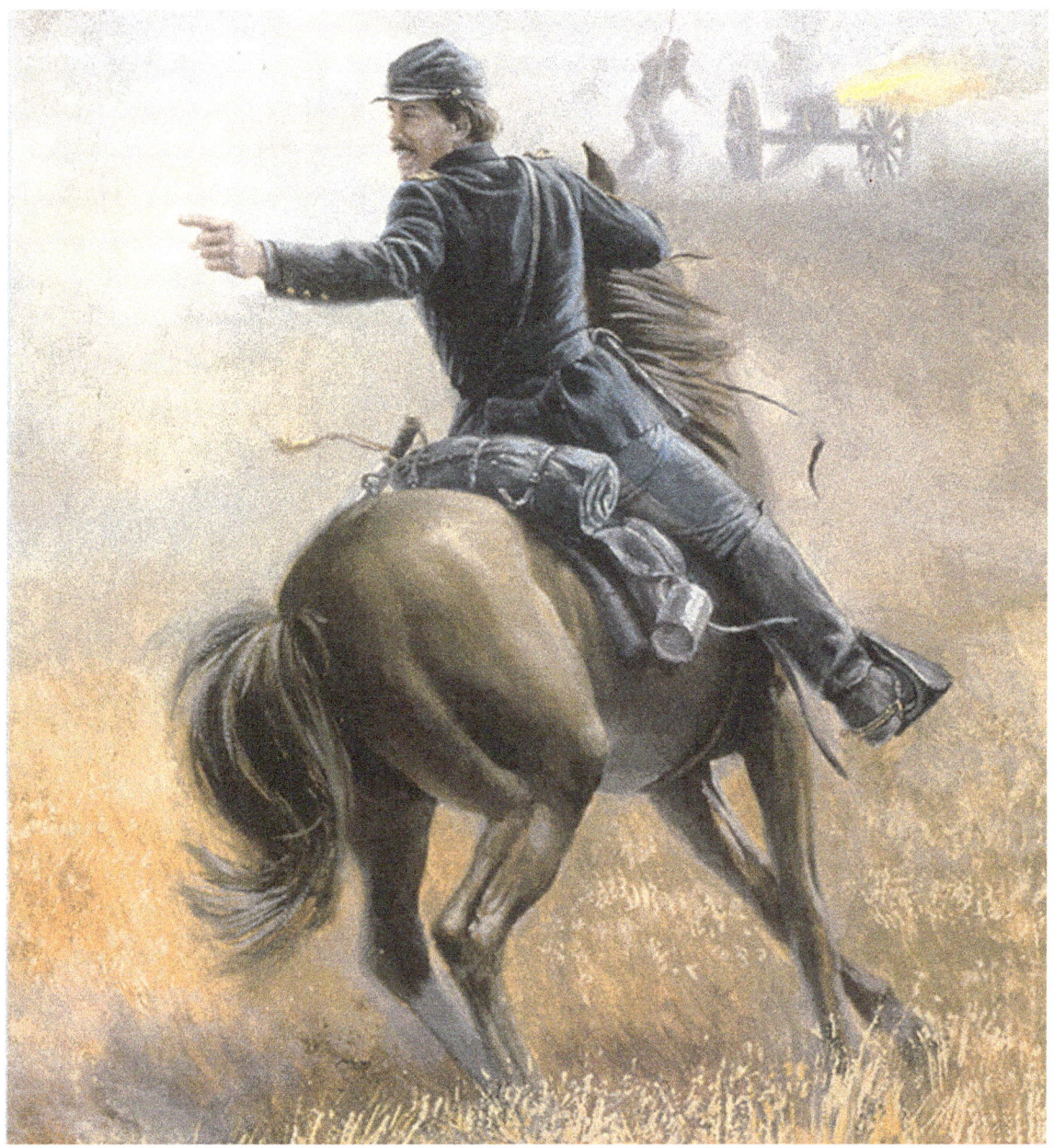

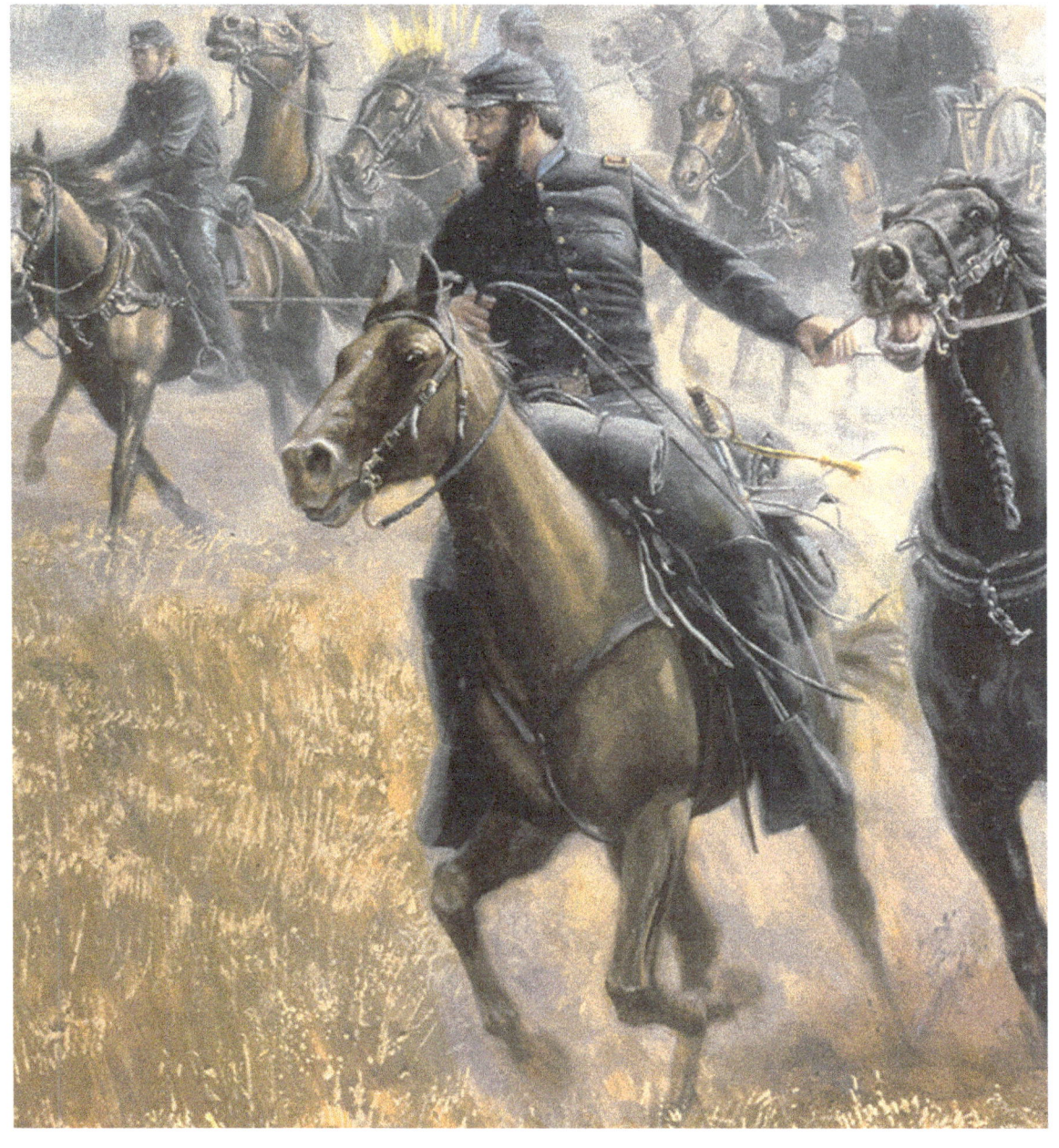

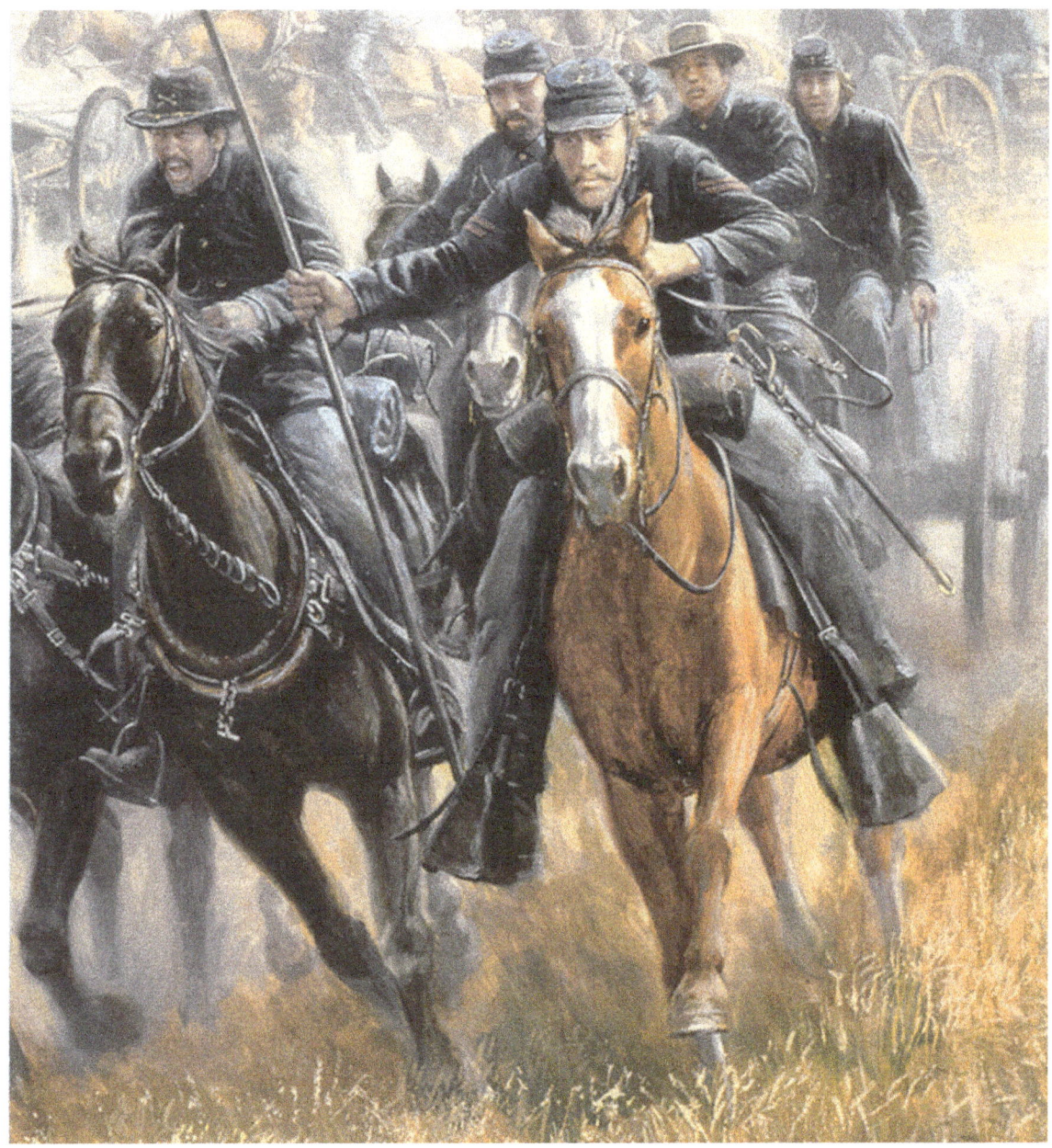

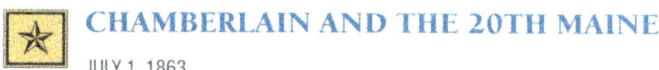

CHAMBERLAIN AND THE 20TH MAINE

JULY 1, 1863

1993, gouache, 16 x 13¼

AMONG THE ELEMENTS OF the Army of the Potomac marching toward Gettysburg was the Fifth Corps, which included the Twentieth Maine and its colonel, Joshua Lawrence Chamberlain—the college professor turned warrior (see volume 2, pages 55–56). In the early afternoon of July 1, the corps crossed the border into Pennsylvania, eliciting a sense of excitement among the ranks of the corps' twelve regiments from the Keystone State. Soon the soldiers heard the low rumble of artillery, then they came upon the town of Hanover and debris from a recent cavalry battle: trampled fields, broken weapons, and dead horses. As the corps prepared to camp, a messenger arrived with news of the desperate battle waged by the First and Eleventh corps, and orders were quickly given to march to Gettysburg without delay.

A new sense of urgency propelled the men forward. When darkness fell, a full moon appeared, and the regimental bands set the pace for the advance. Along the path, farmers and townspeople came out to see the soldiers and offer them water and food. Young girls waved handkerchiefs, sang songs, and flirted with the marching men.

78

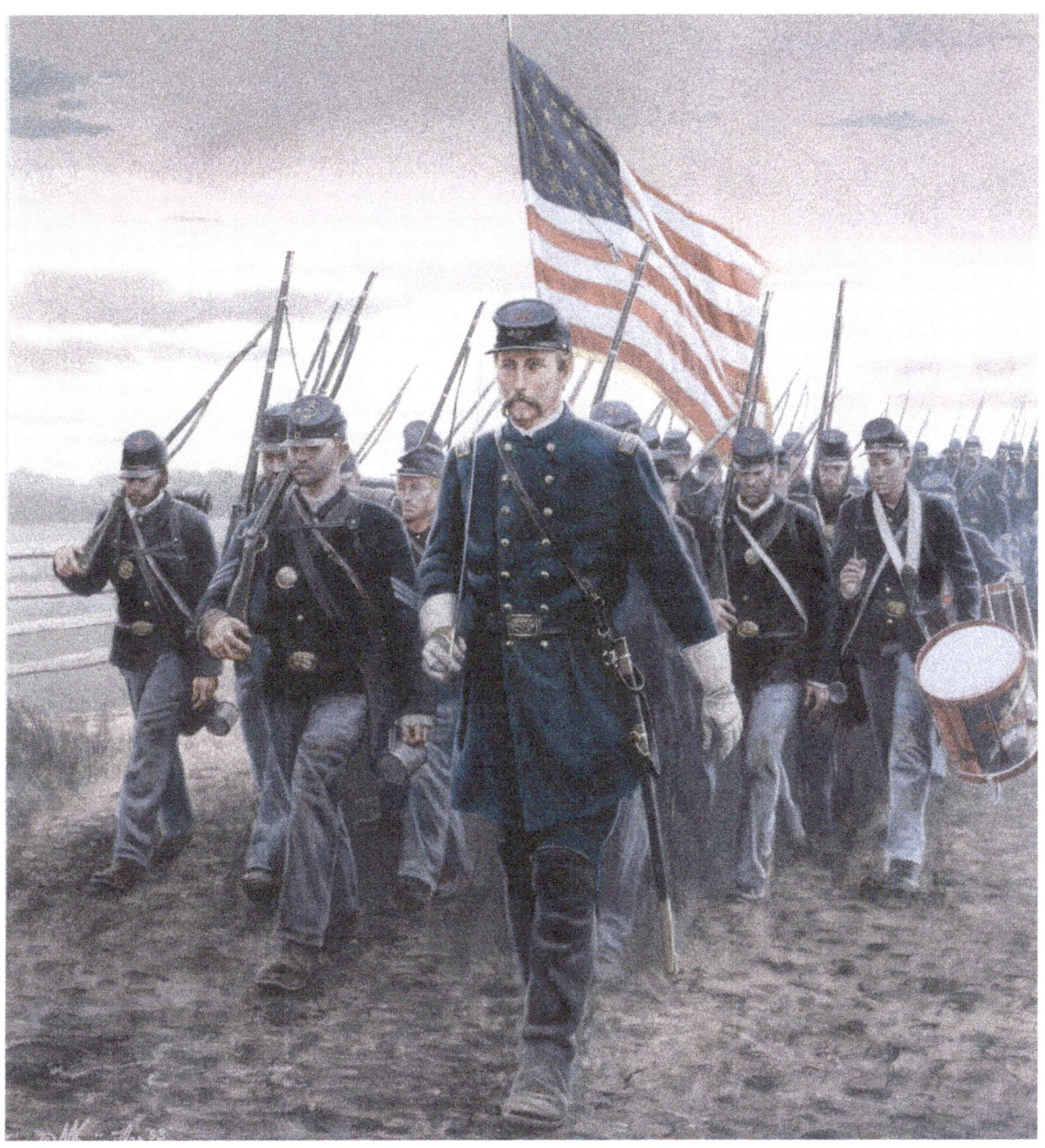

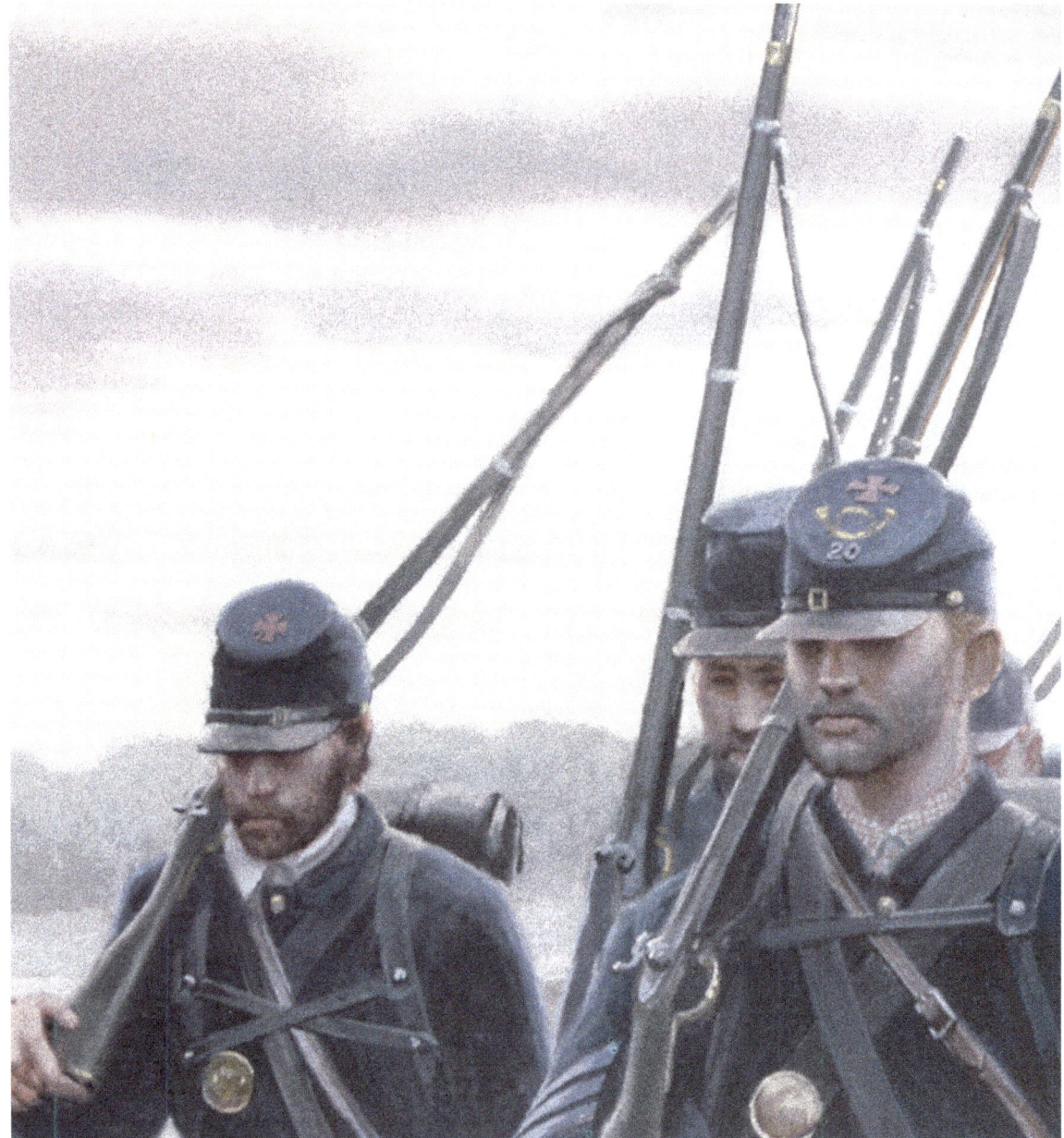

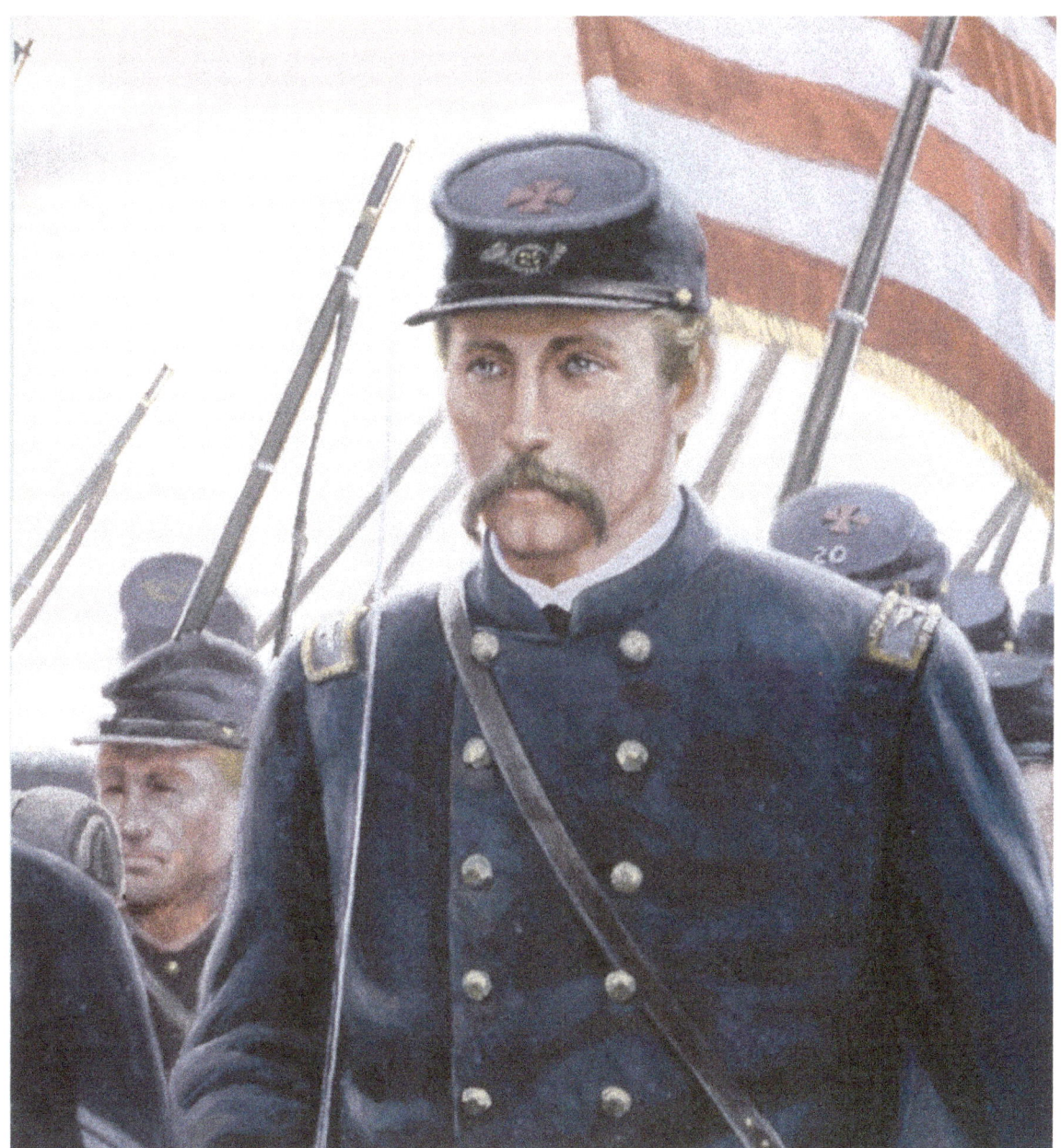

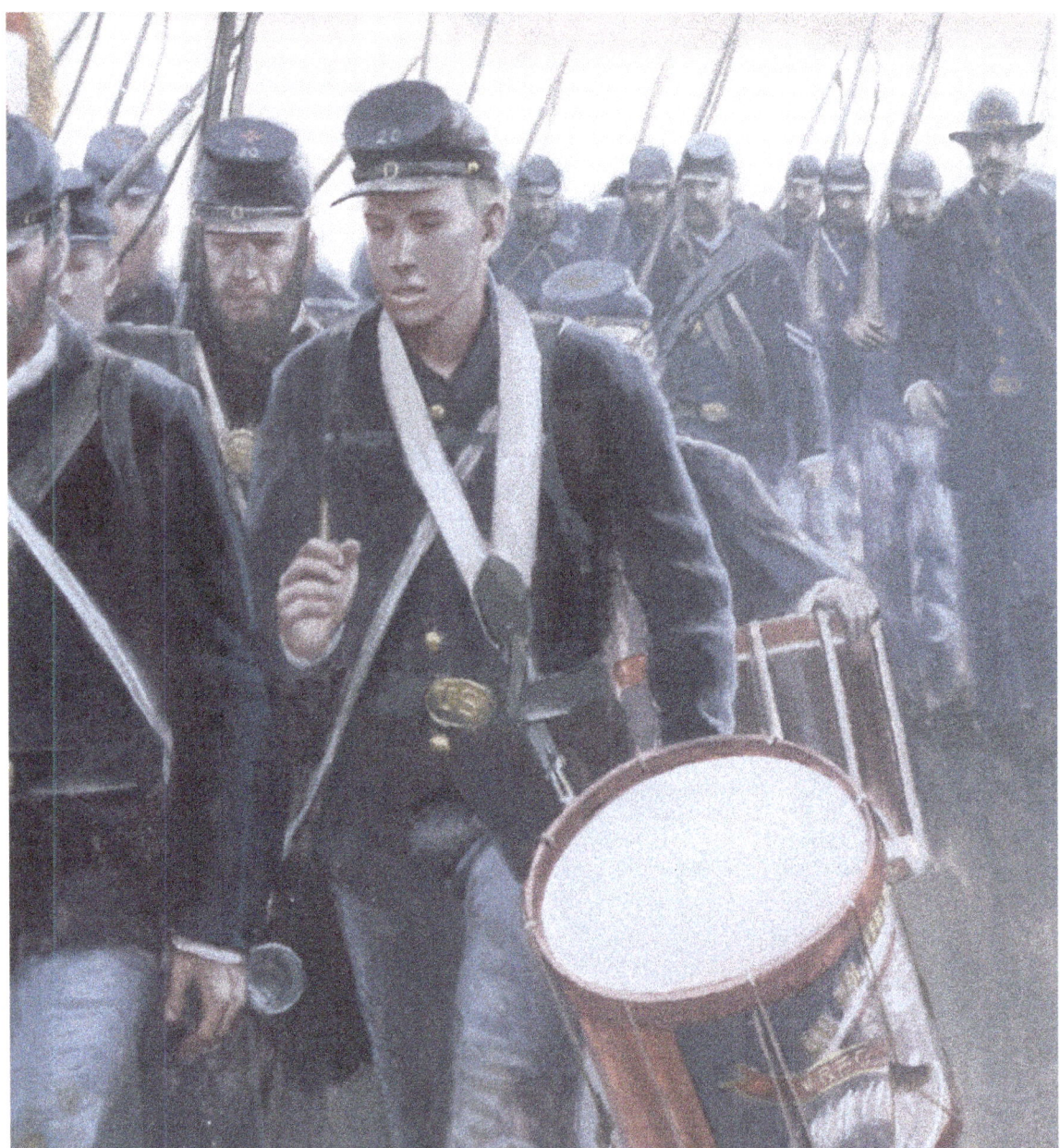

Chamberlain recalled, "All things, even the most common, were magnified and made mysterious by the strange spell of night."

Rumors ran through the ranks, passed from man to man. Some said that George B. McClellan had returned to lead the army (he had not), others claimed that the ghost of George Washington had been seen riding across the fields near Gettysburg.

At midnight, the corps halted, and the men fell asleep at the side of the road, two or three miles from the battlefield. At 3:00 a.m. all were awakened and ordered to resume the march.

They arrived on the outskirts of town around 7:00 a.m. and were directed to the southeast. The men of the Fifth Corps were placed to the rear of the right side of the Union line and continually shifted farther right. Chamberlain kept his men in a line of battle and issued twenty extra rounds of ammunition to each. While the sun and temperature rose in unison, all waited for orders, some dozed, and others searched their haversacks for food.

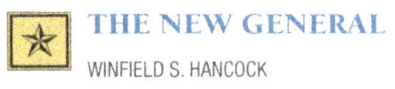
At the end of the first day of battle at Gettysburg, Gen. Winfield Scott Hancock commanded the Union army in the field. Meade did not arrive on site until the evening. John F. Reynolds had been the ranking commander when the First Corps marched into the fighting, but he had been killed within minutes of his appearance at Seminary Ridge. So Meade dispatched Hancock (nicknamed "the Superb") to assess the situation and direct the fighting until Meade was on scene.

Hancock was a Pennsylvanian with a reputation for assessing chaotic conditions and bringing order to them. He was graduated from West Point in 1844 and served in the Indian Territory, the Mexican War, the Third Seminole War, and tumultuous "Bleeding Kansas." When the war broke out, he was in Los Angeles and played a significant role in keeping southern California in the Union. He arrived in Washington in August 1861 while McClellan was reorganizing the army and saw his first action at Williamsburg, during the Peninsula campaign. At Antietam, he ascended to divisional

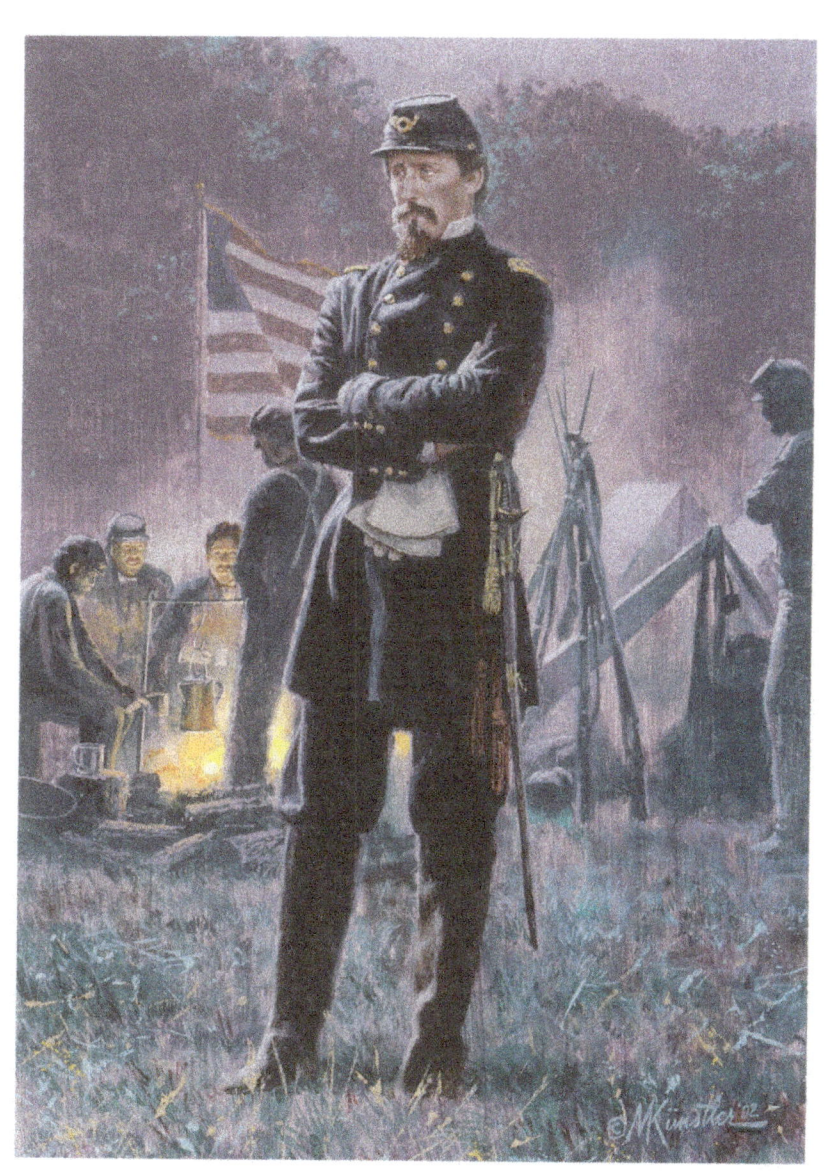

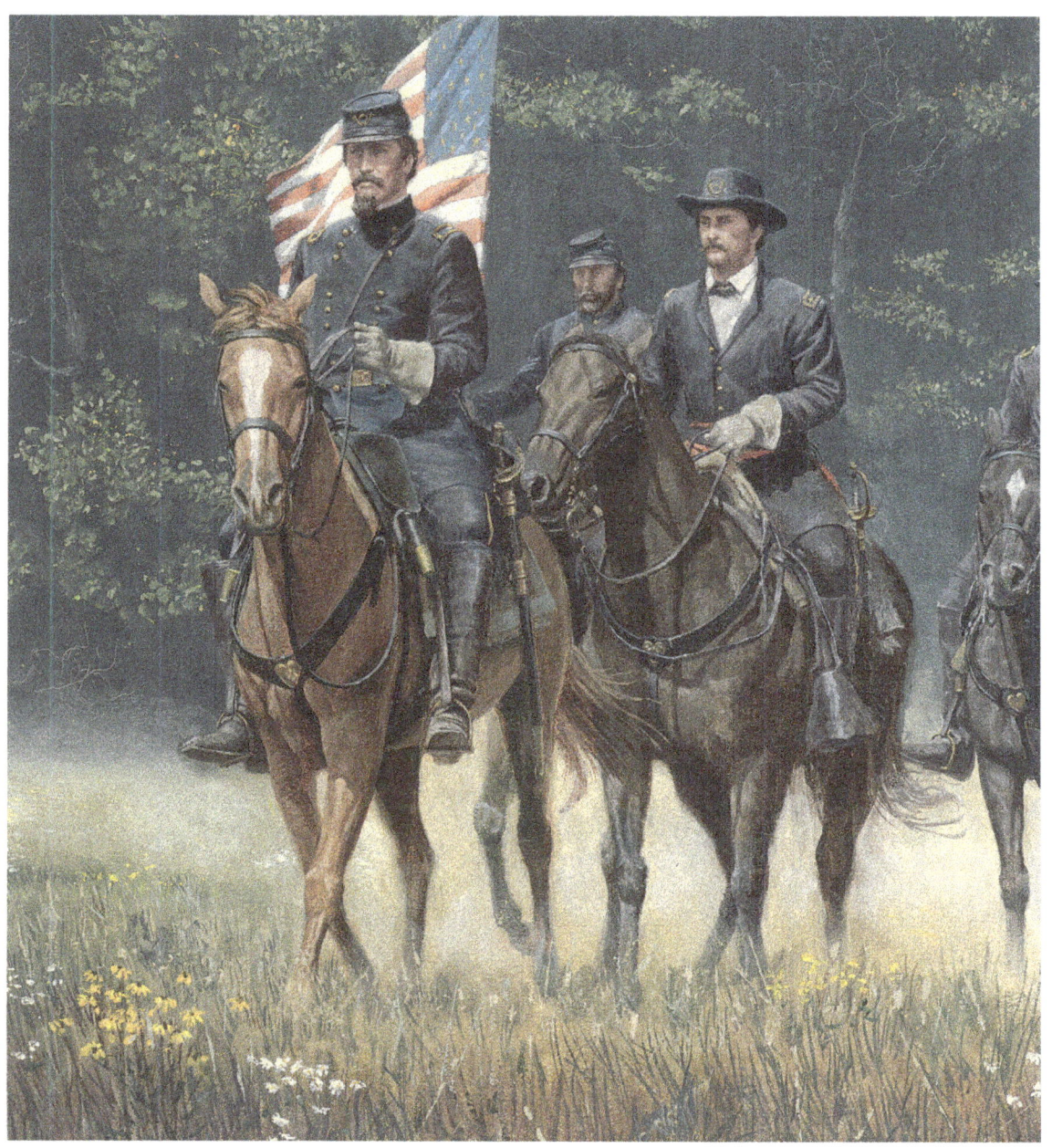

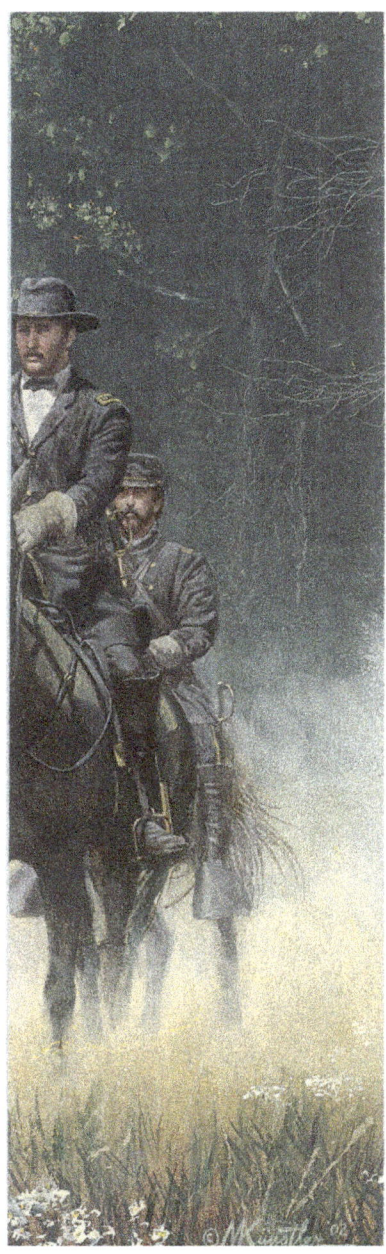

command and led his men into action at Fredericksburg and Chancellorsville. When the commander of the Second Corps resigned after the Chancellorsville disaster, Hancock was named to the command.

The term "fighting general" would apply aptly to Hancock. "He is magnificent in appearance, lordly, but cordial," a staff member wrote. Hancock differed "from other officers I have served with in being always in sight during action."

When Meade ordered Hancock to Gettysburg to take command, Hancock pointed out that Oliver O. Howard, the commander of the Eleventh Corps and already engaged at Gettysburg, had seniority. Meade said that he wanted Hancock to command the situation. "As soon as I arrived on the field," Hancock recalled, "I rode directly to General Howard and said to him that I had been sent to take command of all the forces present. He acquiesced in my assumption of command."

One of Howard's generals commented on the transfer of command, "Howard, in spite of his heart-sore,

THE SOLDIERS OF OLD GLORY

HANCOCK AND STAFF

2002, oil, 11⅞ x 14⅛

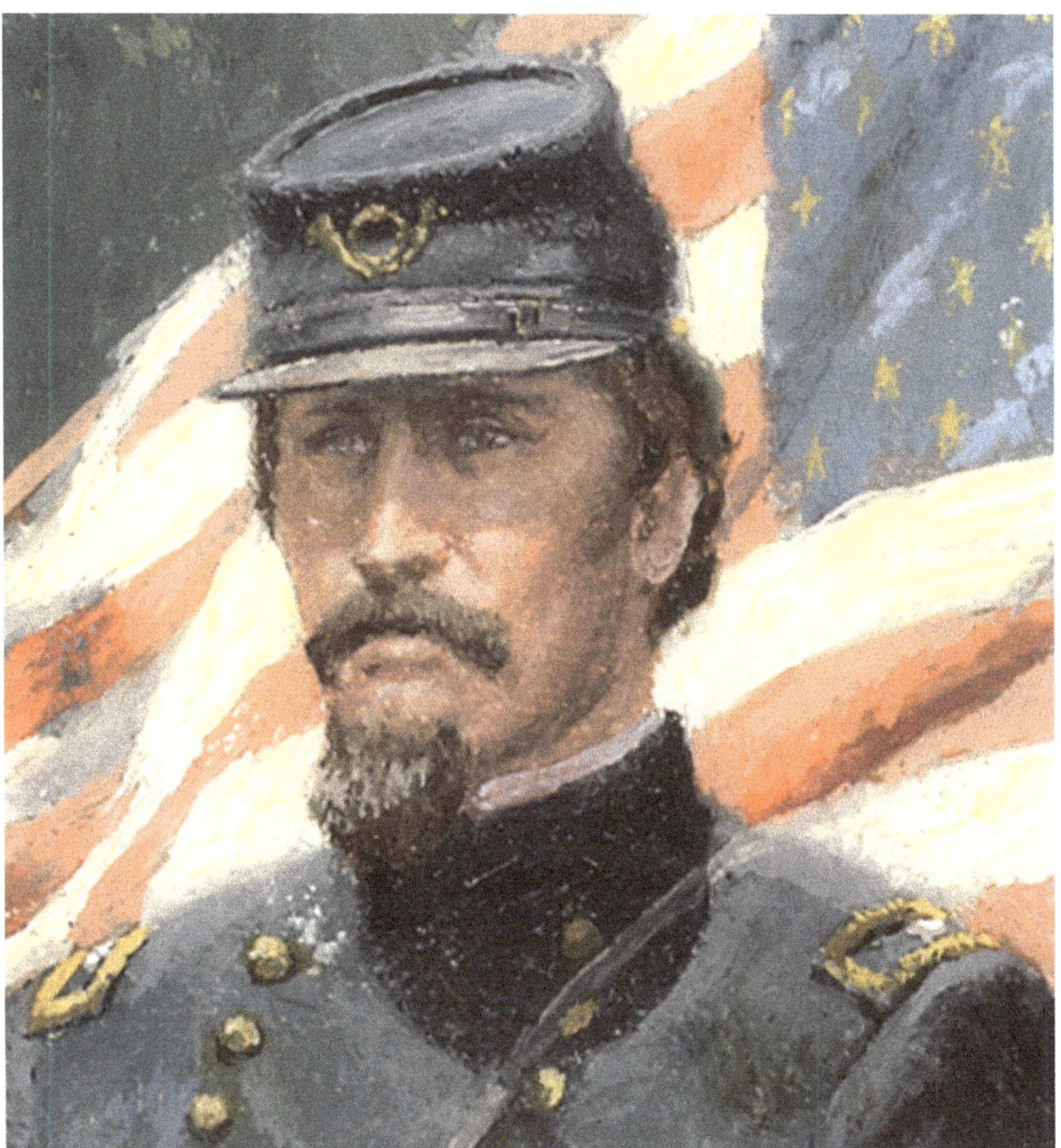

cooperated so loyally with Hancock that it would have been hard to tell which of the two was the commander and which the subordinate."

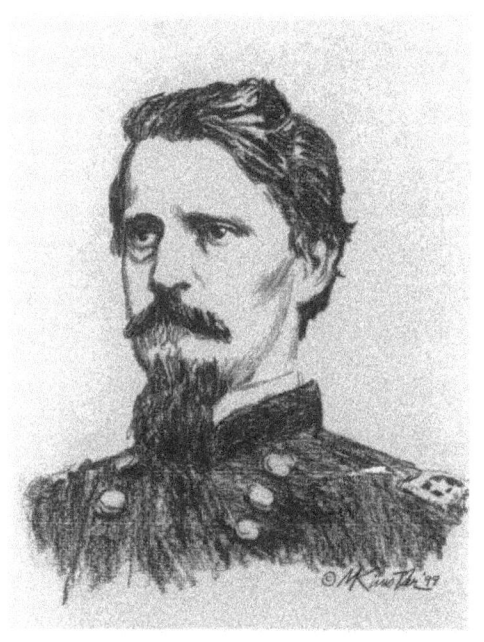

Hancock arrived at Cemetery Hill sometime between 4:00 and 4:30 p.m., which was almost simultaneous with the arrival of most of the Eleventh Corps, which had withdrawn from the fields north and west of the town to this hill southeast of the town.

One of the officers who fell back here recalled, "Directing the placement of troops where we turned up was Hancock, whose imperious and defiant bearing heartened us all."

Immediately, Hancock rallied the army on Cemetery Hill, formed a line, and sent word to Meade that the army should fight on this ground rather than fall back on the contingency plans the army commander was contemplating.

Hancock inspected the ground around Cemetery Hill, then focused on the First Corps and sent word to its commander to occupy Culp's Hill, now the right side of the Union line. After that he scrutinized the Confederate front, anxious to see if an attack was imminent, but none was. The sun set, and he waited for Meade to arrive.

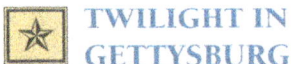

TWILIGHT IN GETTYSBURG

GEN. ROBERT E. LEE, JULY 1, 1863

1993, gouache, 16¾ x 27½

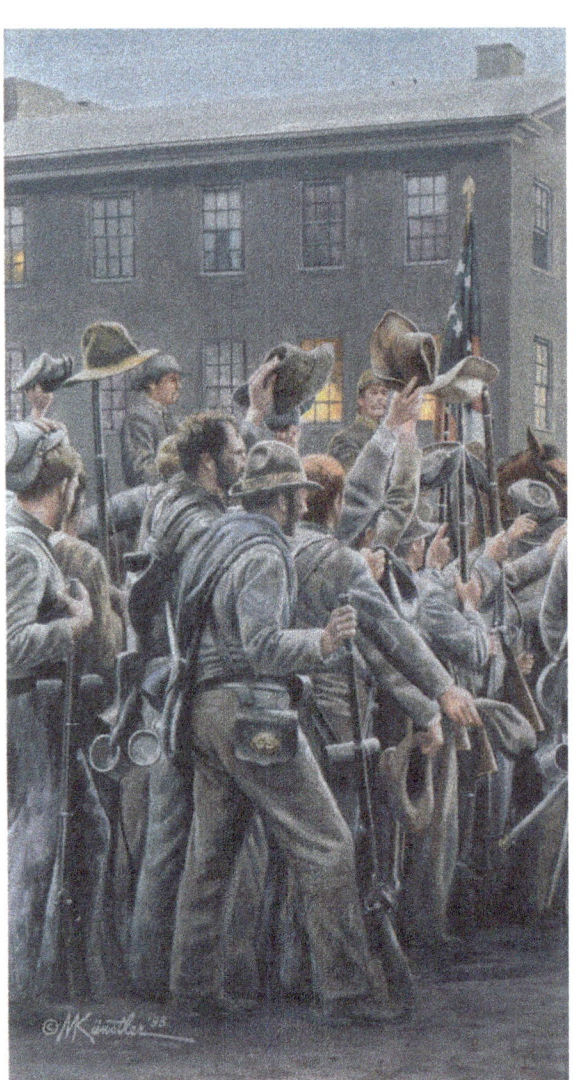

IN THE LATE AFTERNOON, the town square was filled with Confederate soldiers reveling in their victorious efforts of the day. Around 5:00 p.m., Richard S. Ewell encountered the scene and noted the mass of troops awaiting their next assignment, officers rushing from one area to another, and hordes of Union prisoners being ushered to the rear echelons.

Ewell met with his division commanders to determine what they should do next. Then he and Jubal Early rode toward Cemetery Hill to take stock of the situation and assess

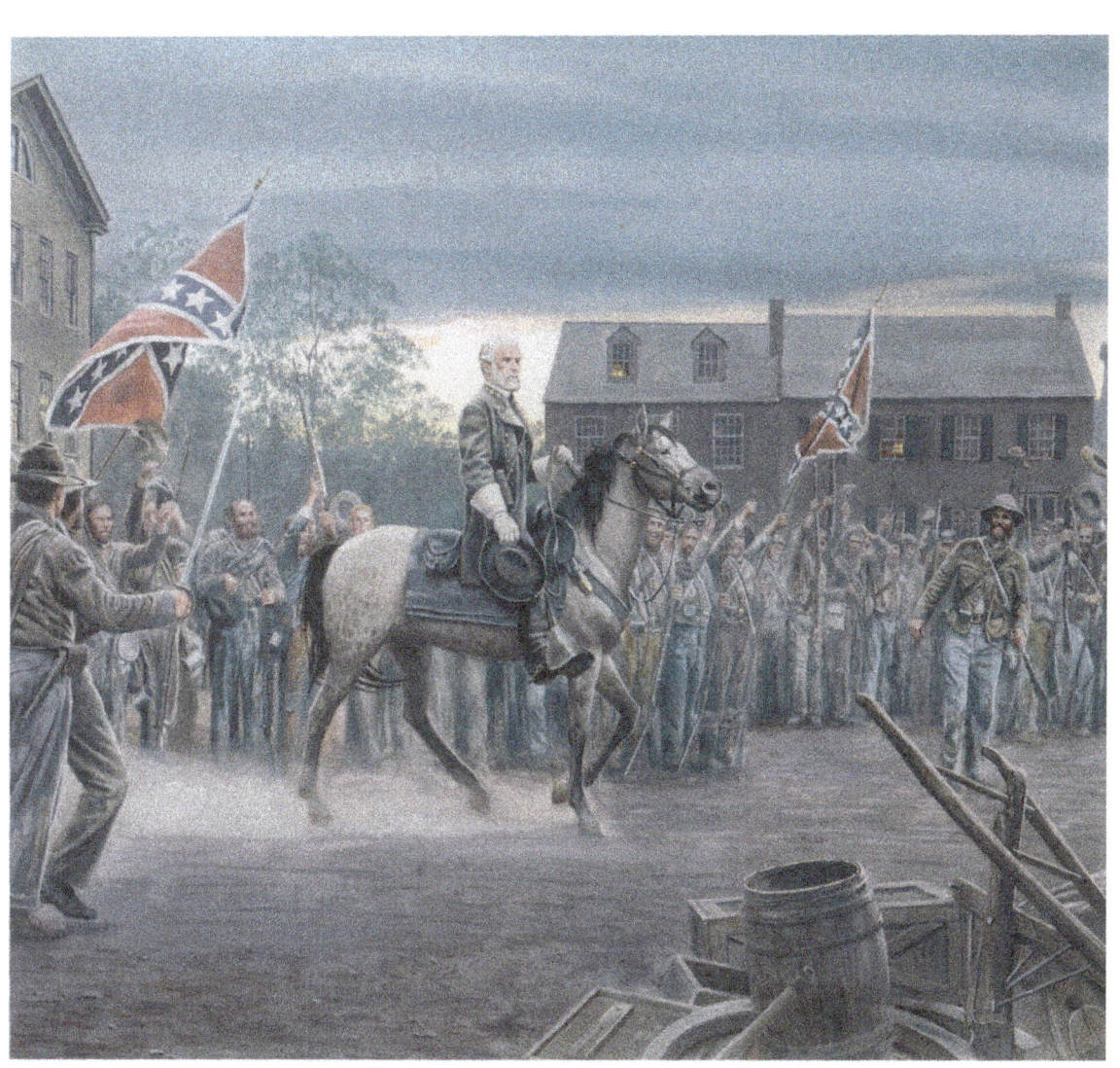

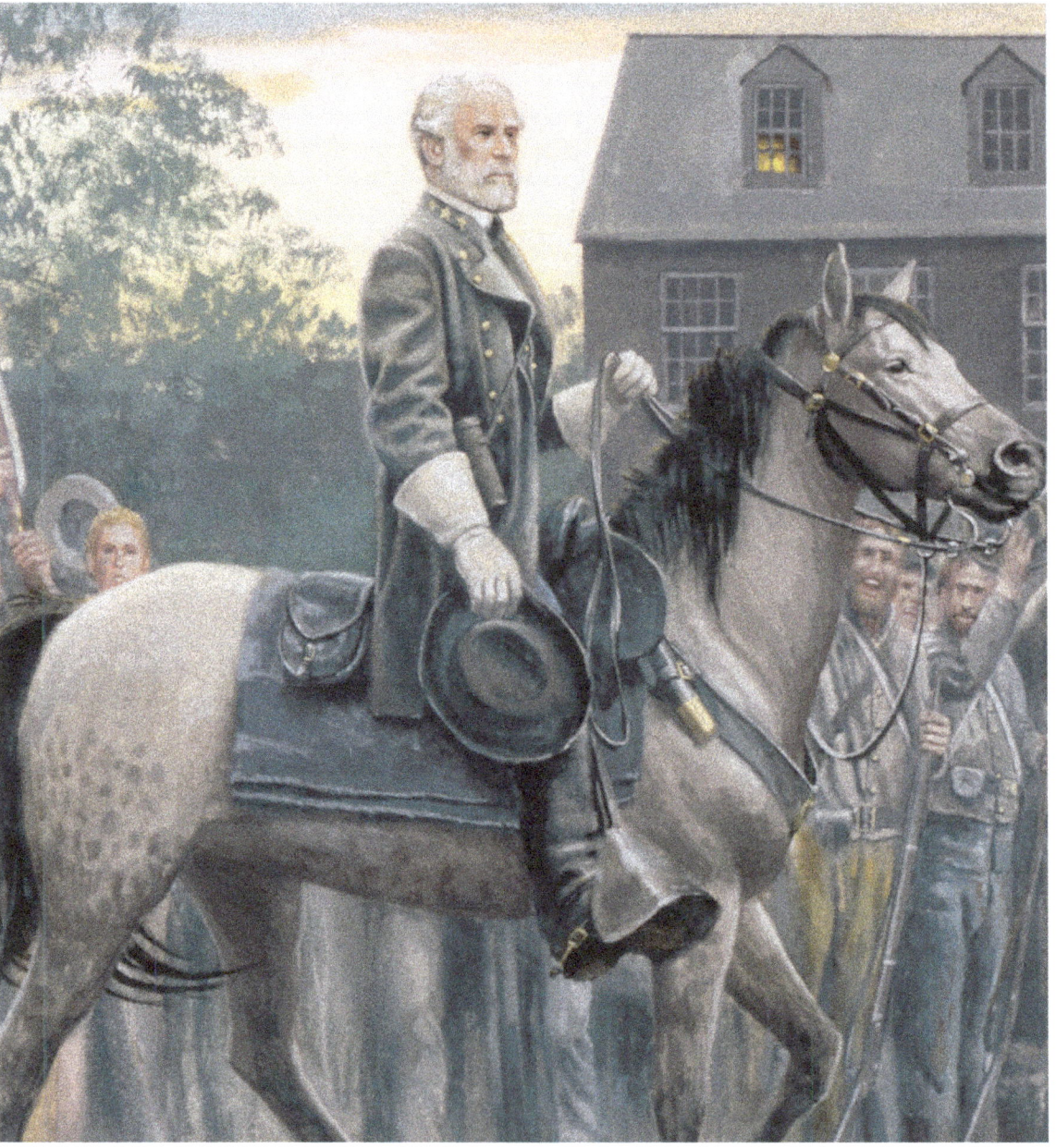

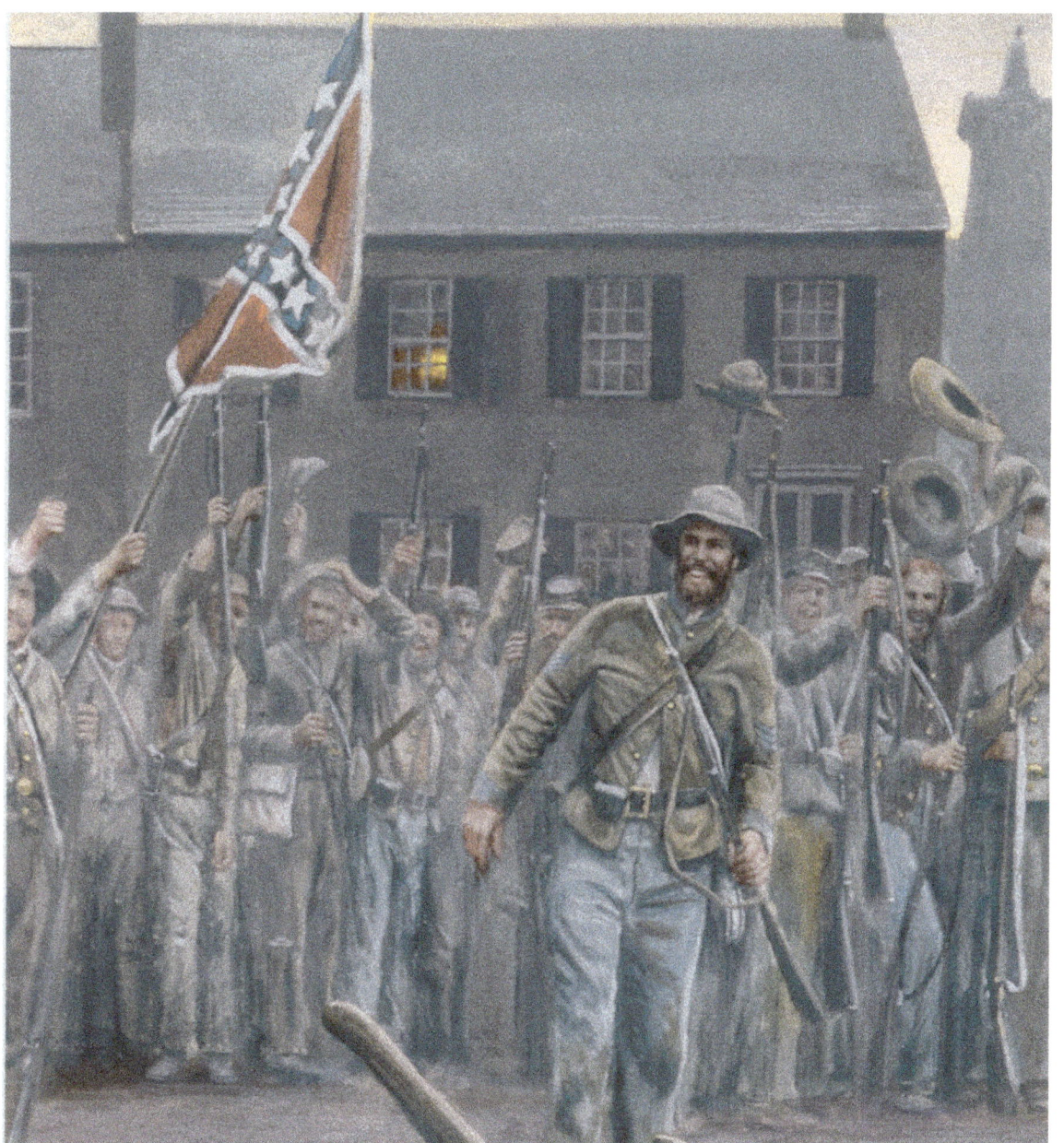

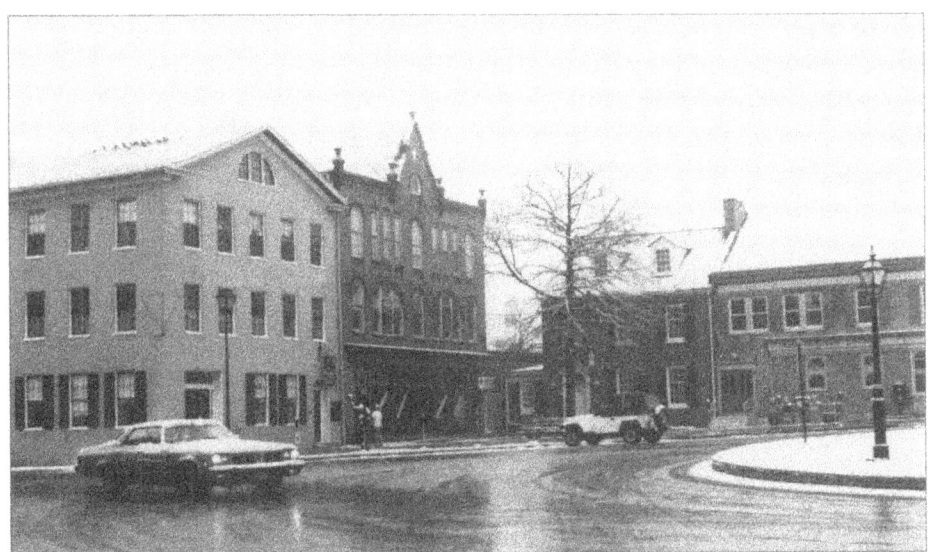

the re-formed Union line. Sharpshooters made their investigation and assessment a difficult task. The Federal batteries arrayed on the heights caught their eye, and they noted that the lines of infantry faced the town to the north and Hill's corps to the west. To attack, Ewell would have to swing his troops around the town rather than advance through the streets, and he would need help from Hill. But he also needed to meet with Lee.

Lee was with Longstreet on Seminary Ridge, and Longstreet's corps was still six miles away. Lee left Longstreet and found Ewell at a house on the outskirts of town, where they discussed the promise of success in attacking Cemetery Hill and how best to assault the right side of the Union line.

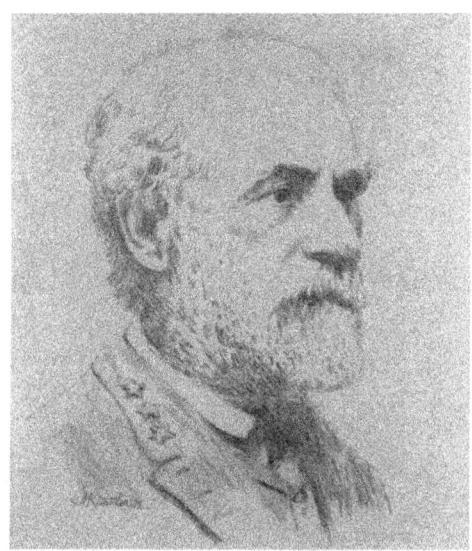

I was delighted to learn that no one had painted this scene of Lee's ride into Gettysburg during the early evening hours of July 1 prior to his conference with Ewell under an arbor behind a house north of town. The troops enthusiastically cheered their commanding general as he passed through the square.

Once I decided to do this painting, I surveyed the town for buildings that were there 130 years ago. While there are many, I believed that Lee's riding through the square would offer the most effective scene for the reveling Confederates, because all four buildings in the painting still stand around the town square and are easily recognizable.

In the left background is the Wills House, famous as the home in which Abraham Lincoln stayed, four months after the battle, on the night prior to the cemetery dedication. The Masonic building that is presently next to the Wills House was not there during the war, and the empty space gave me a perfect opportunity to silhouette Lee against the sky. The two buildings to the right of Lee are there today, looking pretty much like they did then. In the far background, at the extreme right of the picture, is the old courthouse, still easily seen from the square.

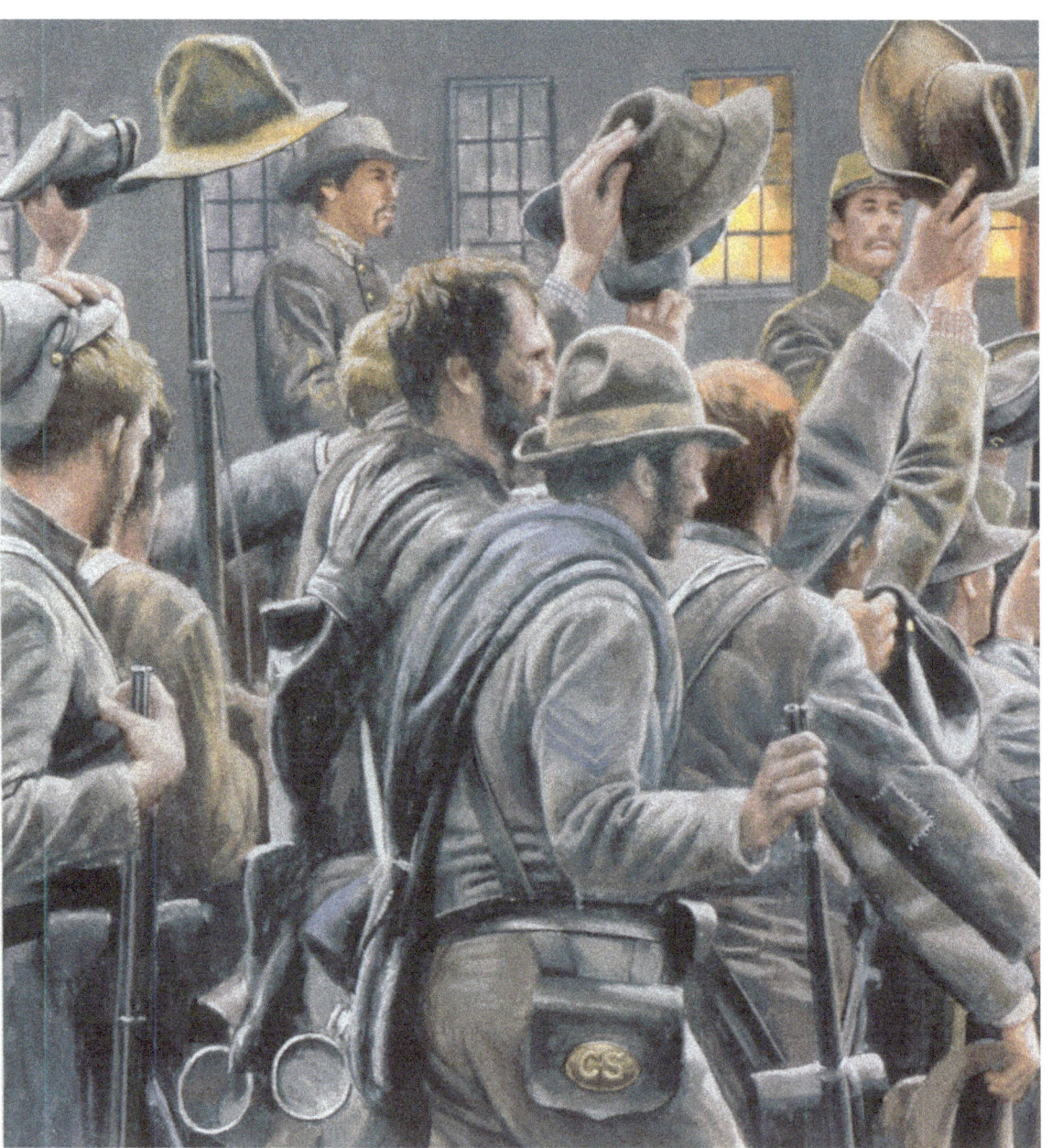

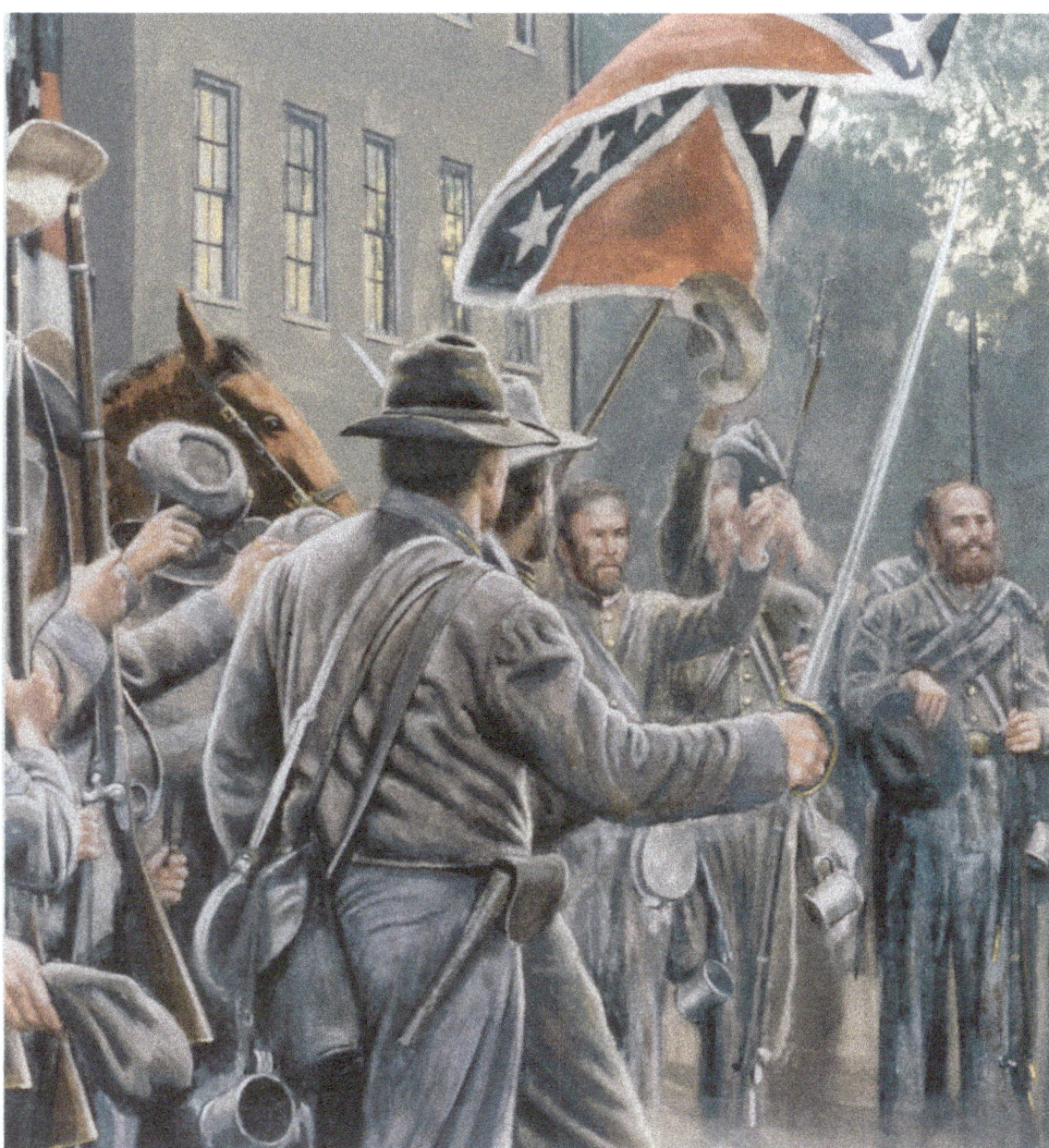

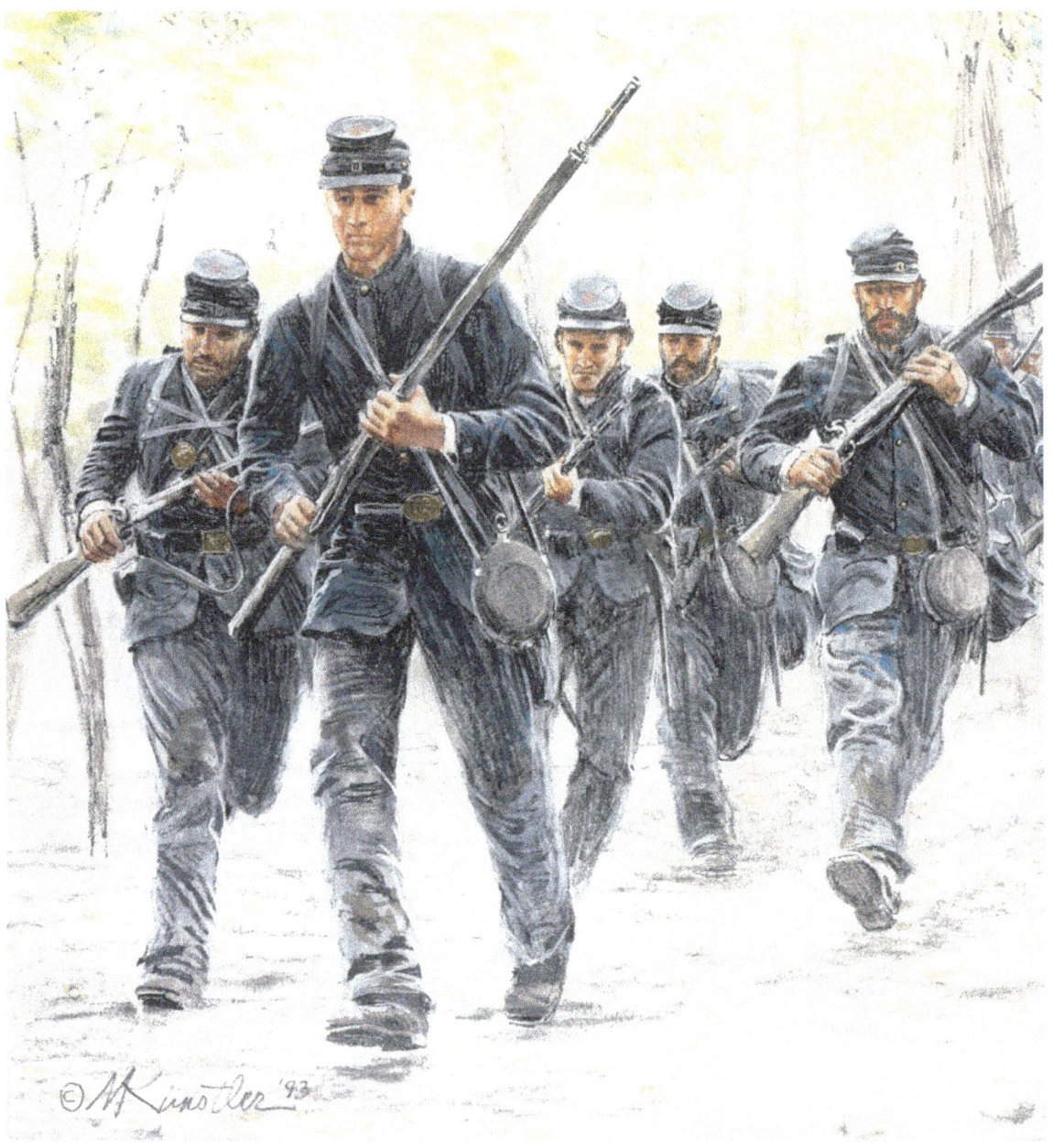

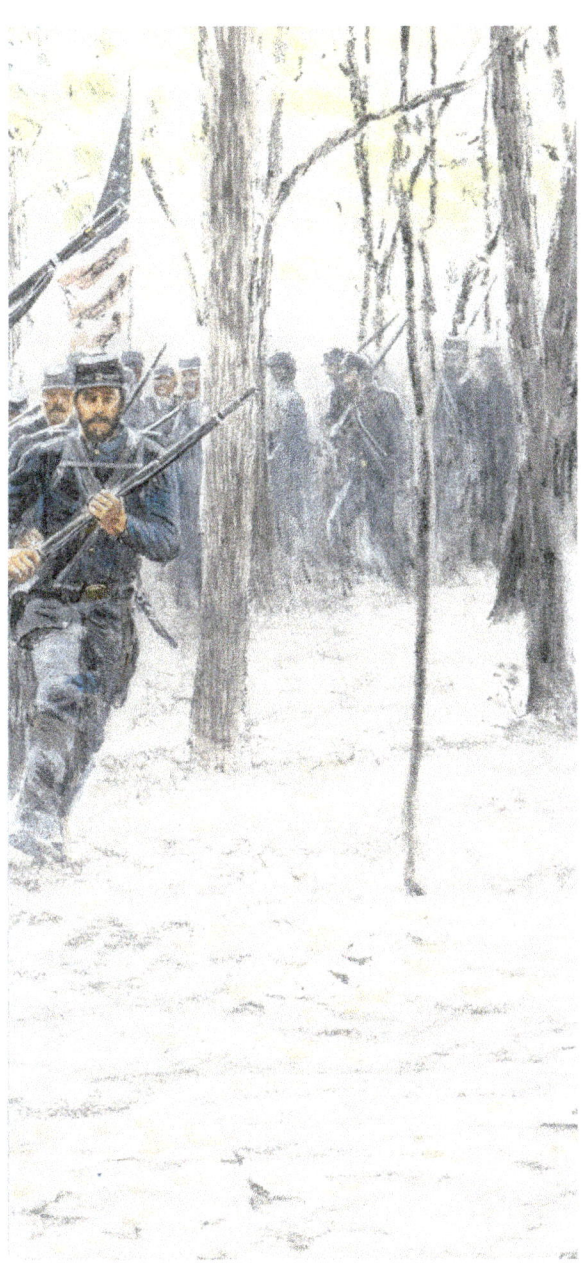

RUSH TO THE SUMMIT

LITTLE ROUND TOP, JULY 2, 1863

1993, mixed media, 11⅞ x 19¼

THE PROMONTORIES ON THE south side of the field came into play on the afternoon of July 2 when Meade's chief of engineers, Gouverneur K. Warren, discovered that the only Federal presence on the most accessible mount—the other was too steep and wooded to occupy easily—were some signalmen. Warren persuaded the commander of the Fifth Corps to release a brigade from the troops being sent to reinforce Sickles and send them double time to occupy Little Round Top. They arrived at the crest just in time to encounter charging Confederates.

99

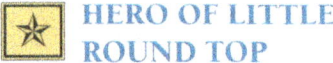
HERO OF LITTLE ROUND TOP

COL. JOSHUA L. CHAMBERLAIN, JULY 2, 1863

1999, oil, 24 x 36

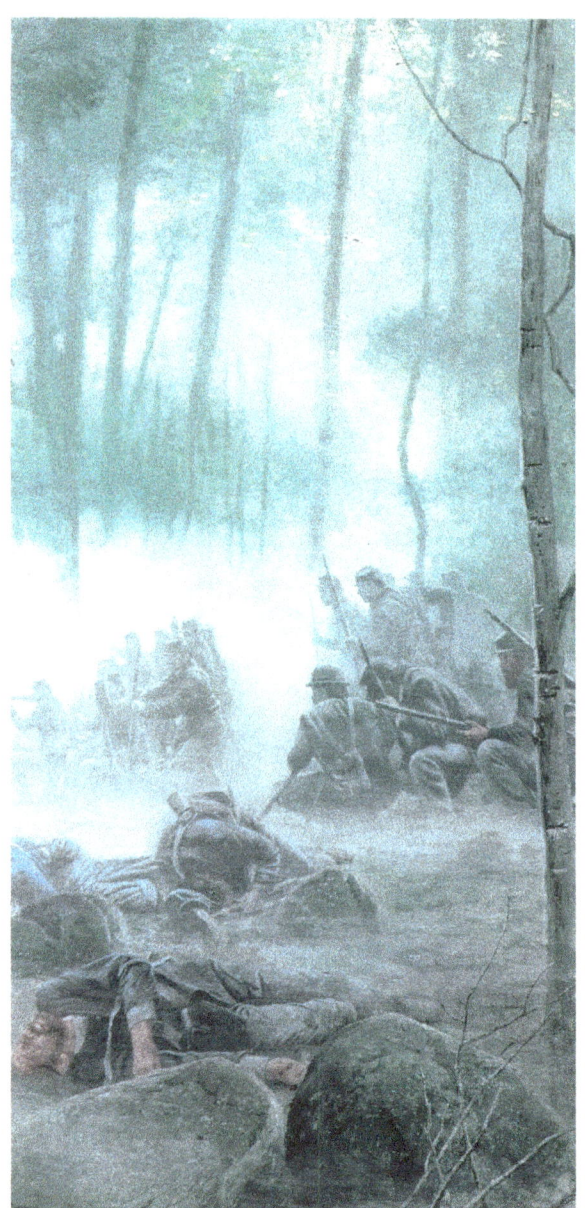

AMONG THE TROOPS ORDERED to the crest of Little Round Top was the Twentieth Maine, which was posted at the far left of the brigade. They were the end of the Union line at Gettysburg, and their orders were to hold this position "at all costs."

Within minutes, Capt. William C. Oates's six companies of Alabamians appeared. Chamberlain's men from Maine unleashed "the most destructive fire I ever saw," Oates recalled.

The Confederates fell back but soon returned to a flurry of bullets that made the Rebel line wave "like a man

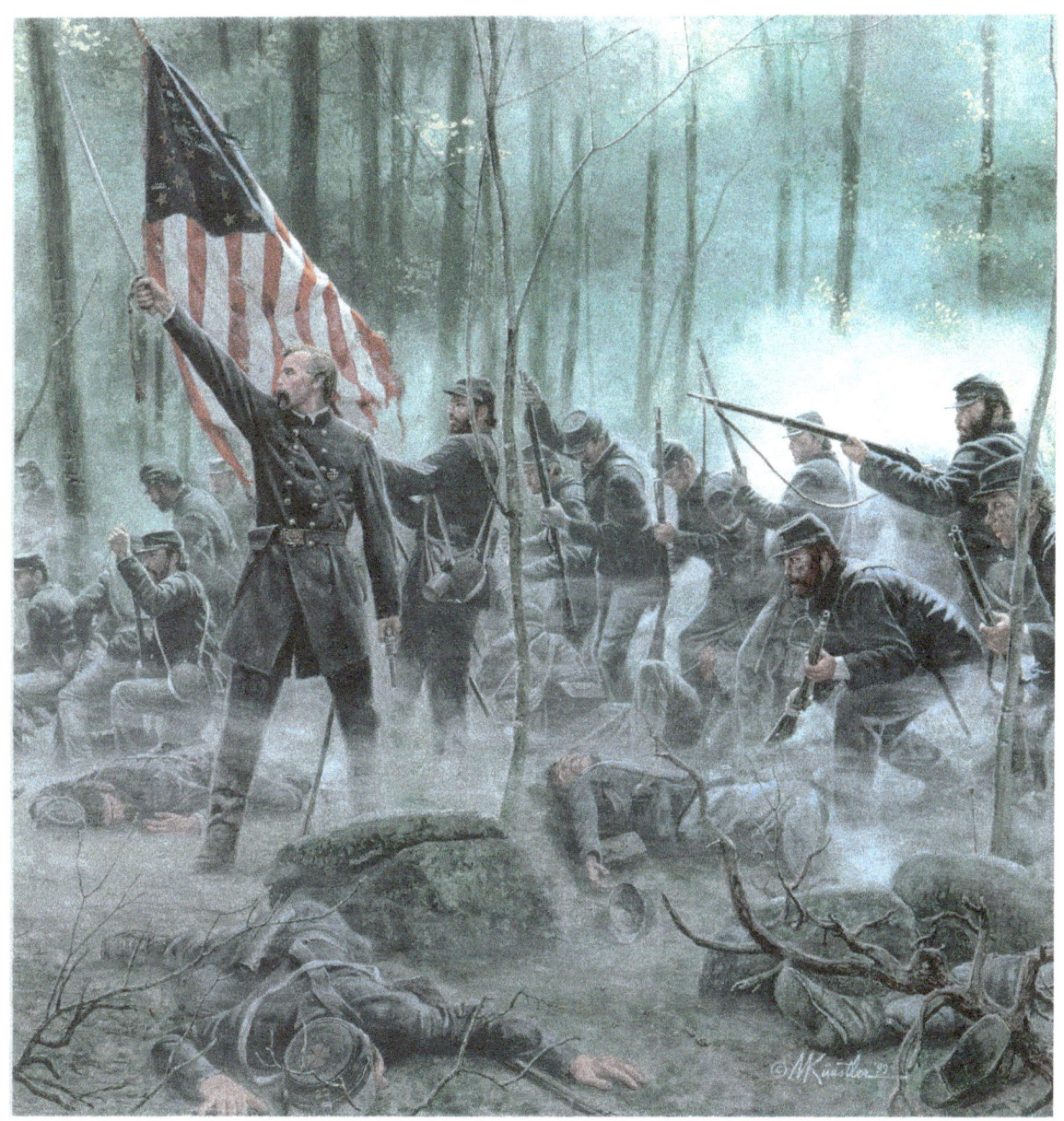

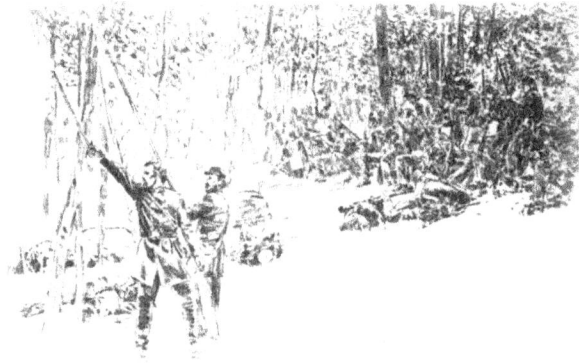

trying to walk against a strong wind."

One of Chamberlain's men recalled the engagement as a "medley of cries, shouts, cheers, groans, prayers, curses, bursting shells, whizzing rifle bullets and clanging steel. The air seemed to be alive with lead. The lines at times were so near each other that the hostile gun barrels almost touched."

Chamberlain himself remembered, "At times I saw around me more of the enemy than of my own men; gaps opening, swallowing, closing again with sharp convulsive energy. All around, a strong mingled roar."

For more than an hour, Oates's men pressed their attack again and again, thinning out their own ranks as well as those of the men from Maine. Oates thought his men had broken Chamberlain's line five times, but the Union troops managed to repulse the Alabamians each time.

Chamberlain's wounded men would not leave their comrades, and so they reinforced the line wherever it weakened. Men who earlier had been charged with mutiny (regarding expired enlistments) pitched in. One of these had been reduced in rank from sergeant to private, but he fought now until he was mortally wounded. His last words were, "Tell my mother I did not die a coward." Chamberlain repaid him by restoring his rank on the spot.

Finally, exhausted and low on ammunition, the Union troops appeared nearing the breaking point. As the determined Southerners renewed the attack on Little Round Top with another assault, Chamberlain realized what was at stake. If his troops faltered, and the Union flank was turned, the Federal army might be destroyed, the battle would be lost.

"FIX BAYONETS!"

COLONEL CHAMBERLAIN, LITTLE ROUND TOP, JULY 2, 1863

1993, mixed media, 12⅛ x 19¼

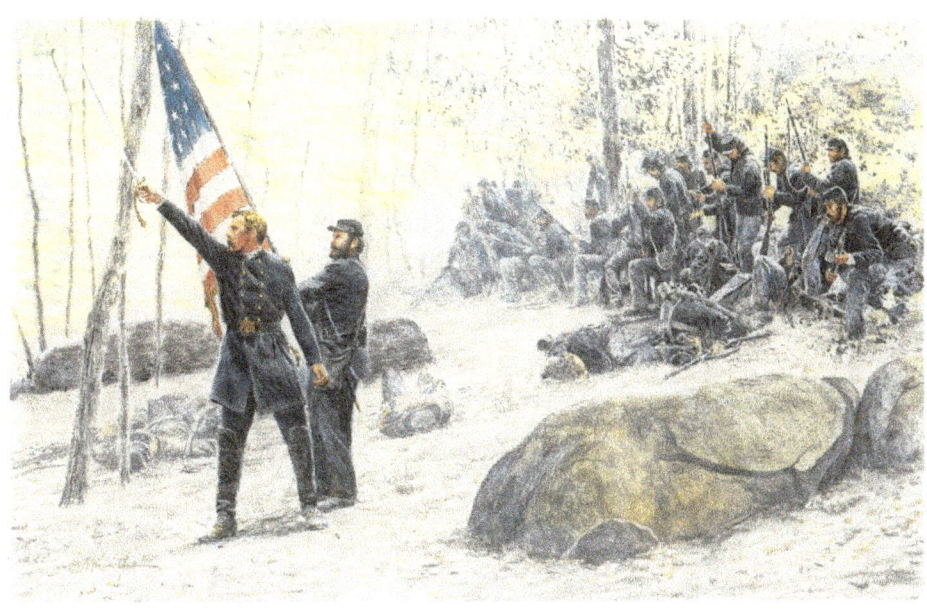

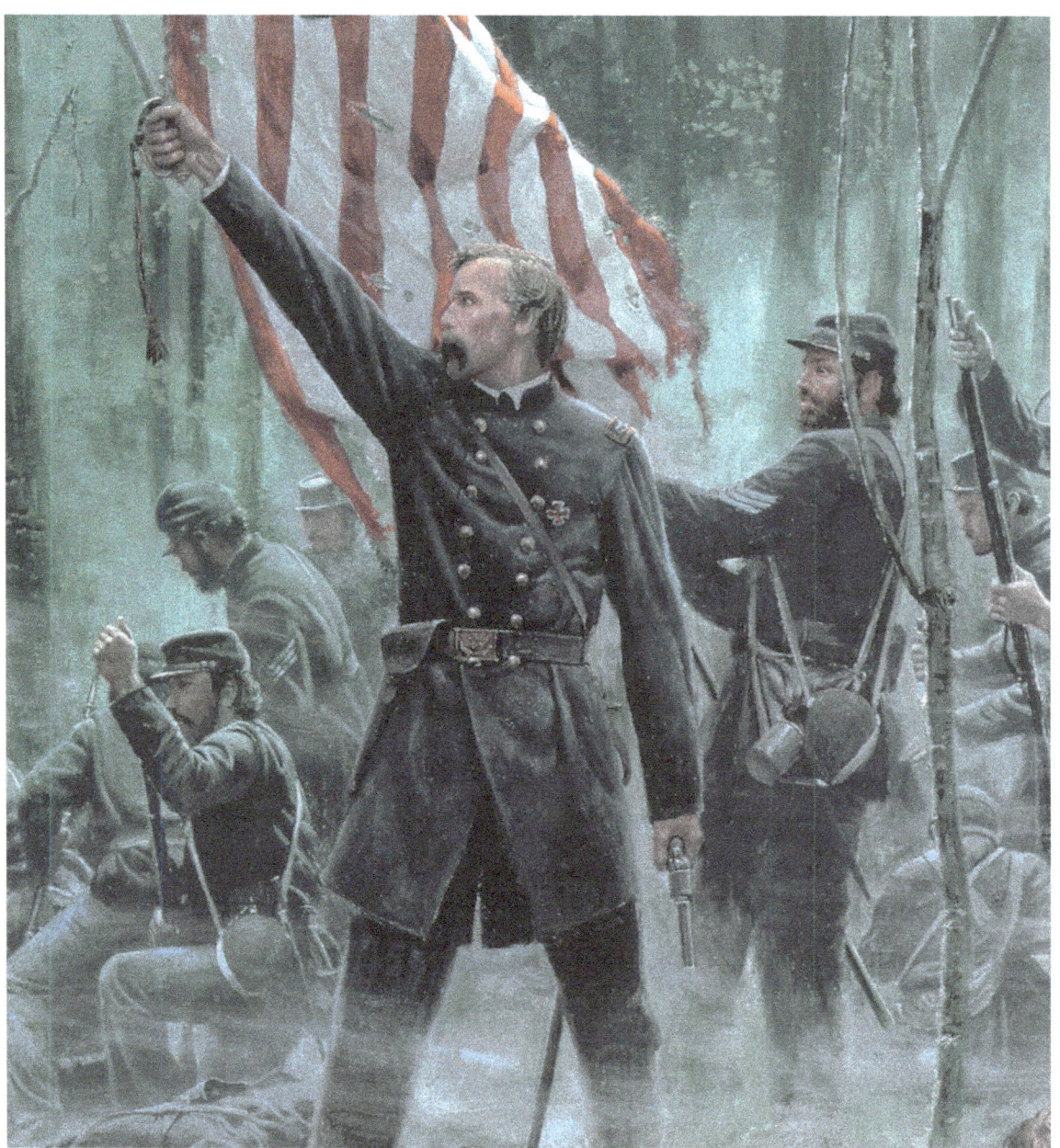

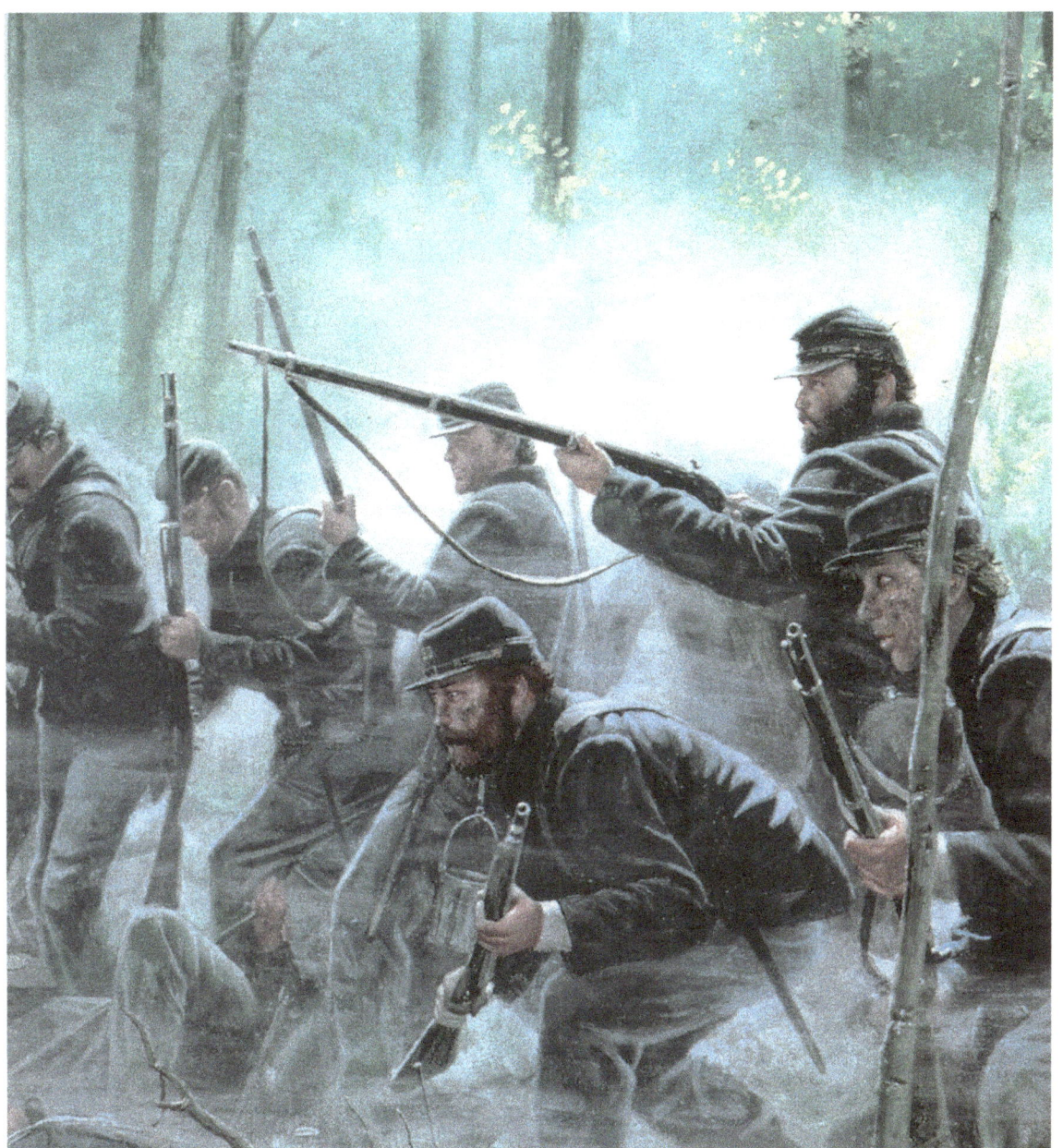

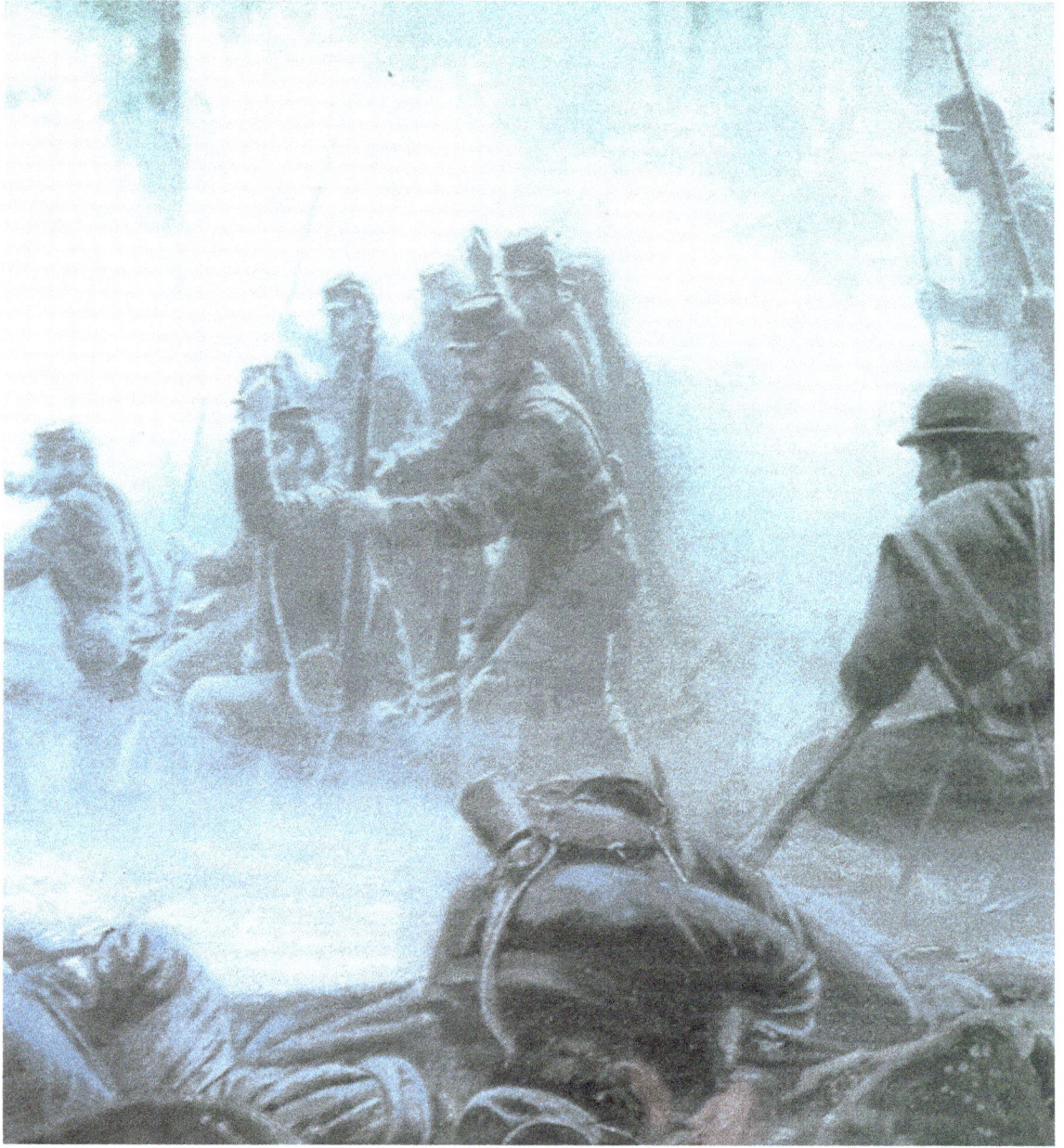

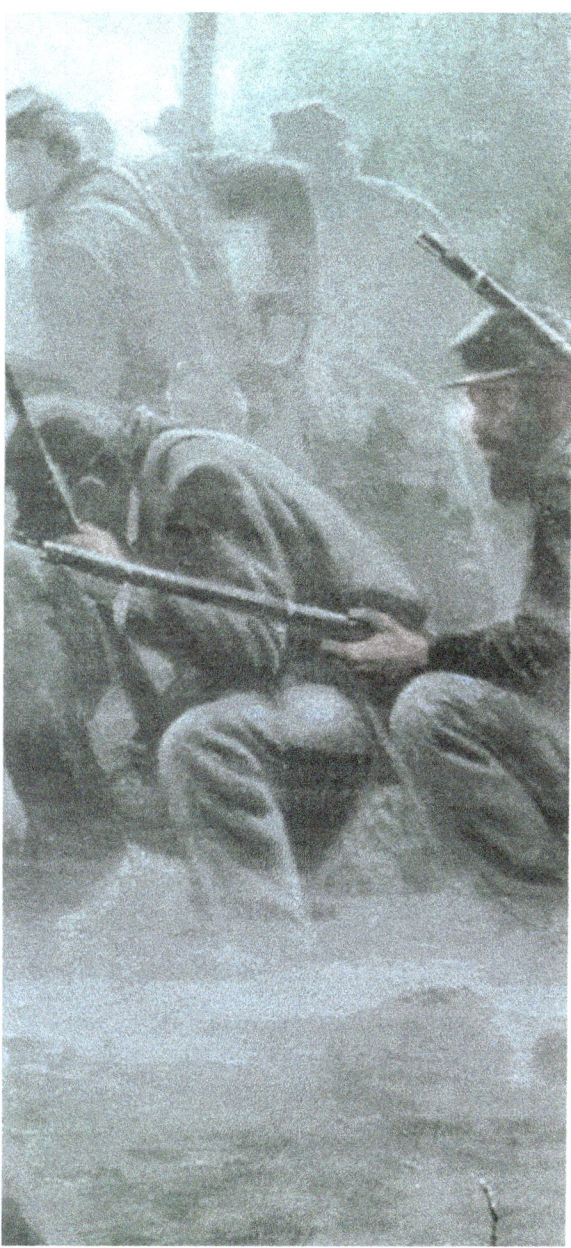

Facing what appeared to be imminent destruction, Chamberlain did the unexpected. At almost 7:00 p.m., he ordered a bayonet charge.

This painting is my second image of Chamberlain on Little Round Top; the first is the next painting, *Chamberlain's Charge*. I realized that the moment just prior to the famous charge was as dramatic as the charge itself. So I chose to portray the moment when Chamberlain ordered his men to fix bayonets.

Although I had some substantial research in hand, I initiated a new round of research for this work. My studies led me to Douglas F. Hawes, curator of historical collections at the Maine State Museum in Augusta. The remnants of the Twentieth Maine's regimental flag are in the museum collection, which enabled me to depict the flag's tears and bullet holes exactly as they exist.

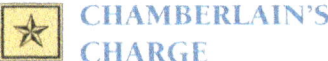
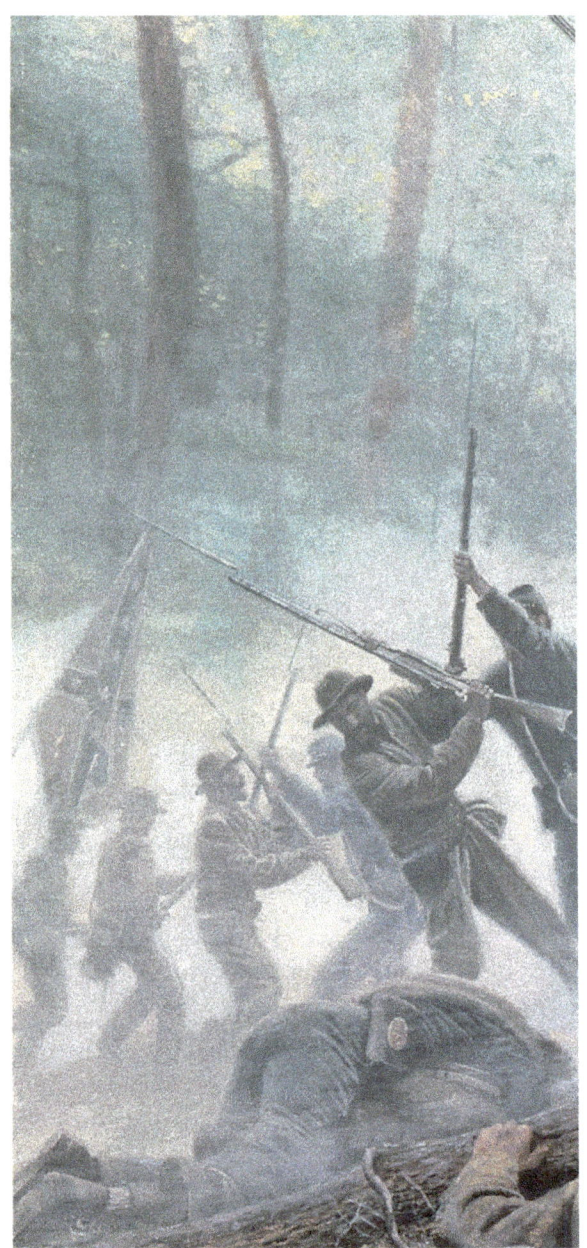

WITH FIXED BAYONETS, THE Twenti-eth Maine proceeded downhill. Chamberlain led them with his sword. The pace was slow at first, with every man trying to keep the line even, and then one of the lieutenants jumped ahead, began to run, and called to his men to follow him. The whole line responded, rushing out of the rock-strewn crest and among the scattered trees.

To the left of the line, Chamberlain had positioned a company of men who saw some Confederates retreat toward them. So they stood, fired a

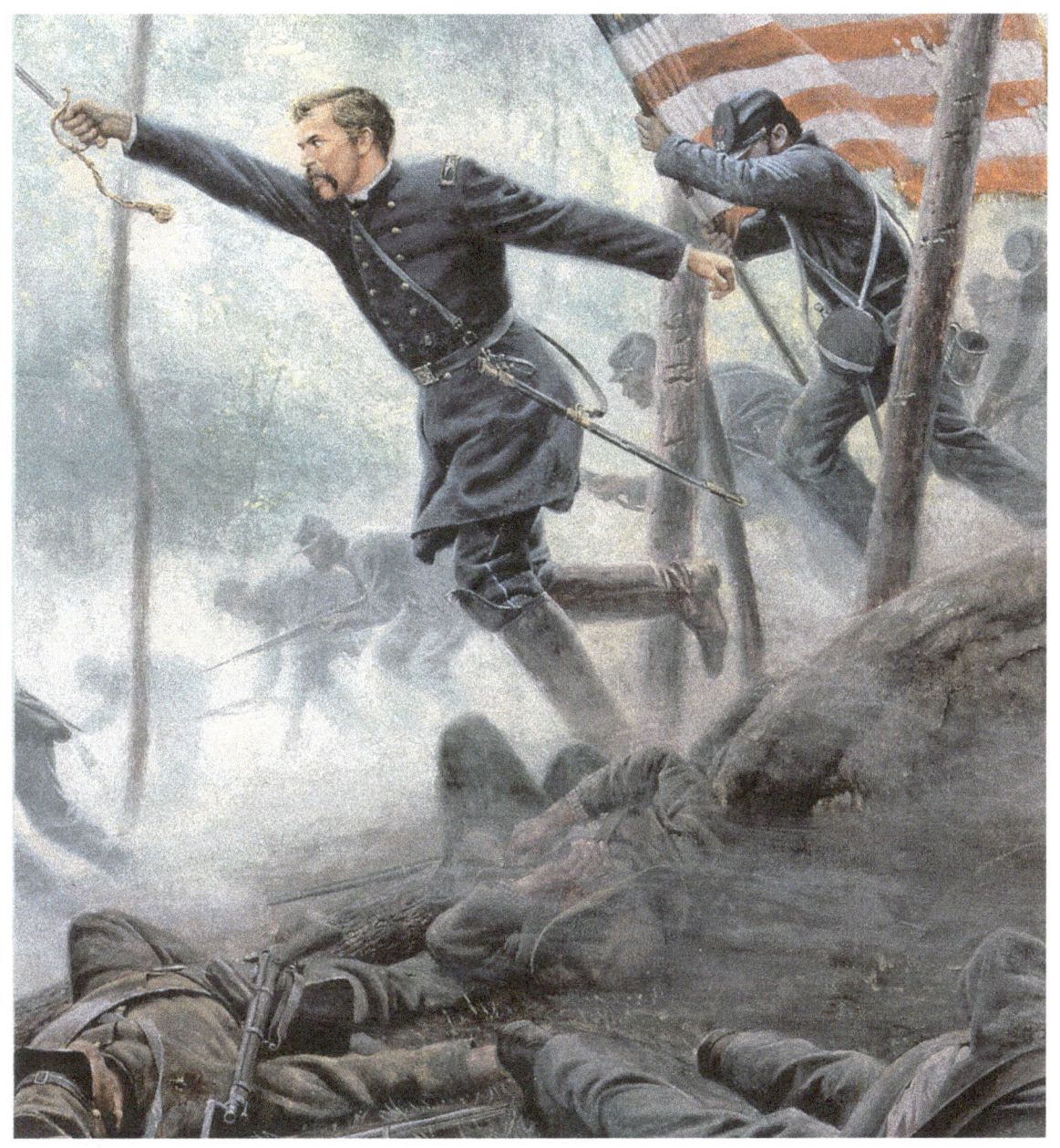

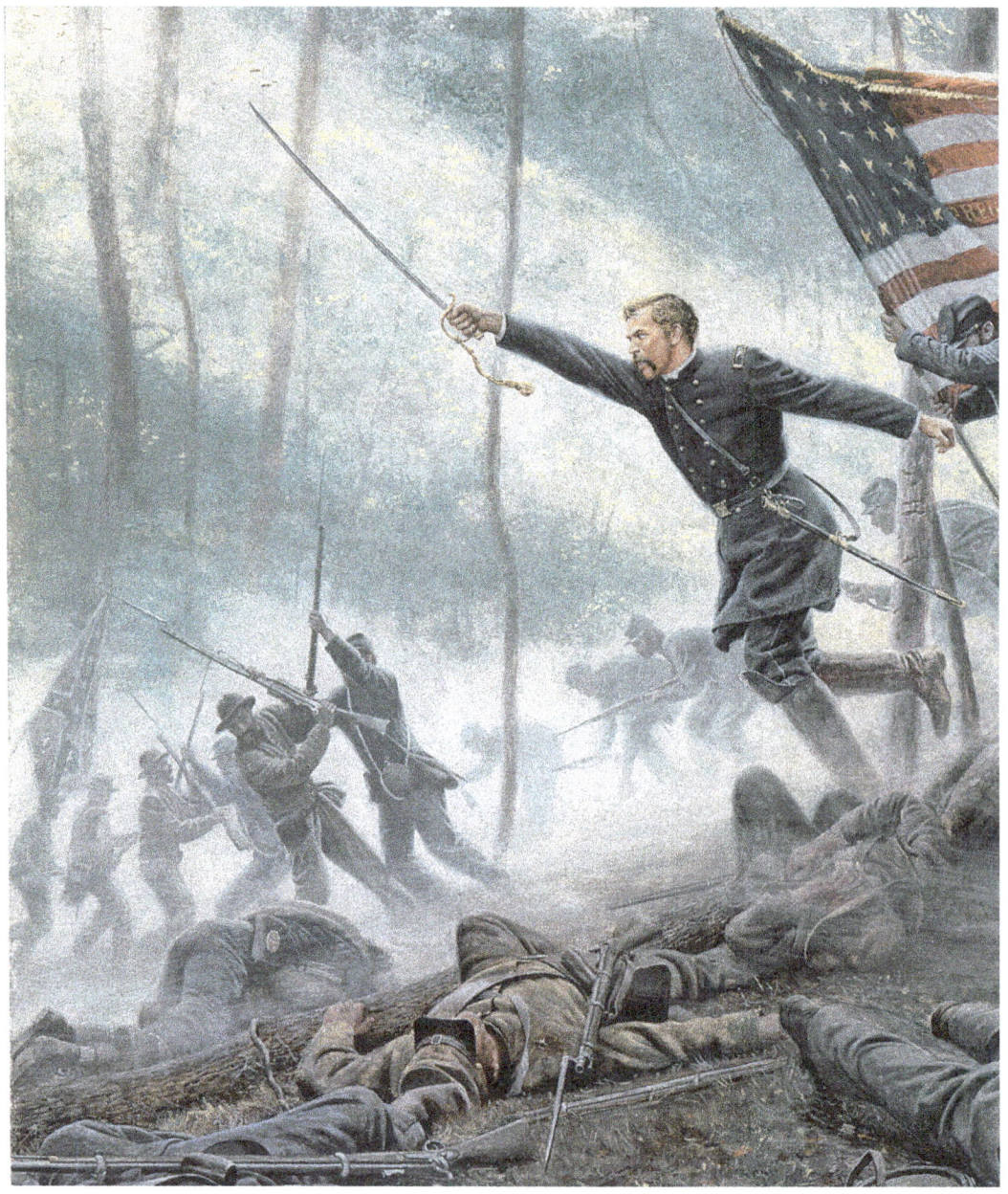

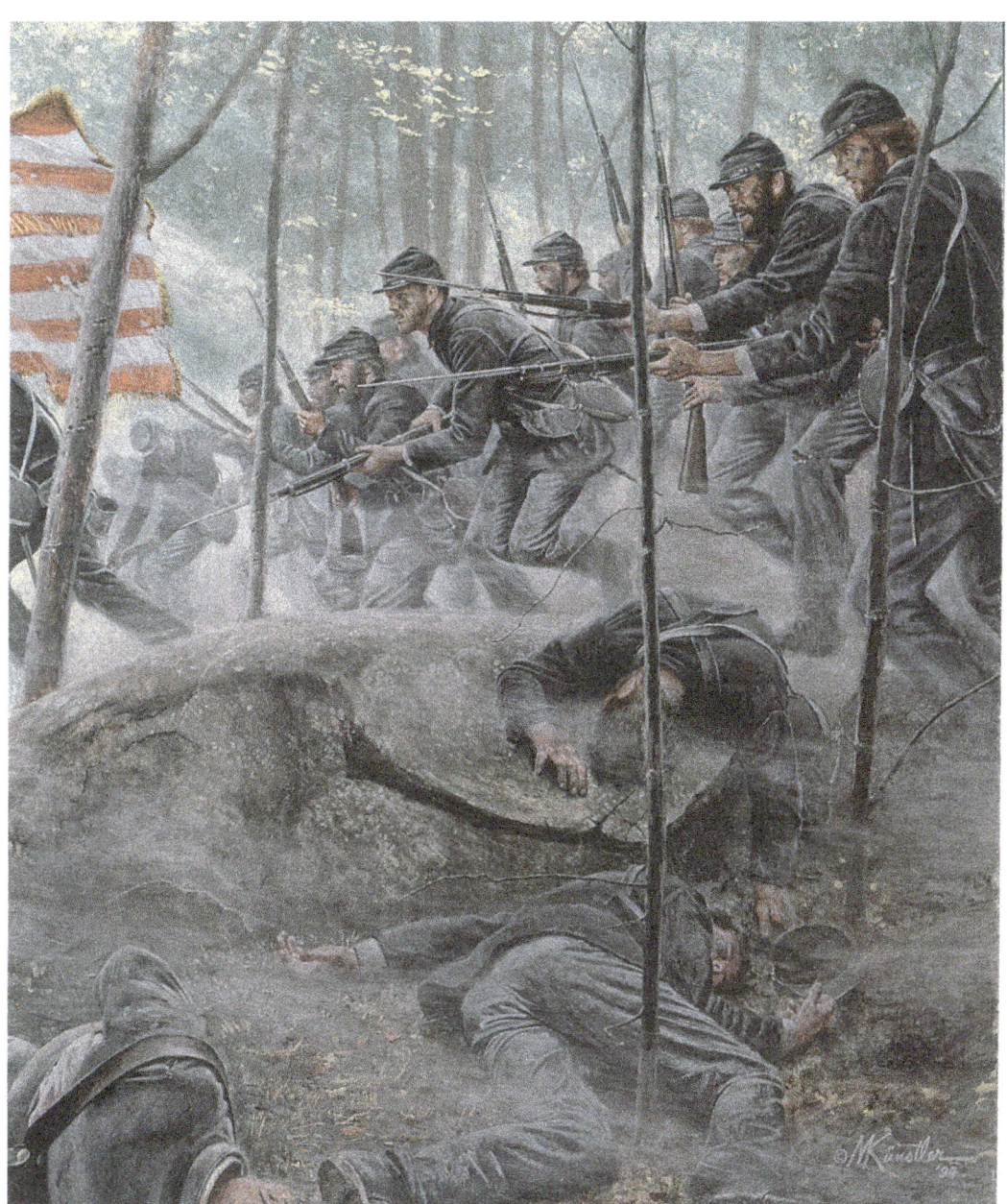

volley, and then threw their numbers into the rest of the Twentieth Maine. Among their ranks were sharpshooters who had been chased up the hill earlier by the Alabamians, and they joined in the charge.

Exhausted by more than two hours of uphill fighting after a twenty-mile forced march the day before, the Confederates were stunned, some firing their weapons and then surrendering. Their commander, Col. William C. Oates, saw men fall all around him. He heard that Union reinforcements had arrived, then he saw the Federals coming toward him from his right and assumed these were the recent arrivals. He knew that he had already lost half of his men, so he ordered a retreat.

In the meantime, the line of the Twentieth Maine began to swing down in an arc, with its right side firmly anchored to the regiment to its right—the Eighty-third Pennsylvania. The maneuver cut off the first line of Confederates, compelling their surrender. The second line fired a volley, then scattered to the west, into the valley, and some tried to escape to the south and the larger mountain. Chamberlain confronted an officer who fired his revolver at him, but the man surrendered his Navy Colt when Chamberlain leveled his sword at him.

The Twentieth continued to sweep down the slope. Within a matter of moments, they took more than 400 prisoners. Rather than press his luck, Chamberlain decided to reclaim the ground they had first occupied. The 386-man regiment had suffered 130 casualties; at their original position they found 50 dead and more than 100 wounded Confederates.

Little Round Top held, and as the sun set, some of the men fell asleep with their weapons in their hands. And then reinforcements arrived.

This painting captures the moment when Chamberlain led the now-famous bayonet charge that halted the Confederate assault on the far left of the Union line. The time of day allowed me to use filtered sunlight through the wooded hilltop and to focus attention on the heroic professor-turned-warrior as he led his regiment down the southwestern slope of Little Round Top. The large boulder in the foreground is still a prominent landmark at the scene of the charge. The trees depicted in the painting are different than

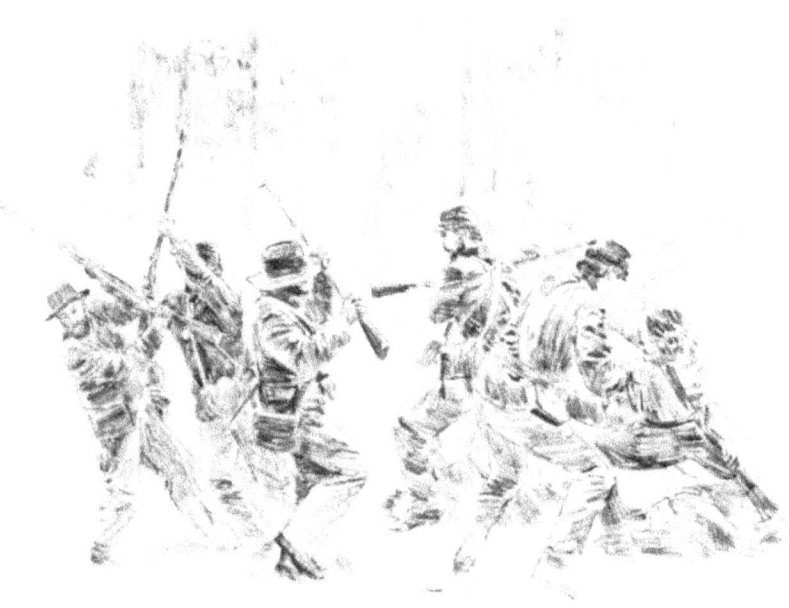

those found on the slope today, but today's forest is a mixture of old and new growth, just as it was in 1863.

The red Maltese Cross on the cap of the color bearer identifies him as a member of the First Division of the Fifth Corps. The "20" on his cap denotes the Twentieth Maine, and the national flag was the only banner the regiment carried into battle that day. The dent in Chamberlain's scabbard shows where it deflected a bullet that day—a deflection that saved him from a serious wound.

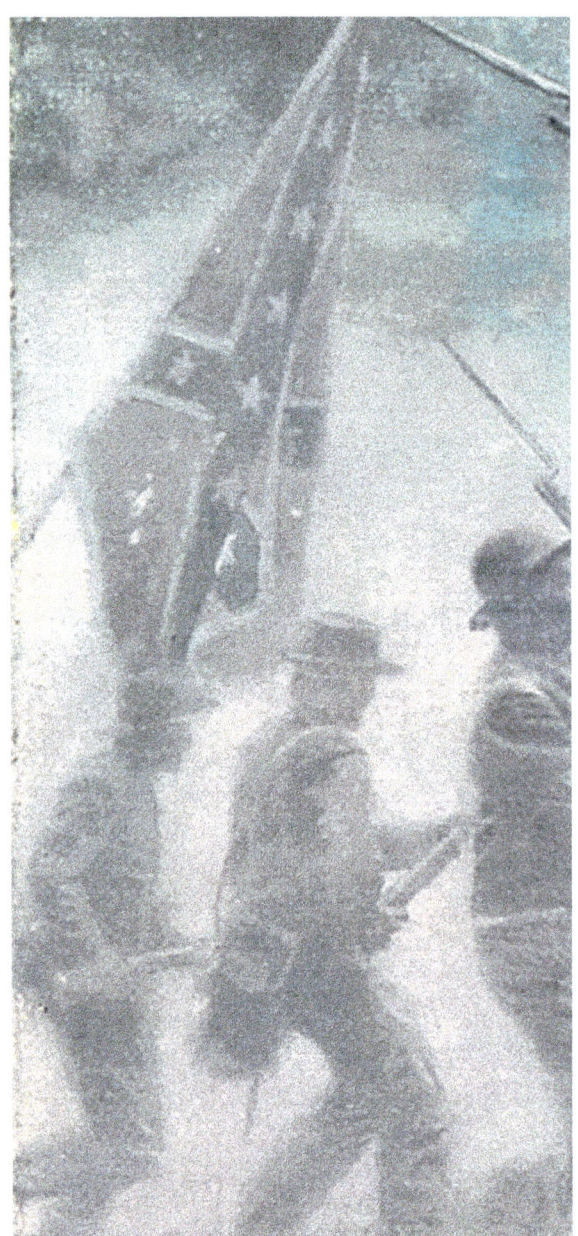

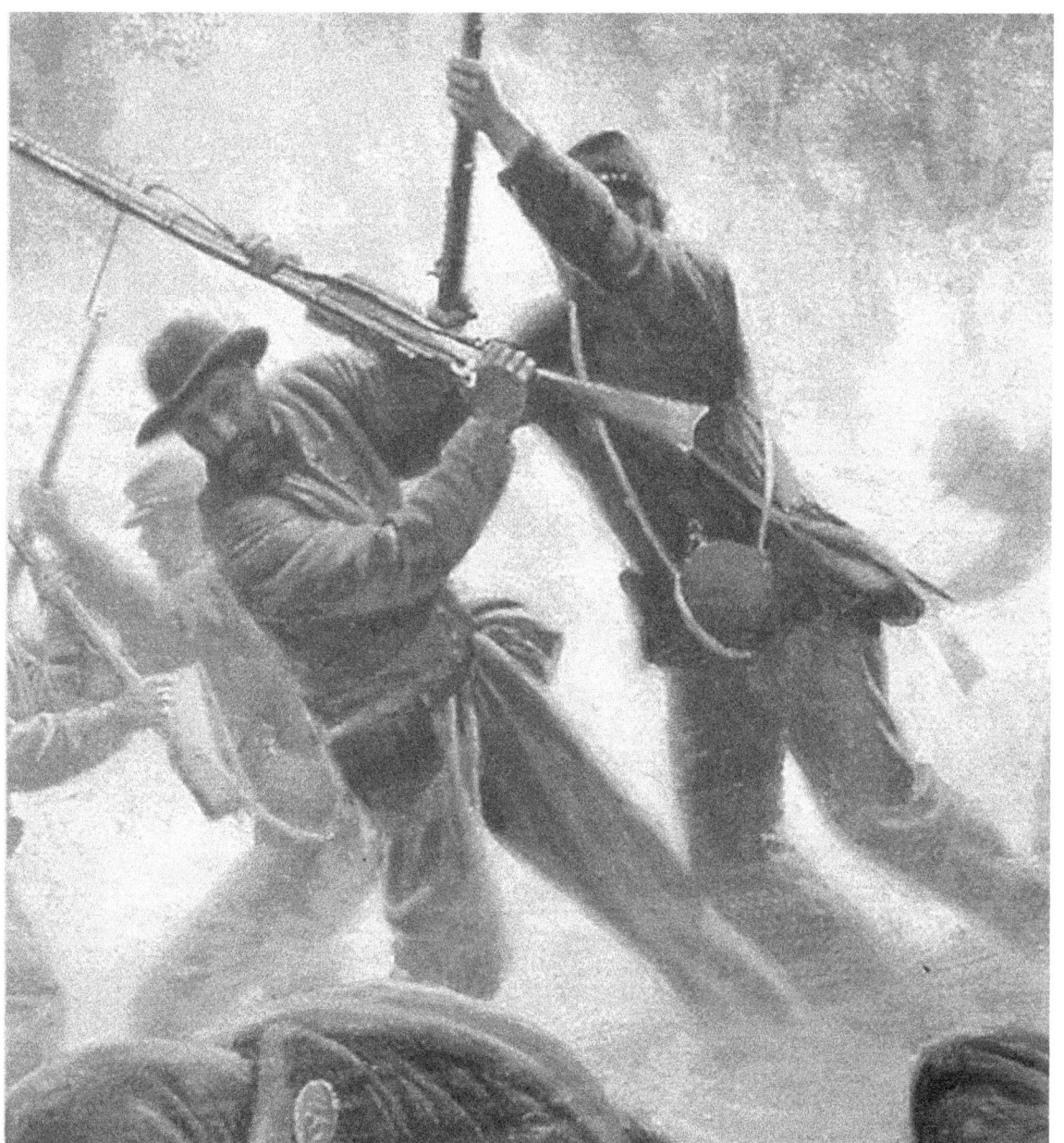

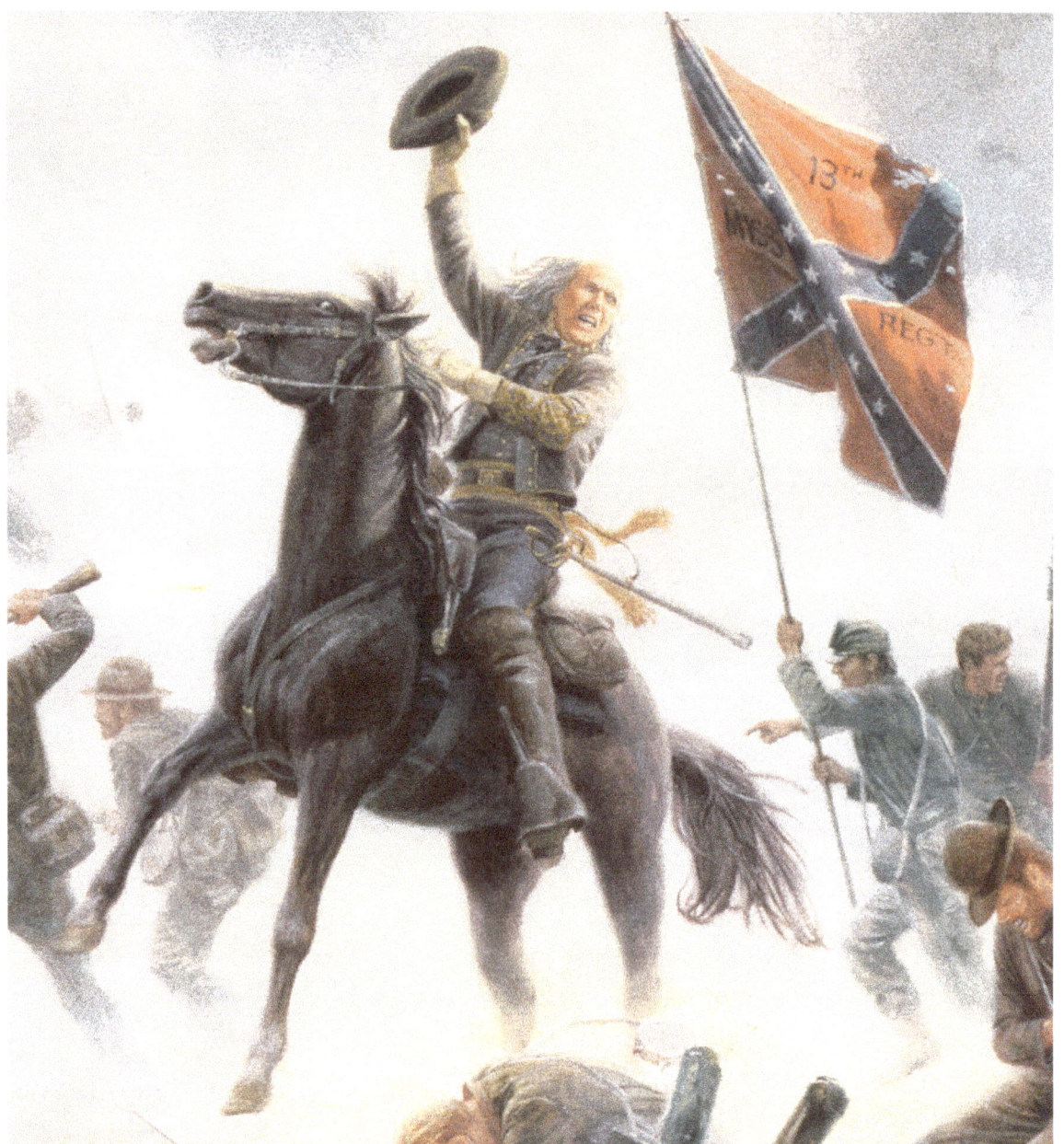

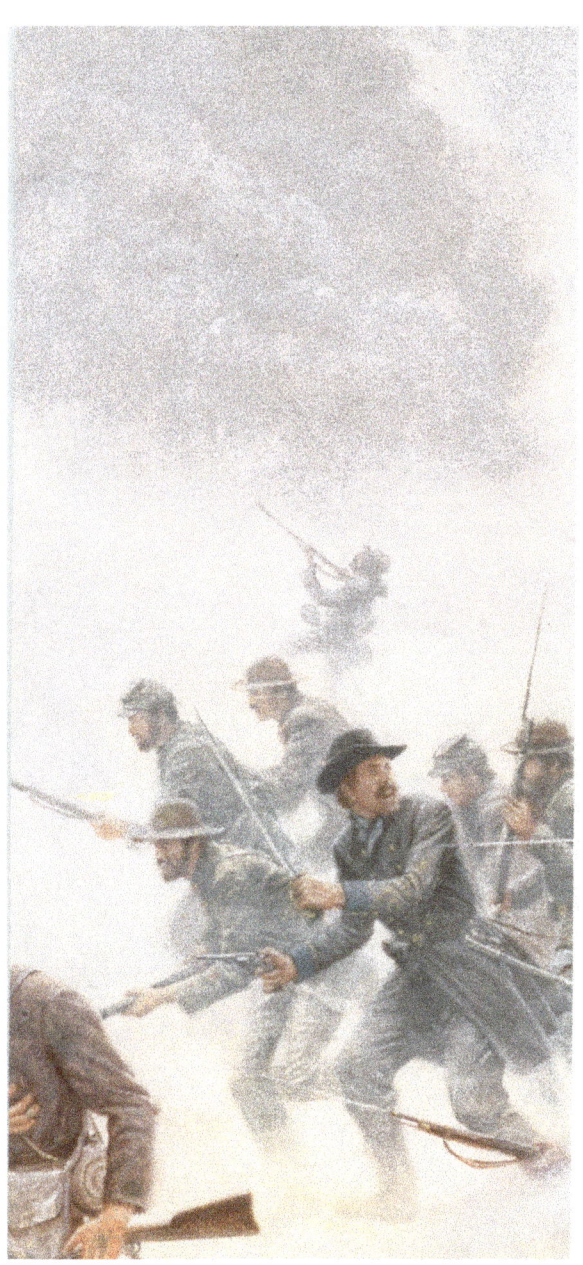

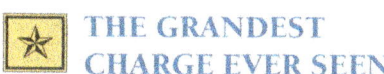

THE GRANDEST CHARGE EVER SEEN

BARKSDALE'S MISSISSIPPIANS AT
GETTYSBURG. JULY 2, 1863

1990, oil, 26 x 48

LEE WAS EAGER TO attack on July 2. His army lacked only George E. Pickett's division and Jeb Stuart's cavalry. But all of Meade's army, except for one corps, was in place. Still, Longstreet still counseled that Lee should maneuver toward a better position between Gettysburg and Washington and induce the Federals to attack.

Lee, however, felt the momentum generated by the successes of the first day would lead to victory on this field. He wanted to attack both flanks of the two-mile-long Union line that stretched from Culp's Hill to the end

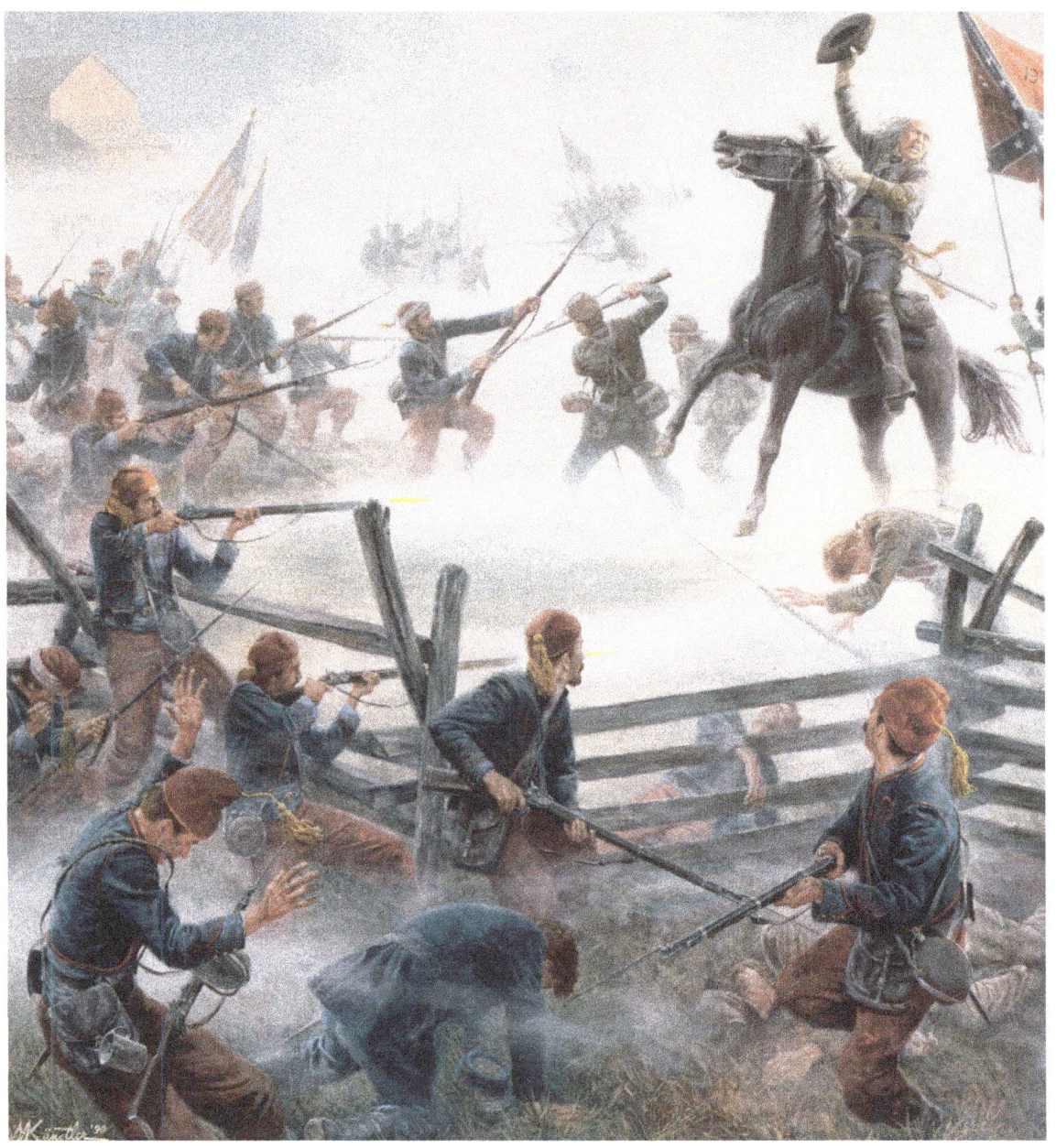

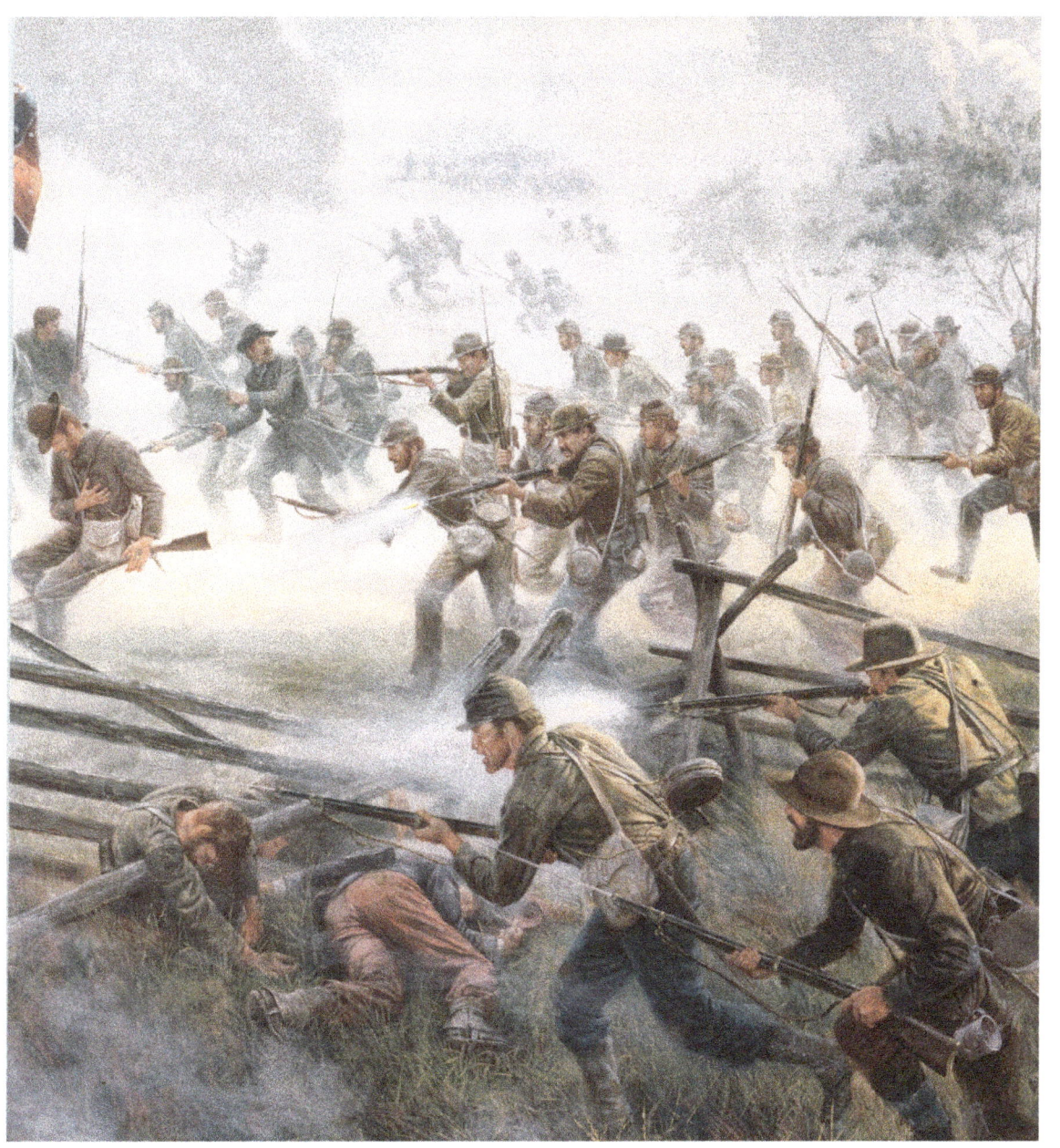

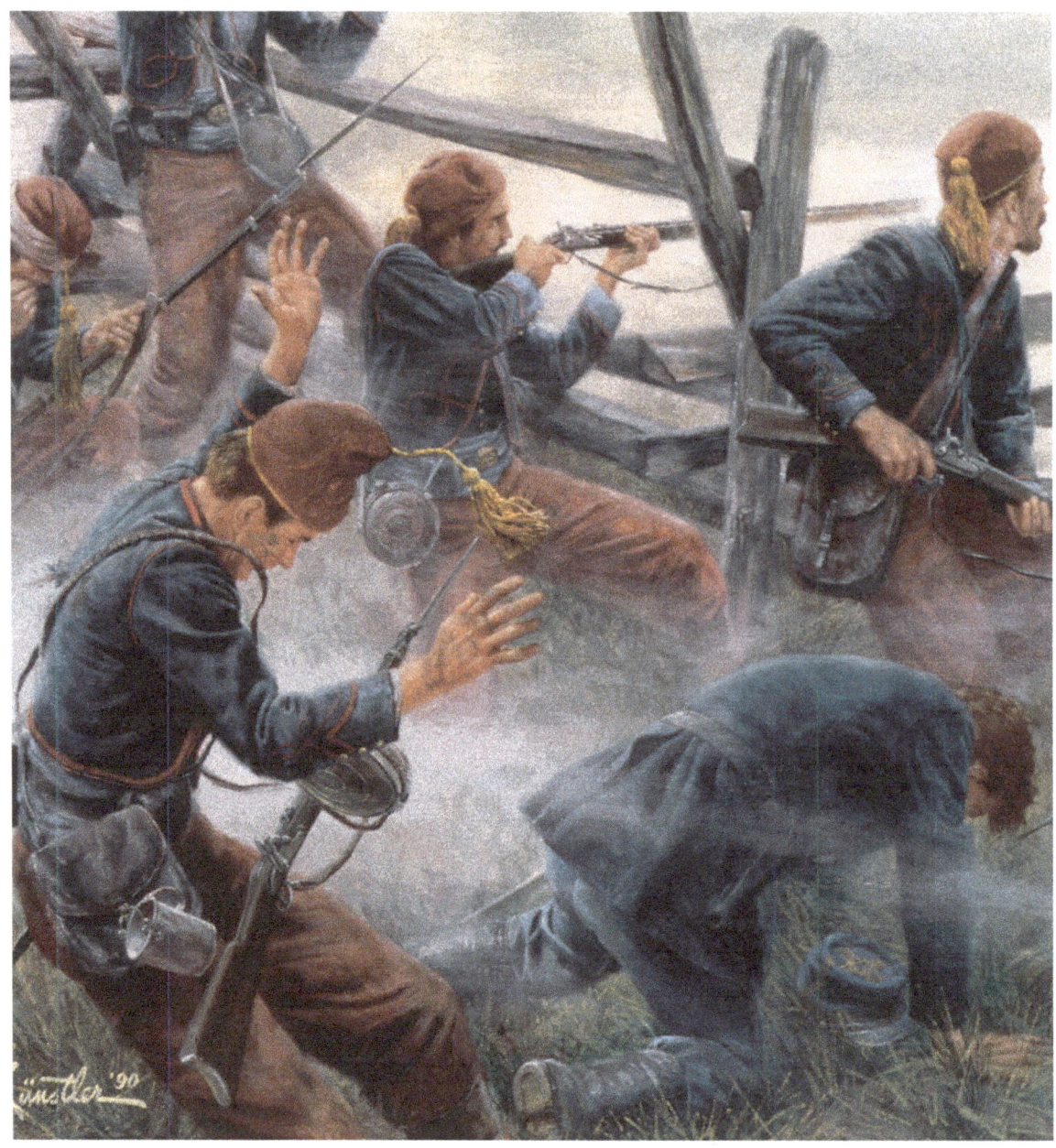

of Cemetery Ridge. Ewell, though, believed an attack on Culp's and Cemetery hills would be futile. So Lee ordered Longstreet to attack the left side of the Union line while Ewell engaged the right side; if Federal troops were shifted from the right to their left to answer Longstreet's attack, Ewell would attack the right side.

Most of the day was lost in getting Longstreet's corps into position on the south side of the field. It was well past noon before his men were in place. In the meantime, the Union left had redeployed. This section of the line was held by the Third Corps, commanded by Daniel E. Sickles. Seeing slightly higher ground to his front, Sickles advanced his corps a mile in front of the line, anchoring one end at a peach orchard near the Emmitsburg Road and the other in a cluster of boulders in front of Little Round Top, known as Devil's Den.

Before Sickles could be ordered back, around 4:00 p.m. Longstreet attacked. For four hours, twenty thousand Confederates engaged ten thousand Federals. Meade and Hancock could only shift troops to support Sickles, but they did not weaken the right side of the line opposite Ewell.

During the fighting, William Barksdale's Mississippi Brigade executed what some have called "the grandest charge ever seen by mortal man" and almost penetrated the Cemetery Ridge line, but it was driven back at a cost of almost half its fifteen hundred men. Among the casualties was Barksdale himself. He was at the front of his troops, his white hair streaming, when he was shot through the legs and chest. He died behind the Union line.

The tale of the Mississippians was much the same for all of Longstreet's brigades: initial successes thwarted by eventual repulse, with nearly 50 percent casualties.

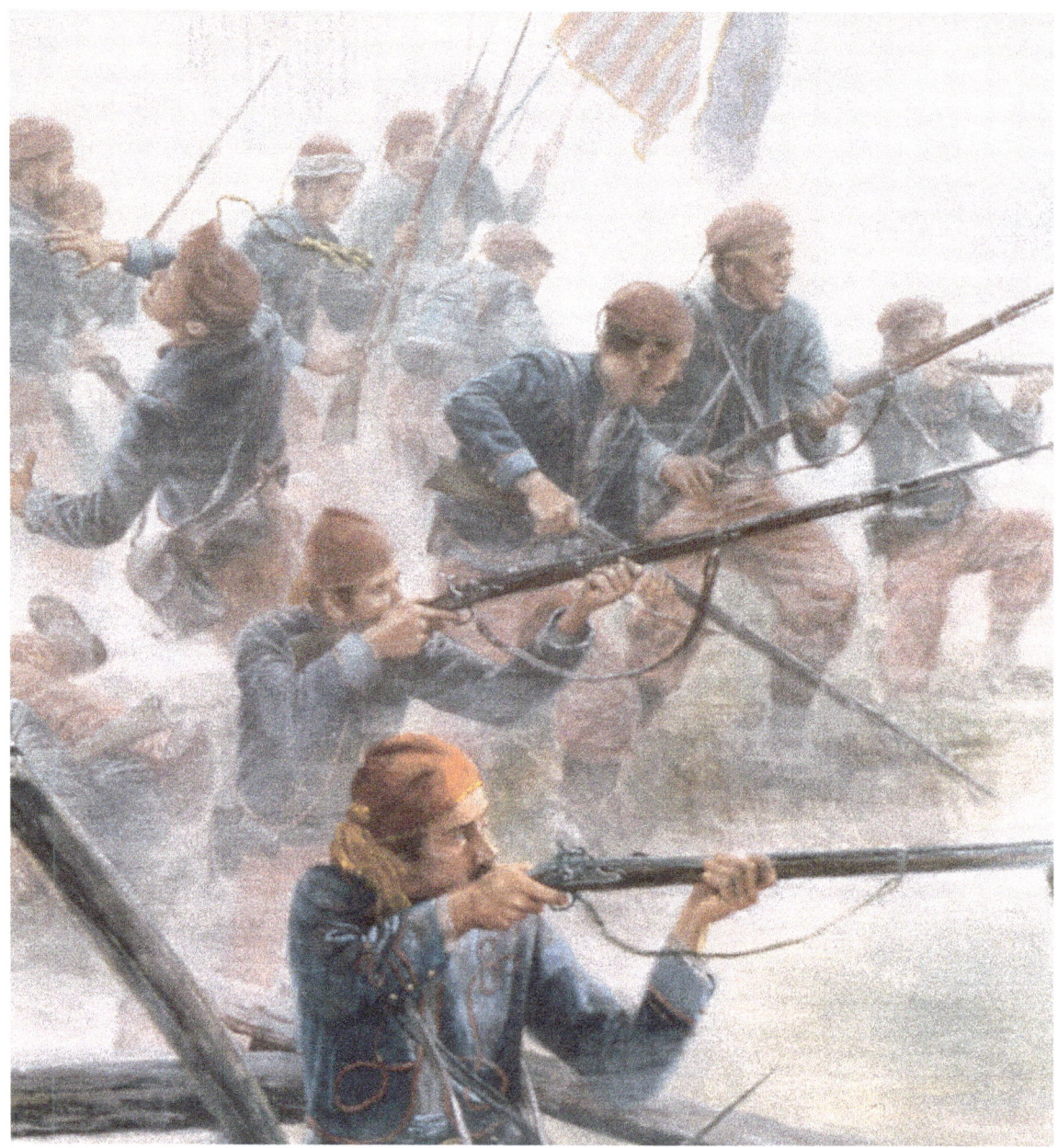

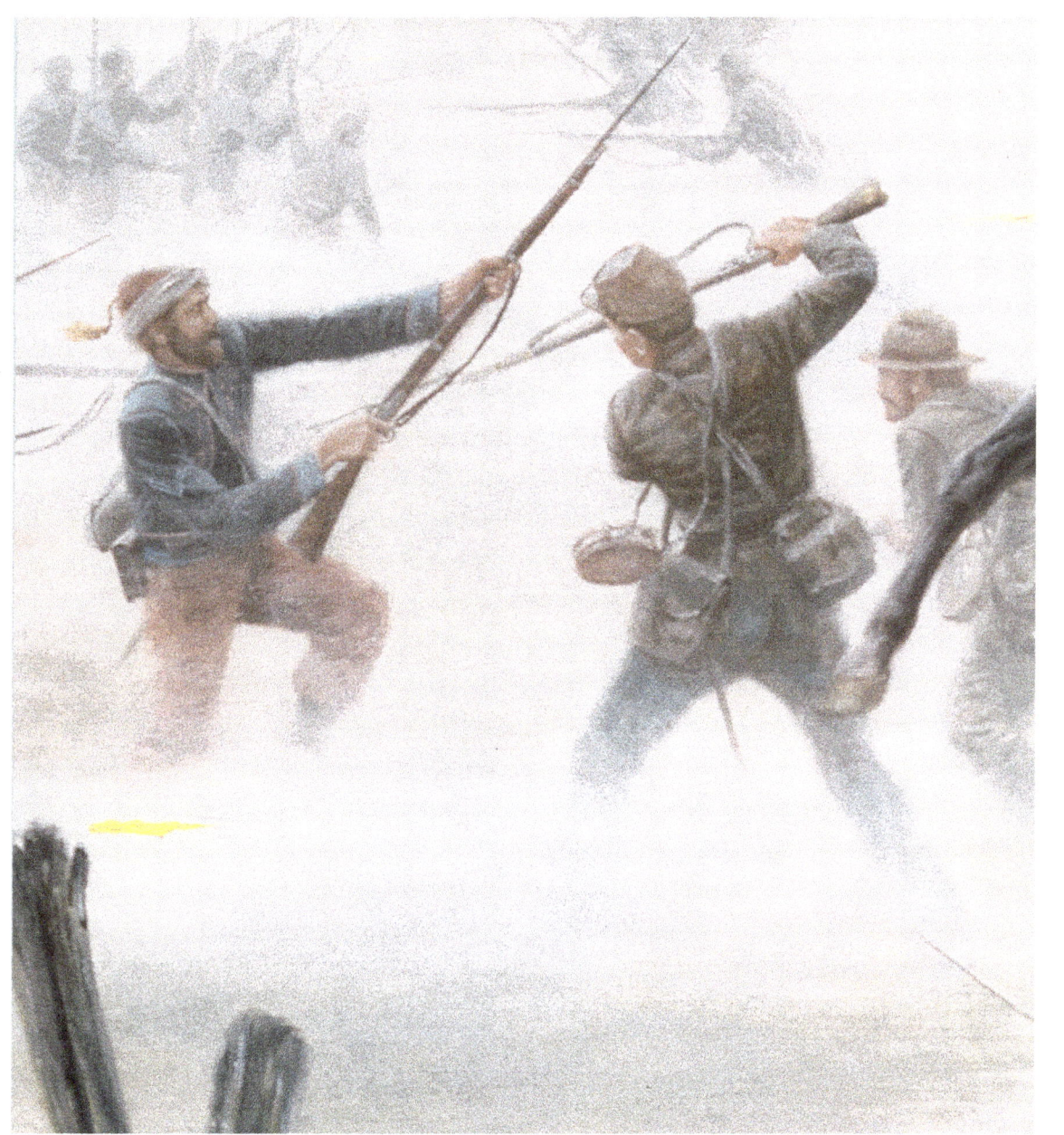

THE RETURN OF STUART

GENERALS LEE AND STUART, GETTYSBURG,
JULY 2, 1863

1993, gouache, 13¾ x 17½

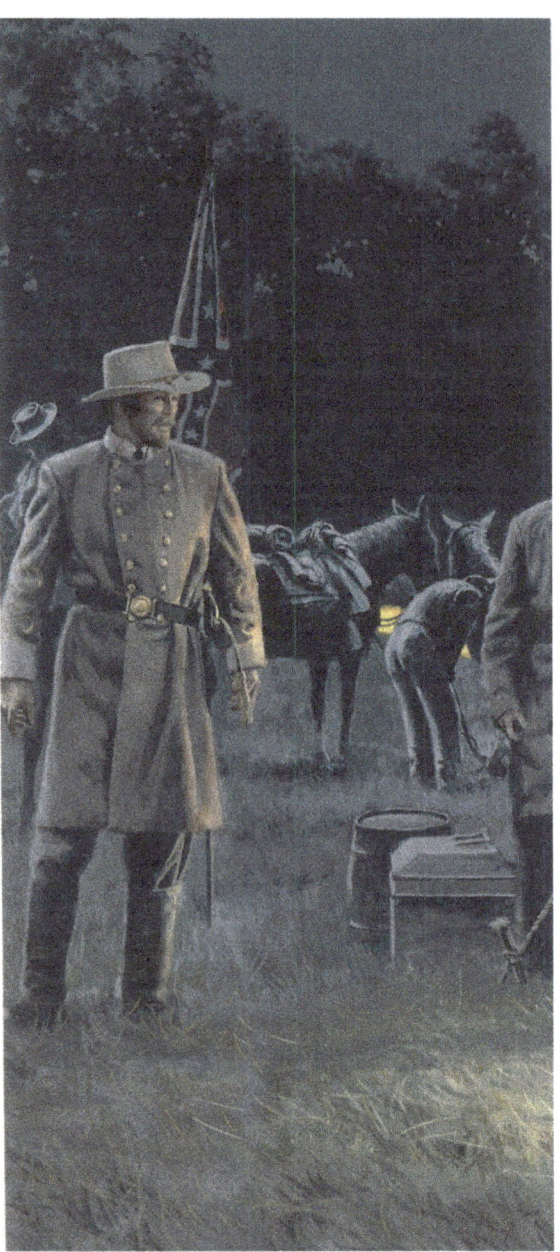

LEE'S GREATEST WEAKNESS AT Gettysburg was the absence of Jeb Stuart. Lee depended on his cavalry to keep him informed on Union troop movements, but in late June 1863, Stuart had taken his horsemen on a raid far away from the action at Gettysburg. As a consequence, Lee lacked crucial information on the expansive, evolving battlefield on which his army fought.

In the late hours of July 2, Stuart finally arrived at Lee's headquarters on Seminary Ridge and was greeted abruptly and coolly by an exasperated army commander. The two men had

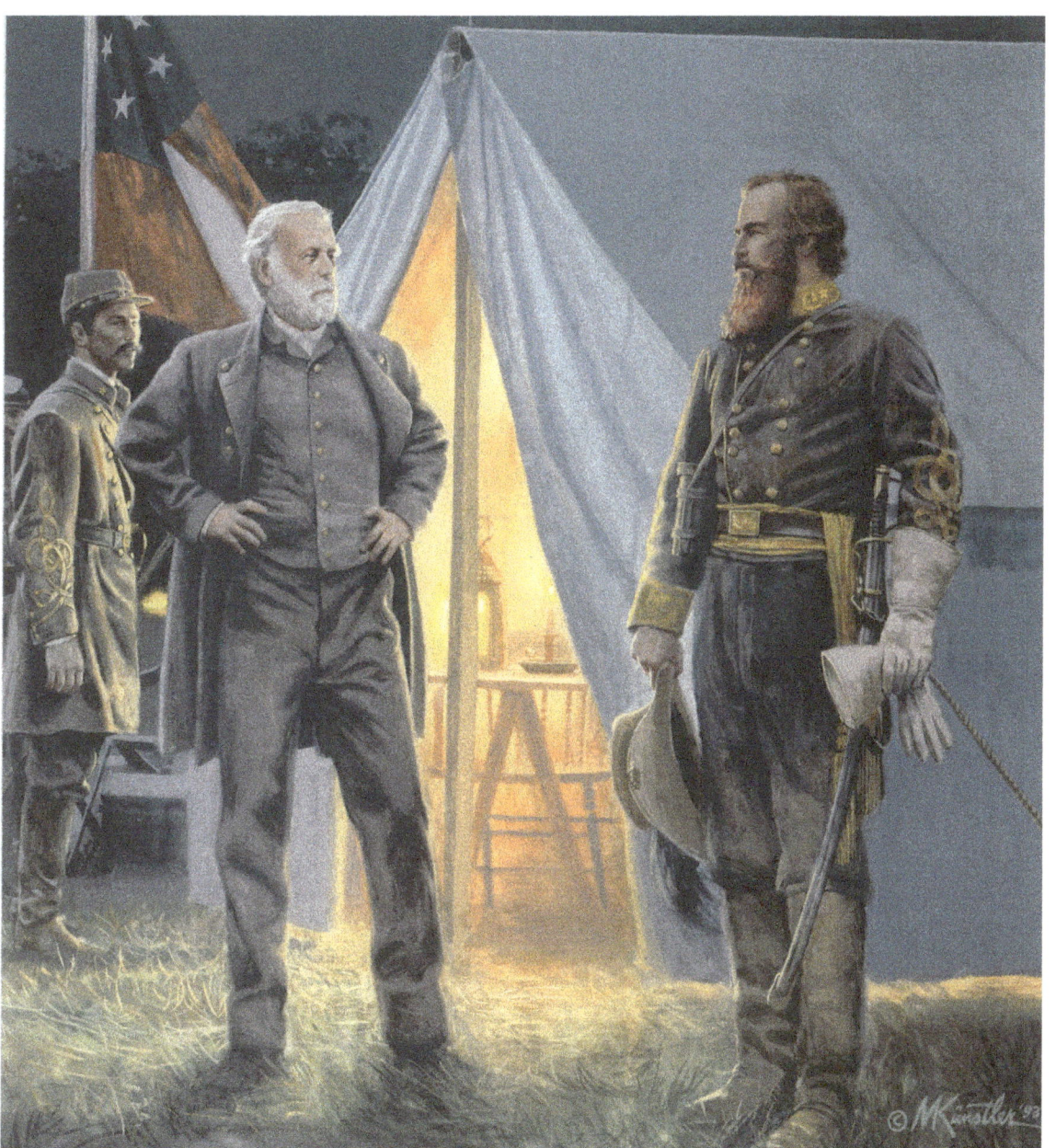

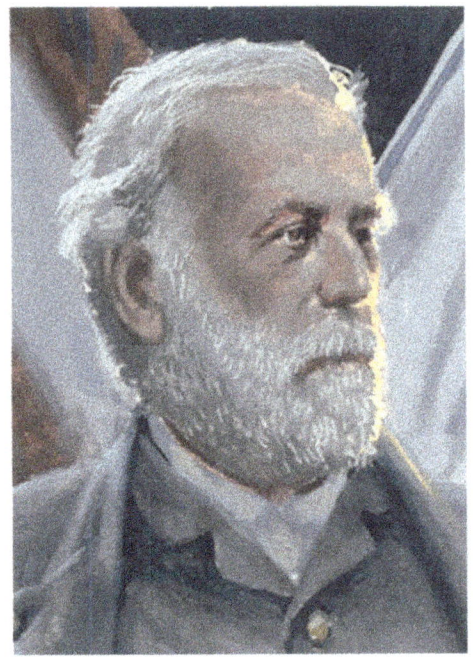

great respect for each other, and this was an awkward moment for both, like a father reprimanding a son.

Lee supposedly said, "Well, General, you are here at last." Stuart understood the words as a rebuke.

Finally, Lee's compassion got the best of him, and he ended the confrontation with words of encouragement for Stuart, who was dispirited about the whole affair.

In trying to capture this dramatic confrontation in a painting, I decided to use the warm light emanating from the tent to illuminate the main characters dramatically and to create a contrast with the cool moonlight effect. By putting Lee's hands on his hips, I implied a feeling of exasperation toward Stuart. Lee was such a gentleman—so dignified and self-controlled—that he seldom showed much more emotion than that.

This is a moving scene, almost like a family scene. When some of my original Gettysburg paintings were displayed at the Gettysburg Cyclorama in the summer of 1993, *The Return of Stuart* proved to be the most popular image of the exhibition.

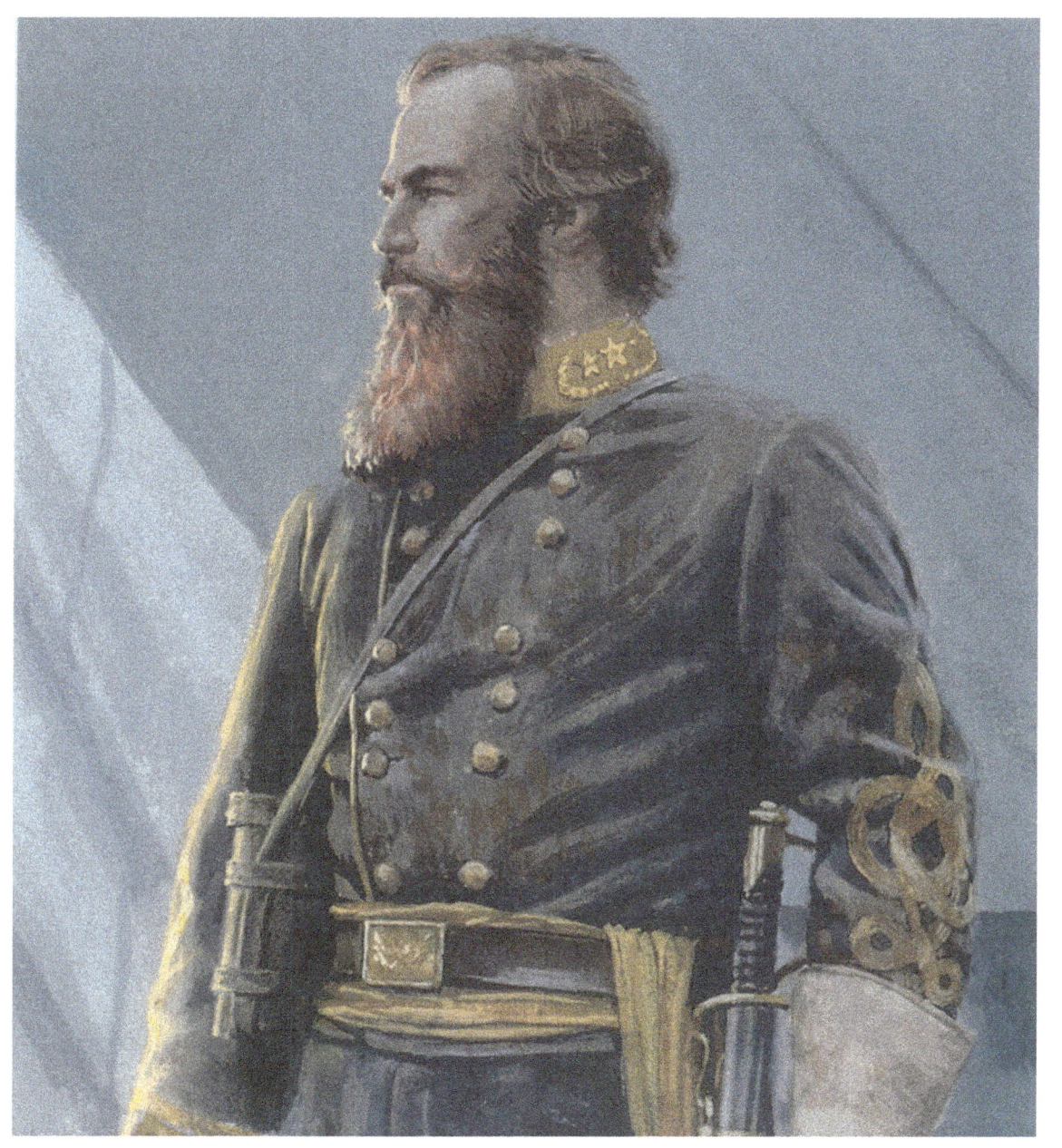

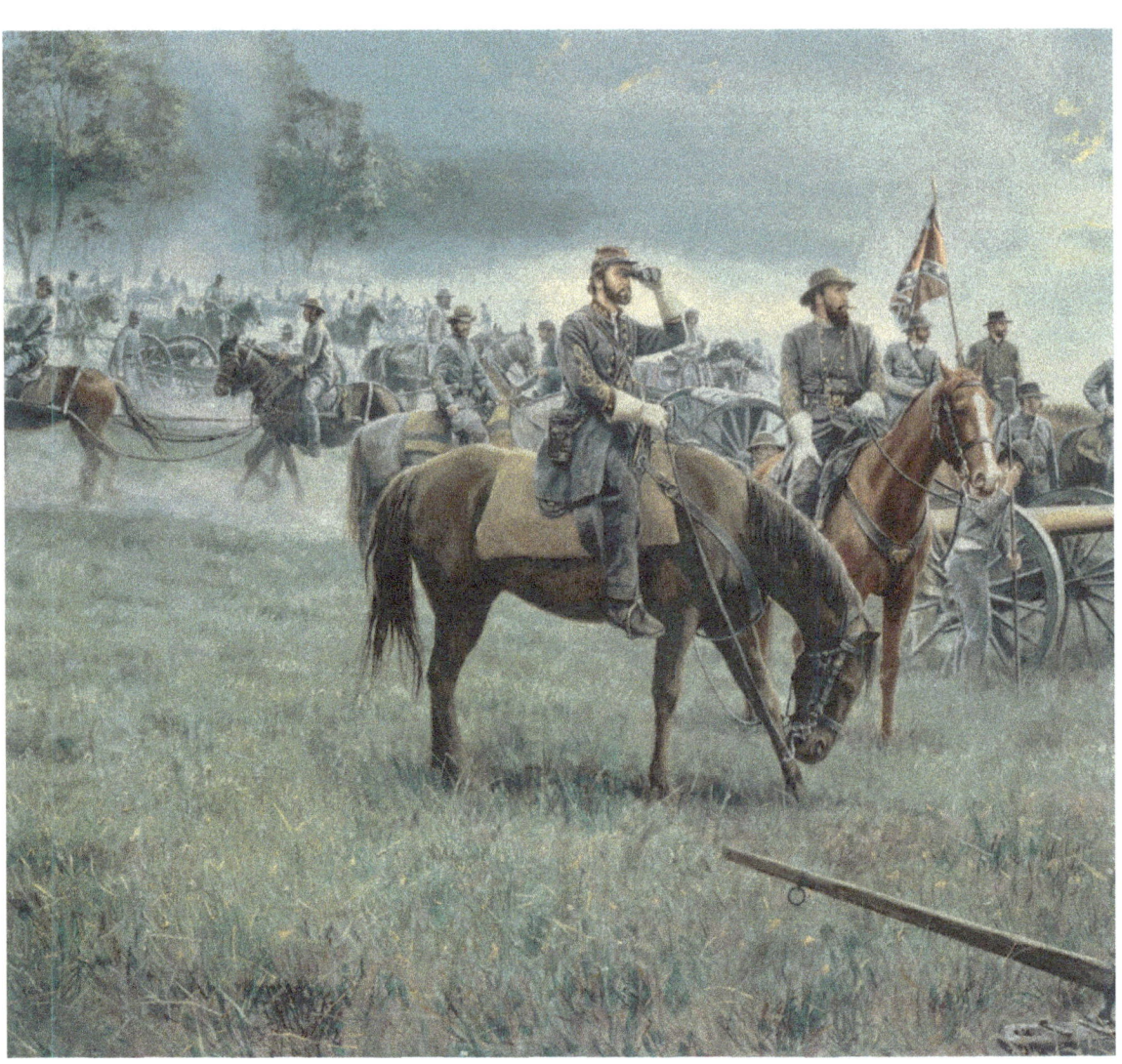

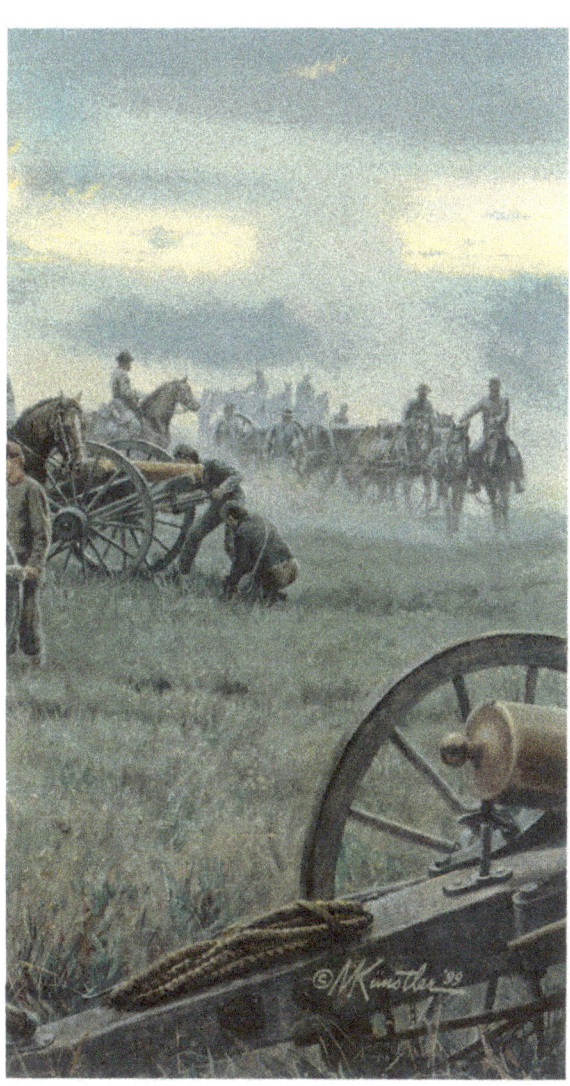

 FORMING THE LINE

COL. E. PORTER ALEXANDER AND
GEN. JAMES LONGSTREET AT GETTYSBURG
JULY 3, 1863

1999, oil, 20 x 34

DURING THE EVENING OF July 2, the Confederates attacked the Union positions on Cemetery Hill, and in the morning of July 3, they attacked the Federals on Culp's Hill—both being on the right side of Meade's line. Lee's battle plan then shifted to the center of the Union line on Cemetery Ridge. Ewell would attack the Union right again, Longstreet would assault the center, and Hill's corps would reinforce whatever breakthrough Ewell or Longstreet achieved.

Ewell's attack began on schedule, but Longstreet's was delayed. After

129

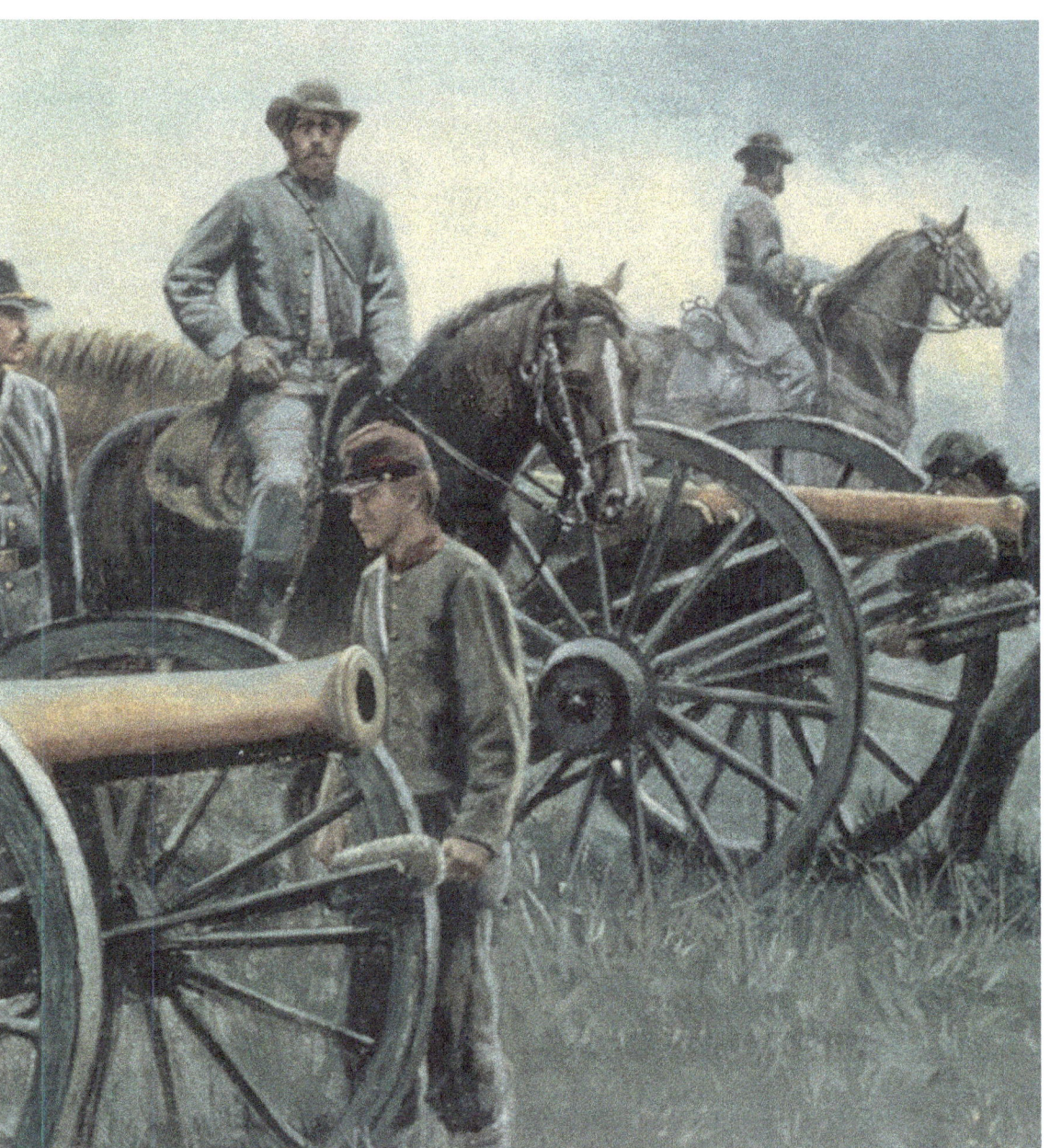

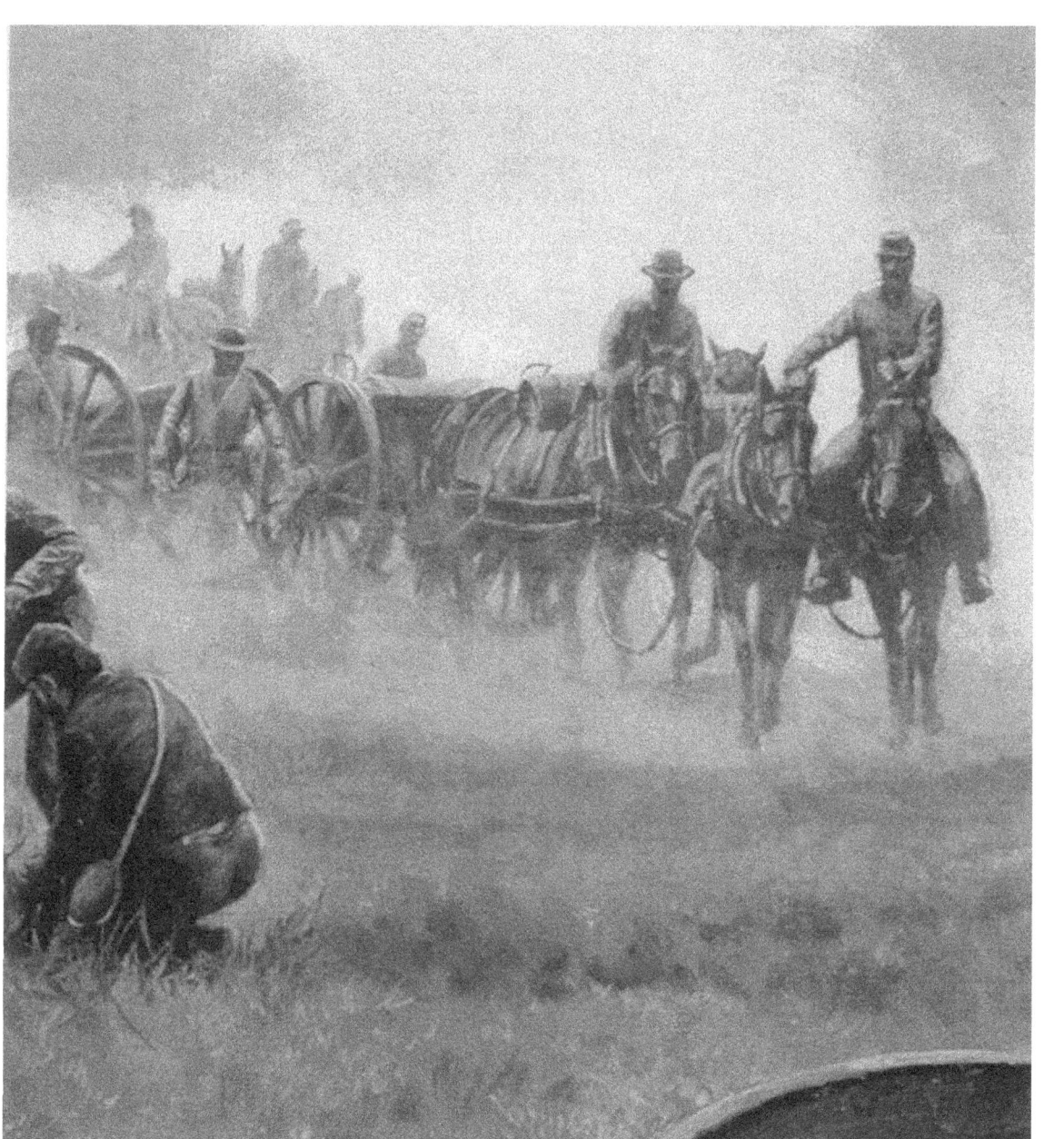

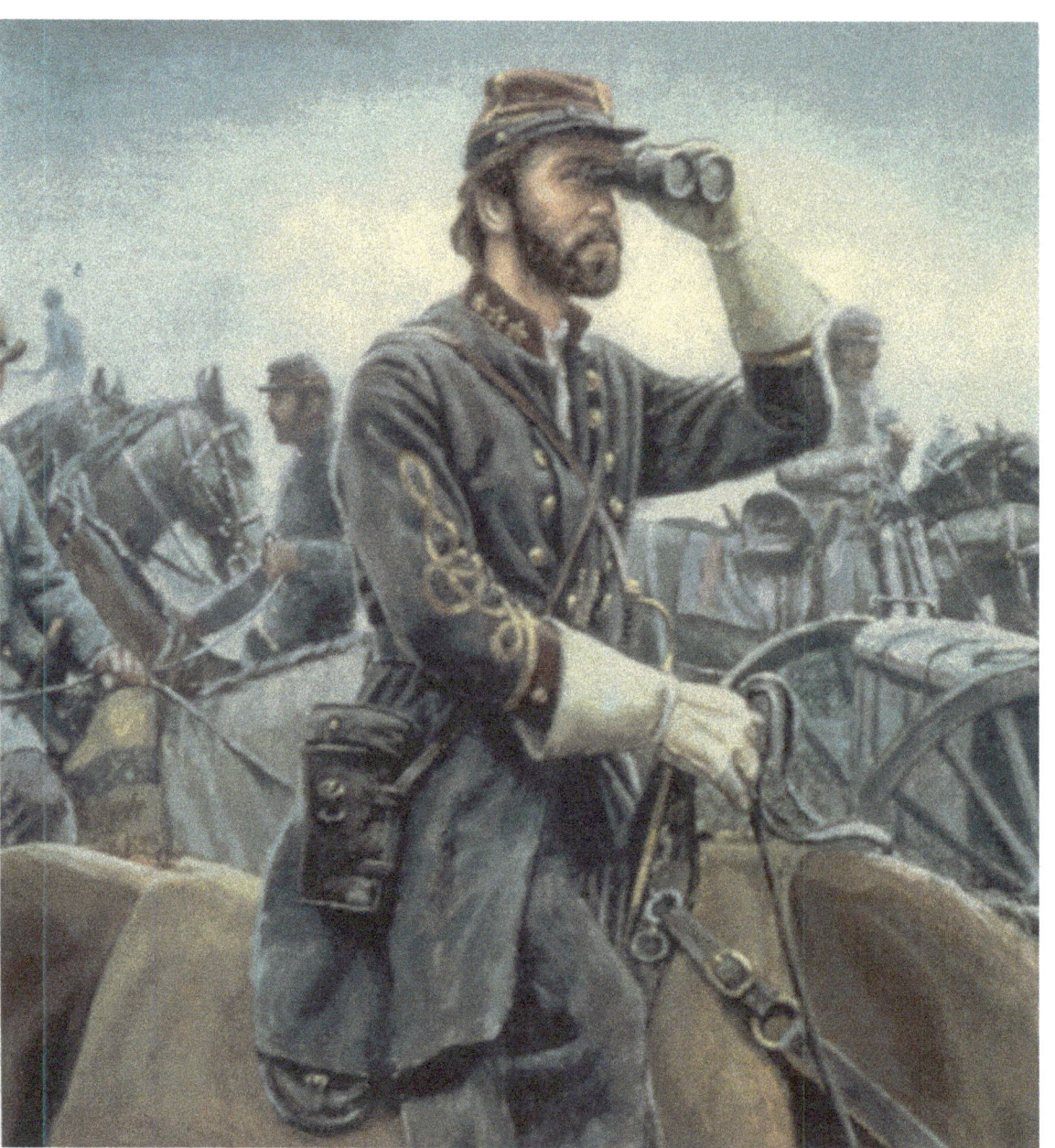

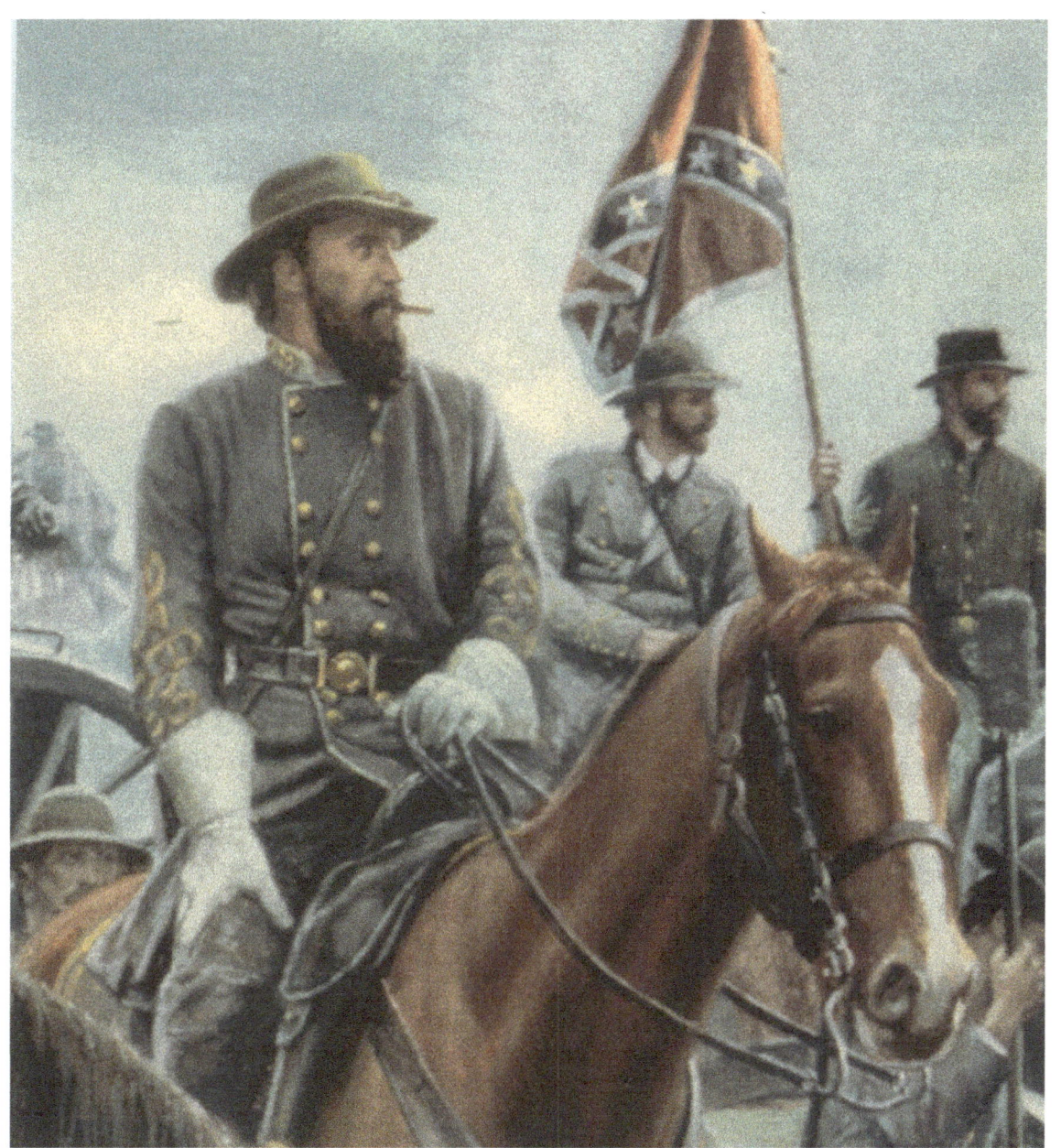

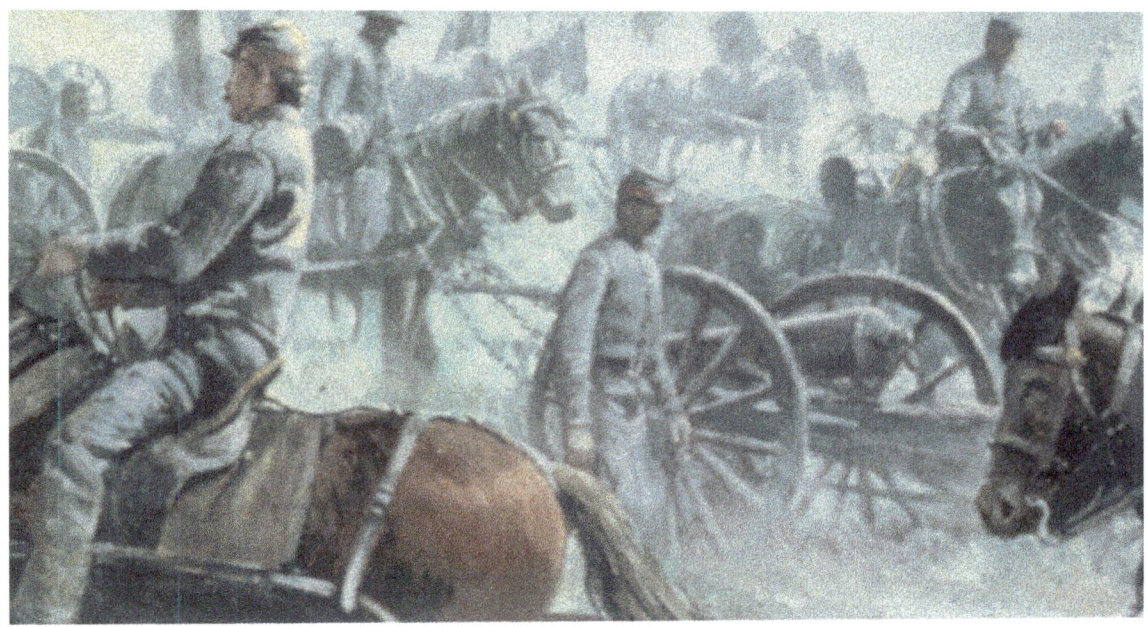

meeting with Longstreet, Lee amended his orders. The attack on the center of the Union line would be spearheaded by George E. Pickett's division, and his advance would be preceded by a cannonade from all three corps.

The bombardment was critical. It was supposed to clear a path for the attackers by overwhelming the Union artillery and demoralizing the Federal infantry. Unfortunately, Lee's chief of artillery failed to coordinate the 163 guns at his command. The most organized gunners on the field were Longstreet's 75 guns, commanded by twenty-eight-year-old Col. E. Porter Alexander.

Most artillery paintings depict the guns in action because smoke and flame are dramatic. Equally dramatic, I thought, was the forming of the line, when the guns are rolled into place, unlimbered, and set up. In this painting, Alexander and Longstreet oversee all of this.

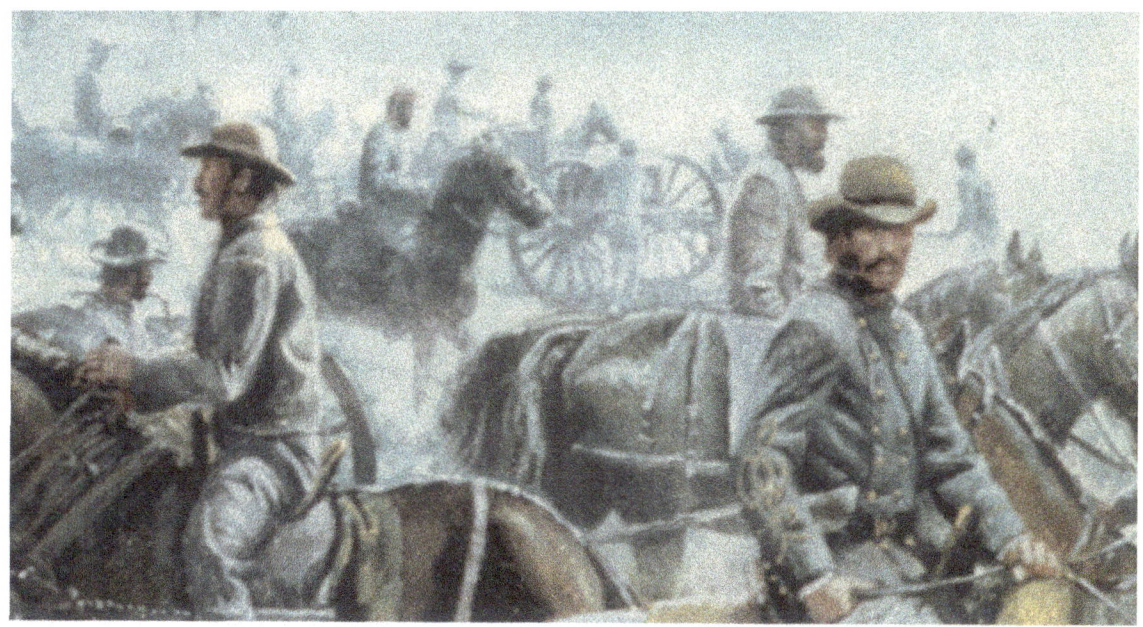

In composing the picture, I wanted to show every phase of Alexander's men as they emplaced the guns. Lt. Col. David Stanley of Raleigh, North Carolina, an expert on horse-drawn artillery, was of invaluable help in describing for me the maneuvers, the positioning of the men, the appearance of the harnesses, and so on.

In the extreme right foreground, a bronze Napoleon stands unlimbered, with the handspike in place. Near the middle of the picture, directly behind Longstreet, the crew of another Napoleon maneuvers it into firing position. Farther back, behind the staff officers, another crew works on a recently unlimbered gun; the horse team is in the extreme left of the painting, moving right to left, pulling the caisson to the rear. The teams in the extreme left background, moving left to right, are bringing up additional guns.

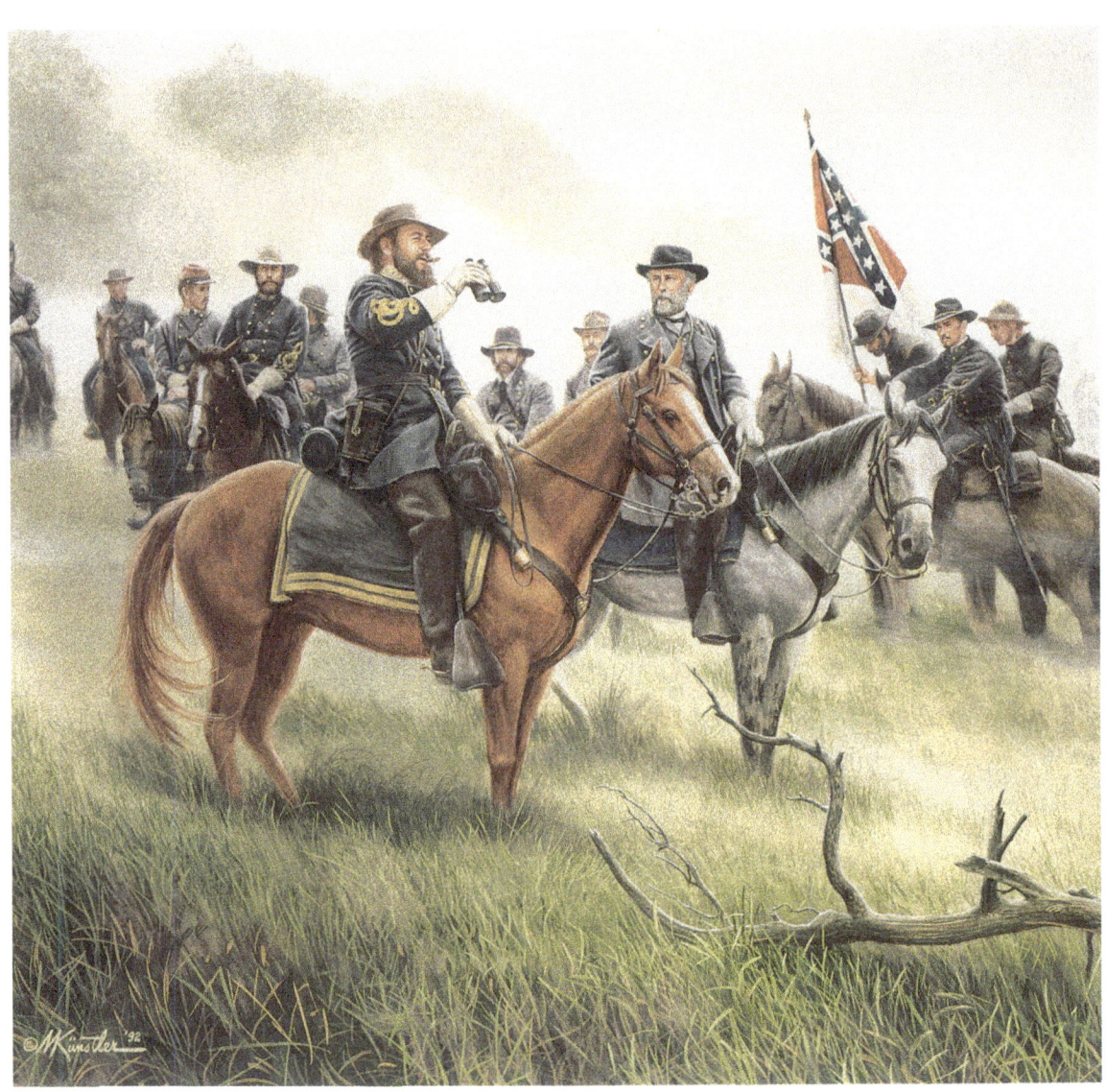

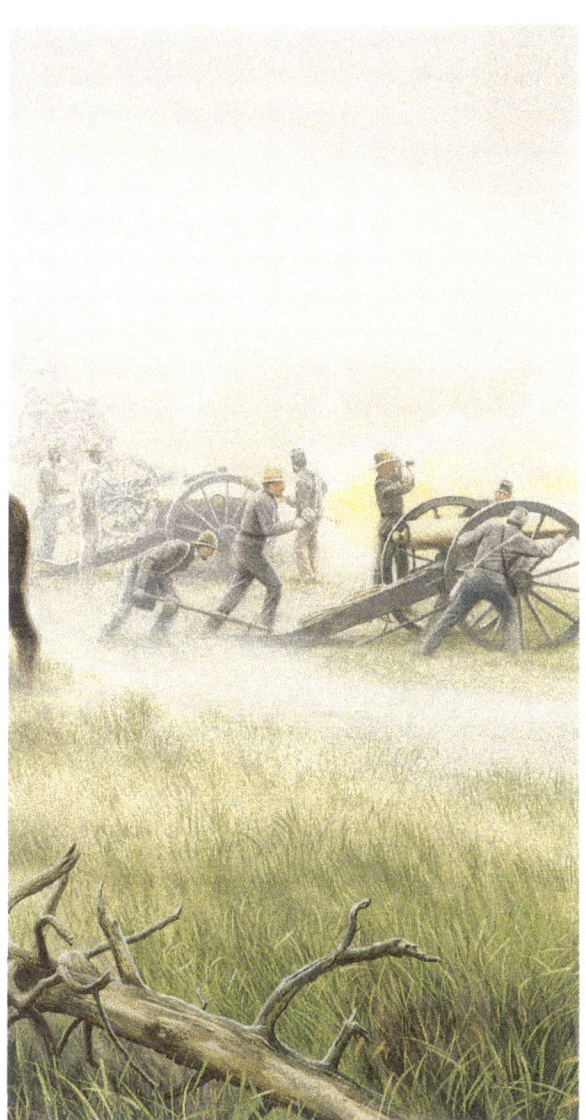

LEE'S "OLD WAR HORSE"

GENERALS LONGSTREET AND LEE
GETTYSBURG, JULY 3, 1863

1993, gouache, 16½ x 27

ROBERT E. LEE AND James Longstreet are the two central Confederate figures in the story of Gettysburg and how the Army of Northern Virginia performed during that engagement. Even after nearly 150 years, no one can explain exactly what happened or why these two commanders seemed to stumble on what so many Southerners saw as the threshold of victory.

Some historians see Lee as uncommunicative, directing the battle with as little input from his senior commanders as possible. Heady from the successes of the past year, most recently at

Chancellorsville, he seemed to believe that his army could accomplish whatever he asked of it. Lee may have dismissed Longstreet's council to find better ground from which to fight (perhaps seeking to reenact his greatest victories at Second Manassas and Fredericksburg) because Longstreet had not been with the army when Lee achieved the unlikely victory at Chancellorsville. For his part, Longstreet may have reacted to Lee's fixation on attacking the Federals on Cemetery Ridge by parsing his orders, following them to the letter, rather than exercising his discretionary authority as a corps commander to reinterpret orders as opportunities presented themselves on the battlefield.

What better way to show Longstreet, Lee's "Old War Horse," than as he is sizing up the enemy position while Lee awaits his opinion? Perhaps this is the moment that Longstreet claimed to say: "I have been a soldier all my life. I have been with soldiers engaged in fights by couples, by squads, companies, regiments, divisions, and armies, and should know as well as anyone what soldiers can do. It is my opinion that no fifteen thousand men ever arrayed for battle can take that position."

On the morning of July 3, Lee and Longstreet rode the line out to the Confederate right. Some sporadic fire from A. P. Hill's artillery broke out in front of Henry Heth's division but died away shortly after noon. The artillery piece in the foreground is a bronze Napoleon. Next to it is a Napoleon in action. I used the flame of the muzzle flash to silhouette the artillery officer observing the results through his field glasses.

With Lee and Longstreet, of course, are their respective staffs: officers, couriers, flag bearers, etc. Within this entourage are some recognizable members of both staffs. Above Traveller's head, between the flag bearer and another soldier, is Lt. Col. Walter Taylor, one of Lee's aides throughout the war. Immediately to the left of Lee is Lt. Col. James Corely. To Longstreet's left, I placed Lt. Col. W. H. Stevens, viewing the two generals, watching the give and take between these two extraordinary commanders. The staffs mingle, conversing and waiting for orders.

THE GUNS OF GETTYSBURG

1993, mixed media, 9¼ x 12

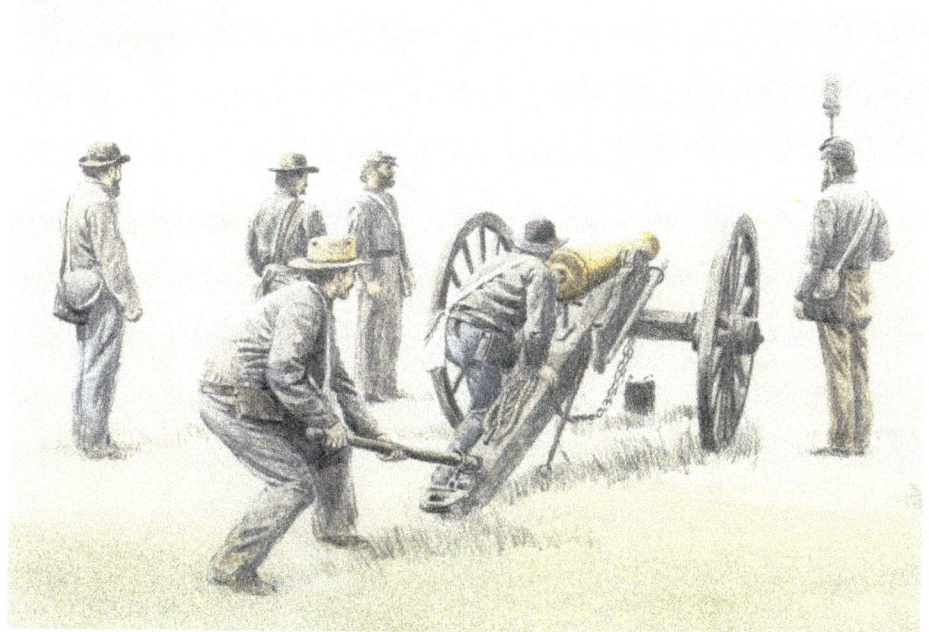

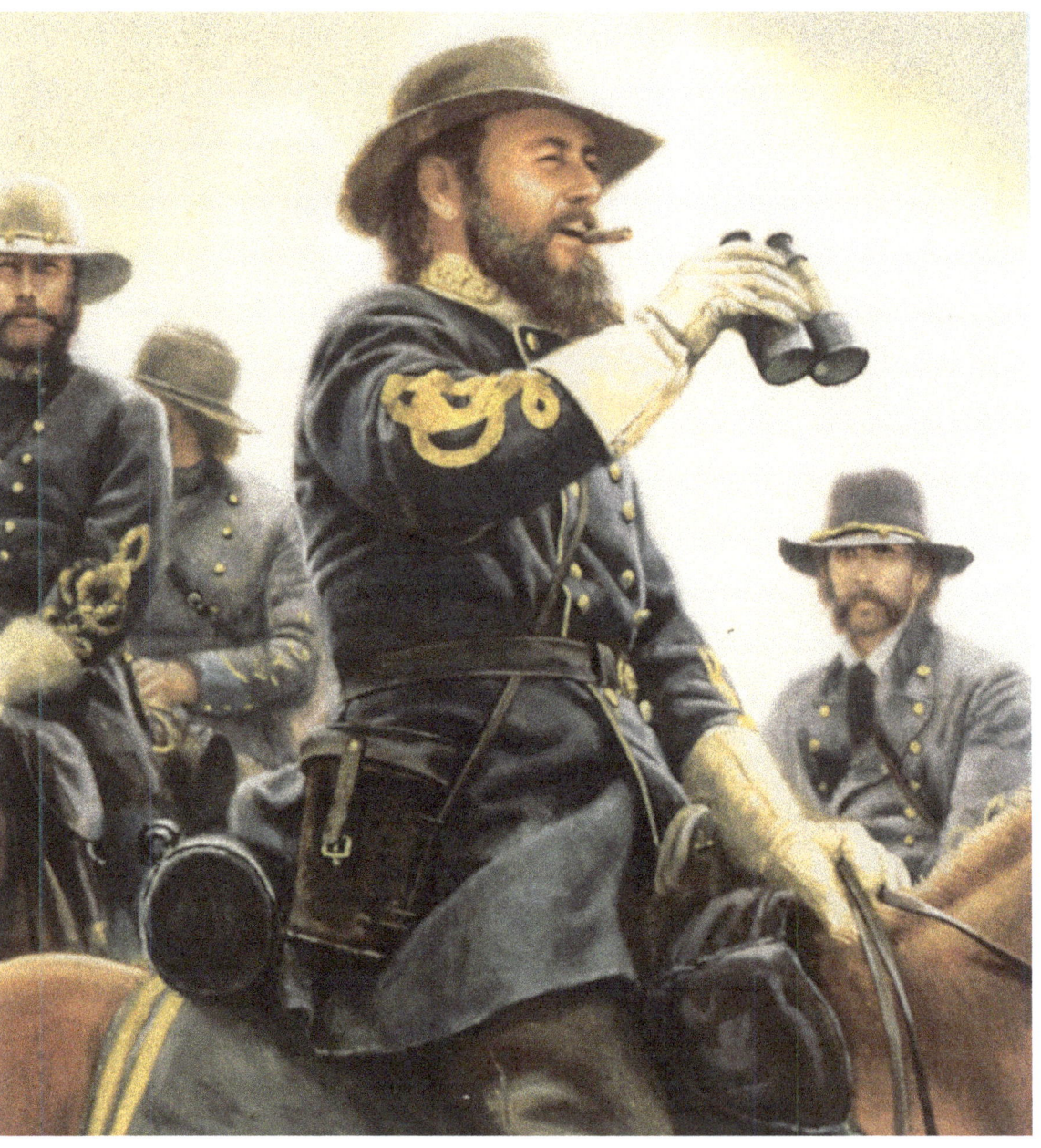

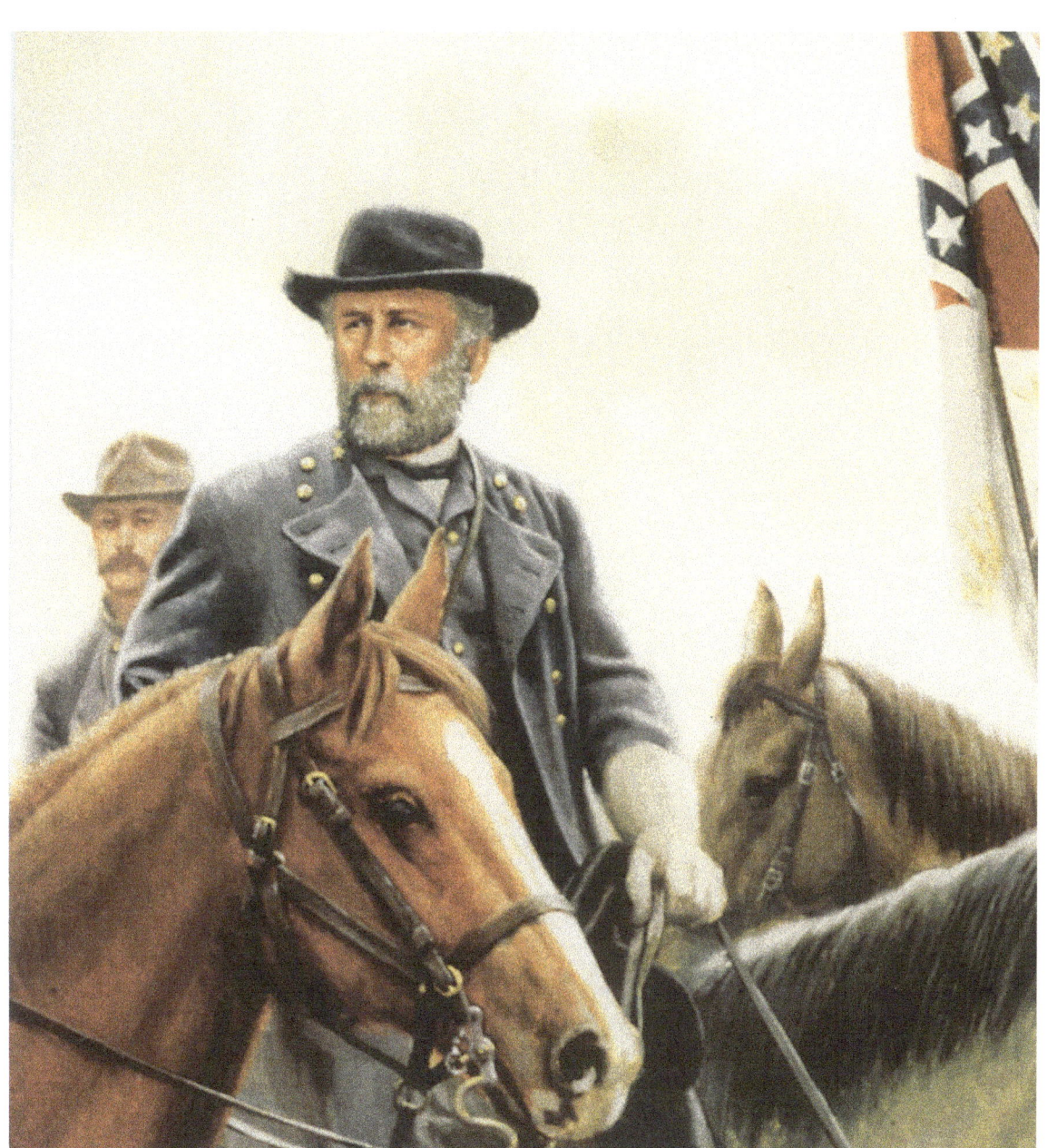

"KEEP TO YOUR SABERS, MEN!"

GENERALS CUSTER AND HAMPTON, GETTYSBURG, JULY 3, 1863

1992, oil, 24 x 60

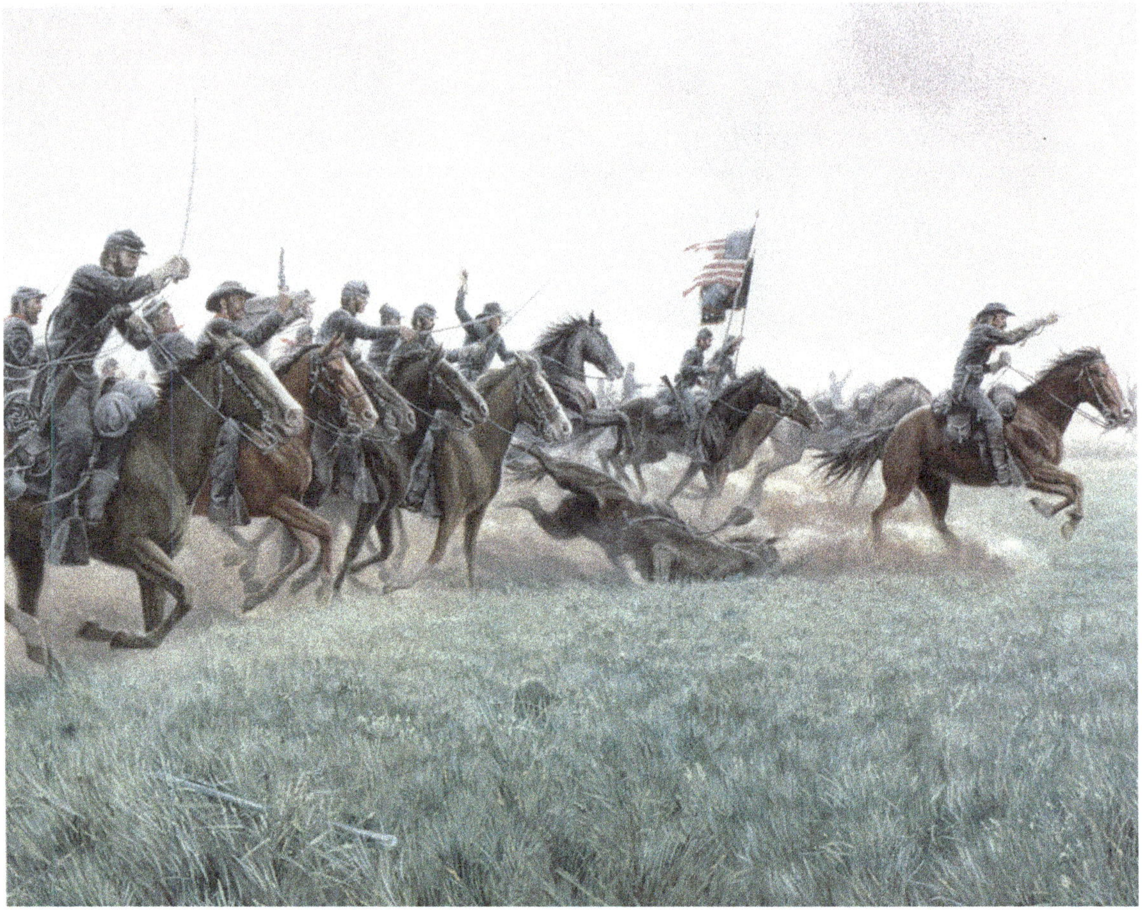

THERE WAS TO BE a third part to Lee's battle plans for July 3: a coordinated cavalry attack. If the infantry assault succeeded in breaking the Union line, a Confederate cavalry thrust at the enemy's rear would wreak havoc on the Federals'

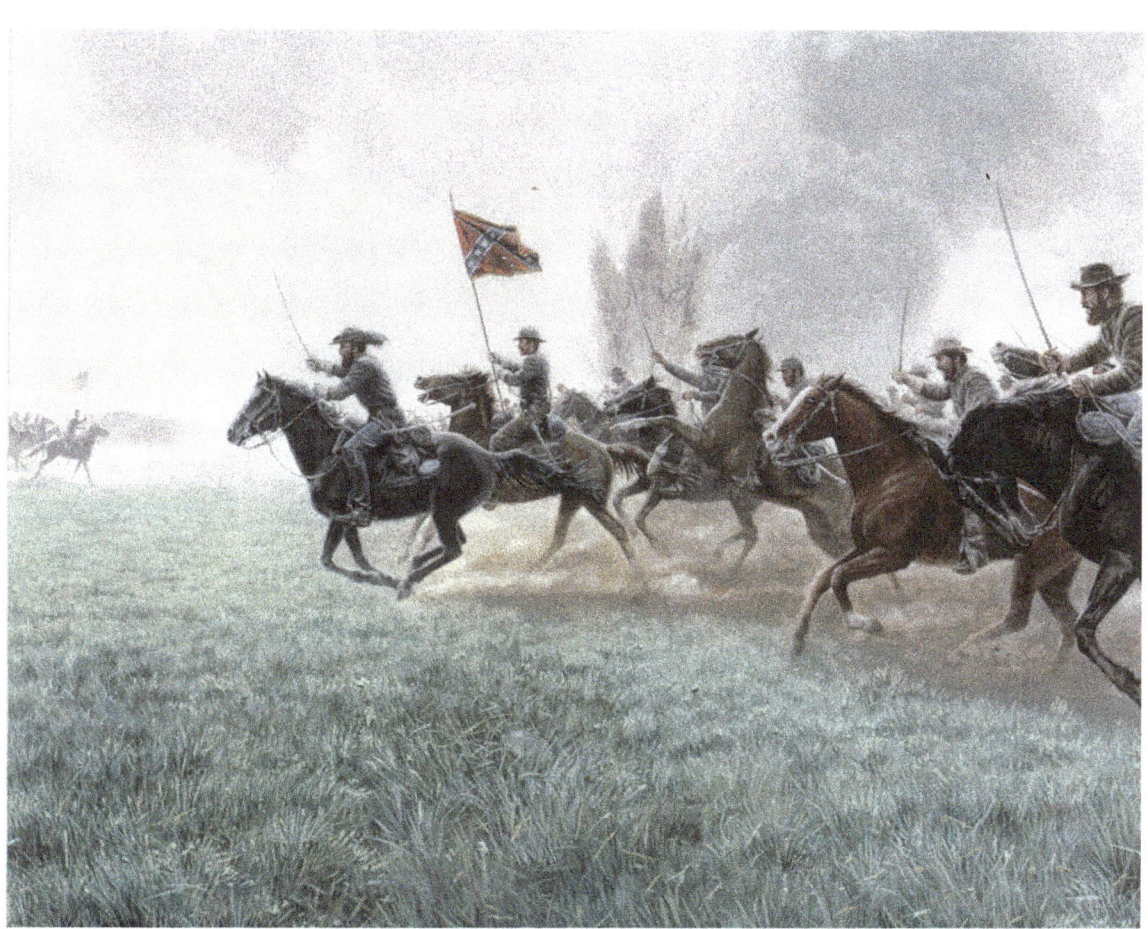

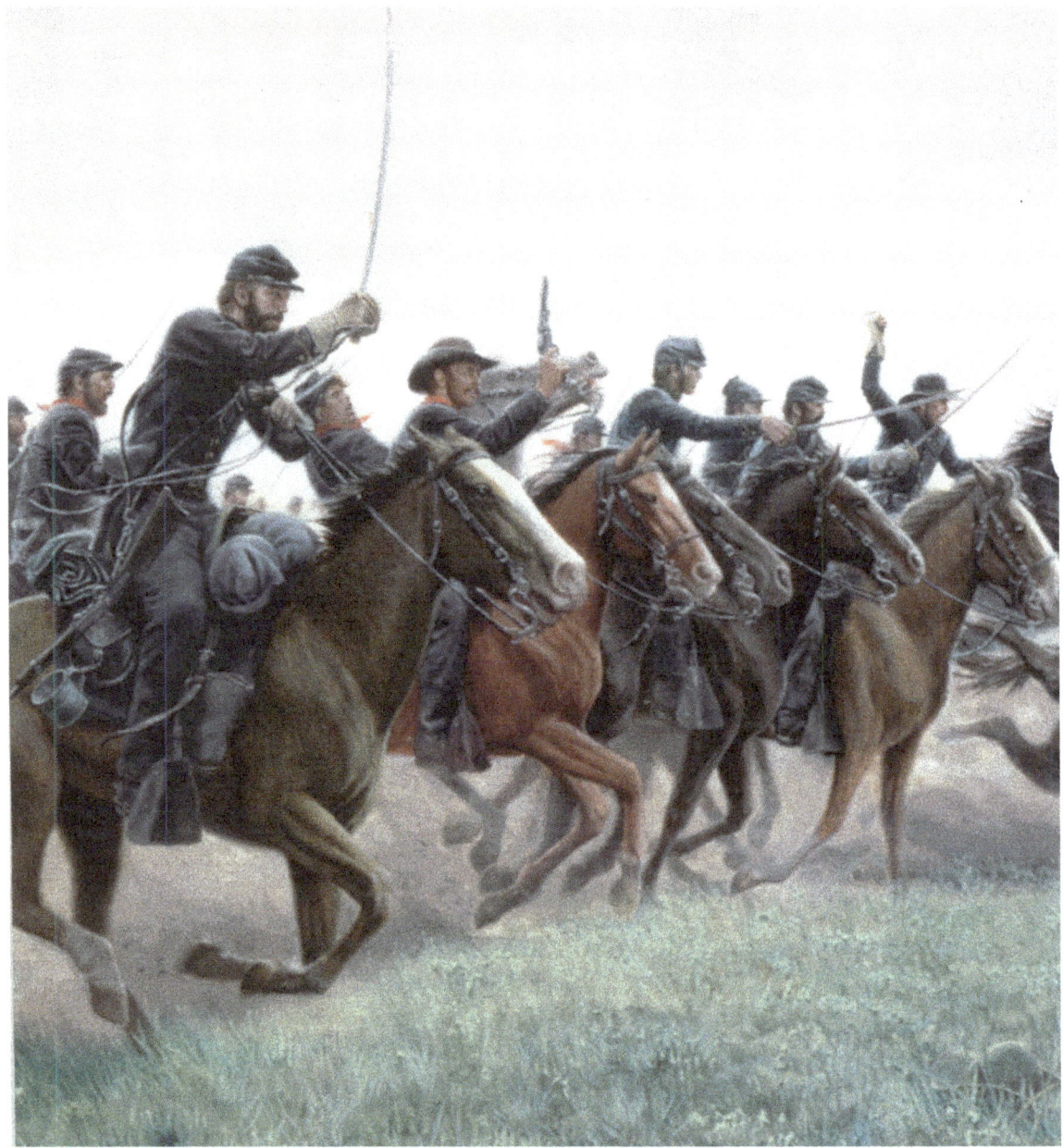

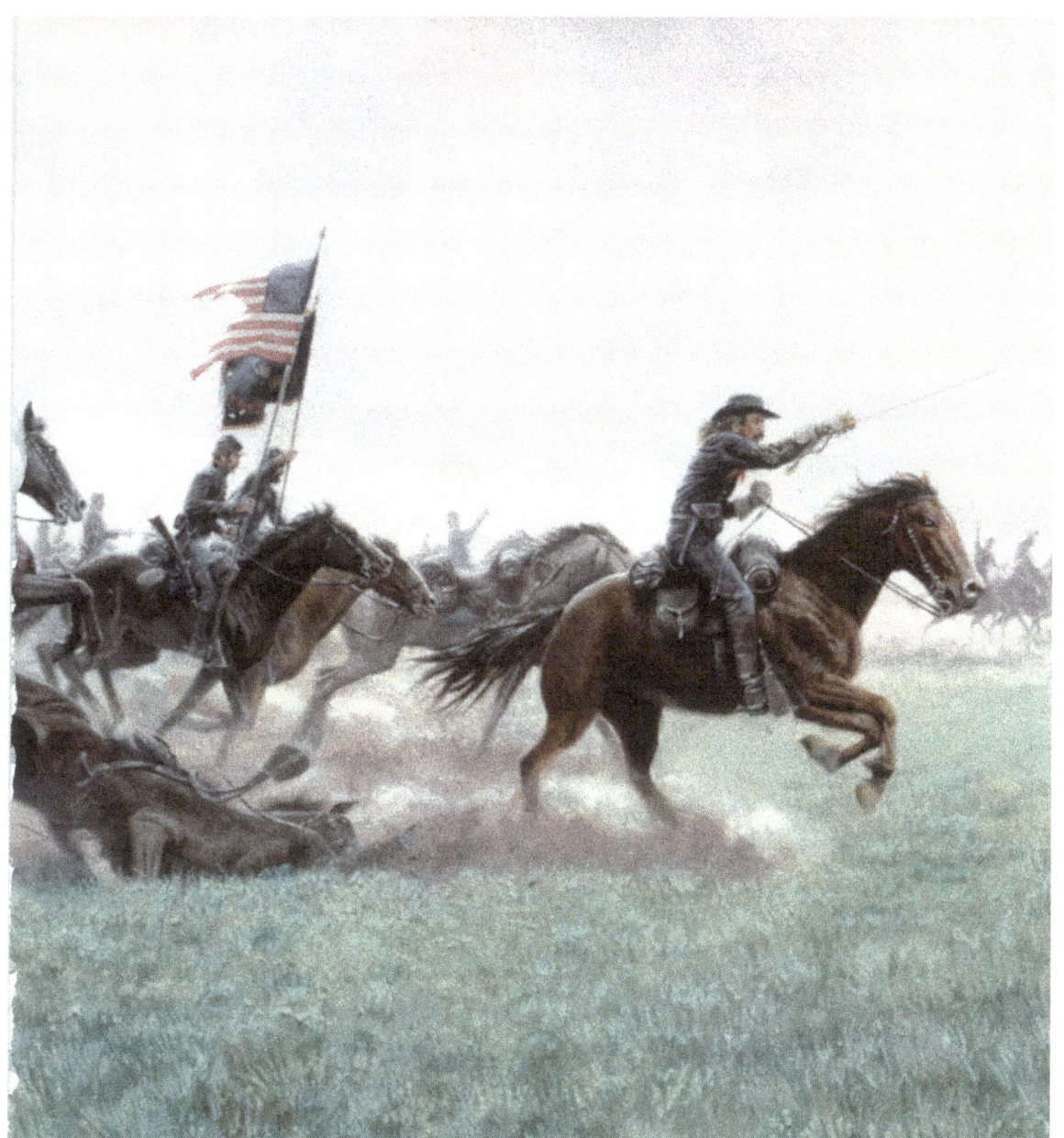

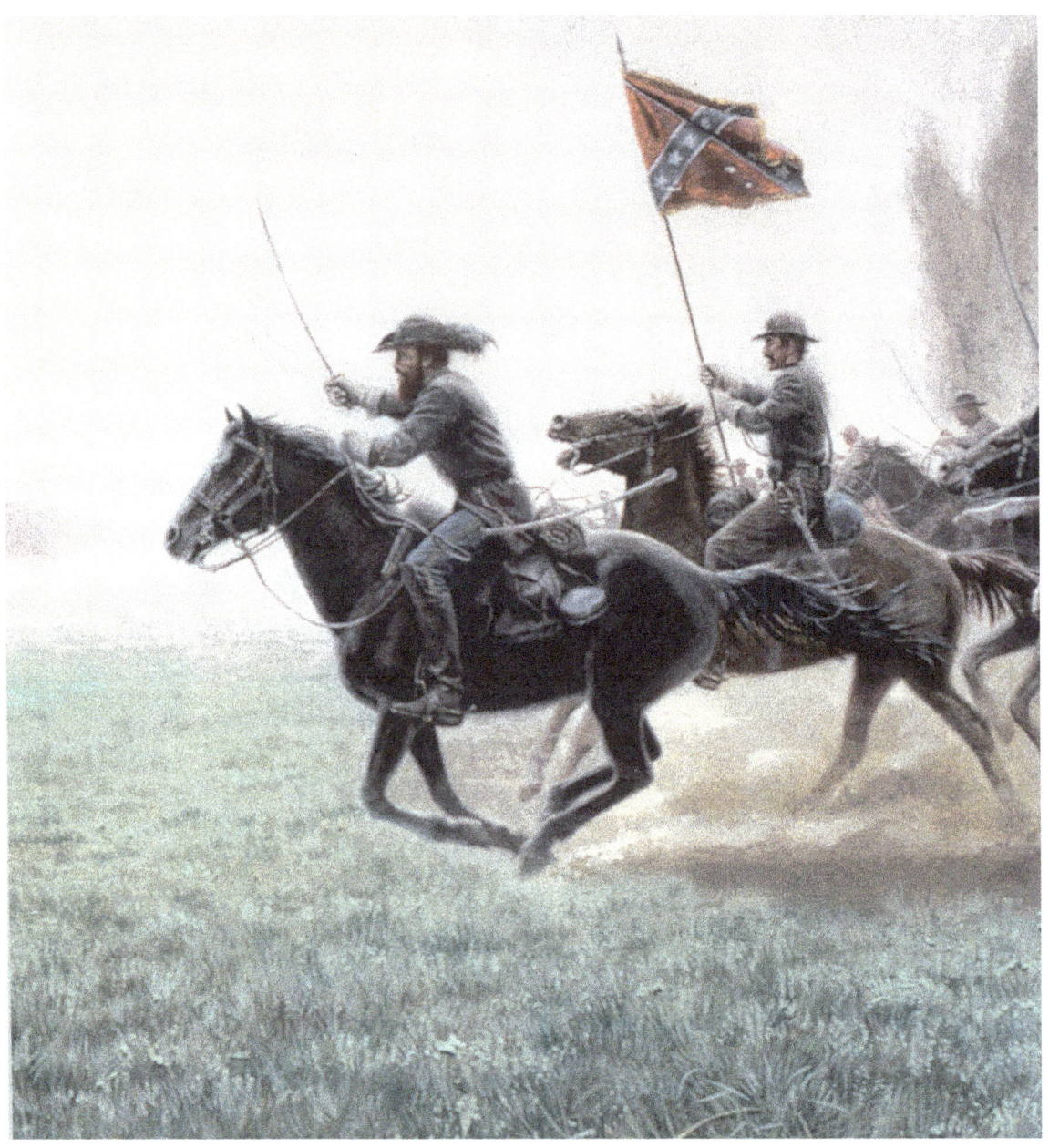

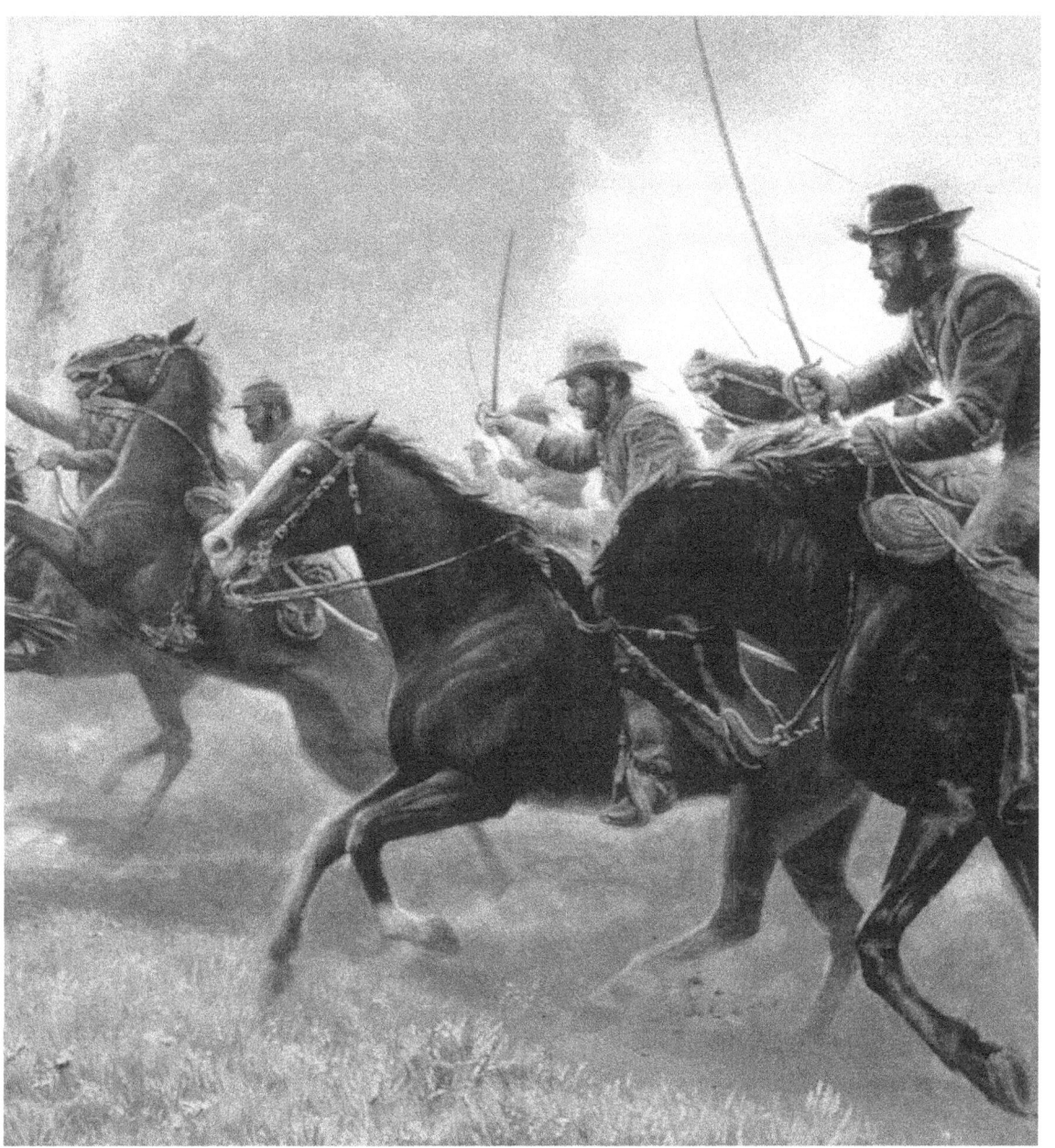

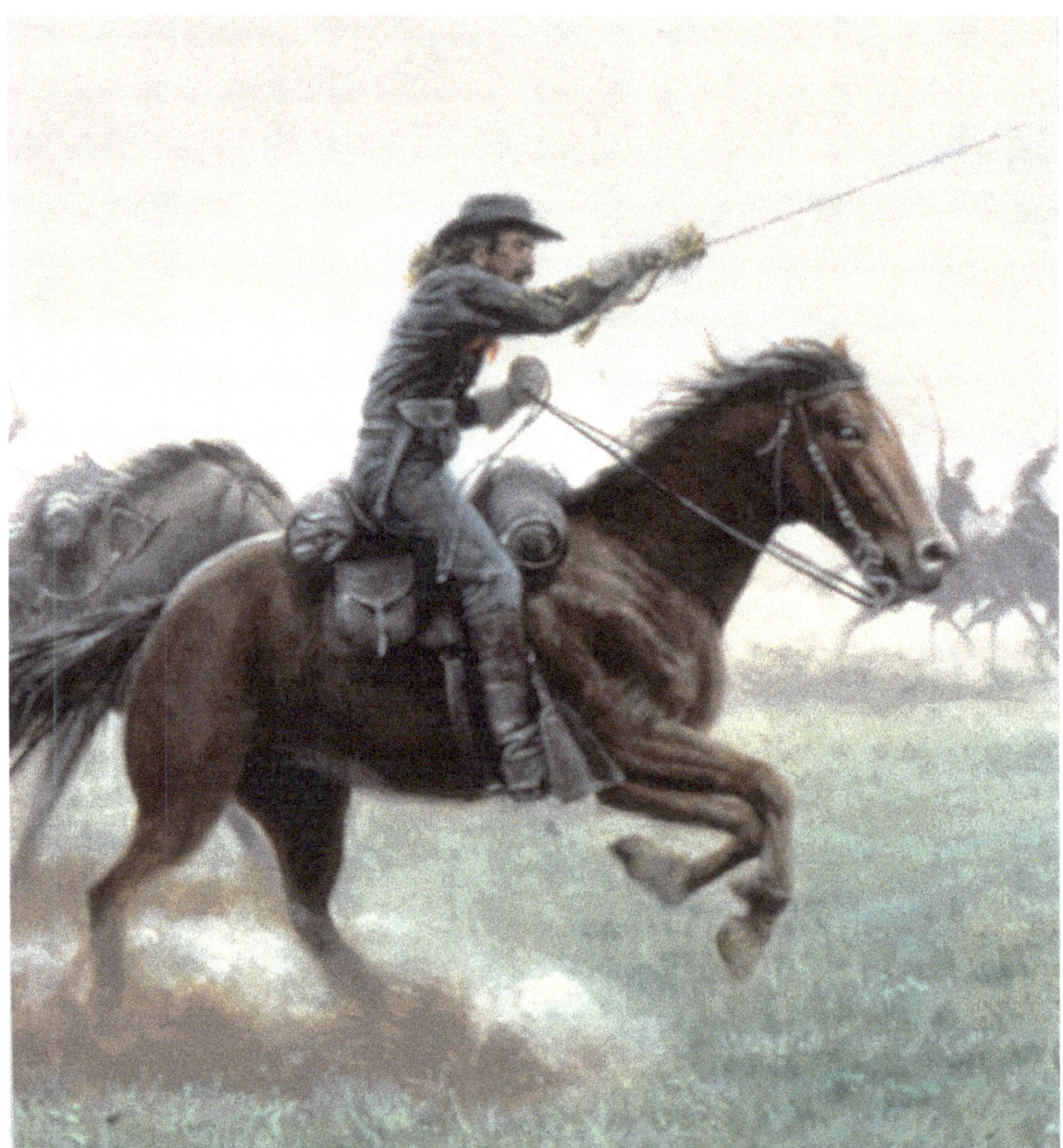

interior lines and sow confusion amid the Union troops, thus giving the Confederates a better chance of victory. The plan called for a charge on the center of the Federal position and a portion of the cavalry to pressure the Union flank.

Late that morning, Jeb Stuart led four brigades (about three thousand cavalrymen) to the east, planning to circle around the Union line. About three miles from Gettysburg, he encountered Union cavalry: David M. Gregg's division and George Armstrong Custer's Michigan Brigade (about thirty-two hundred horsemen).

At first, they fought dismounted, but then Stuart charged and Gregg countercharged. Neither had an advantage until Stuart's men formed long, narrow squadrons on the field. They were an impressive sight, but the formation was susceptible to artillery fire, and Union gunners blew gaps into the long columns. Charging through the Federal fire, Wade Hampton's brigade found Custer's brigade rushing toward it.

Twenty-three-year-old Custer, at the time the youngest general in the Union army, led his men with the now-famous battle cry, "Come on, you Wolverines!"

The Confederate cavalry's traditional weapon of choice at close quarters was firearms, but in this action, sabers—the preferred weapon of the Union cavalry—were used. At the head of his troops, Hampton was heard to shout above the din, "Keep to your sabers, men! Keep to your sabers!"

The Union charged from the northeast, the Confederates from the southwest, with the sun behind them. Federal artillery fired on the Southerners, but Hampton's horsemen continued undaunted. When the two lines met, some said that the impact was heard a mile away.

A Pennsylvania captain recalled, "As the two columns approached each other, the pace of each increased, when suddenly a crash, like the falling of timber, betokened the crisis. So sudden and violent was the collision that many of the horses were turned end over end and crushed their riders beneath them. The clashing of sabers, the firing of pistols, the demands for surrender, and cries of the combatants, filled the air."

Initially, the advantage was with the South, but Federal pressure on the Confederate flanks crumpled their formations. The Union flank held, and the Confederates pulled back, ruining any chance for a successful attack against the rear of the Northern line. Hampton was badly wounded in the ensuing melee, and Custer was credited by some with personally capturing Hampton's battle flag.

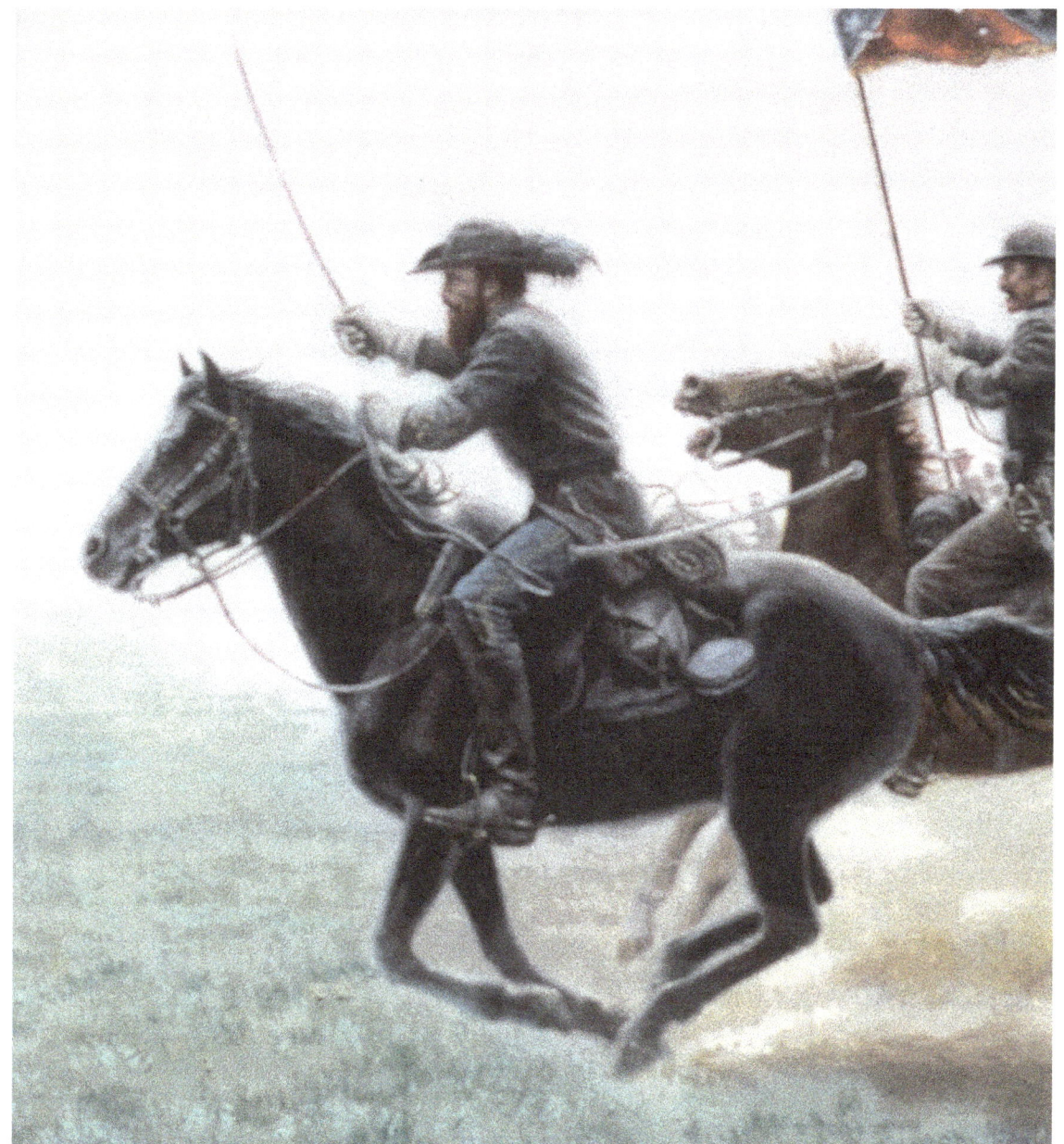

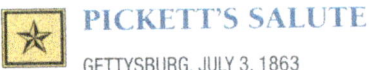

PICKETT'S SALUTE

GETTYSBURG, JULY 3, 1863

1993, mixed media, 10¼ x 9½

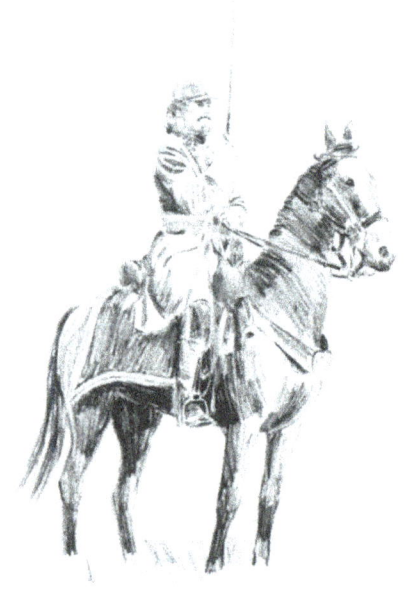

GEORGE E. PICKETT WAS graduated from West Point at the bottom of the Class of 1846 (his classmates included George B. McClellan and Thomas J. Jackson). He was a protégé of Longstreet's, but Pickett had been out of action for more than a year. He had been wounded at Gaines's Mill during the Peninsula campaign and had been promoted to major general and made a division commander in the interim. On July 3, he was anxious to prove himself as the commander of the pending charge against the Union center.

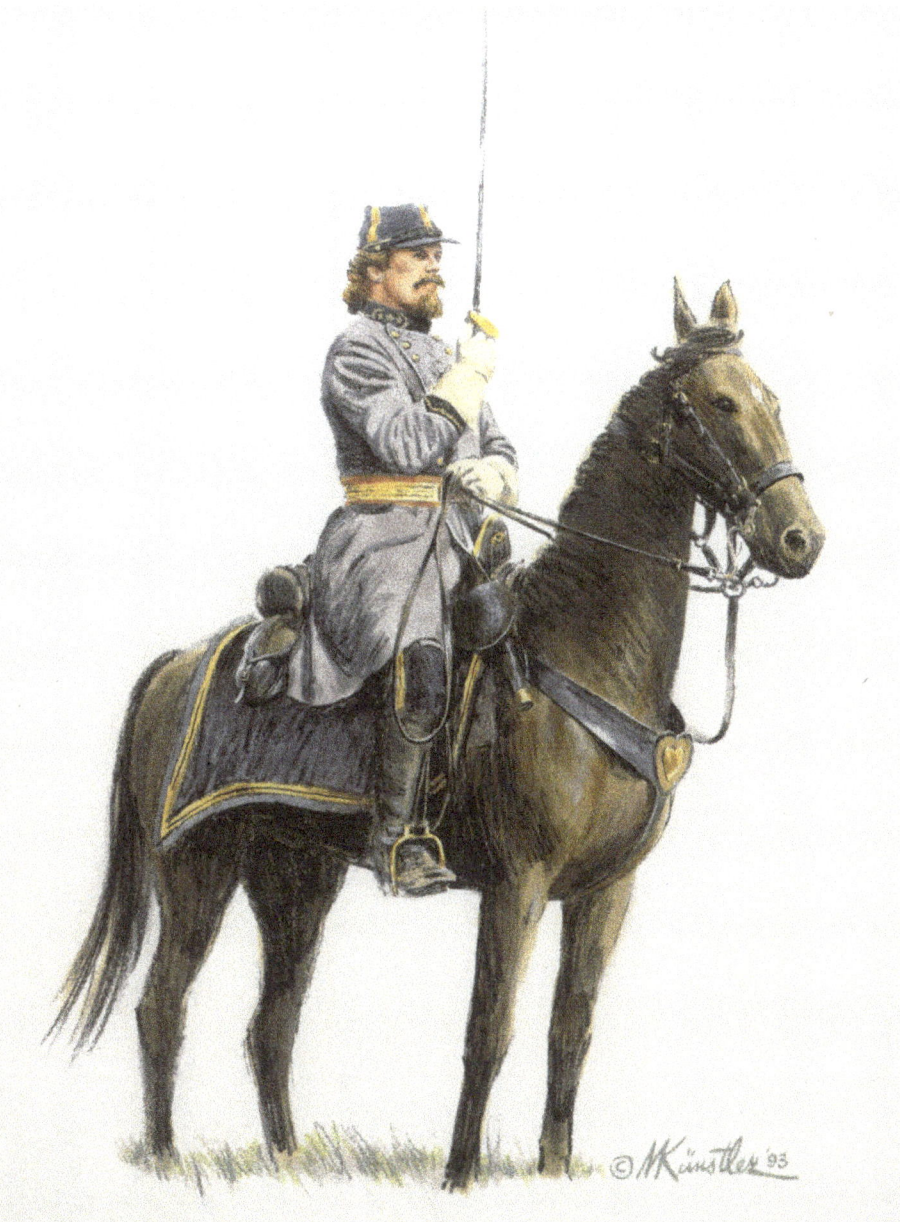

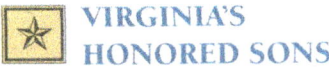

VIRGINIA'S HONORED SONS

GENERAL PICKETT
GETTYSBURG, JULY 3, 1863
1993, mixed media, 11½ x 19

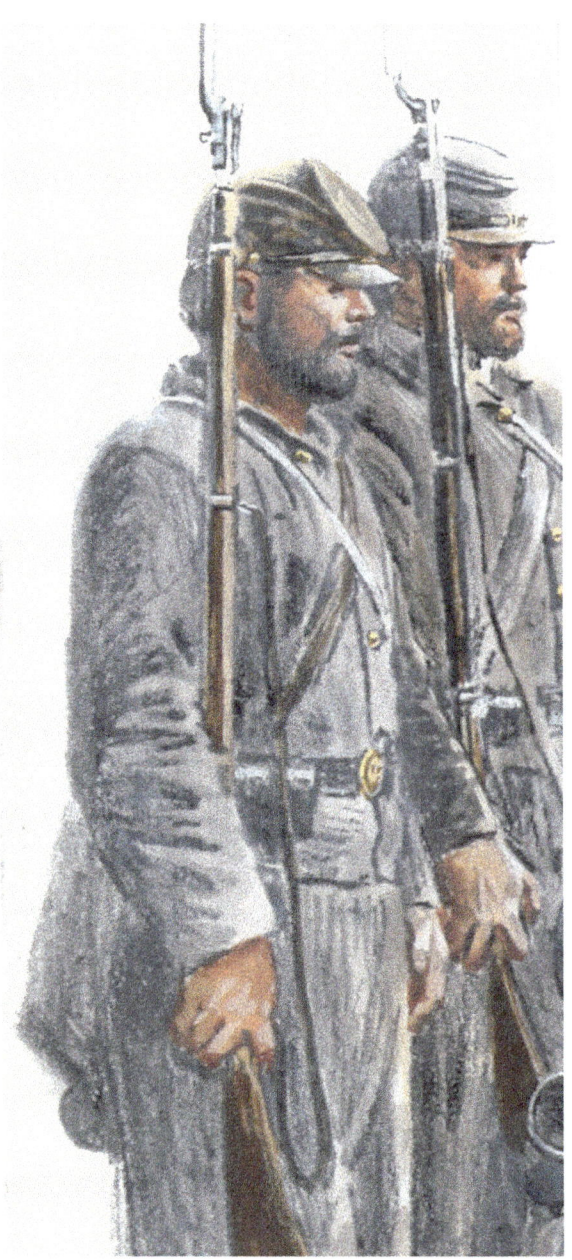

THE CONFEDERATE CANNONADE designed to soften up the Federals began a little after 1:00 p.m. and continued for more than an hour. Return fire slackened when the Union artillery chief decided to conserve ammunition; Porter, Longstreet's artillery commander, was running low too. He sent word to Pickett to begin the attack.

"Up men, and to your posts," George E. Pickett called out to his troops as they prepared to step off into immortality. "Don't forget today that you are from Old Virginia!" Pickett's Charge began around 2:30 p.m.

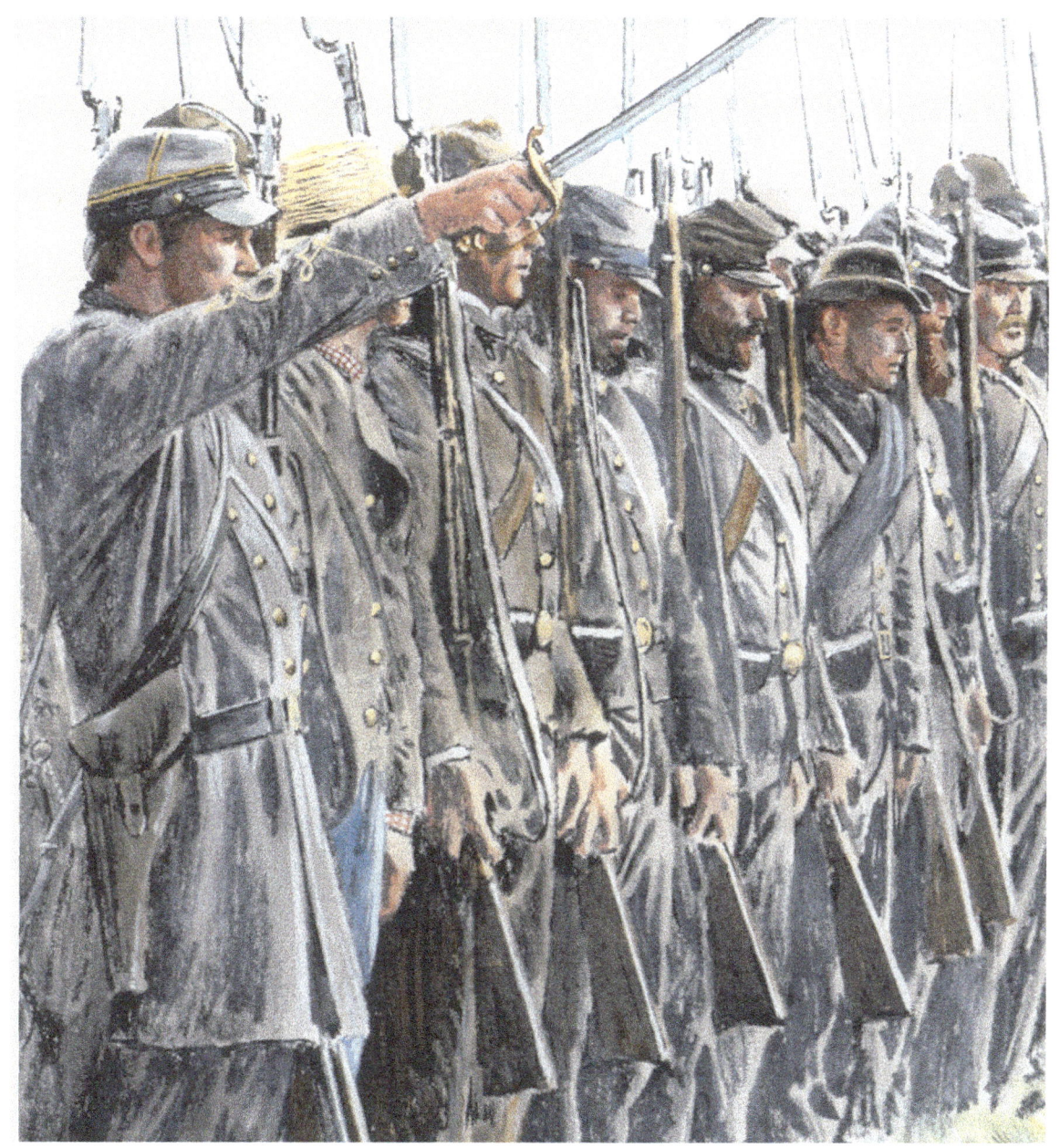

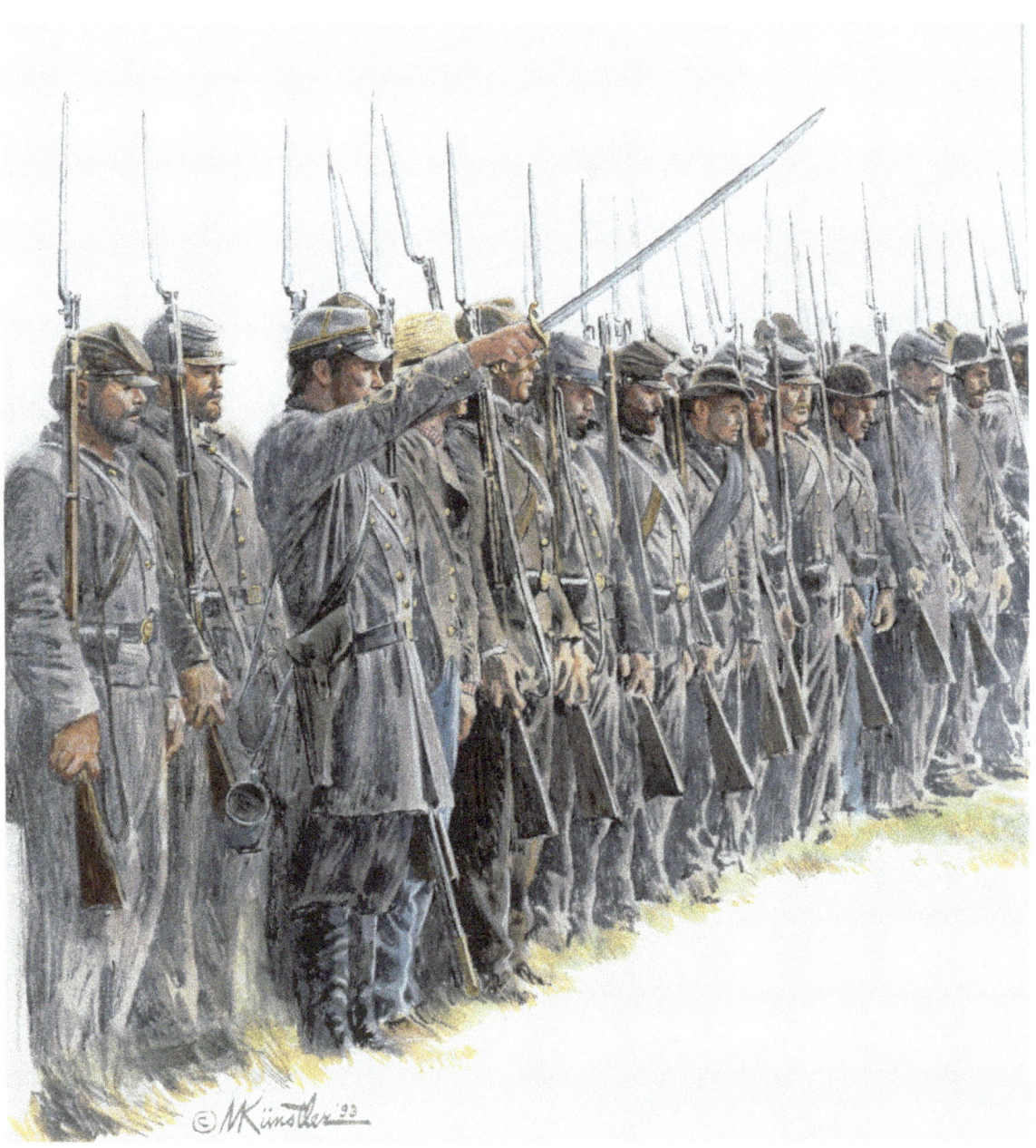

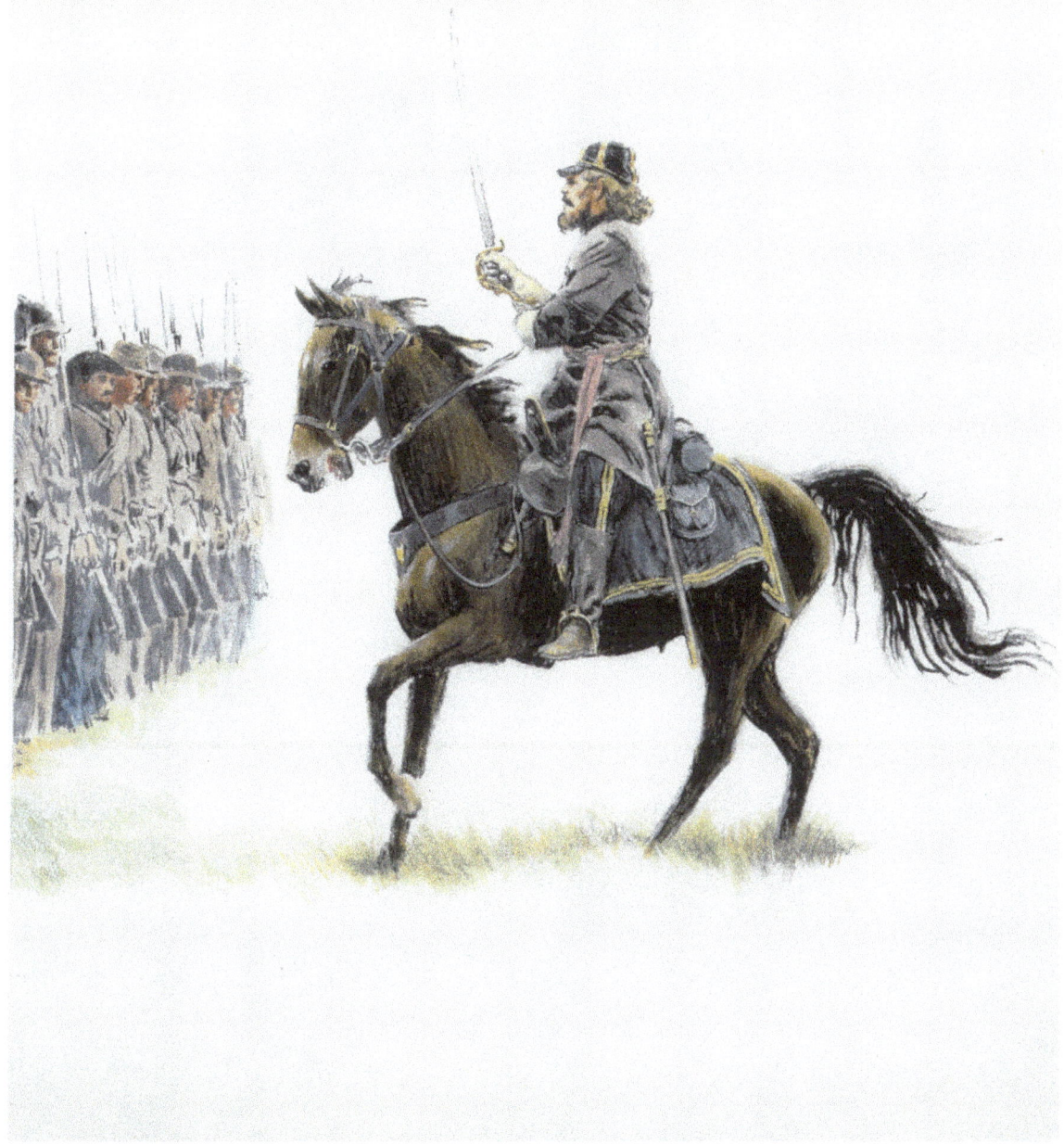

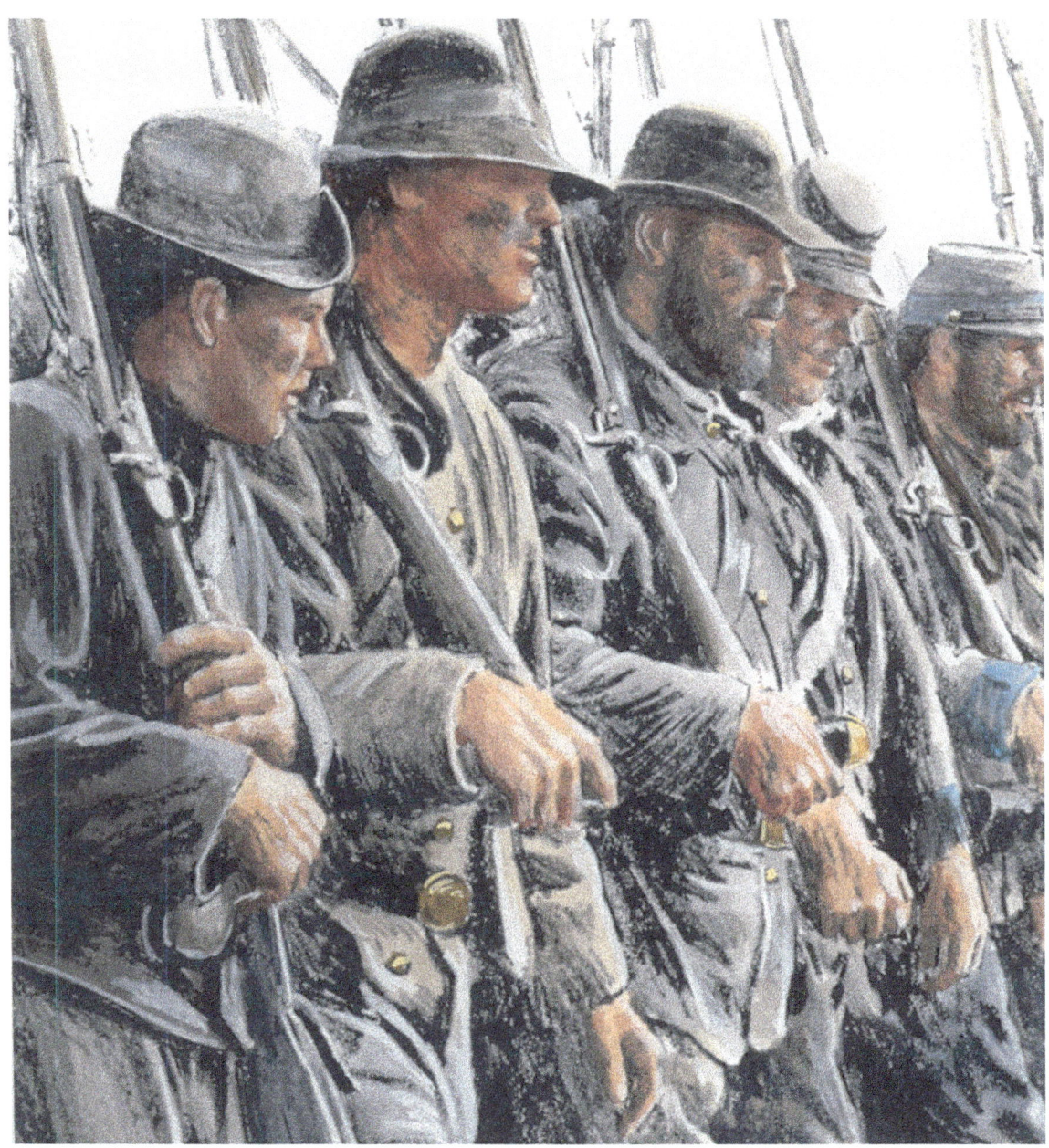

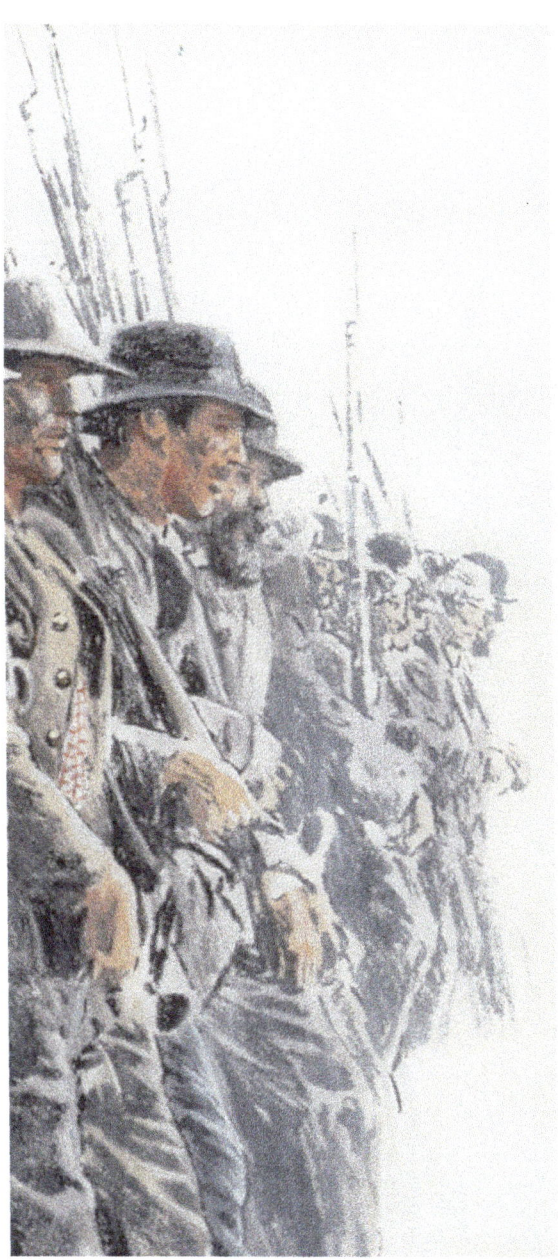

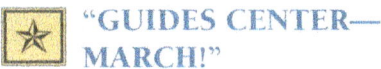 ## "GUIDES CENTER— MARCH!"

GENERAL GARNETT, PICKETT'S CHARGE

1993, mixed media, 13¾ x 18¾

ALTHOUGH ORDERS HAD BEEN issued that line officers should advance on foot with their commands, Richard Garnett rode at the head of his brigade. He explained that a horse had kicked him, and he could not walk. Others noted that Garnett was wearing a new uniform and inferred that he chose this highly visible gesture of leading his men on horseback in an effort to atone for the charge of dereliction of duty brought against him in 1862 by Stonewall Jackson, during Garnett's command of the Stonewall Brigade at the battle of Kernstown.

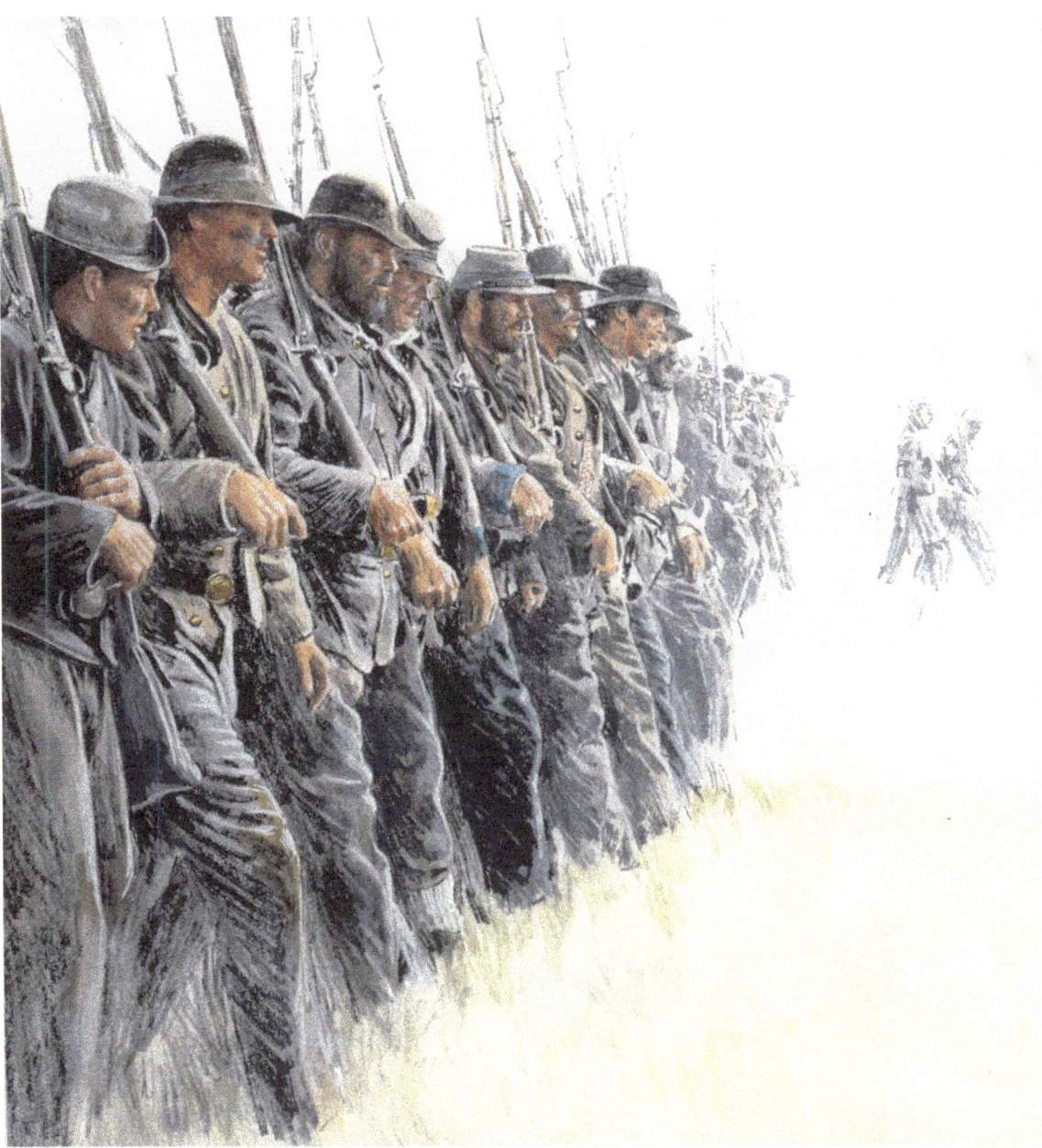

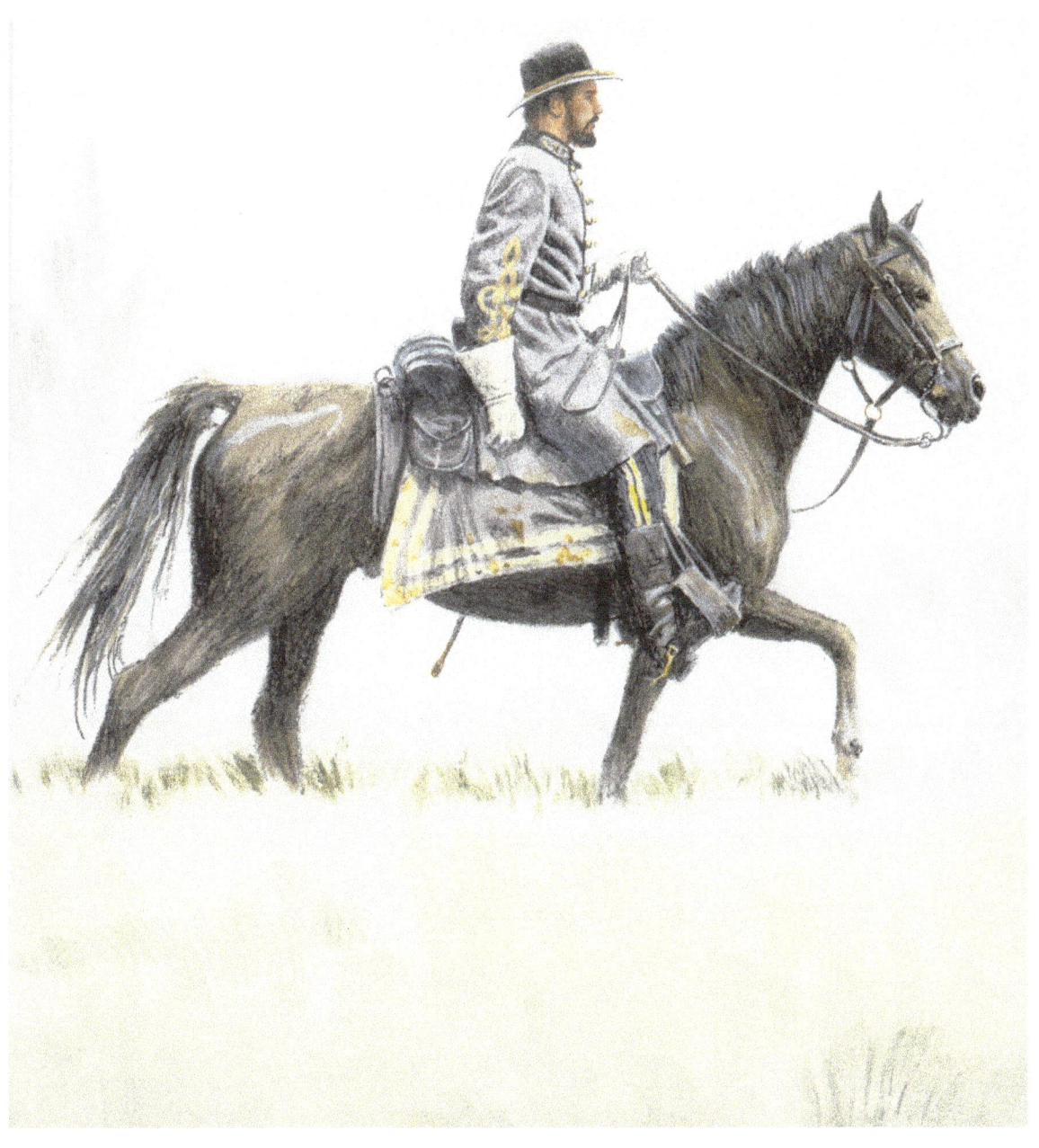

"STEADY, BOYS, STEADY!"

GENERAL ARMISTEAD, PICKETT'S CHARGE

JULY 3, 1863

1993, gouache, 14 x 37½

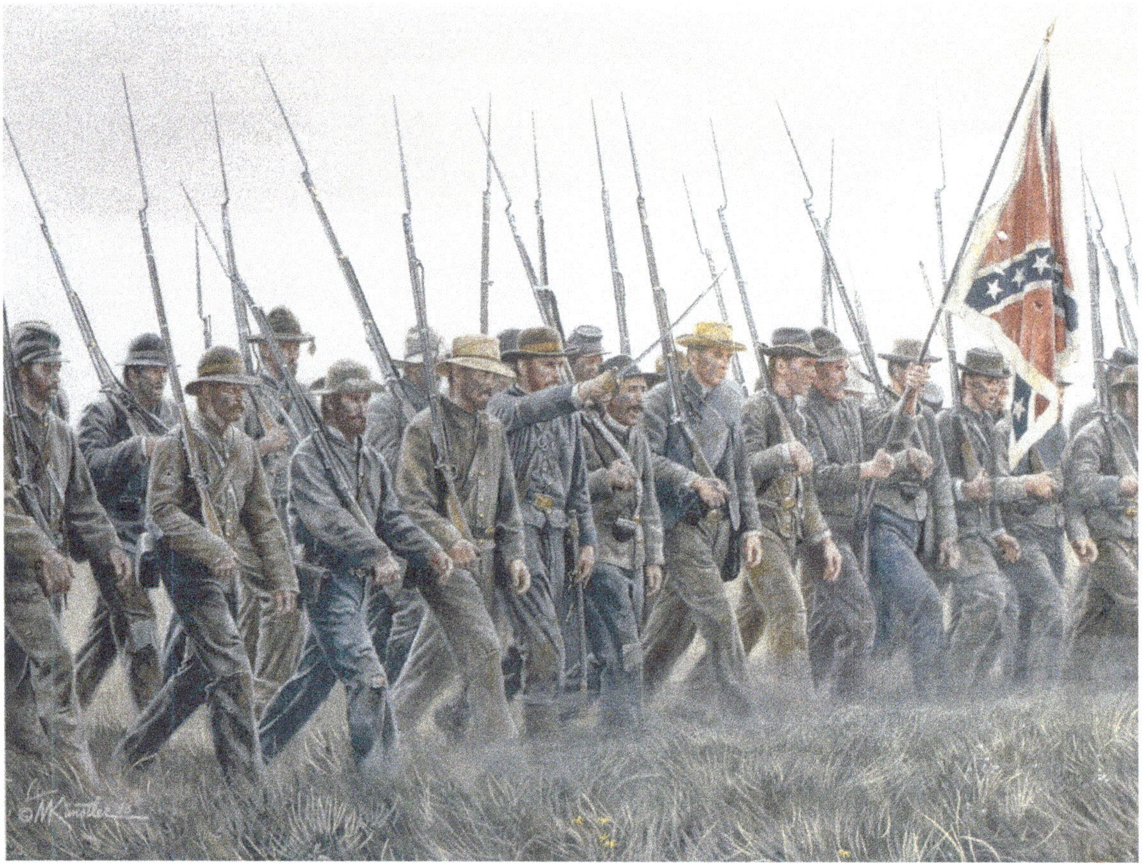

ALL OF PICKETT'S BRIGADES deployed in a single line, two ranks deep. Garnett's was on the left, James L. Kemper's was on the right, and Lewis A. Armistead's followed roughly eighty yards behind them. Of these three brigade commanders, only Armistead led his men on foot. When the order to

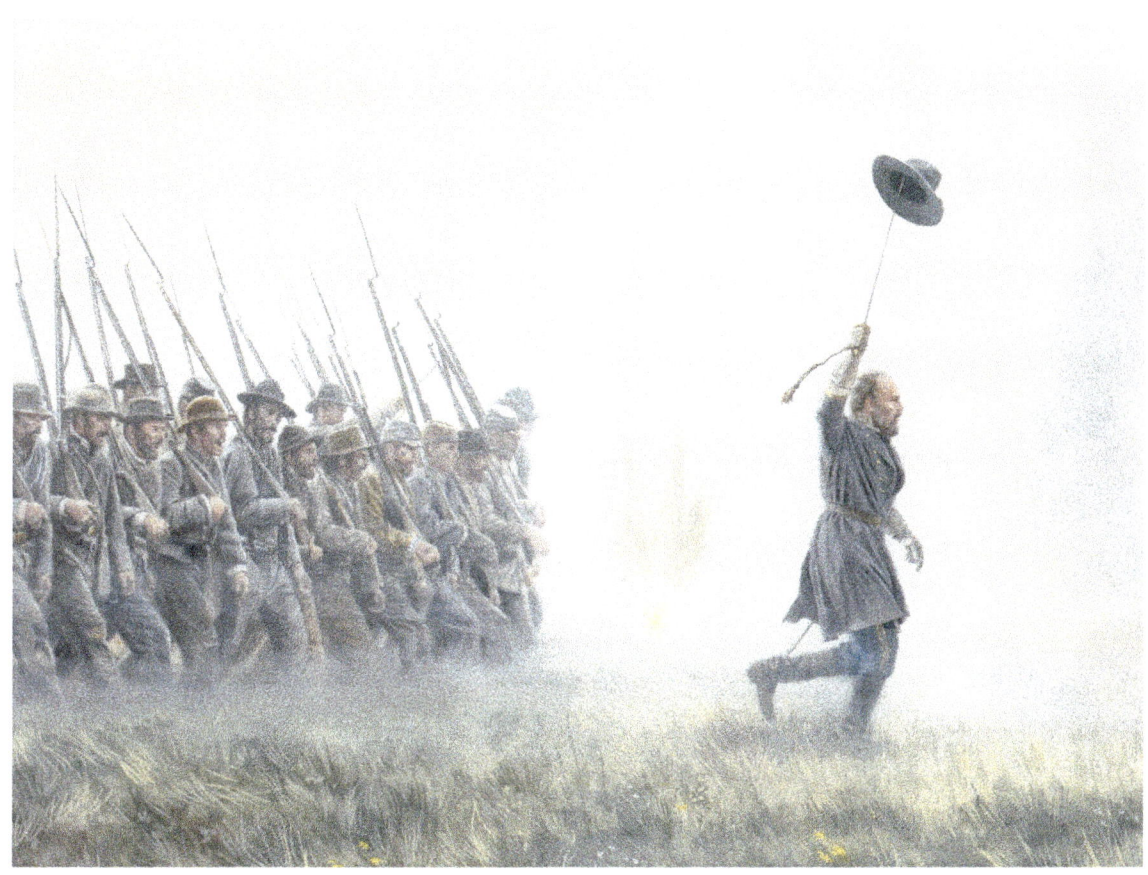

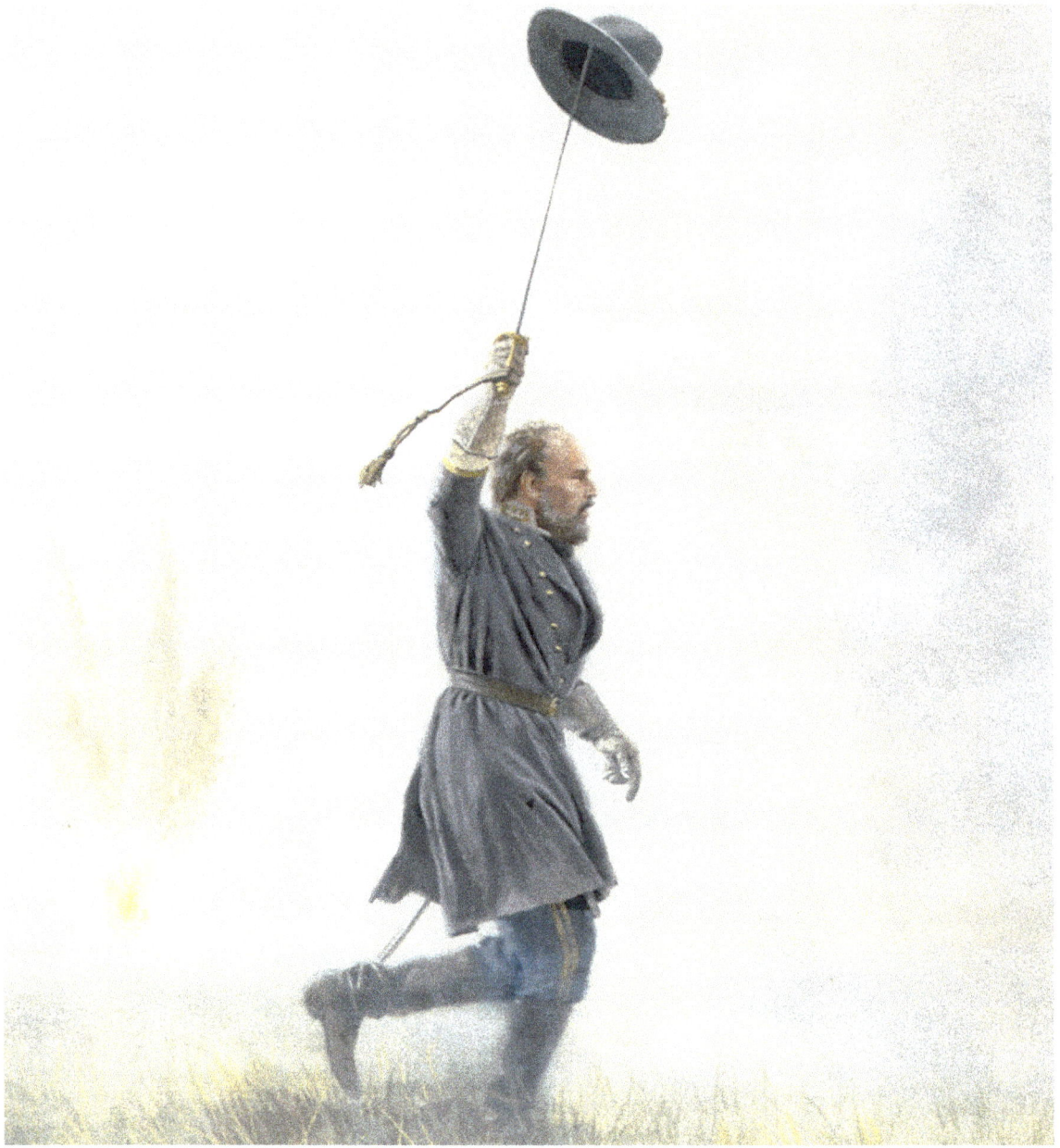

advance was given, Armistead drew his sword and called out, "Men, remember what you are fighting for! Your homes, your firesides, and your sweethearts! Follow me!"

Armistead's family had no little prominence. His father and five brothers served during the War of 1812; one brother was the commander of Fort McHenry during the British attack on Baltimore. The family also was related to four U.S. presidents: James Monroe, William Henry Harrison, John Tyler, and Benjamin Harrison.

Armistead had served in the old army twenty years before the war. He had been dismissed from West Point, either because of poor grades or because of an altercation with classmate Jubal Early. He joined the army in 1839 and saw action in the Seminole wars and the Mexican War before he was posted to the frontier. Among his closest friends from those days was Winfield Scott Hancock—currently the commander of the Union Second Corps and on the opposite side of the field across which Armistead now led his men.

Pickett's men had to advance at an angle across the field in order to align with Pettigrew's division. The angled march, however, made them prime targets for Union artillery, and Federal gunners wasted no time in showering the Confederates with shell and canister. When Virginians in the first ranks fell, the rear ranks continued on and closed the gaps.

With a copse of trees behind the Union line as their aiming point, Pickett's division was on course to immortality. Kemper rode back to Armistead to coordinate their next movements and confirm Armistead's support. After Kemper returned to his brigade, Armistead placed his hat on his sword point so his men would have no problem distinguishing him on the field in front of them.

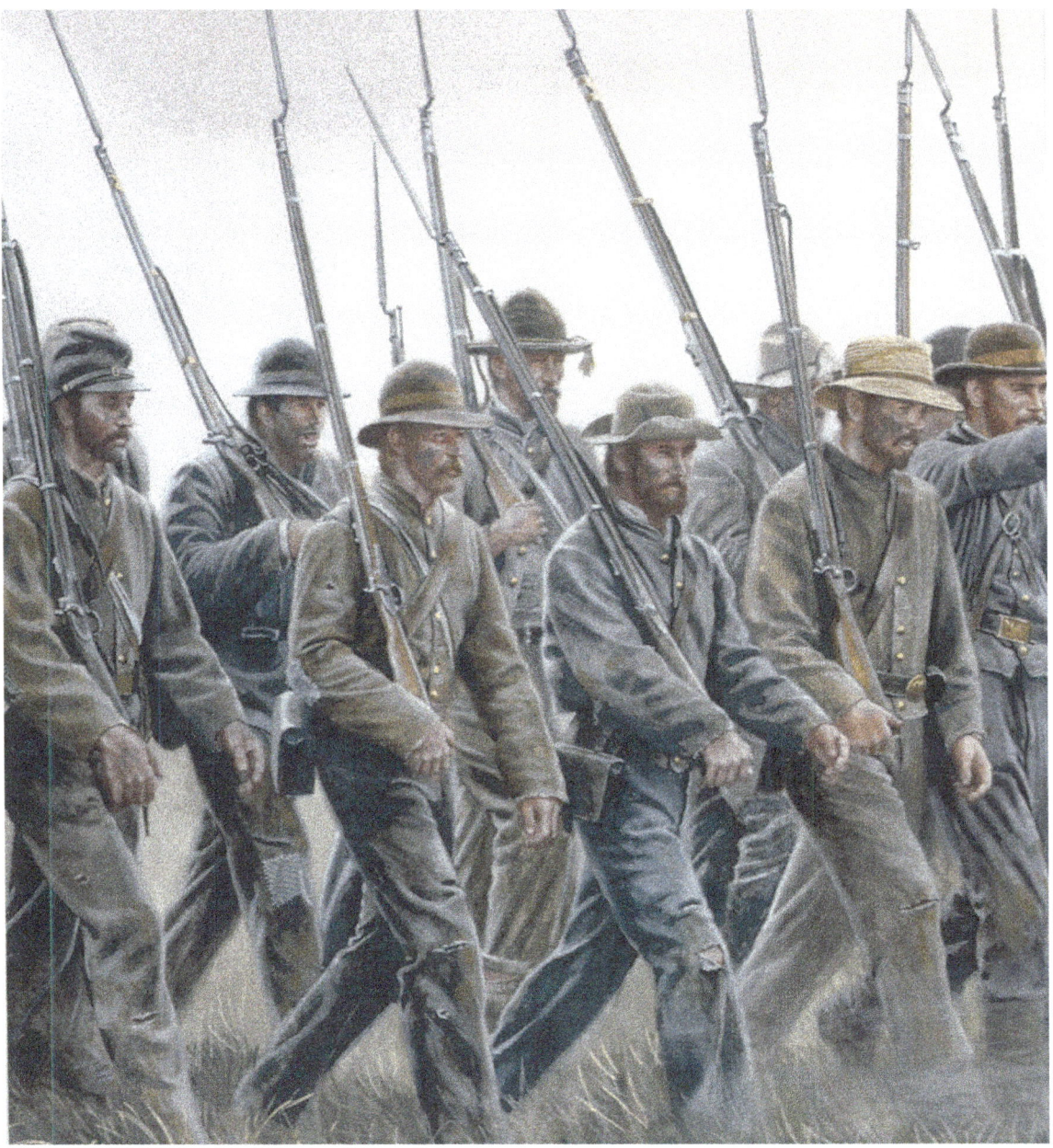

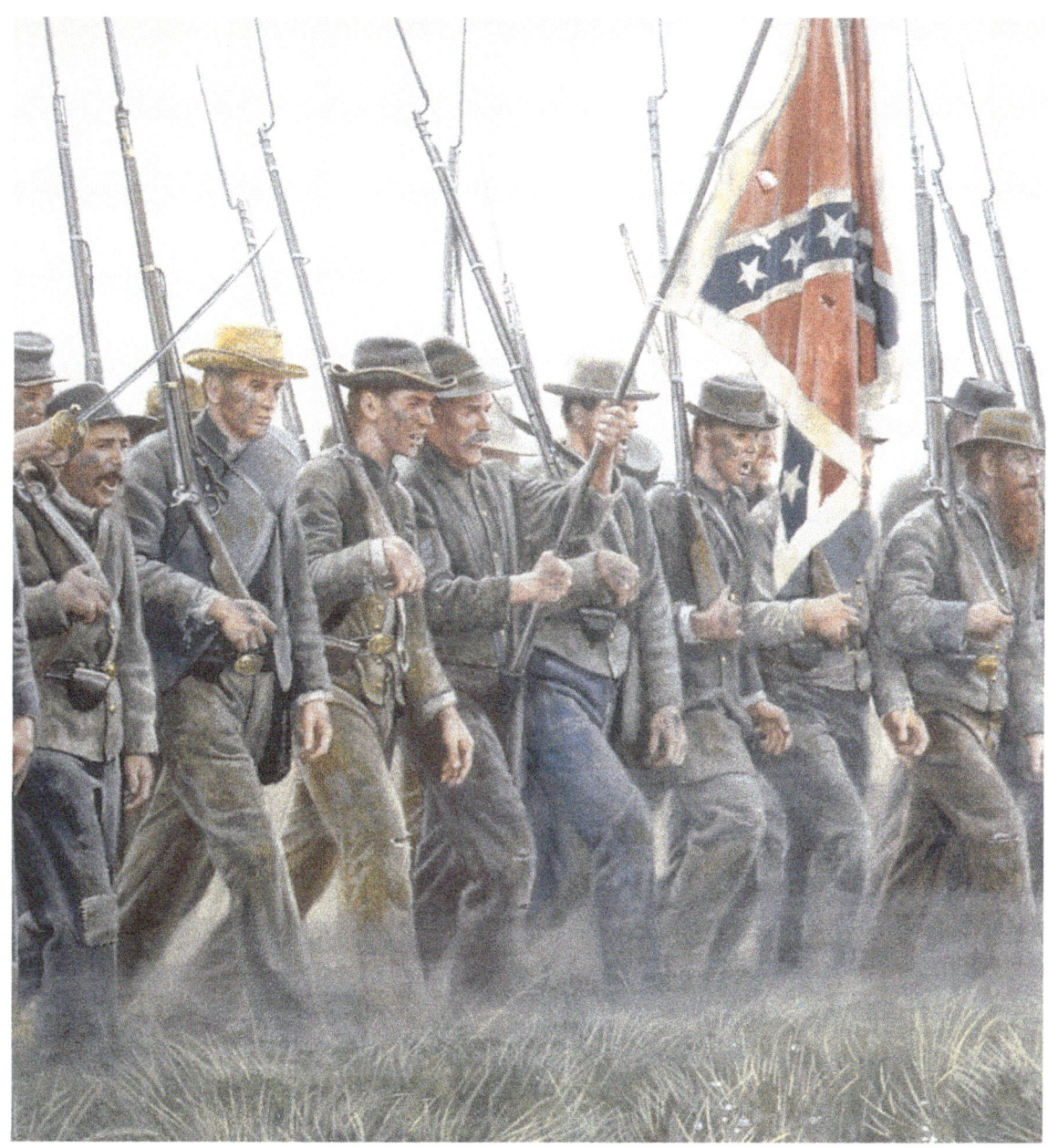

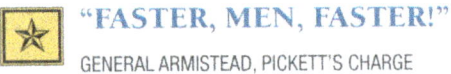

"FASTER, MEN, FASTER!"

GENERAL ARMISTEAD, PICKETT'S CHARGE

1993, mixed media, 12¼ x 19½

J. Johnston Pettigrew's and Isaac R. Trimble's six brigades set off from Seminary Ridge at the same time that Pickett's three brigades began their march. At first, a quarter-mile gap separated the two formations, but the brigades slowly merged into a single advancing line. In all, forty-two regiments stepped off toward Cemetery Ridge, each with its colors flying and poised at regular intervals among the rows of advancing soldiers.

Confederate soldiers had almost no reputation regarding martial displays such as parades. After the war, one

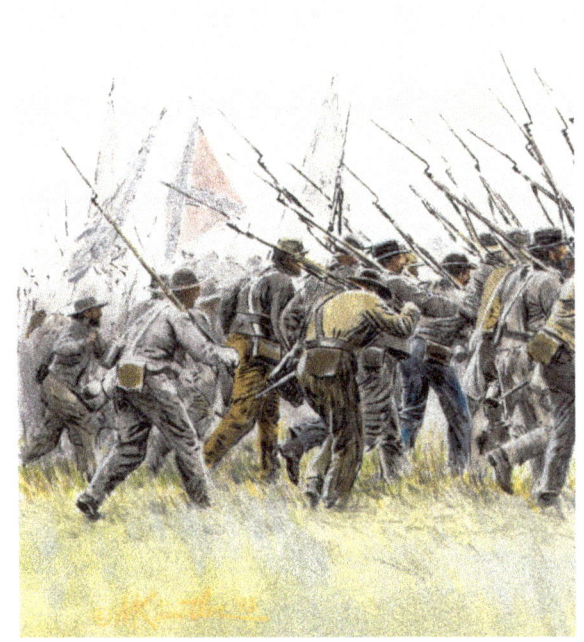

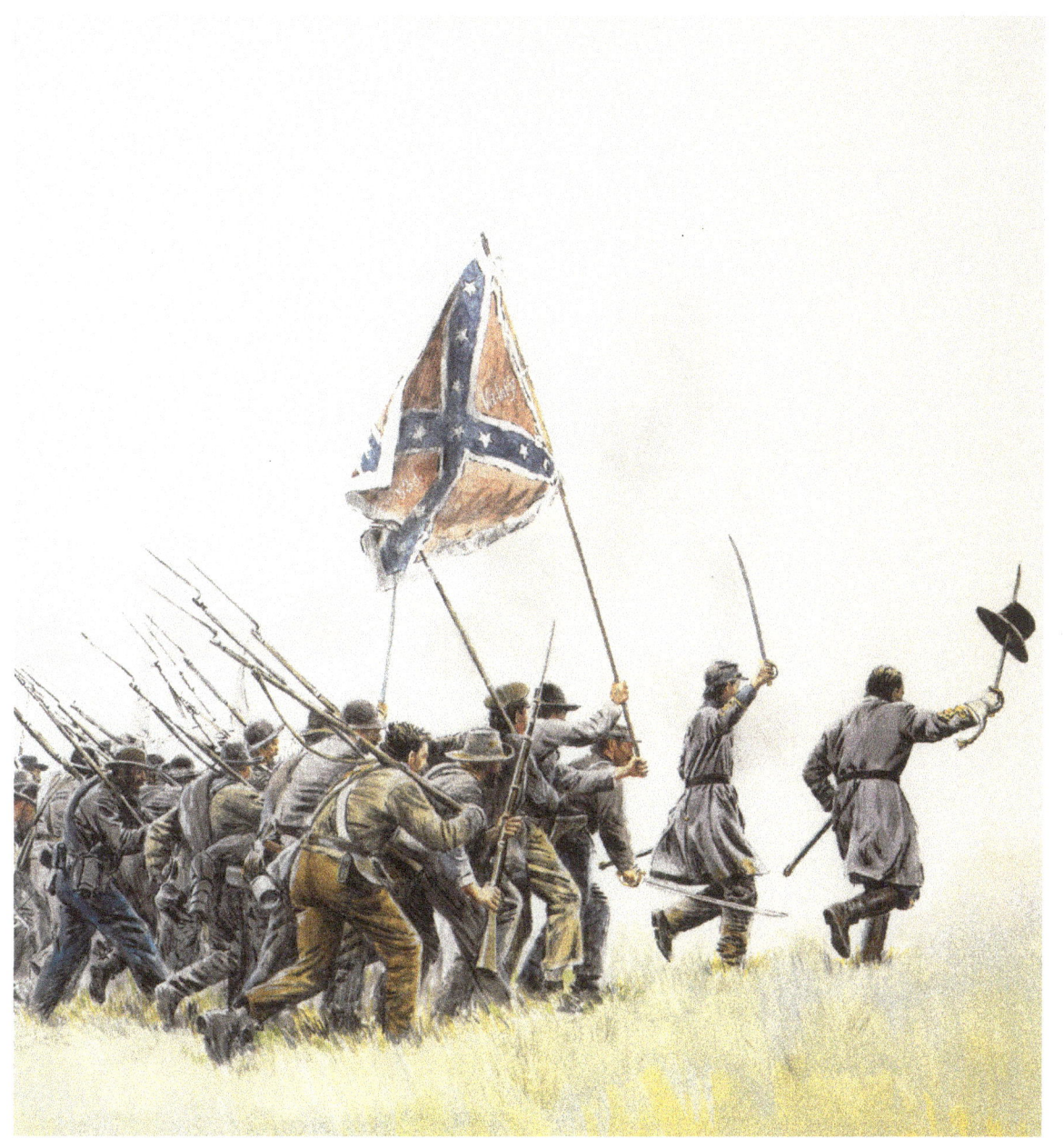

Southern commander commented on the discipline of individual Southern soldiers: "Of shoulder-to-shoulder courage, spirit of drill and discipline, he knew nothing and cared less. Hence, on the battlefield, he was more of a free-lance than a machine. Whoever saw a Confederate line advancing that was not crooked as a ram's horn? Each ragged rebel yelling on his own hook and aligning on himself."

The line advancing toward Cemetery Ridge, however, was an exception. These men had been ordered to maintain a uniform step and forbidden to fire their rifles or shout the Rebel Yell, and so they concentrated on maintain-

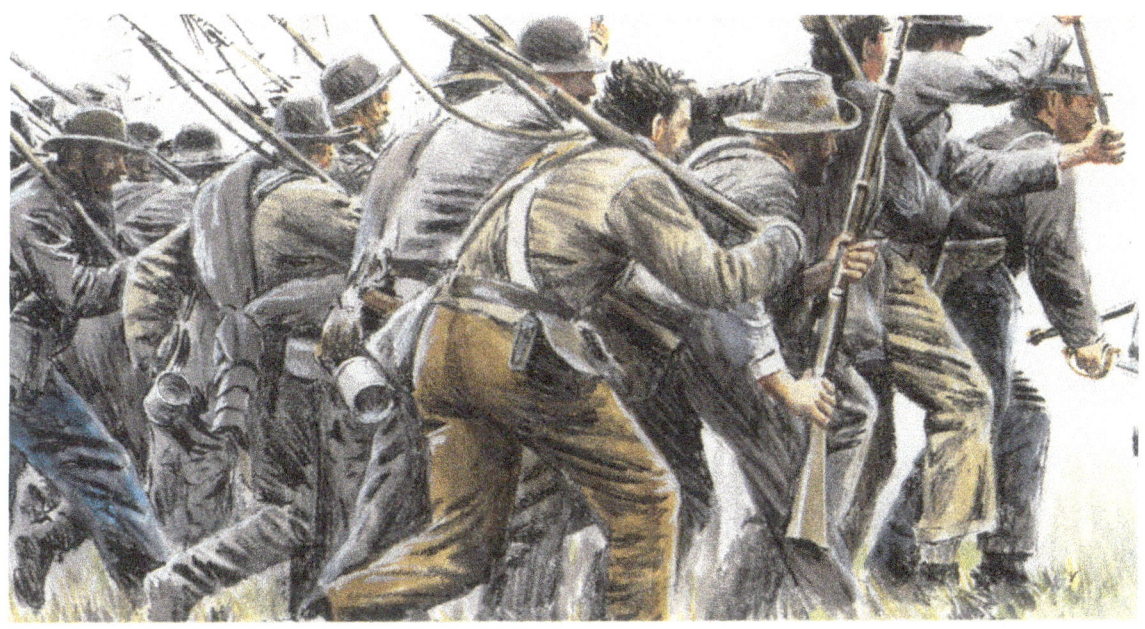

ing their alignment, perhaps to awe the enemy and even unnerve him. One of the Union officers crouched in the field in front of the oncoming horde recalled a "glittering forest of bayonets," the troops "in superb alignment," the "murmur and jingle" of trousers and equipment, the "rustle of thousands of feet amid the stubble" that stirred up dust and chaff "like the dash of spray at the prow of a vessel."

The Confederates advanced steadily, about one hundred yards a minute. From behind, Longstreet, perched on a fence, marveled at the sight of near parade-ground perfection. Perhaps, he wondered, they might achieve what he doubted they could accomplish.

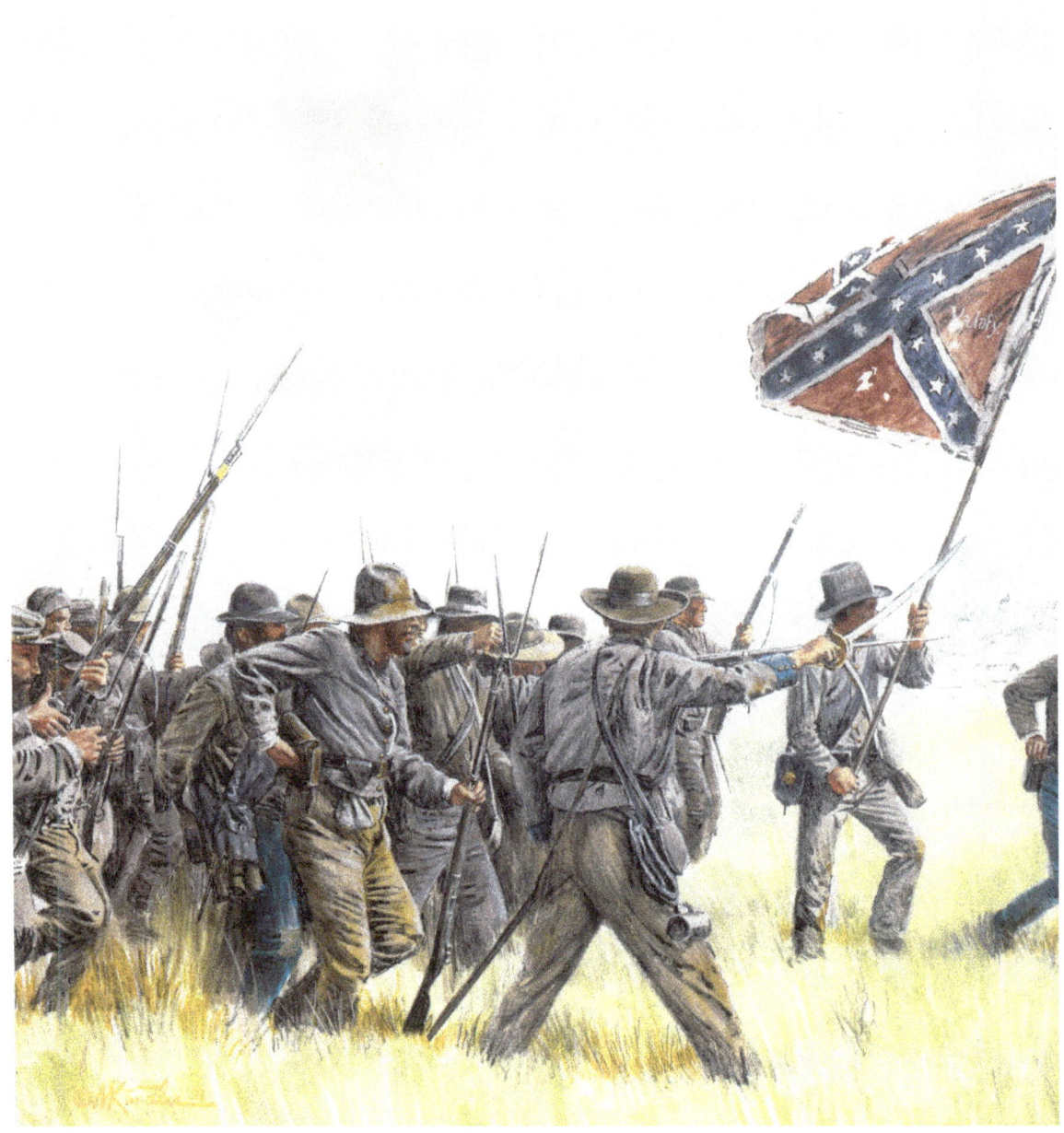

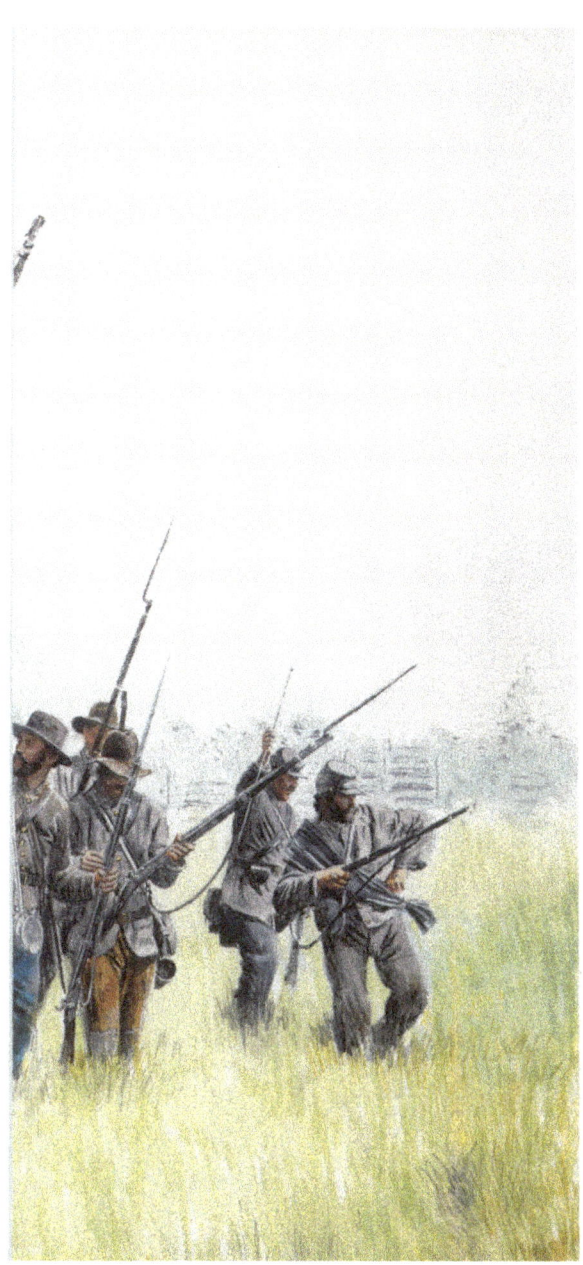

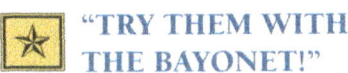 ## "TRY THEM WITH THE BAYONET!"

PICKETT'S CHARGE, JULY 3, 1863

1993, mixed media, 12 x 19½

WHEN PICKETT'S AND PETTIGREW'S divisions came together, they had covered a little more than half the distance to the Union line. They paused in a slight depression in the field, partially protected from enemy fire, and redressed their lines. Brigade commanders passed the word down the line to align with one another, thus completing the convergence of the battle line about fourteen hundred feet in front of the enemy.

173

THE COPSE OF TREES

GETTYSBURG, JULY 3, 1863

1993, mixed media, 9 x 19

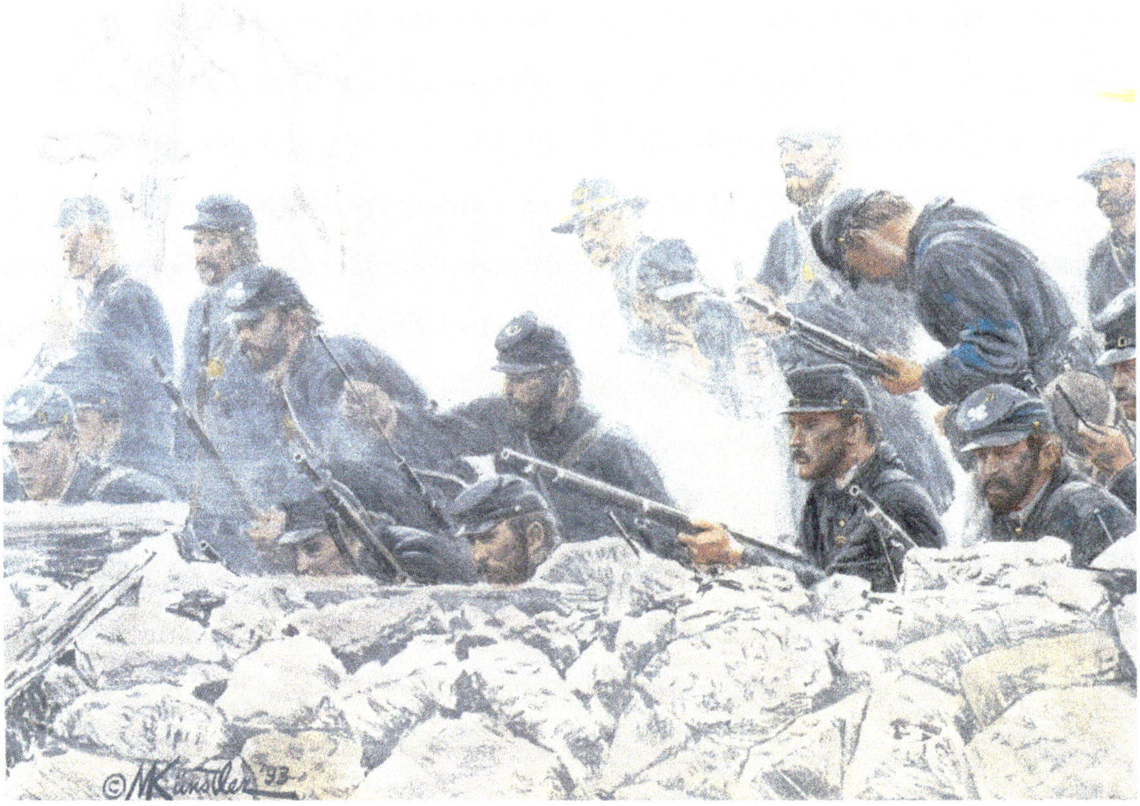

UNION TROOPS ON THE targeted ridge were galled at the Confederates' pause at midfield. "My God, they're dressing the line," some exclaimed, more in outrage than admiration. A few stood up and fired at the enemy a half mile away—until their officers roughly told them to hold their fire until the Confederates were within range.

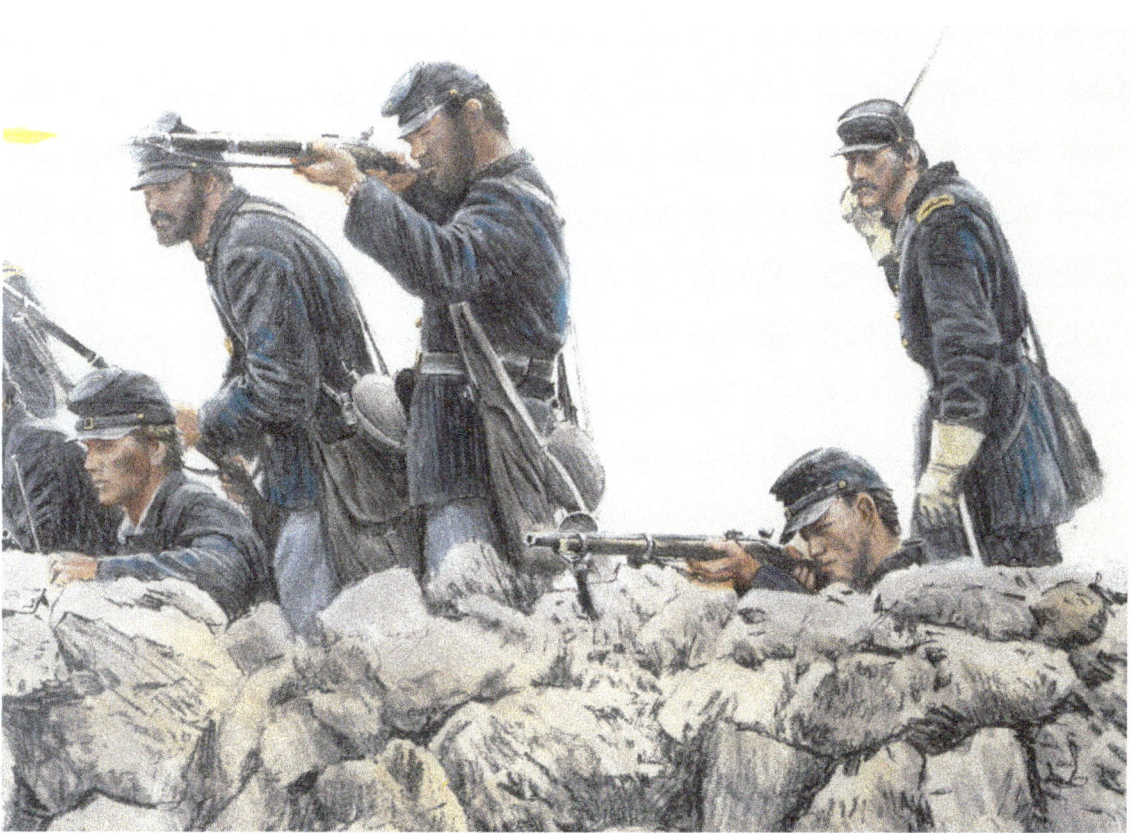

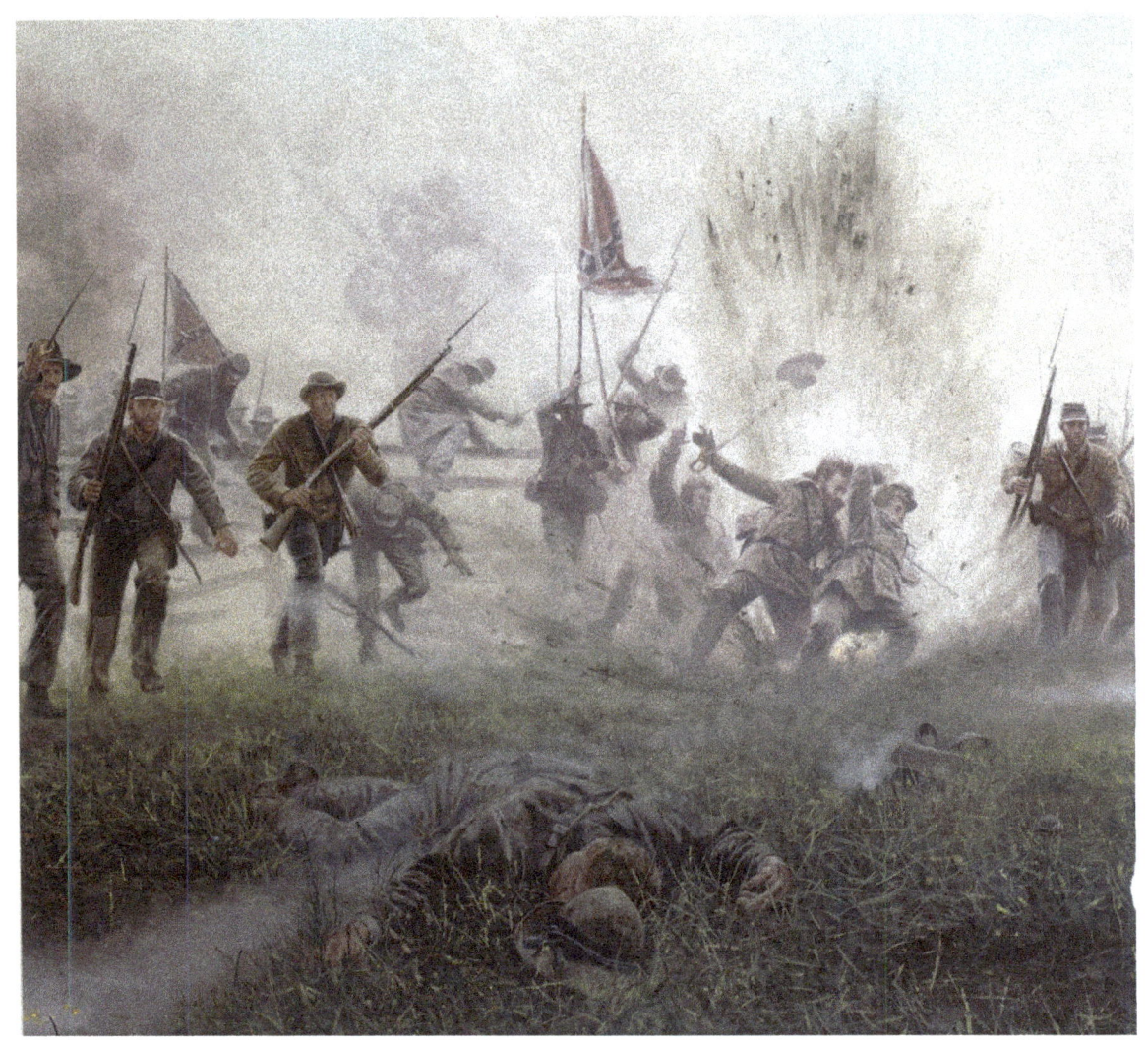

PICKETT'S CHARGE, JULY 3, 1863

2004, oil, 20 x 44

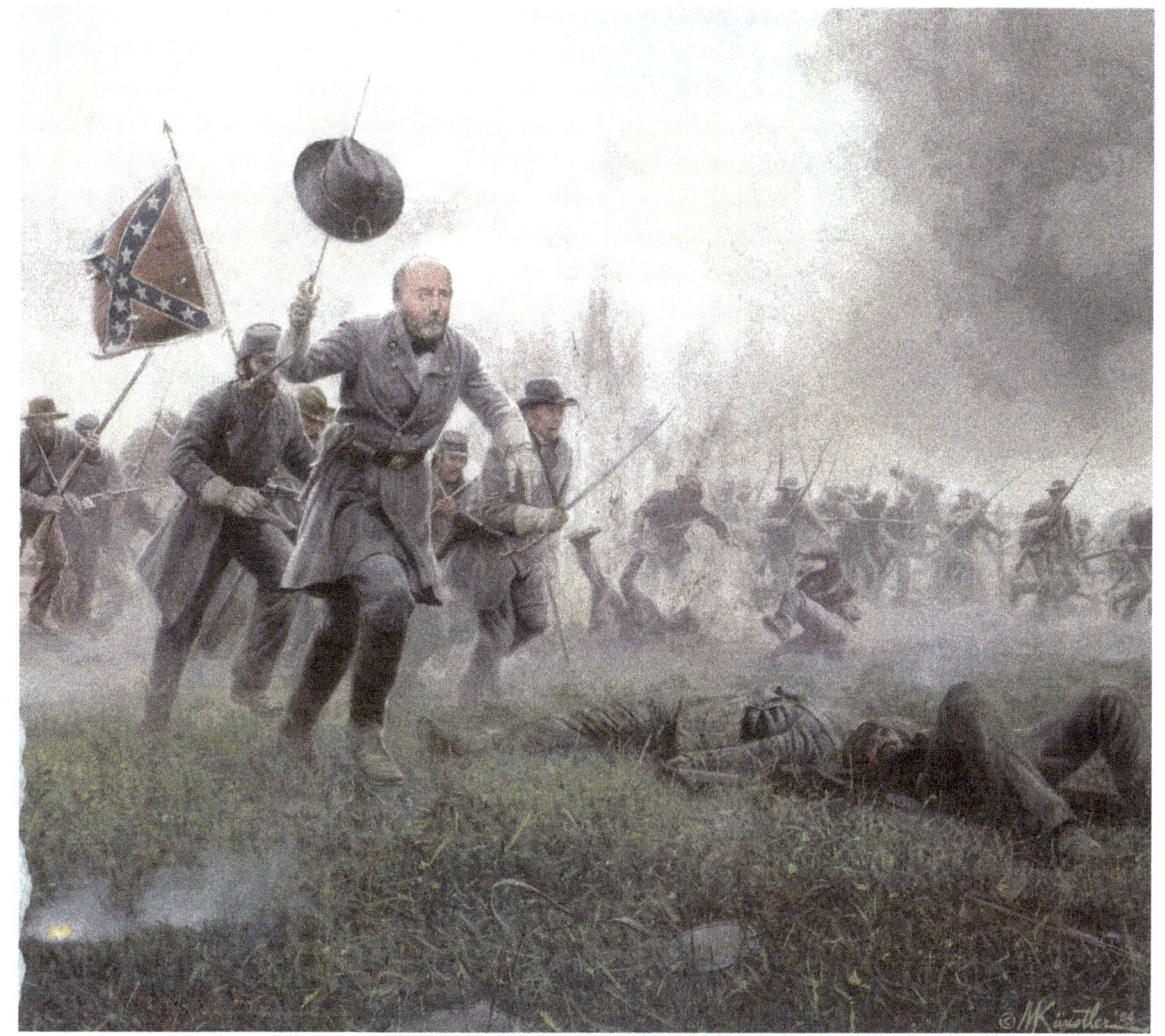

O N THEY CAME WITH flags flying," a Northern officer marveled. "In open sight of friend and foe, over the green valley, they marched in battle's stern array." Stout hearts, however, would not be enough for Lee's soldiers this day.

The Emmitsburg Road posed an almost insuperable obstacle to the Confederate advance. Pettigrew's troops stalled along the northern stretch of road, which was hemmed on both sides with strongly built fences: post and rail on the west side and post and plank on the east. His left flank was also exposed to Union infantry in addition to artillery fire. Thus his men could not take the time to pull down the fences; they could only climb over them.

"The time it took to climb to the top of the fence seemed to me an age of suspense," recalled one of Pettigrew's Tennesseans. "It was not a leaping over; it was rather an insensible tumbling to the ground."

Between the fences, the roadway was about two feet lower than the surrounding ground. So some men tried to use the slightly sunken roadbed for cover. Ahead they saw a rail fence and a stone wall that would further impede their progress.

Many in Pettigrew's division advanced no farther than the Emmitsburg Road. One officer estimated that two-thirds of the front brigades that reached the road did not go past it. Another regimental commander reported that only half of his men reached the road, and only half of those went beyond it. Several of Pettigrew's brigades had been reduced to a line of skirmishers.

Afterward, someone examined a sixteen-foot-by-fourteen-inch board from one of the fences. He counted 836 bullet holes in the lumber.

The roadway filled with corpses and wounded men, so much so that the following formations were fragmented while trying to pass over them. Many more soldiers crouched in the roadway and fired from there.

Slightly farther to the south, Pickett's Virginians did not all have to contend with roadway fences nor such close quarters with enemy infantry.

"TO THE WALL!"

GEN. LEWIS A. ARMISTEAD, PICKETT'S CHARGE, JULY 3, 1863

1993, mixed media, 10⅛ x 19⅛

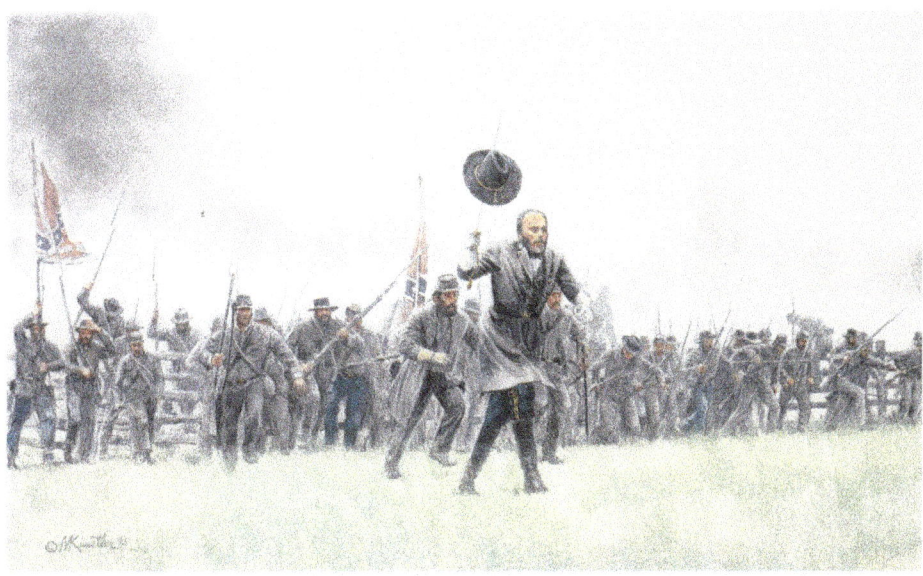

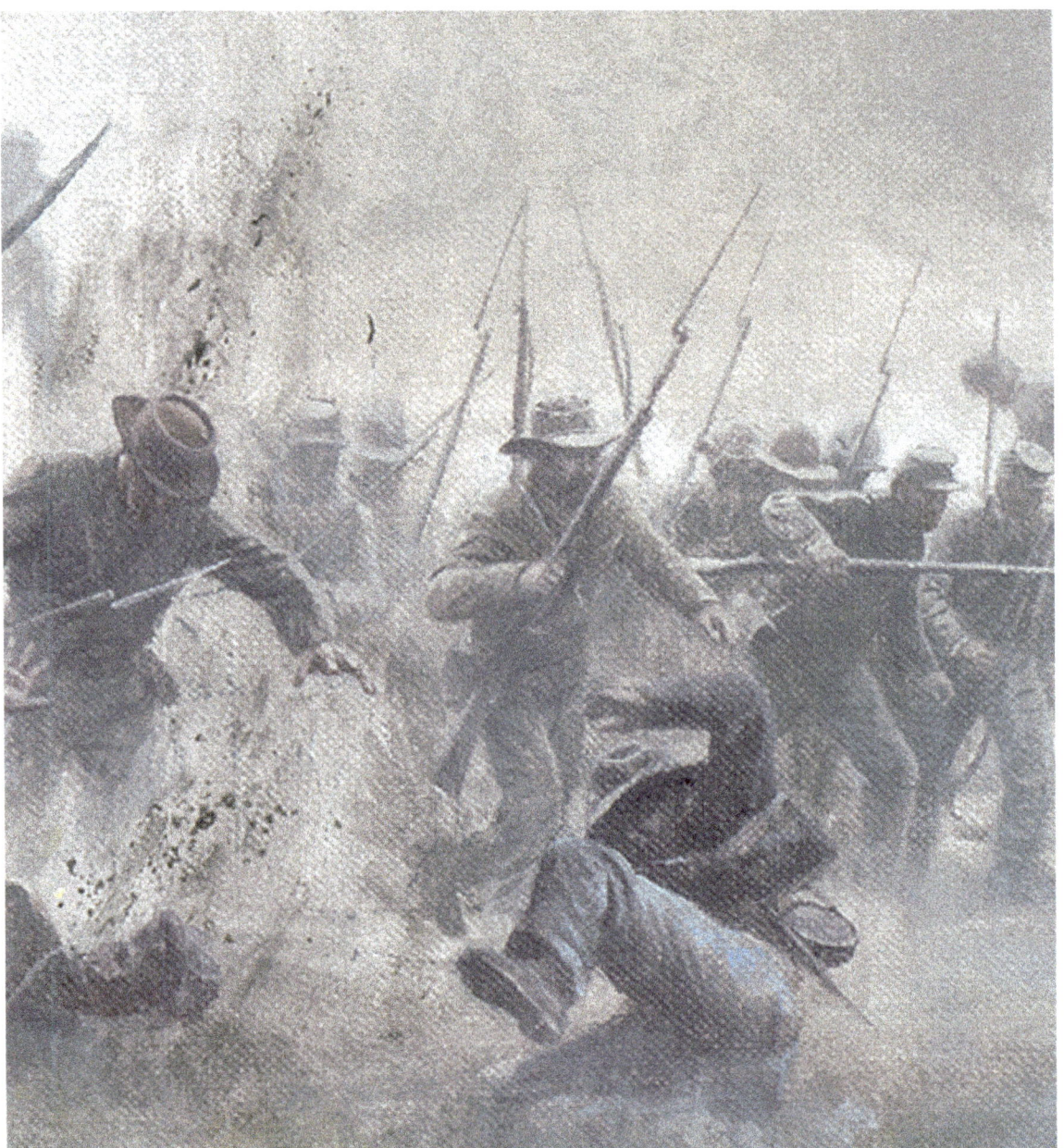

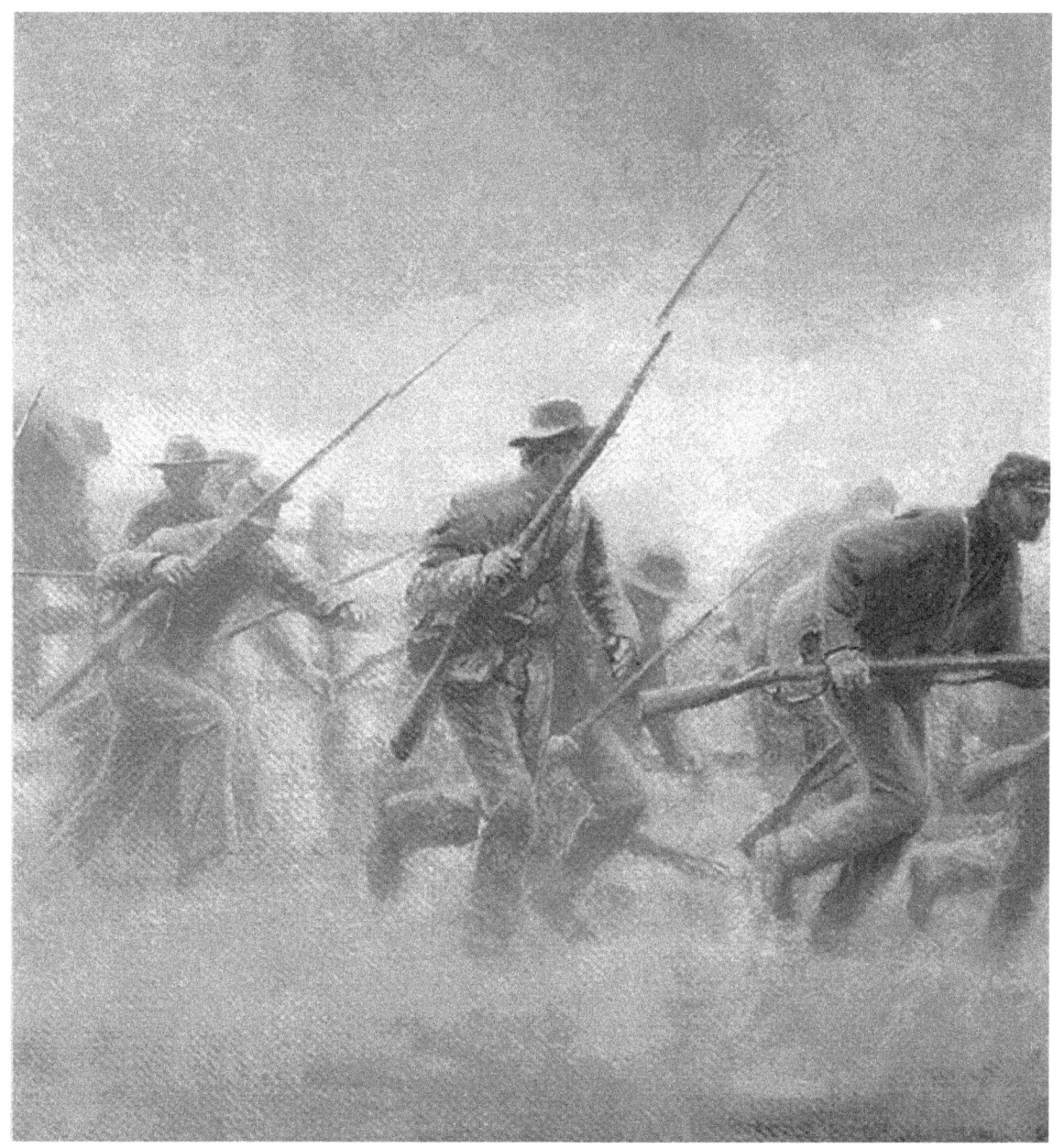

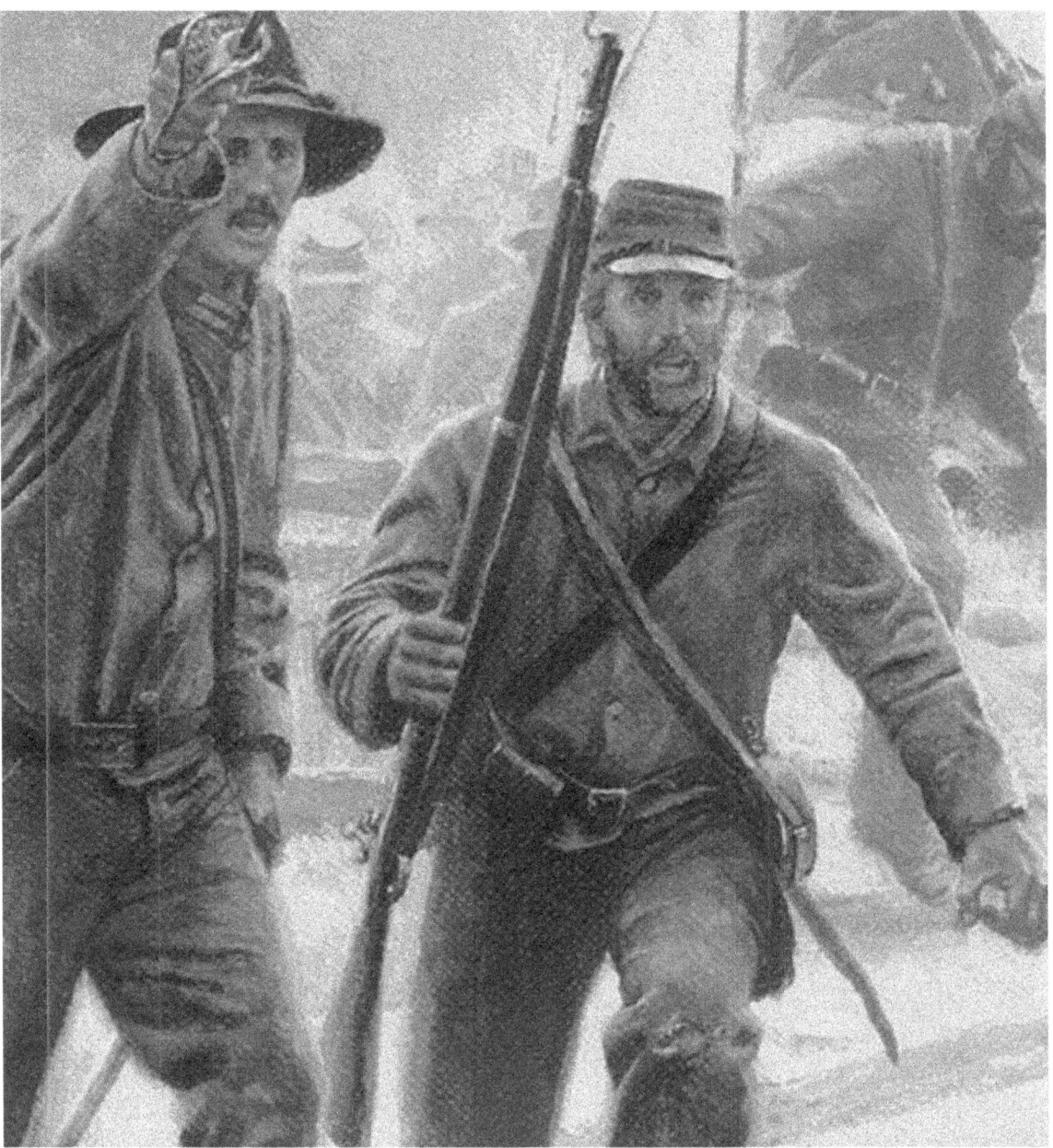

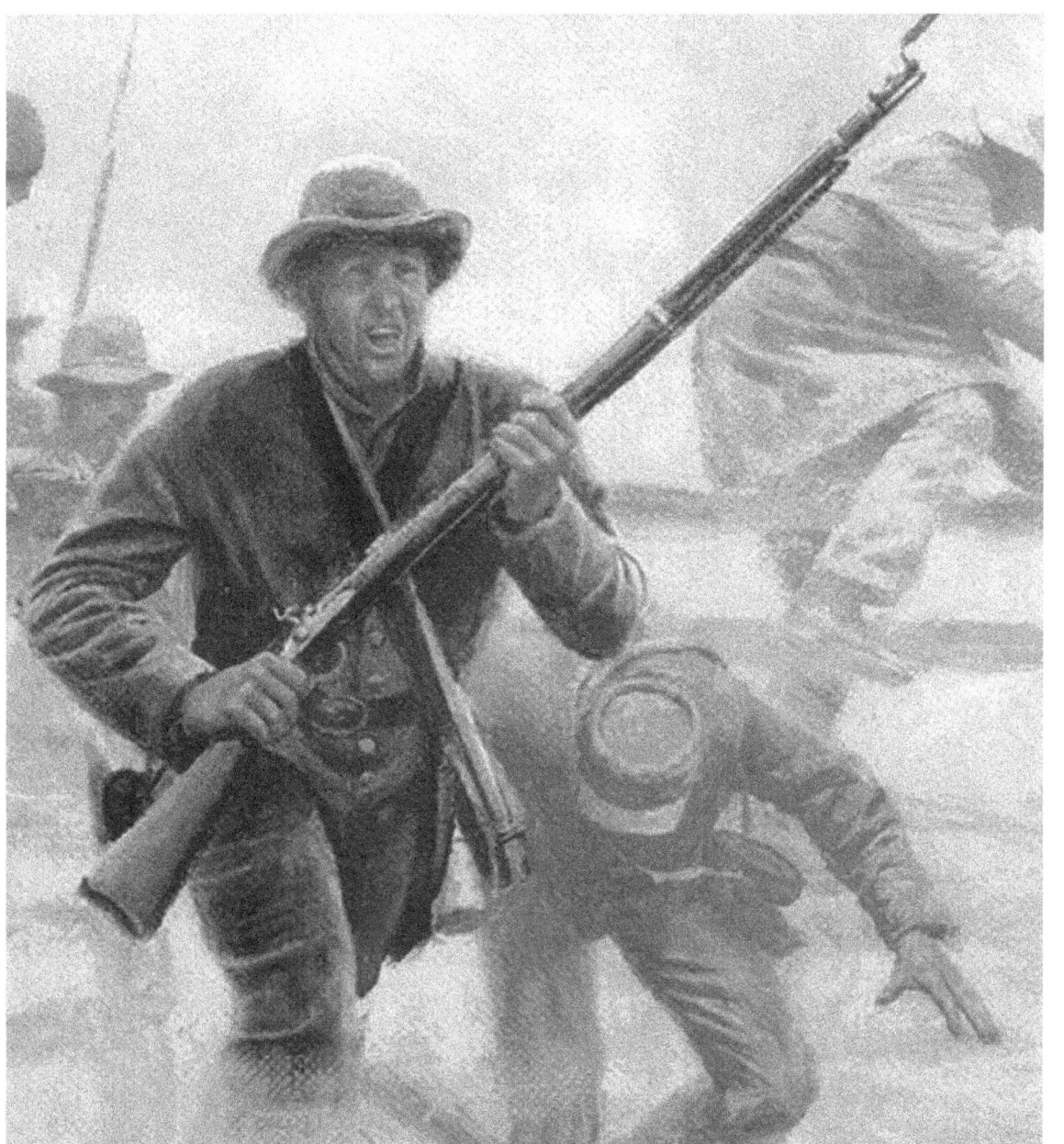

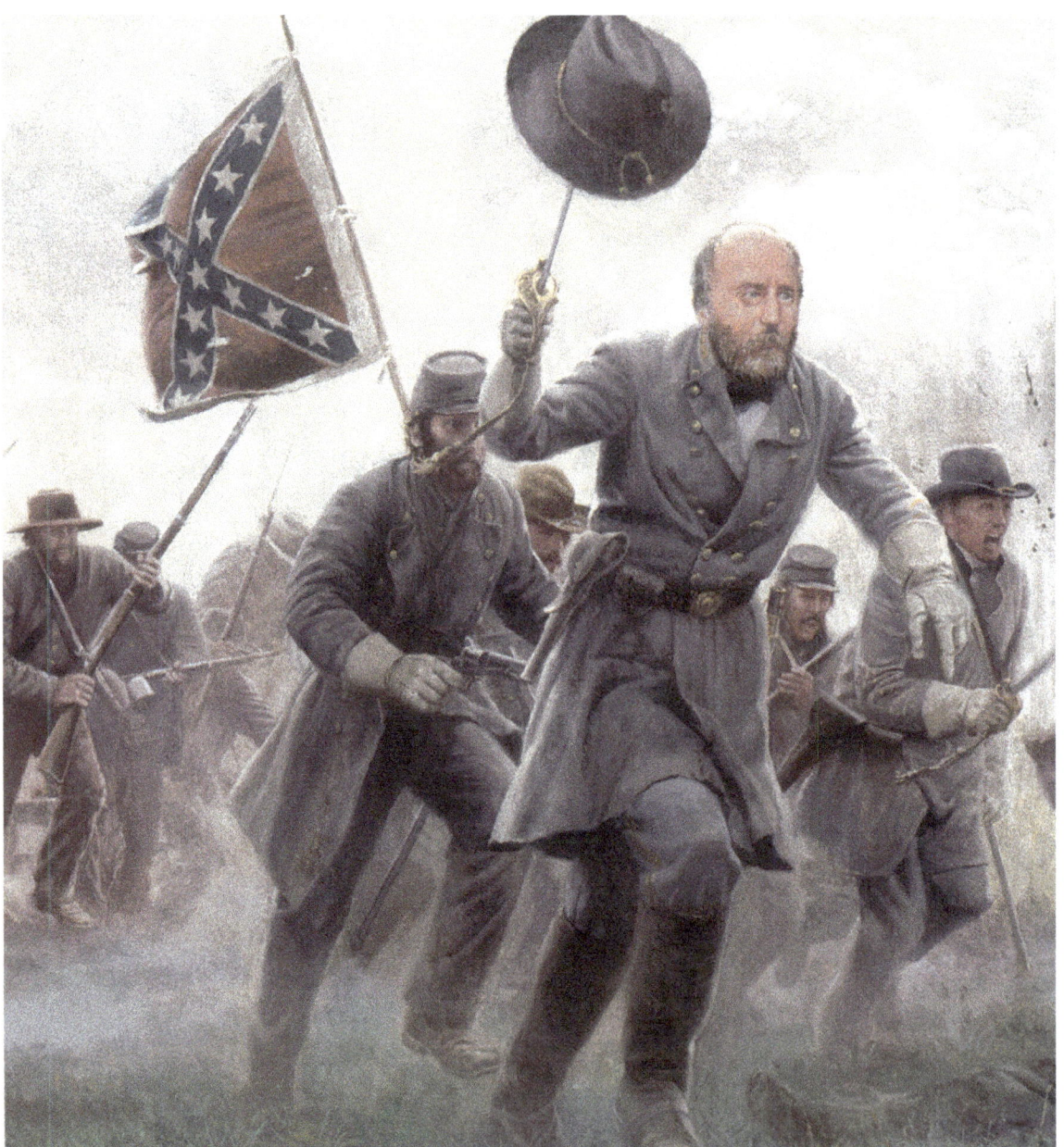

Instead, they endured murderous artillery fire, against which they could do nothing.

When Pickett saw his lead brigades mesh with Pettigrew's survivors and surge into the field beyond the Emmitsburg Road, he noted their heavy casualties. If the survivors were to achieve General Lee's objective, they would need reinforcements, and he sent word to Longstreet to send in the reserves.

On the battlefield, the five brigades mixed as they were swept up in the chaos of combat, still marching forward. All held their fire until Richard Garnett gave the order and the counsel to take good aim and fire low. Shortly after giving that order, Garnett was shot out of his saddle.

Moments later, James Kemper turned to shout to Lew Armistead, "I am going to take those heights and carry them, and I want you to support me!" Armistead acknowledged, and then Kemper fell wounded to the ground.

Pickett's men had only a single brigade commander left in action on the field—Armistead—and he kept going. His leadership was both harrowing and heroic, and that's what I wanted to convey in this painting. The historic elements are here: the assault route, the artillery fire, the post-and-rail fences, the weapons, the accoutrements, the chaos of being under fire.

I paint in a realistic style, using a technique that conveys the full experience through light, colors, shadows, objects, and motion. The composition of this painting is like a pyramid, arranged so that it draws the viewer's eye to the central focus of the scene: Armistead, his hat, and the flag. I believe this is the first painting of Armistead near the Emmitsburg Road during Pickett's Charge.

"FOLLOW ME, BOYS!"

GENERAL ARMISTEAD, JULY 3, 1863

1994, oil, 22 x 34

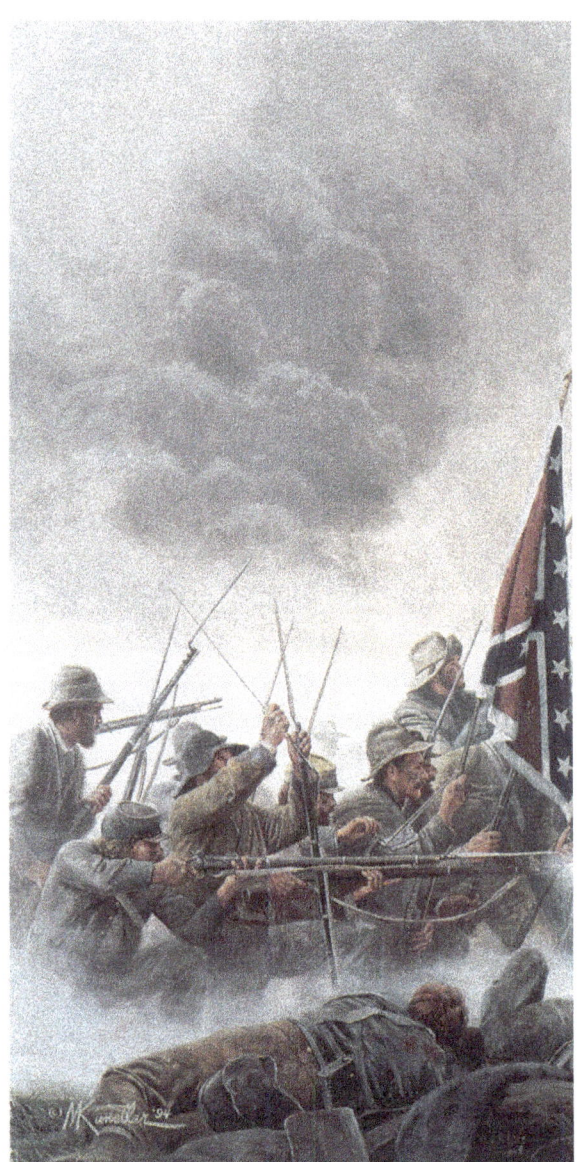

PICKETT'S BRIGADES ABANDONED THEIR carefully maintained order, and the men bunched in clusters. The closer they came to the stone wall that marked the center of the Union line, the less distinction there was between units. Later recollections described the oncoming horde as a mass of men as they closed on the wall.

Shouts pierced the din of rifle- and cannonfire, but it was not the Rebel Yell, for the men were too occupied to render that ear-splitting cry. Some described it as a guttural roar amid the powder smoke swirling and spreading along the battle front. Nothing could

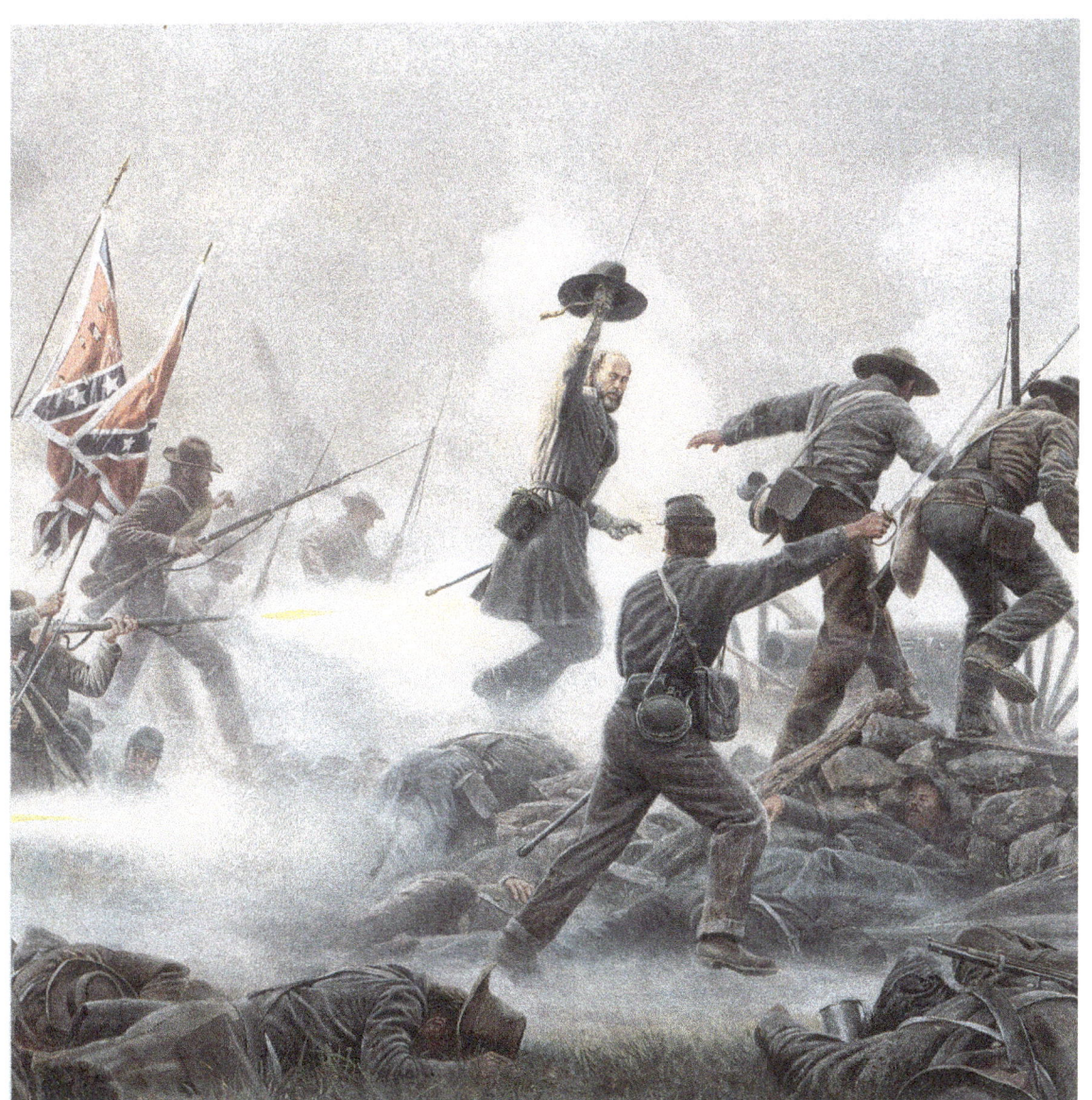

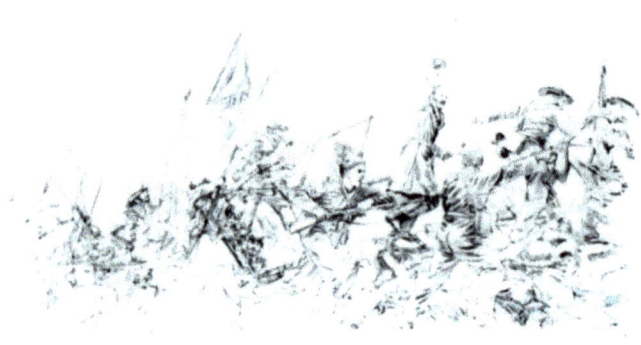

be seen clearly, and few orders or shouts could be distinguished.

Kemper's brigade was devastated by heavy fire from the front and right side. Garnett's was the next to draw fire on its flank. One soldier recalled, "At one time I saw two men cross their muskets, one fired to our right and the other to our front." Still, the ragged groups of men followed their flags toward the center of the Union line.

Back on Seminary Ridge, British observer Lt. Col. Arthur Fremantle was awed by what he could see of the fighting in the distance. To James Longstreet he said, "I wouldn't have missed this for anything!" But Longstreet could only respond, "I would like to have missed it very much."

Armistead, meanwhile, discovered two gaps in the Union line in front of him. One was nearly fifty feet wide at an angle in the stone wall that marked the Federal front; the other was below the copse of trees that had served as his aiming point for the assault. Both gaps occurred when Union regiments fell back from the fire of the oncoming Confederates. The latter gap exposed a Federal battery that could only fire its last load of canister and pull back. A nearby Union soldier recalled, "I never saw such slaughter."

The gap at the Angle (as it became known after the battle) was larger, more Confederates were closer to it (Kemper's brigade was in ruins, but Armistead's and Garnett's brigades totaled twenty-five hundred or three thousand men at this point), and fewer Union troops were there to stop them. Garnett's and Armistead's brigades could focus solely on the Federals in front of them: the Sixty-ninth Pennsylvania and Alonzo Cushing's two 3-inch

"FOLLOW ME, BOYS!"
STUDY

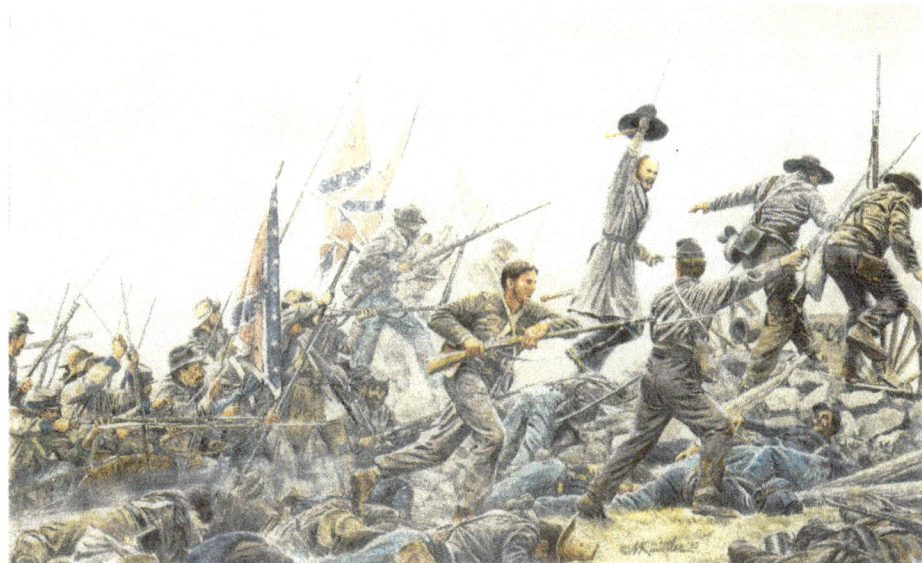

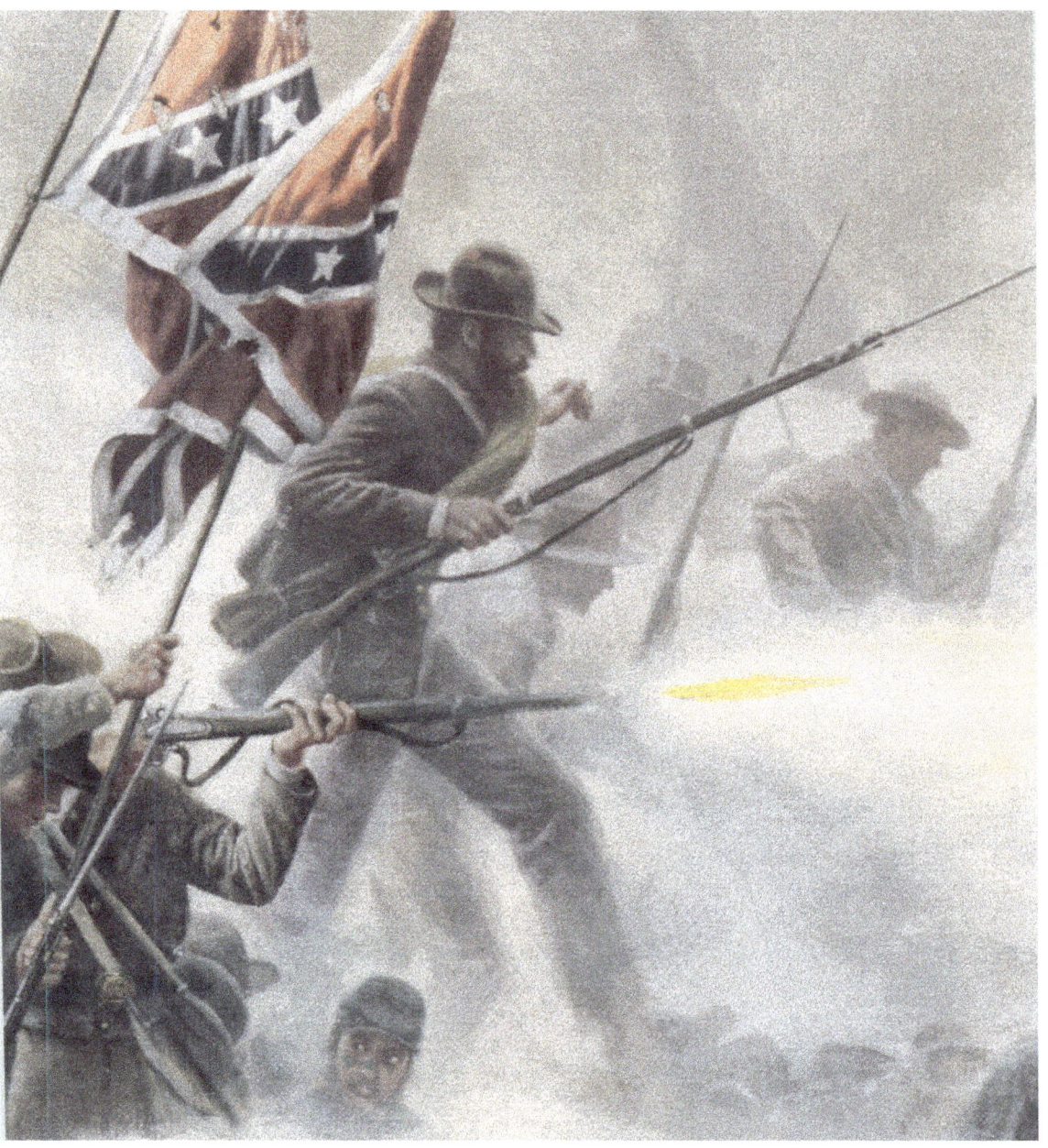

ordnance rifles. The regiment's colonel reminded his men of an earlier heroic battle when he admonished them not to fire until they could see "the whites of their eyes." The approaching Confederates were only fifty yards away when the Pennsylvanians loosed their first volley. A Virginia officer noted that his regiment "recoiled under the terrific fire that poured into our ranks."

Cushing was shot down while directing the fire of his two guns. For their last shot, the gunners waited until the Confederates were twenty yards away before they fired and abandoned their guns.

Armistead rushed for the wall, directly toward Cushing's guns. He turned to his men and called out, "Come forward, Virginians! Come on, boys, we must give them the cold steel! Who will follow me?"

More than a hundred men plunged over the wall with Armistead. Three Union companies turned to counter the breakthrough, but one was overrun and captured by the Virginians. Other men rushed to Cushing's guns and turned them to fire on the Federals, but there was no ammunition for them.

Behind the Union lines, Winfield Scott Hancock reviewed the situation on his right flank, near Ziegler's Grove. Pettigrew's brigades had been shredded here, victims of combined Federal infantry and artillery fire. Since the danger seemed to have passed here, Hancock rode fast for the center of his line. The angle in the stone wall created an awkward position for some regiments, placing some of his troops well forward of his main line.

En route, Hancock was hailed by a colonel whose regiment was being held in reserve.

"They have broken through," he informed the general. "The colors are coming over the stone wall. Let me go in there."

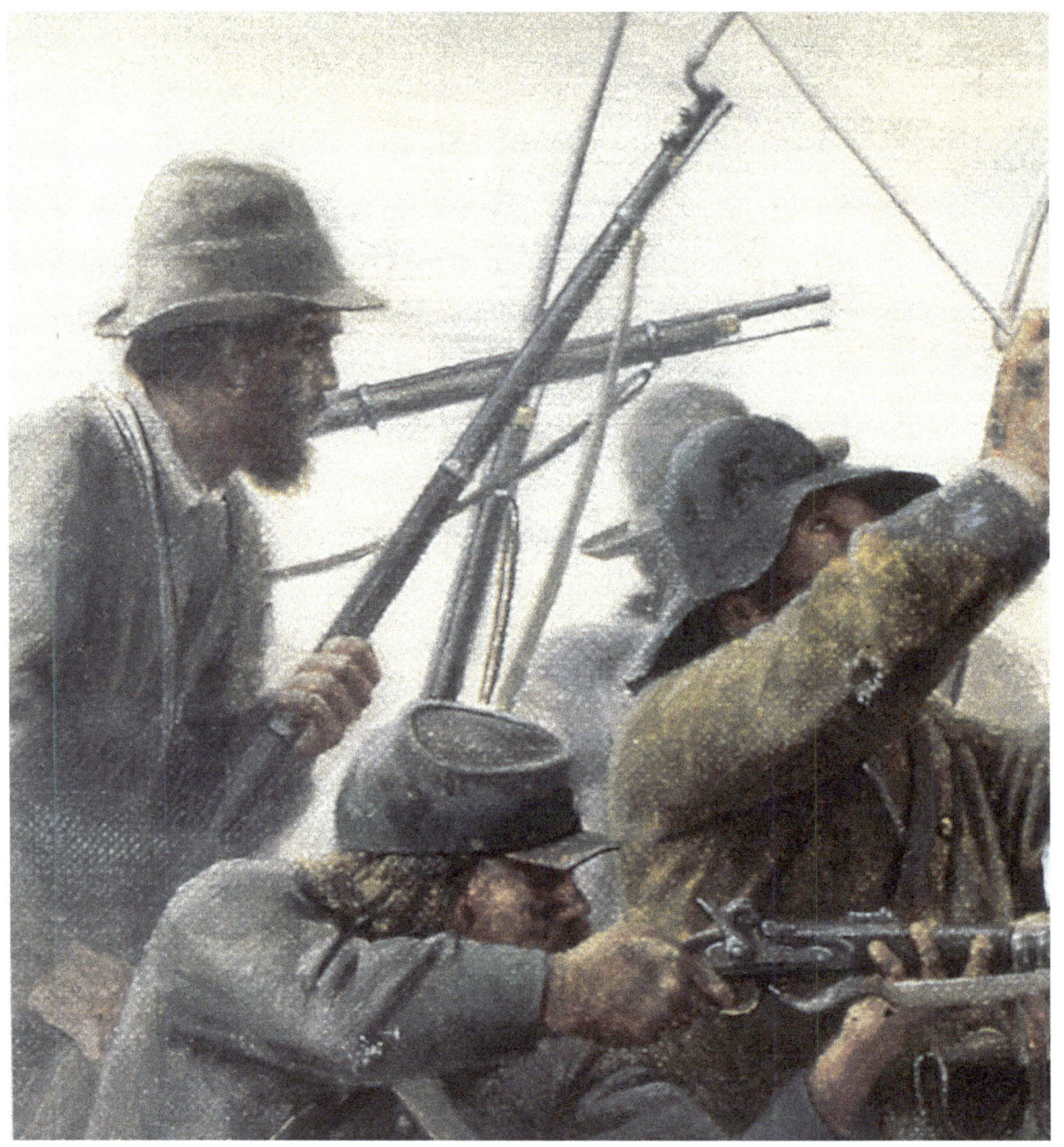

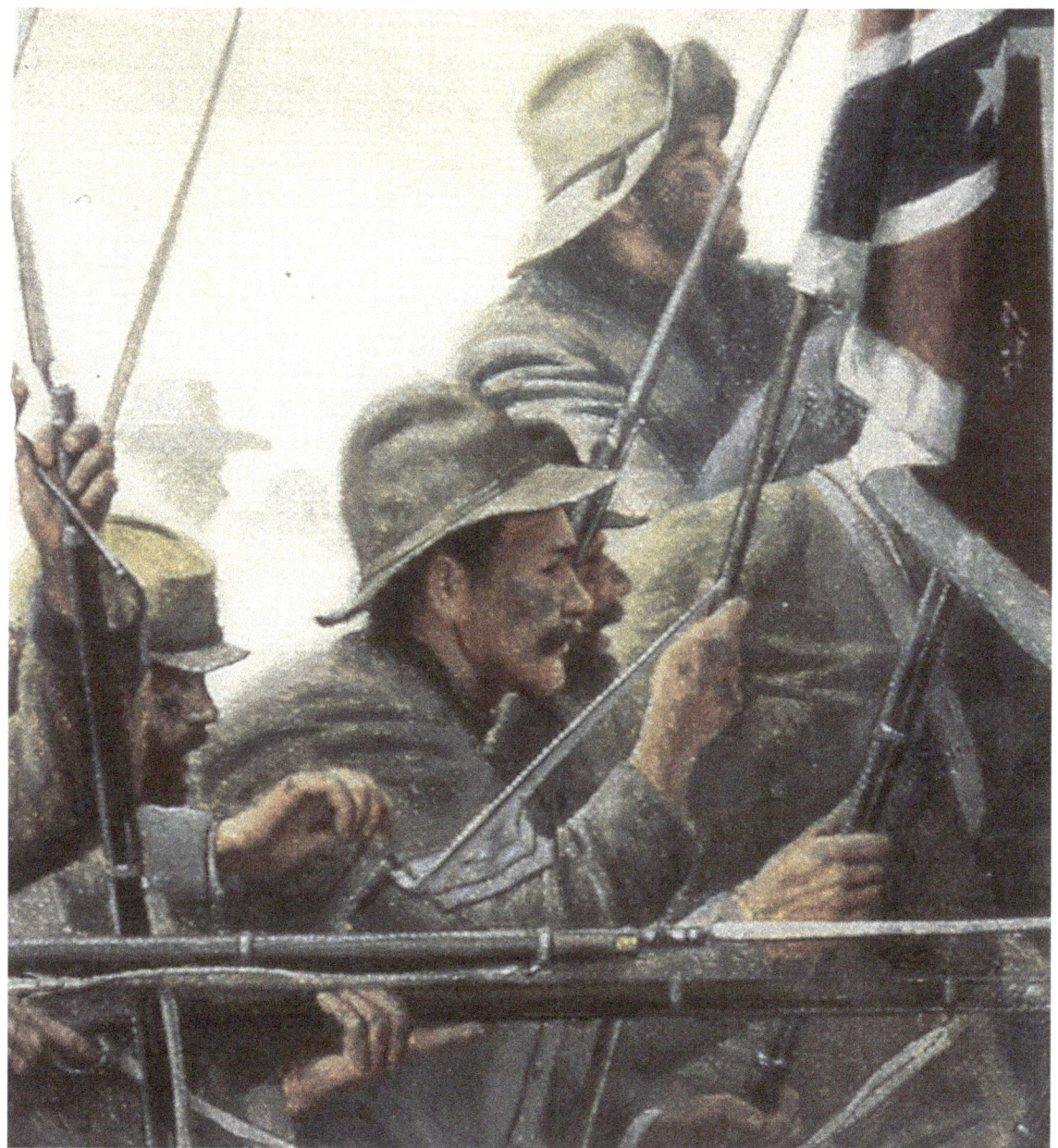

From less than two hundred yards away, Hancock saw a cluster of Confederates clambering over the wall behind a gray-haired man whose hat was poised near the hilt of his sword. "Go in there pretty . . . quick!" he commanded, then spurred his horse to find other regiments to send toward the breakthrough.

One of the most difficult problems an artist can face is to present a scene that has been done many times before. A new painting automatically calls for comparison with the other works. Such a scene is this of Armistead, hat on his sword, leading his brigade over the stone wall at Cemetery Ridge.

I had done a pencil sketch that I used as a study for a mixed-media painting for my earlier book on Gettysburg. Shortly after that book was published, I decided to do a major oil painting of the scene.

I used sunlight, in the left of the painting, breaking through the powder smoke, to catch the tops of the two battle flags and Armistead. The light play dramatically calls attention to the center of interest. The smoke in the background heightens this effect as well. I believe this is one of the most dramatic works of all my paintings.

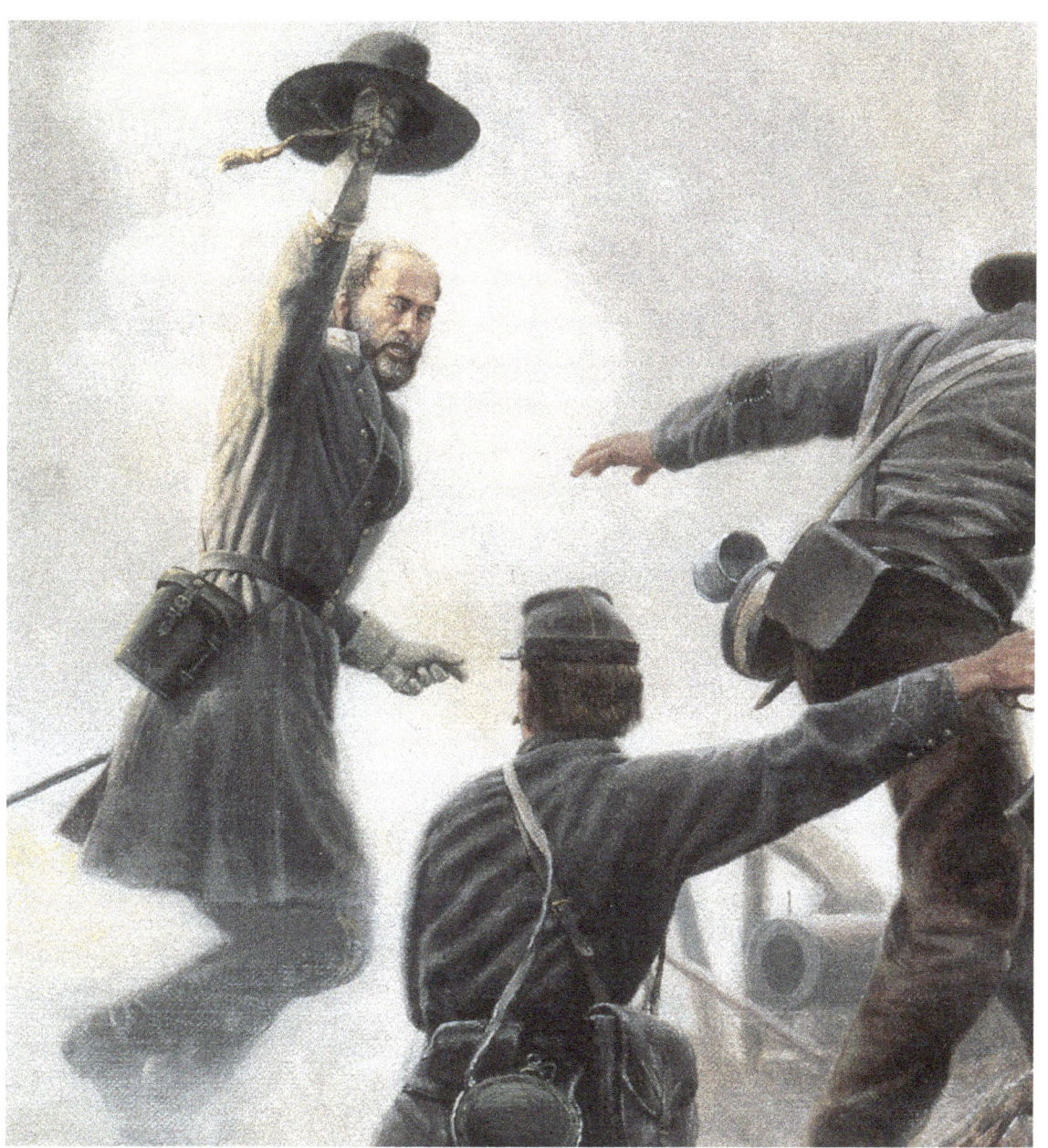

THE HIGH WATER MARK

GETTYSBURG, JULY 3, 1863

1988, oil, 30 x 56

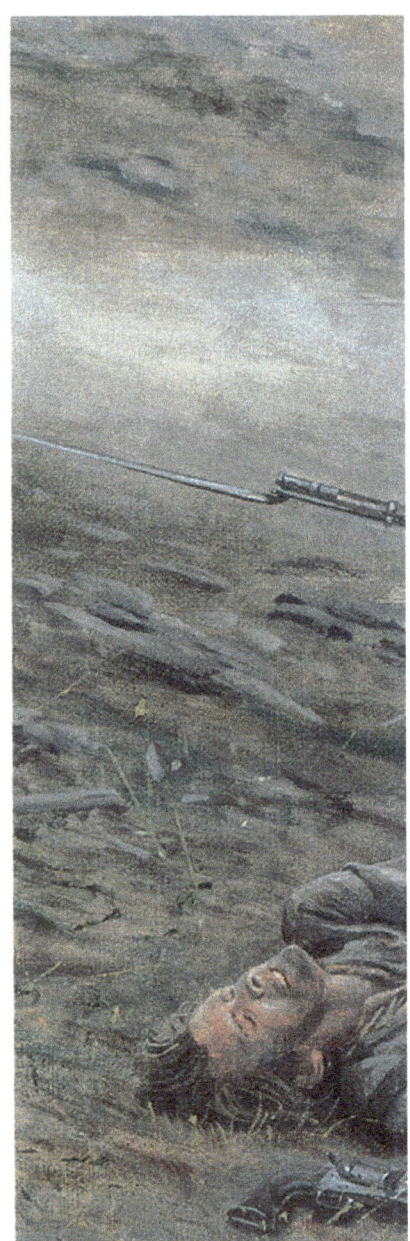

WHILE ARMISTEAD'S VIRGINIANS STRUGGLE at the Angle, farther to the north a North Carolina regiment tries to reach the Union line. In the right foreground, the Twenty-second and Twenty-sixth North Carolina charge headlong at the Fourteenth Connecticut. In the right middle ground, a soldier in a shell jacket and blue pants, with his back toward the viewer, wears an Iron Brigade hat he took from a fallen Union soldier in the fierce fighting of two days earlier. Pennsylvania regiments battle in the Angle with the Virginians as the Garibaldi Guard rush in from the left as reinforcements. The cannon, firing double canister, takes its deadly toll. This was the moment when Southerners either surrendered or retreated. This was the high-water mark of the Confederacy—and my first painting of Gettysburg.

196

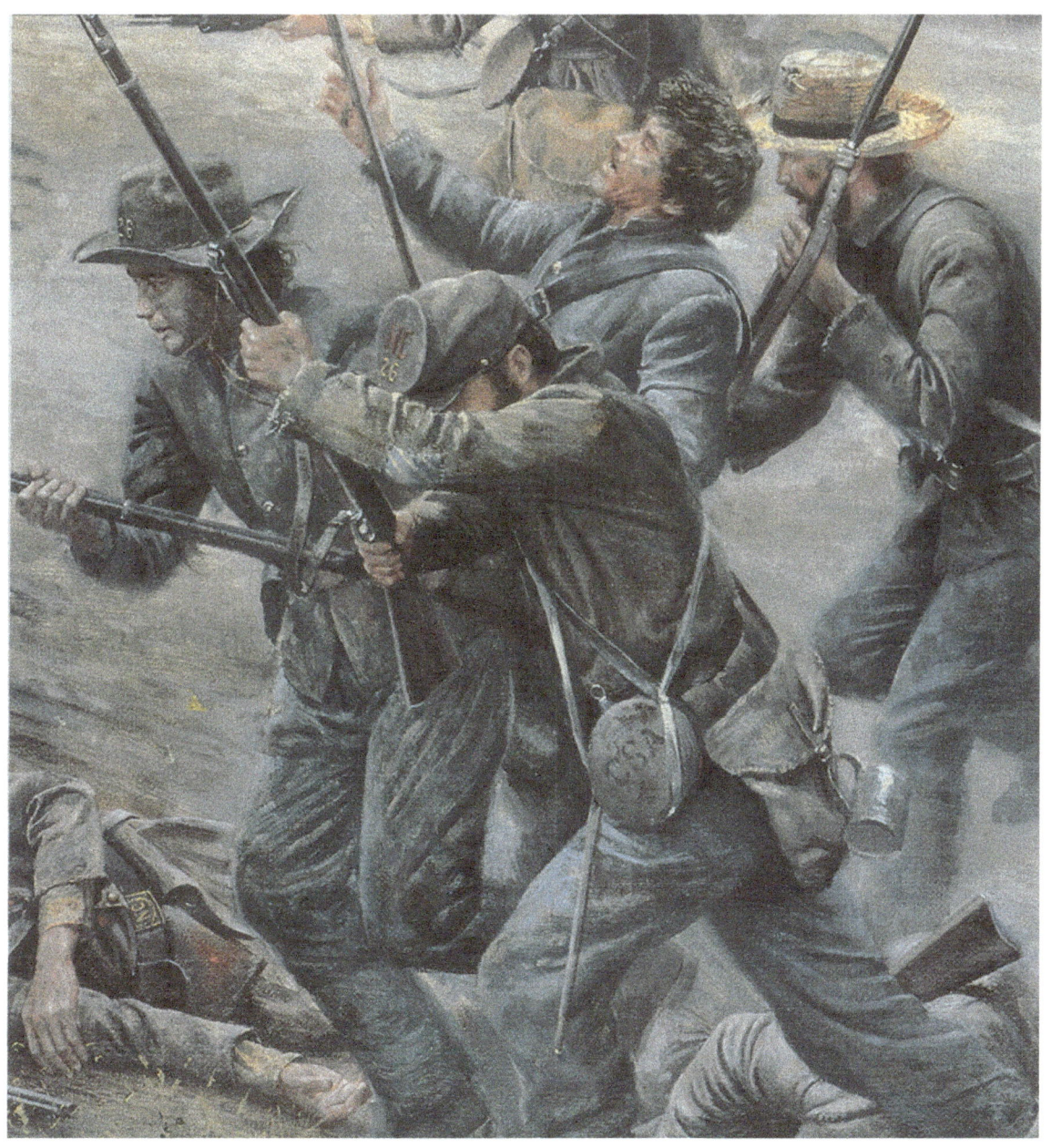

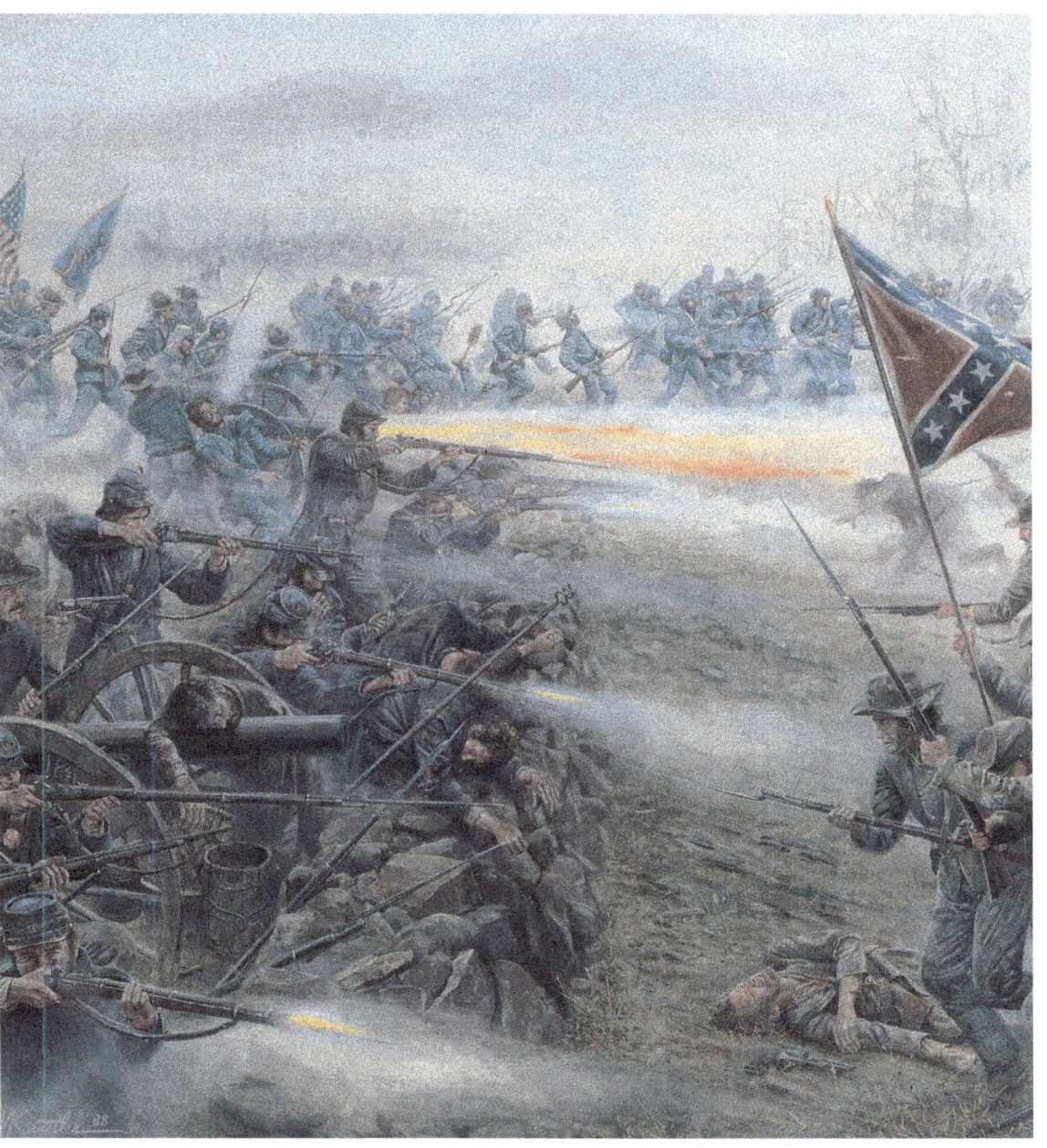

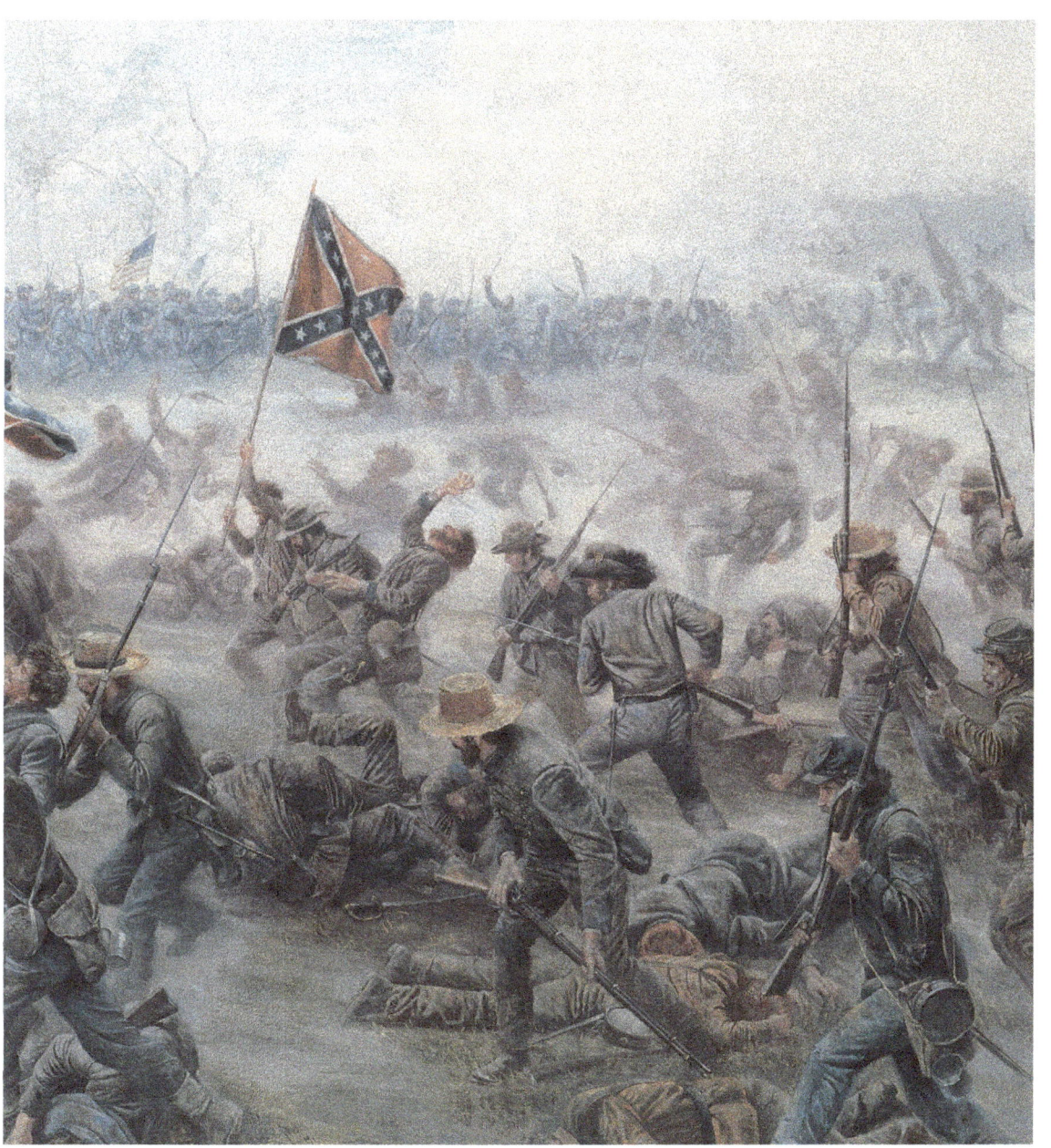

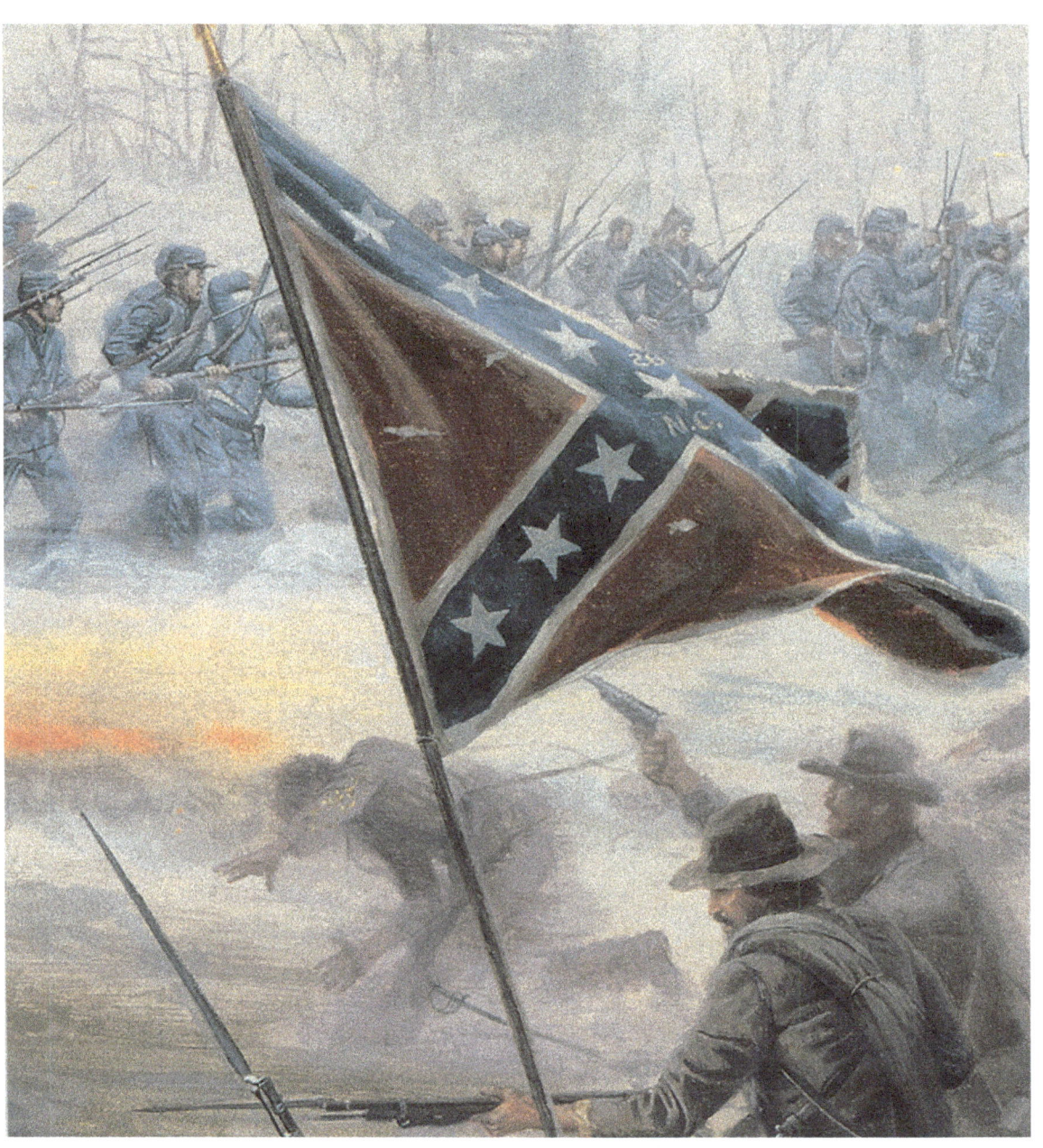

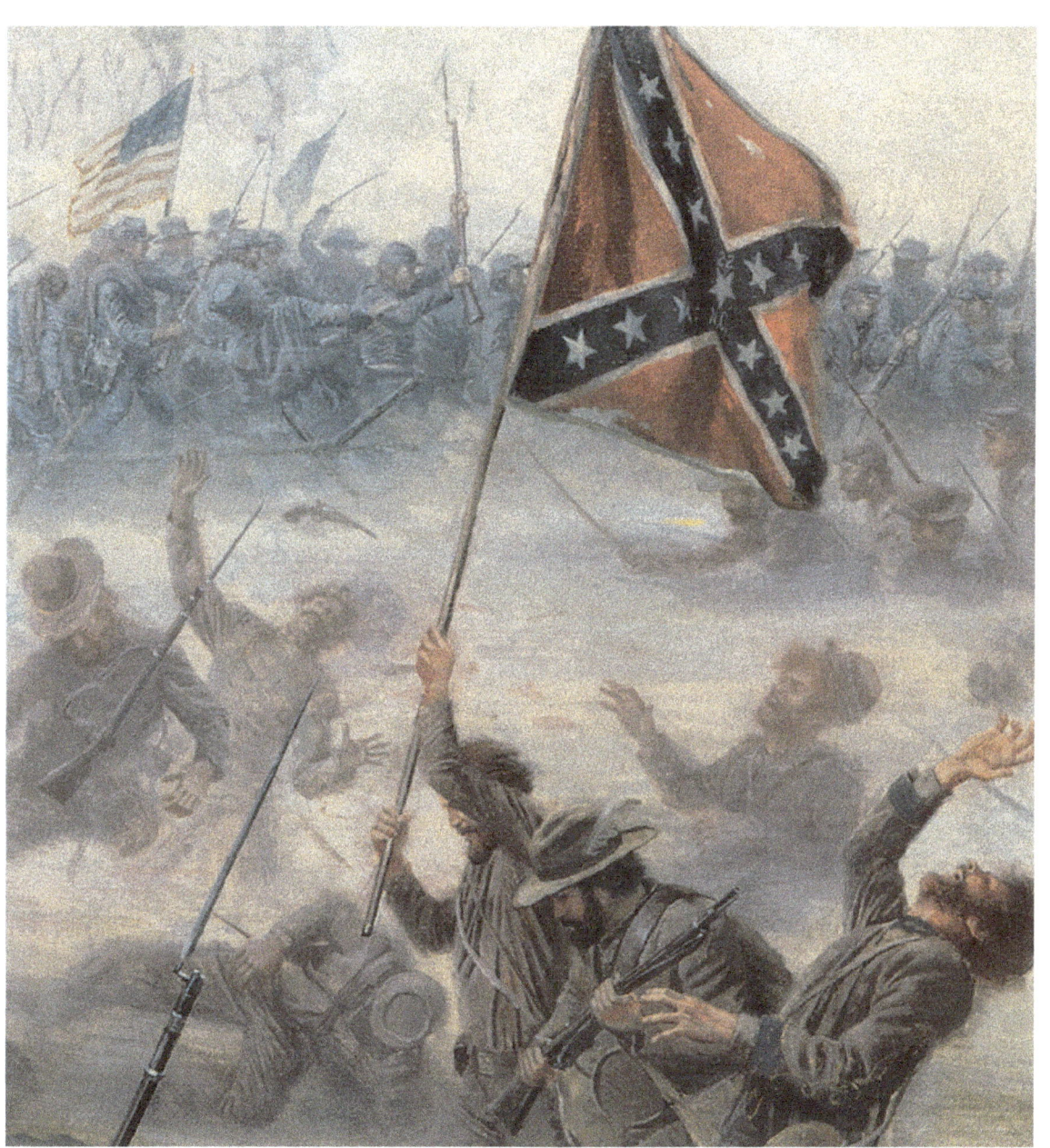

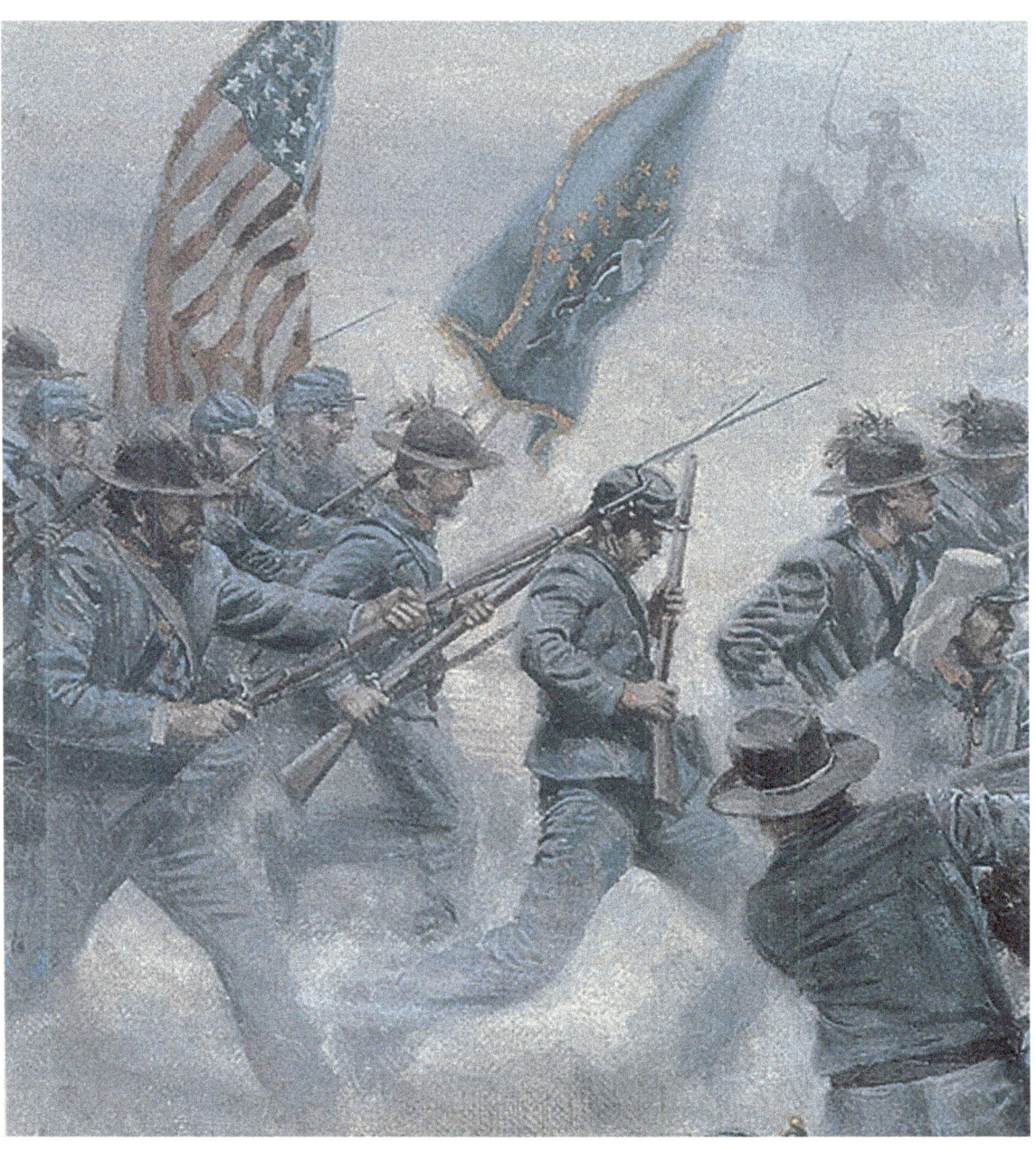

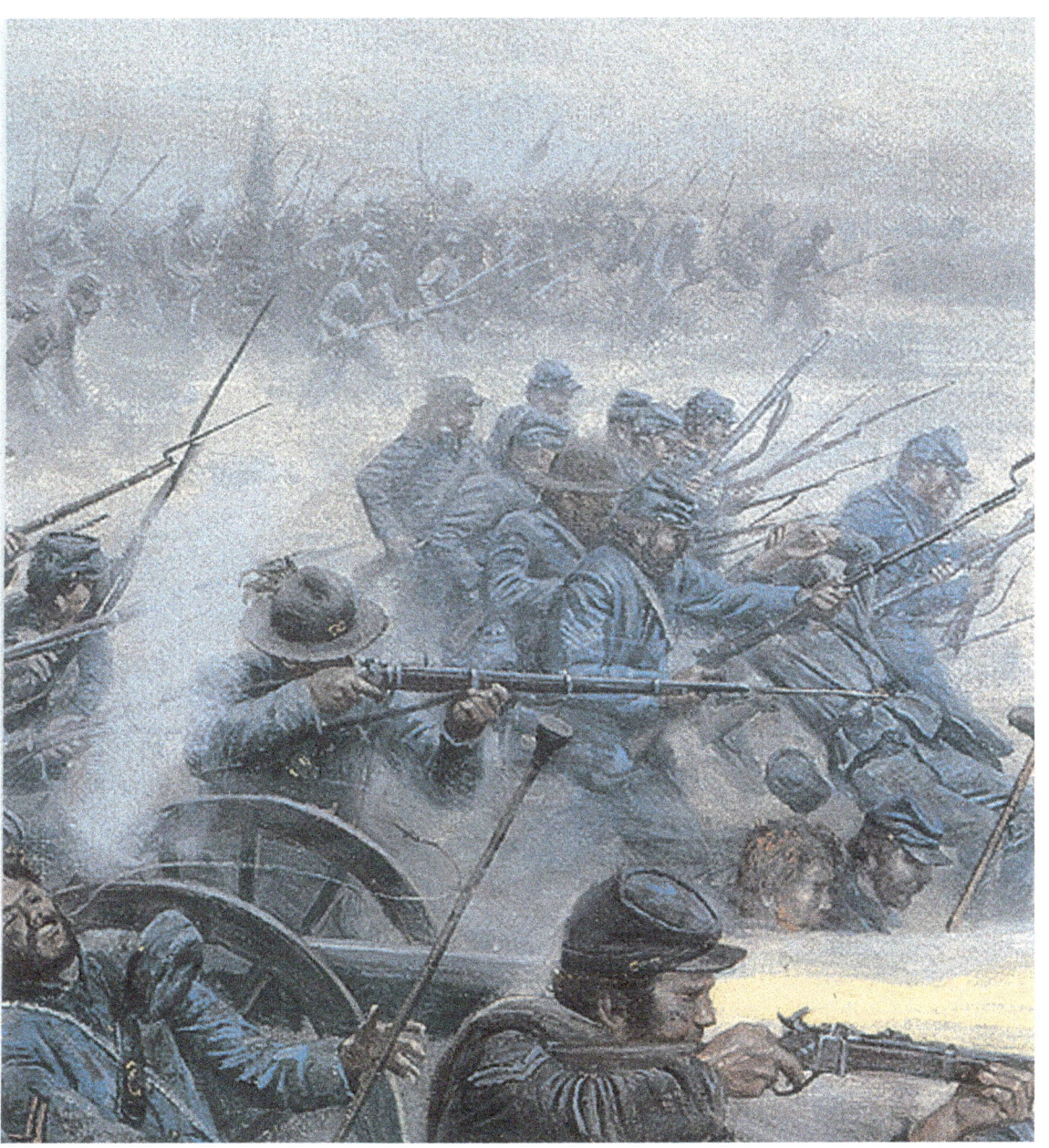

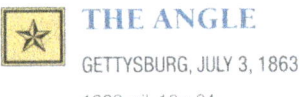

THE ANGLE

GETTYSBURG, JULY 3, 1863

1988, oil, 18 x 24

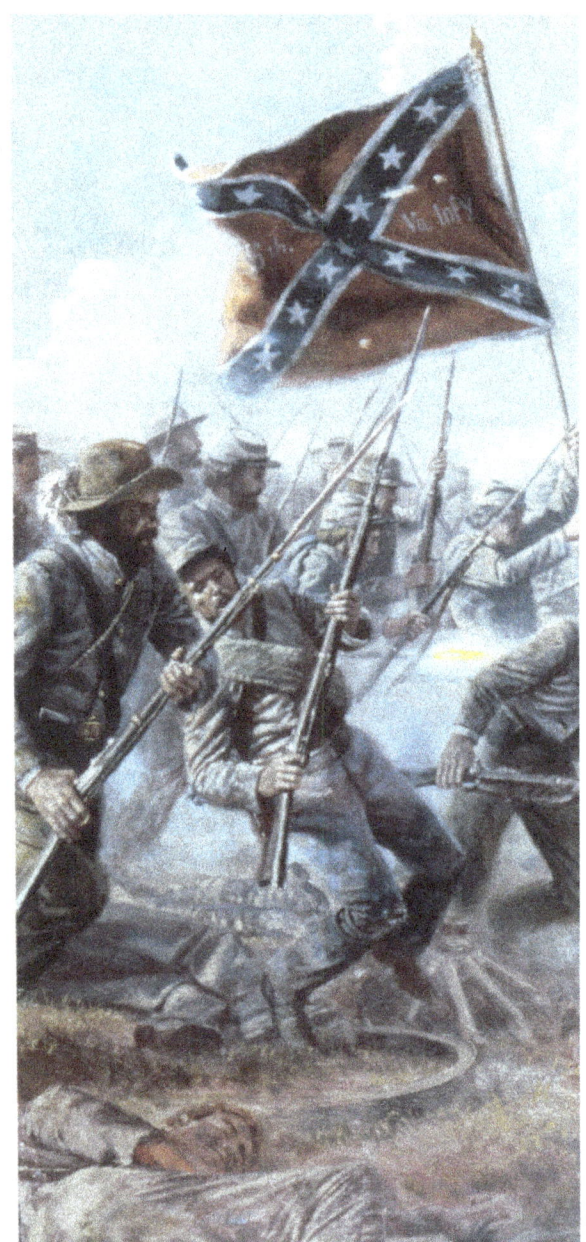

AFTER CAPTURING A UNION company and two cannon without ammunition, there was little else Armistead's men could do. To their right was the determined Sixty-ninth Pennsylvania, fighting hand to hand with clubbed muskets and fists. To their front was the Seventy-second Pennsylvania. They were responding to a plea to come up from another regimental commander. His men had fled their position at the wall, creating the gap that Armistead's men had exploited.

Drawing fire from these regiments to their front and right, the Virginians'

204

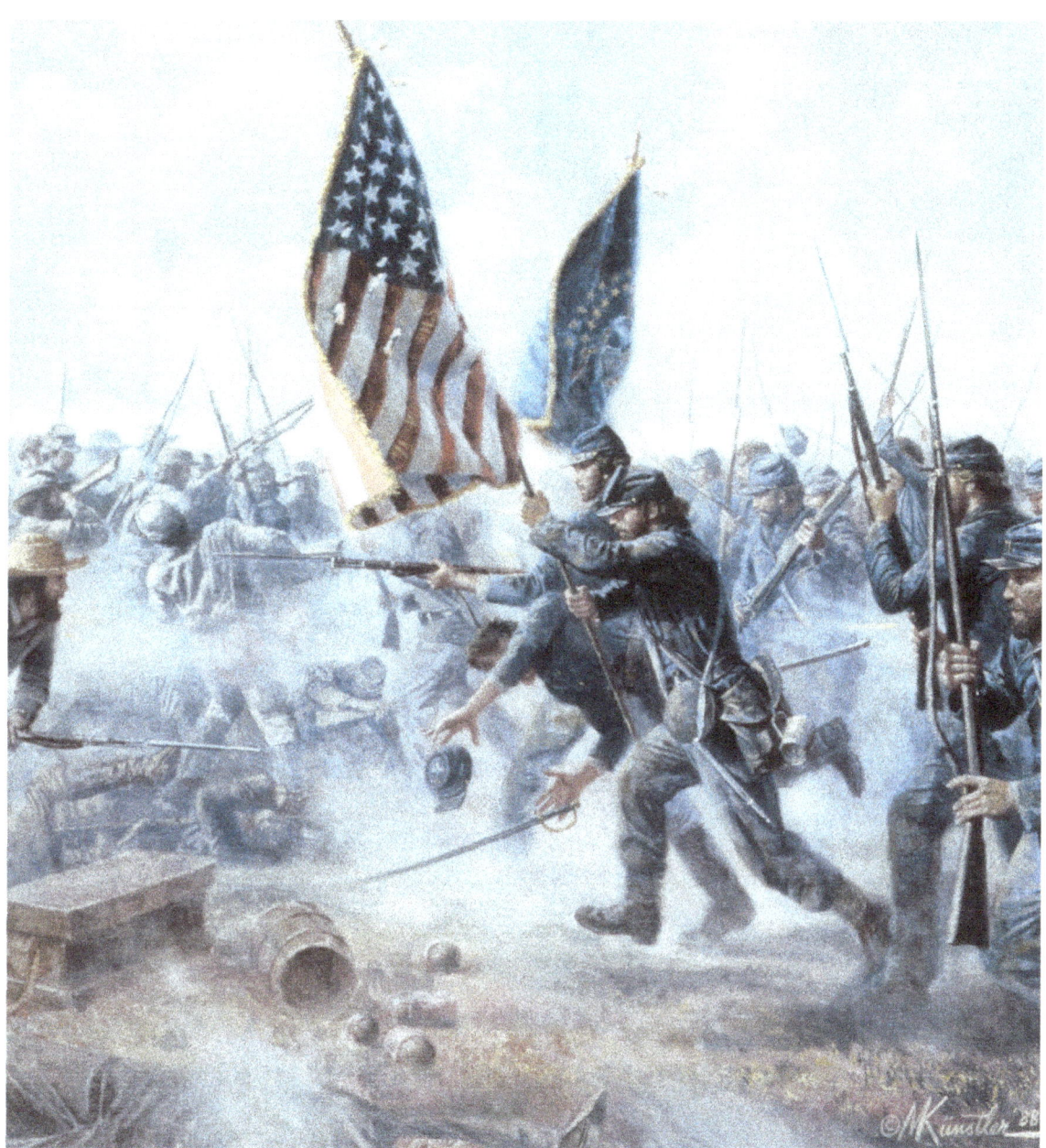

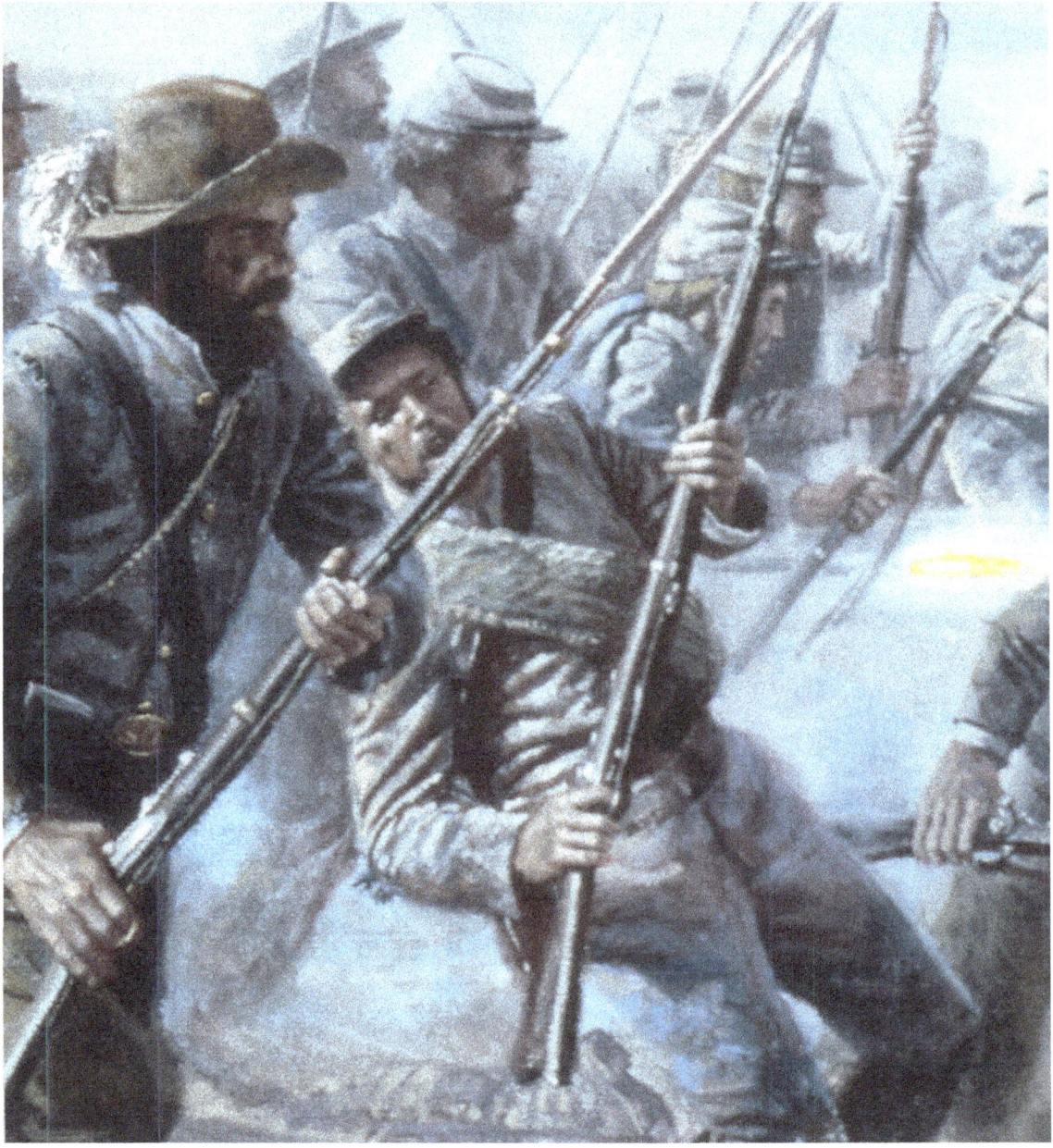

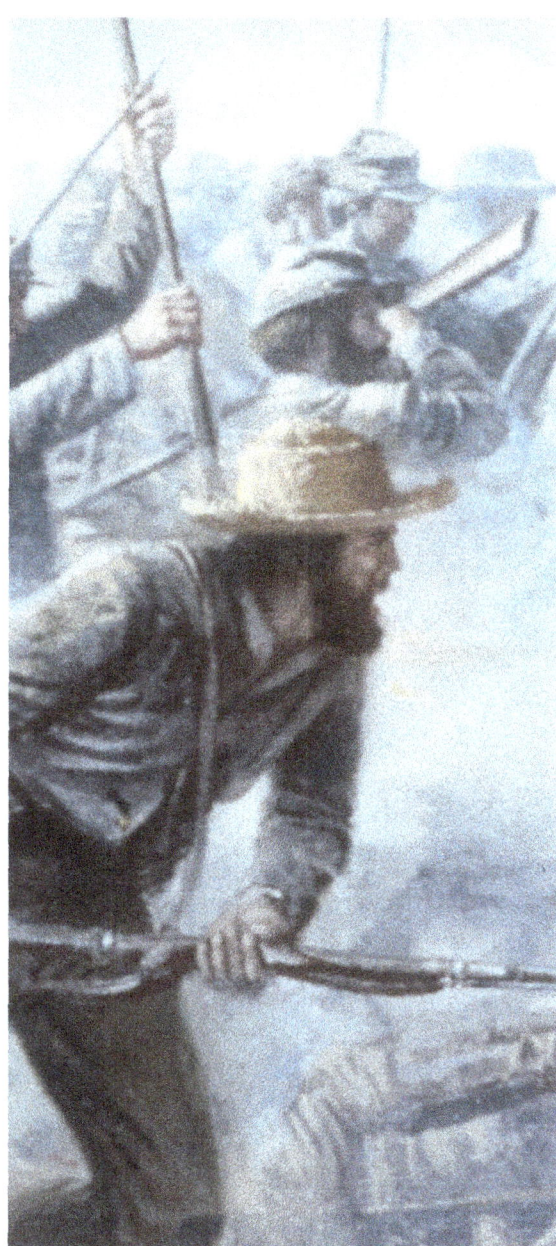

brief breakthrough closed behind them. Three bullets struck down Armistead, and he fell mortally wounded to the ground near one of Cushing's guns. The rest of his men were shot down, captured, or retreated over the wall. The breakthrough had lasted roughly ten minutes.

Still, fighting raged along the wall from the Angle to the copse of trees. The Confederates had come this far, and although they could not breach the wall, they were determined to fight there. Both sides fired at point-blank range, but the Northerners could not dislodge the Southerners. A Virginia officer glanced back toward Seminary Ridge, expecting to see the rest of the army rushing to reinforce the men in front of the wall; instead, he saw "nothing but dead and wounded men and horses on the field behind us. . . . It was a grievous disappointment."

One of the Union generals fighting at the wall commented, "That halt at the wall was the ruin of the enemy, as such halts almost always are; yet so natural is it for men to seek cover that it is almost impossible to get them to pass it under such circumstances."

Federal reinforcements arrived, and the fighting swung in their favor. The regiment whose colonel responded to Hancock's "Get in there . . . quick!" arrived along with two other regiments. Meanwhile, Hancock had been wounded when a bullet struck his saddle and drove splinters and a nail into his thigh. A tourniquet temporarily halted the bleeding, but Hancock would not allow stretcher bearers to remove him from the field until the breakthrough threat passed.

I conceived *The Angle* after I had done *The High Water Mark*, which illustrated Pickett's Charge from a southern viewpoint. I wondered how I could stage this scene differently from the way many other artists had painted it. I looked at *The High Water Mark* and decided to portray everything from the opposite direction, reversing my view. While the view in *The High Water Mark* was from above, looking down and to the south from the north, in *The Angle*, the scene is drawn at eye level, from the south looking north. This created a reverse-angle picture. It brought the action in the far background of *The High Water Mark* into the foreground and allowed me to portray intense hand-to-hand fighting in detail. It also enabled me to place the Union and Confederate flags close to each other.

The fighting at the stone wall along Cemetery Ridge turned to hand-to-hand combat. It was here that a few hundred Tennesseans and Virginians penetrated the Union line, and here that they were cut down or captured.

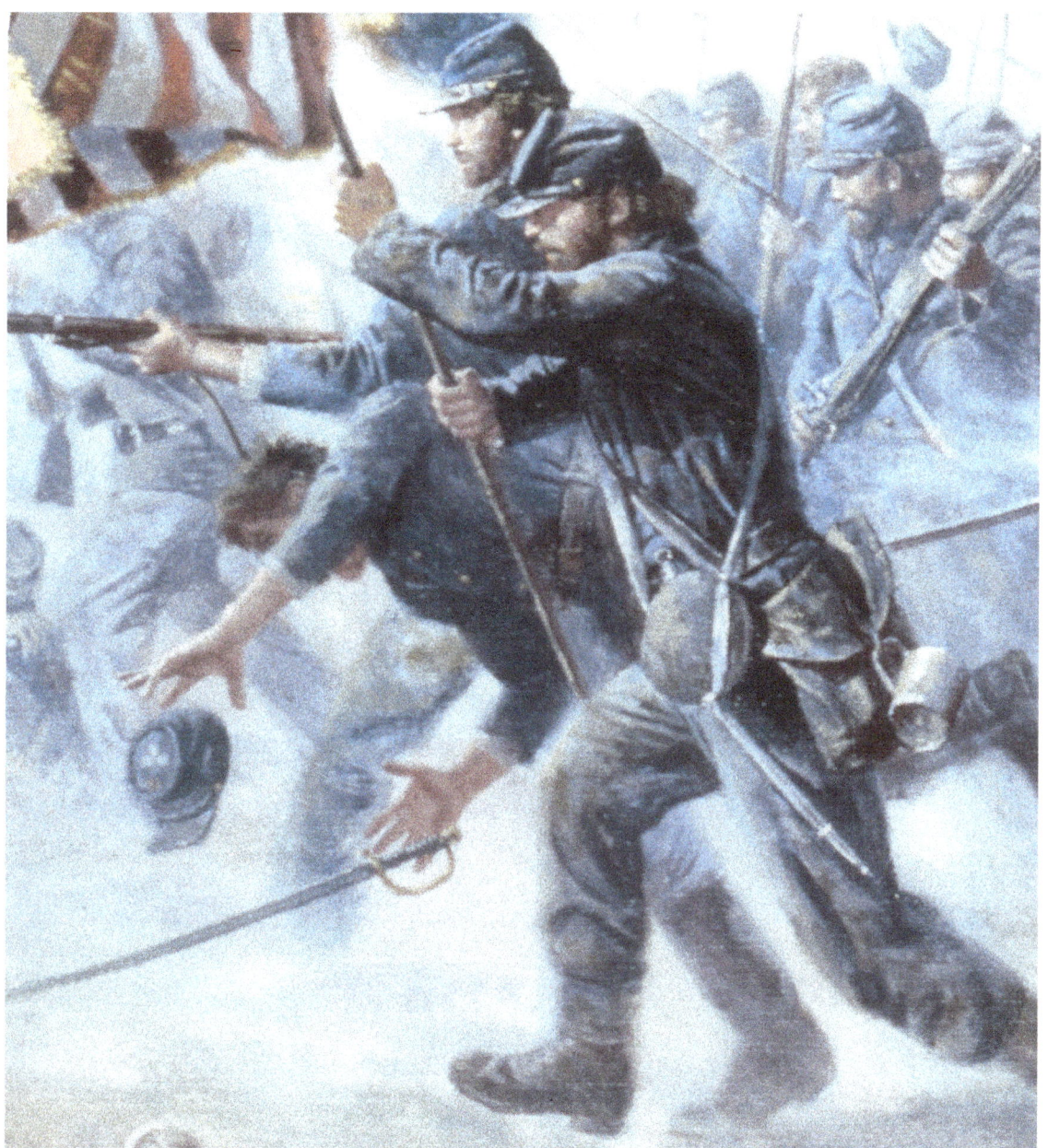

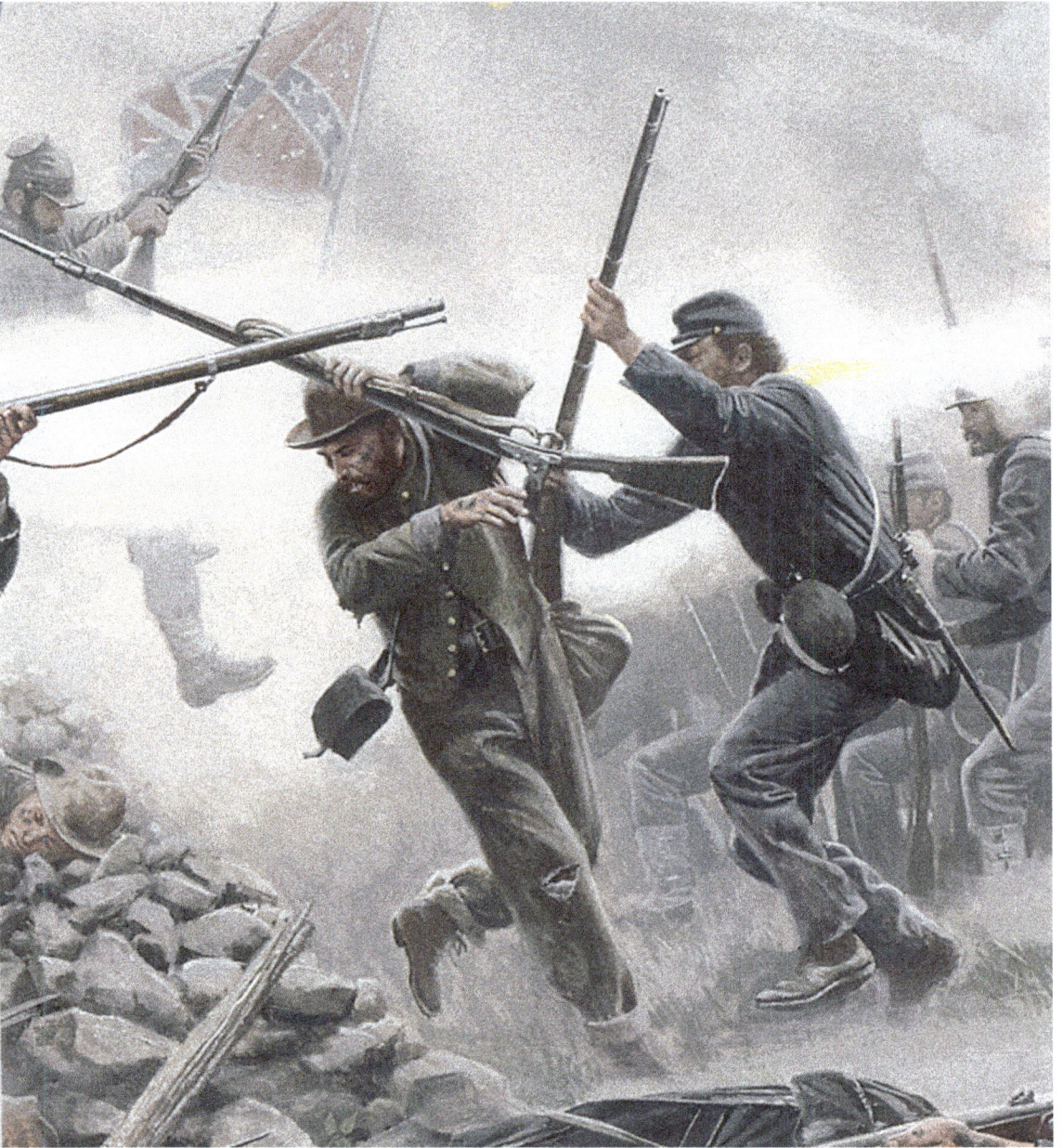

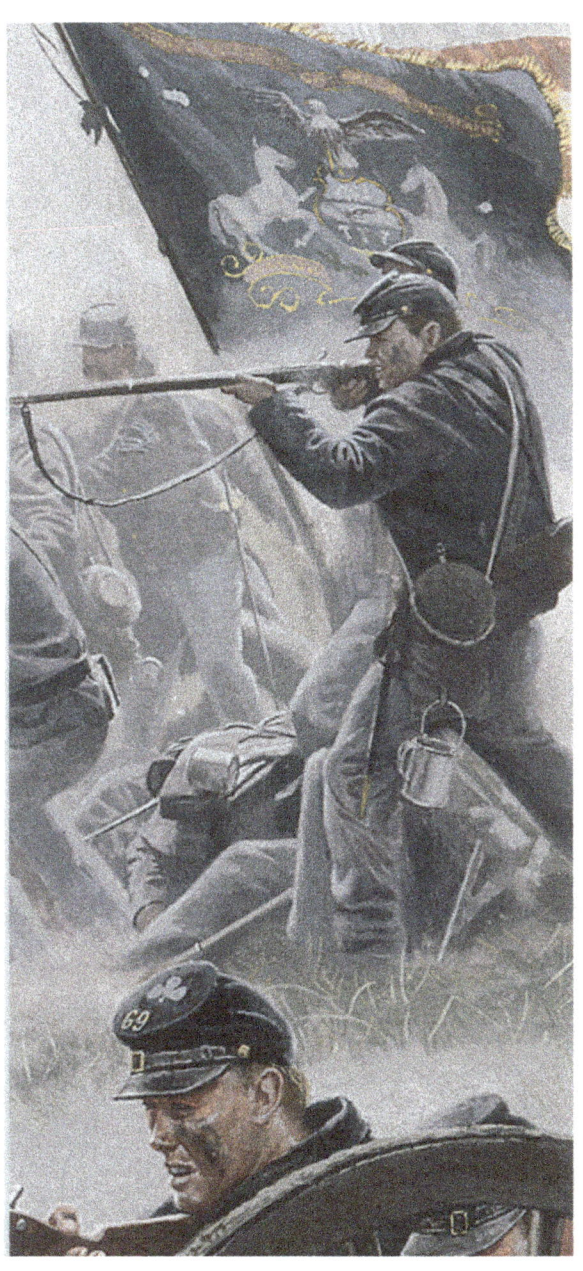

THE HIGH TIDE

GETTYSBURG, JULY 3, 1863

1993, gouache, 16 x 28¾

THREE MORE UNION REGIMENTS were sent quick-timing toward the one-hundred-yard battle zone along the stone wall between the Angle and the copse of trees. The reinforcements more or less raced one another to the scene, arriving in clusters rather than units. They pushed forward to fire, then pulled back to reload. Some even threw rocks at the Confederates. Slowly, the Southerners' battle line began to crumble.

In pondering this painting, I was looking for a way to show this dramatic moment in a different way than

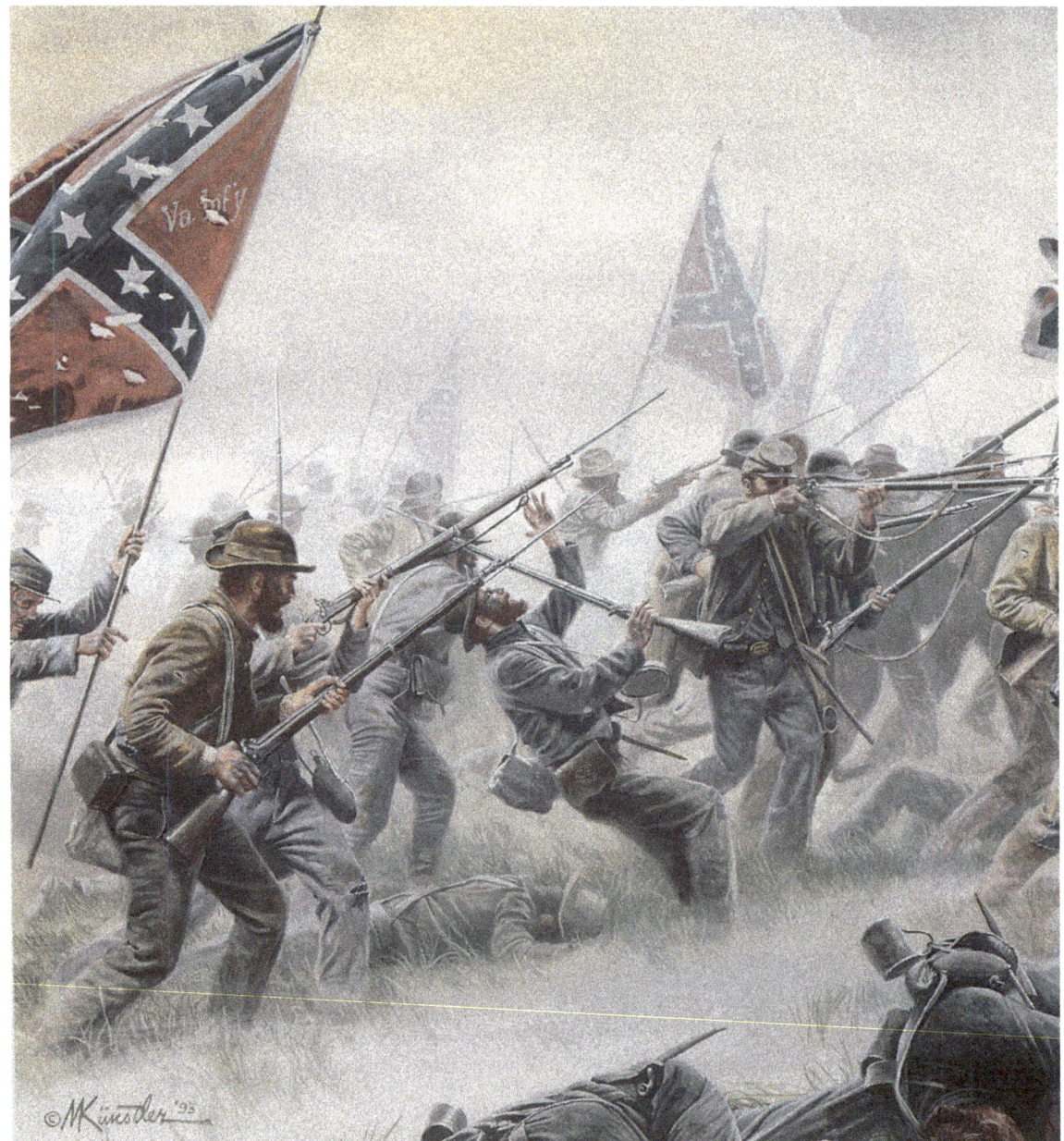

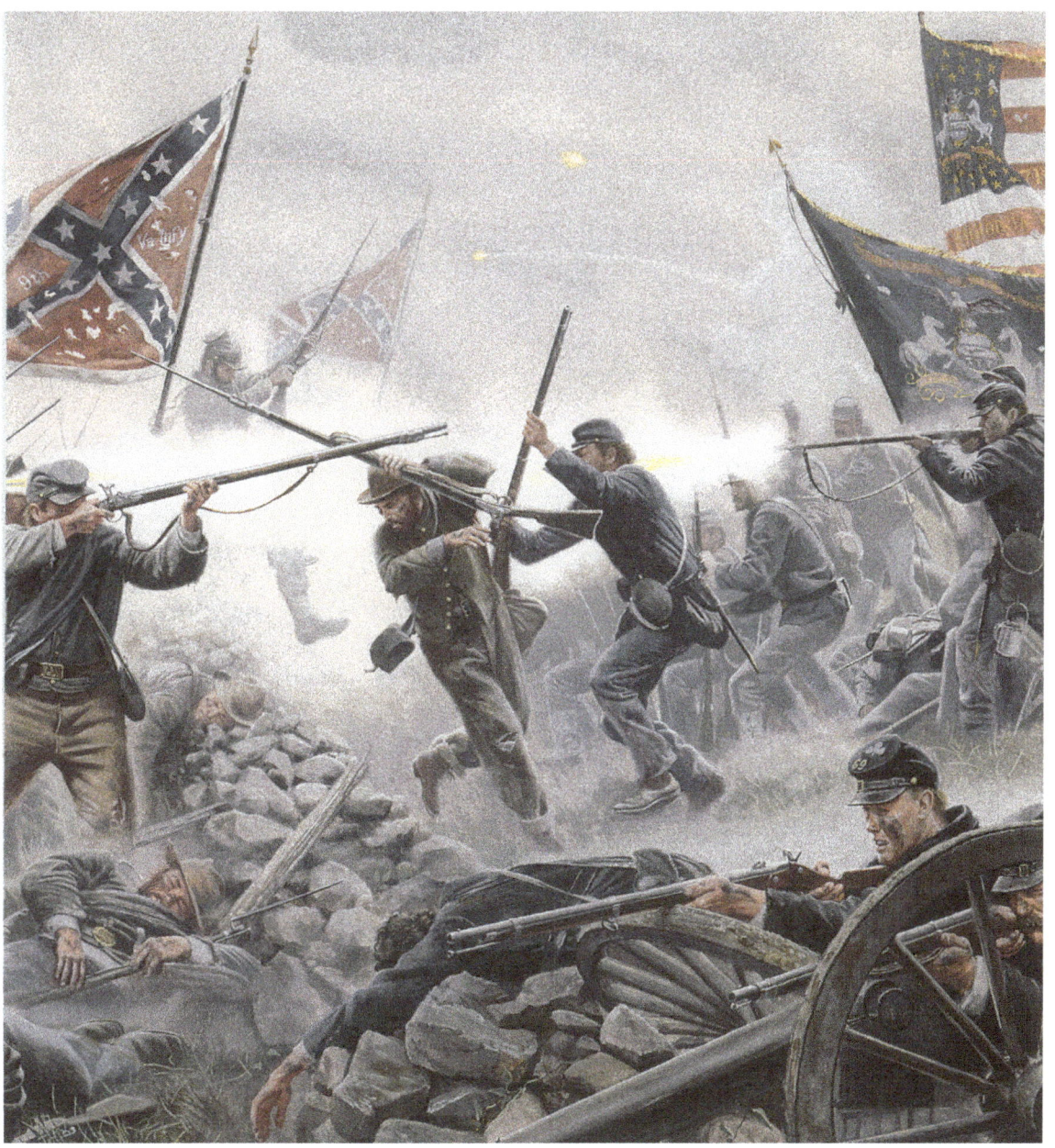

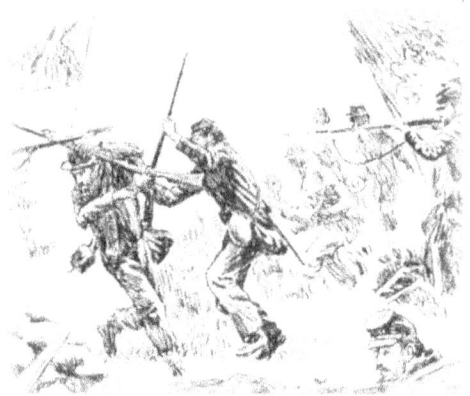

I had in my first Civil War painting, *The High Water Mark*. By looking north, I was able to show the Confederates coming from the left instead of the right. I also decided to come in tighter on the scene and not have as much of a panoramic effect as in my previous painting. I dropped the eye level to give the painting a different look.

Most of the flags shown in this painting are standard Confederate battle flags, with the Ninth Virginia Infantry seen in the center and the Fifty-sixth Virginia Infantry found in the background. To the right is the regimental flag of the Seventy-second Pennsylvania and the state-issue flag of the Seventy-first Pennsylvania. The Seventy-second Pennsylvania was a semi-zouave regiment but had lost most of their distinctive uniform by this time. The only remnants of those garish costumes were the low white-canvas gaiters containing four buckles on each side. These can be seen on two of the soldiers in the right background. The cloverleaf and the "69" on the headgear of the soldier in the right foreground identifies his unit as the Sixty-ninth Pennsylvania.

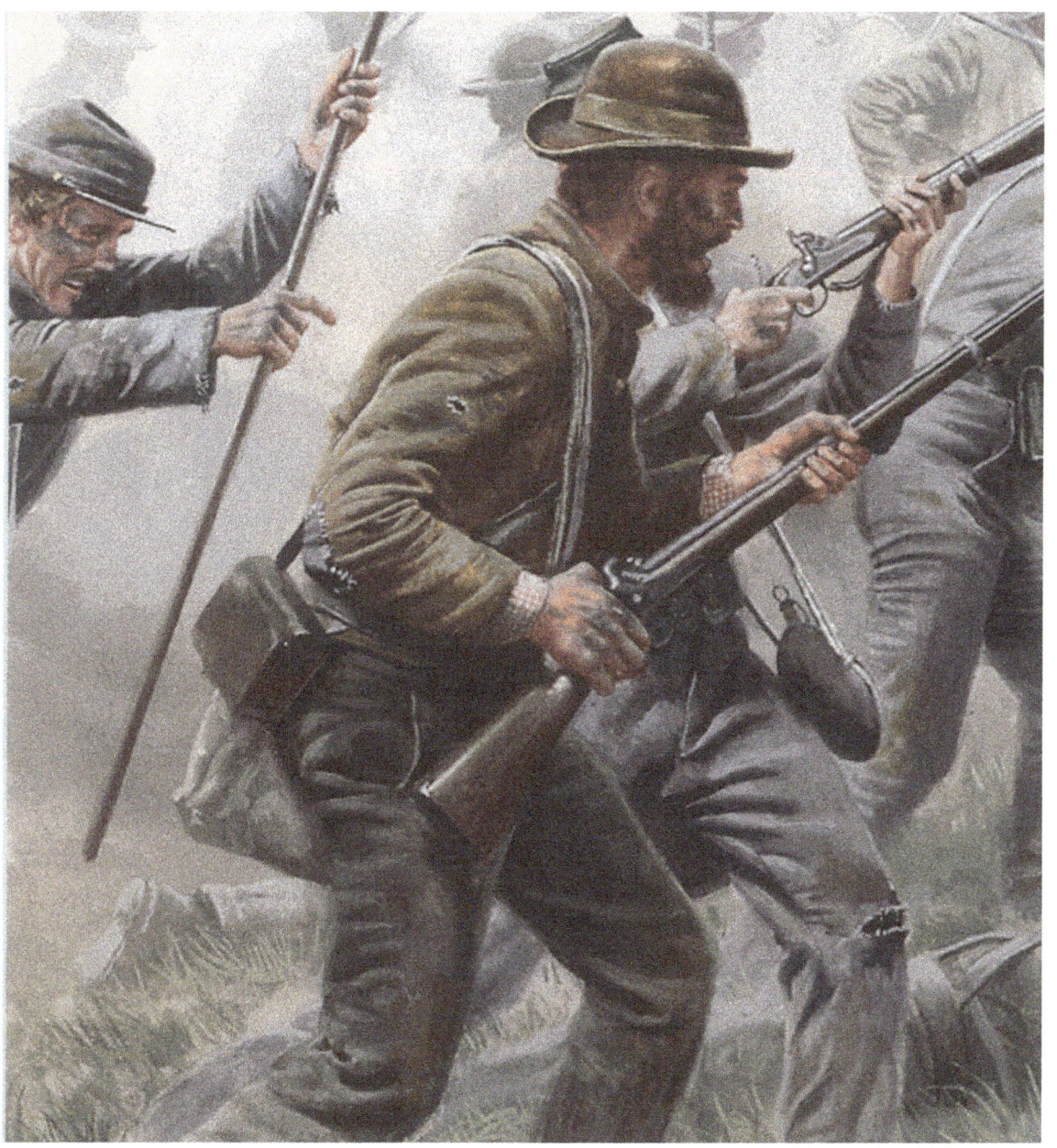

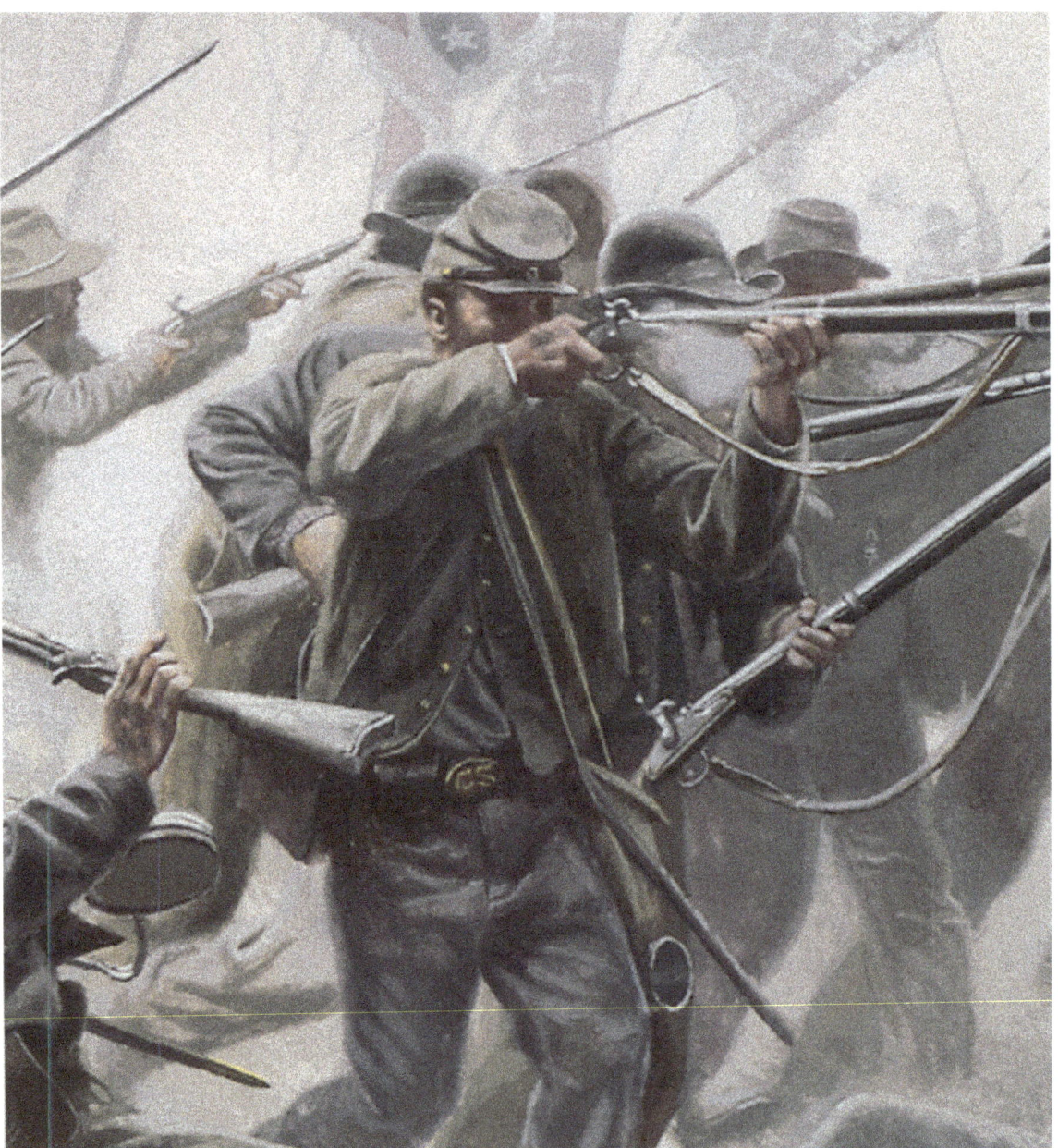

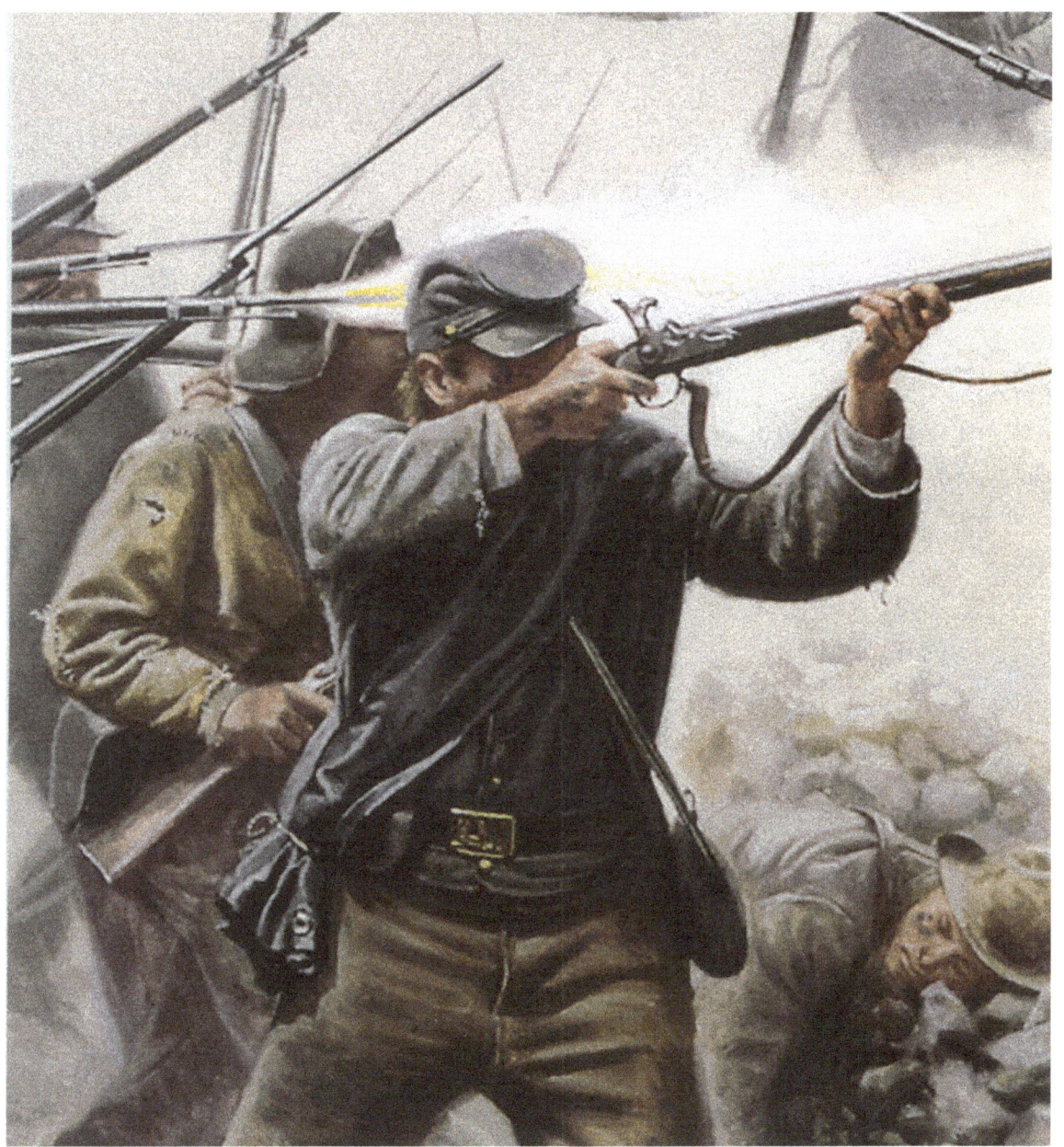

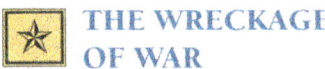
THE WRECKAGE
OF WAR

GETTYSBURG, JULY 3, 1863

1993, mixed media, 13 x 14

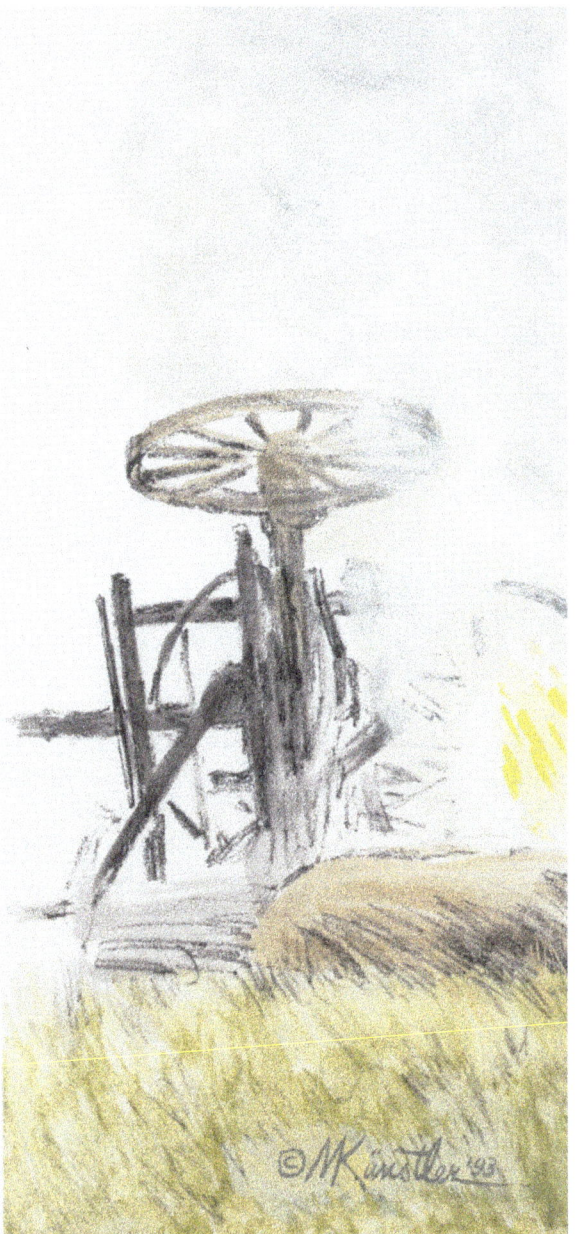

CONFEDERATE GEN. ISAAC R. TRIMBLE had been wounded during the charge, although he was well back from the stone wall. When an aide reported that his men were starting to fall back and suggested rallying them, Trimble replied, "The best these brave fellows can do is to get out of this."

A Union commander noted, "The rebels behaved with as much pluck as any men in the world could; they stood there, against the fence, until they were nearly all shot down."

next page ⋁

THE REPULSE

GETTYSBURG, JULY 3, 1863

1993, mixed media, 10¾ x 19½

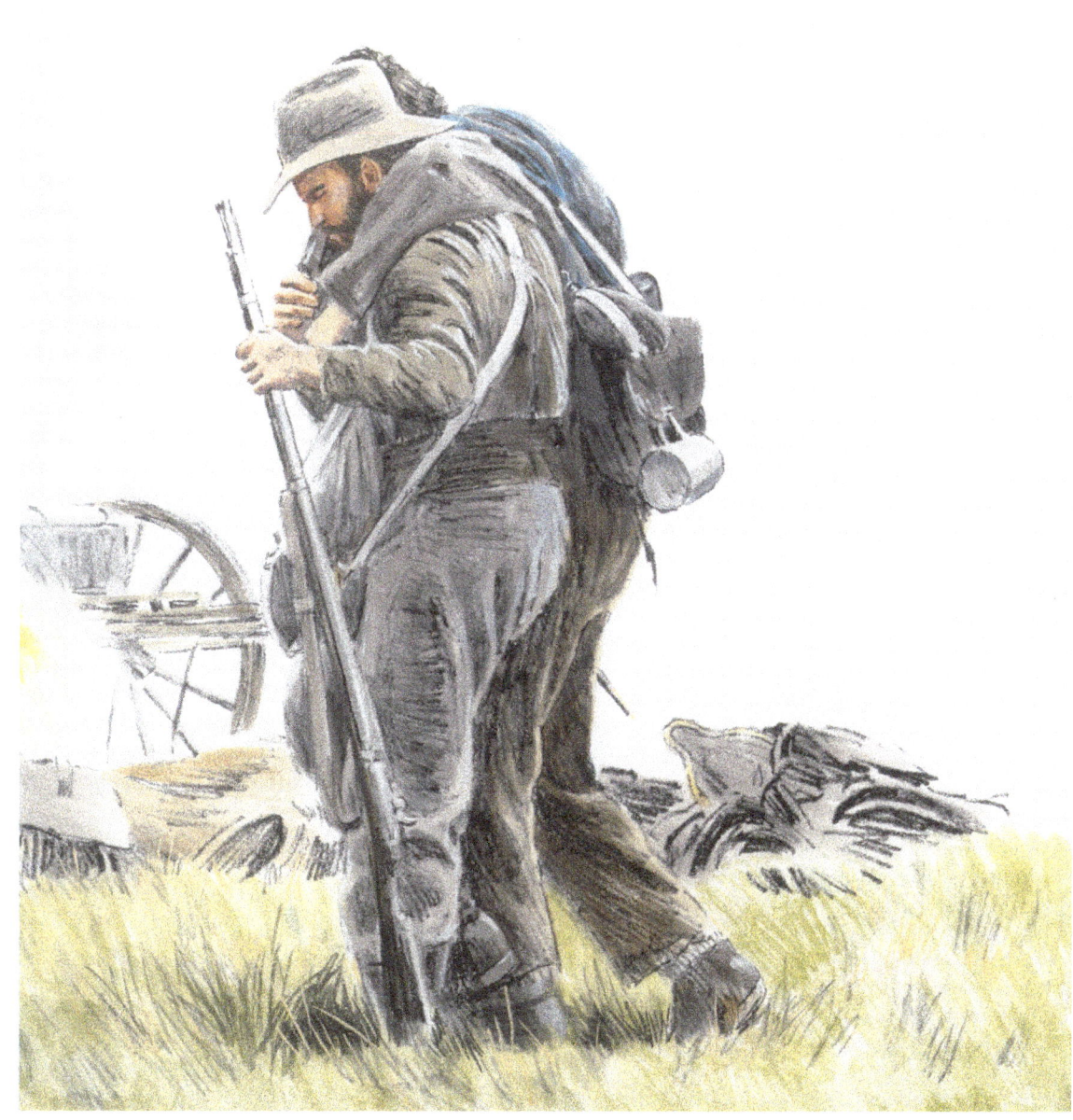

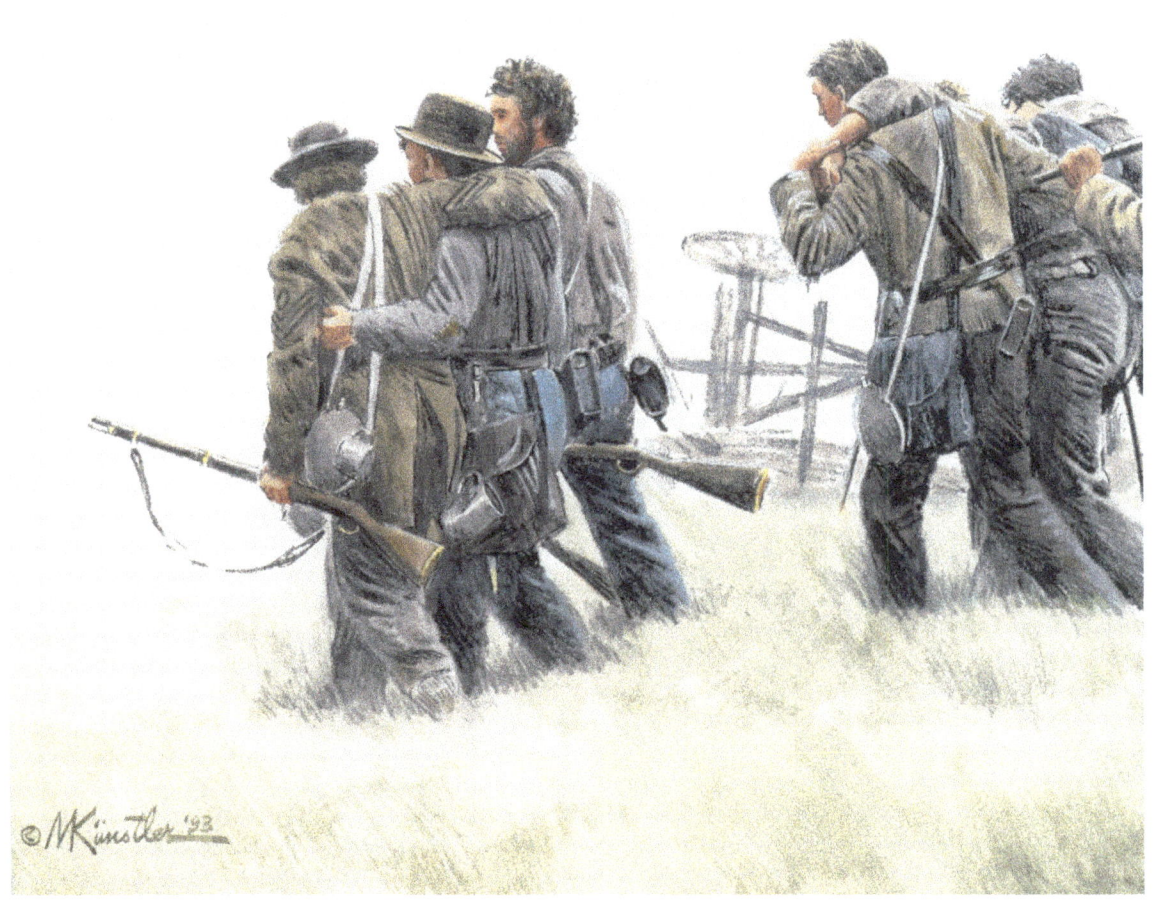

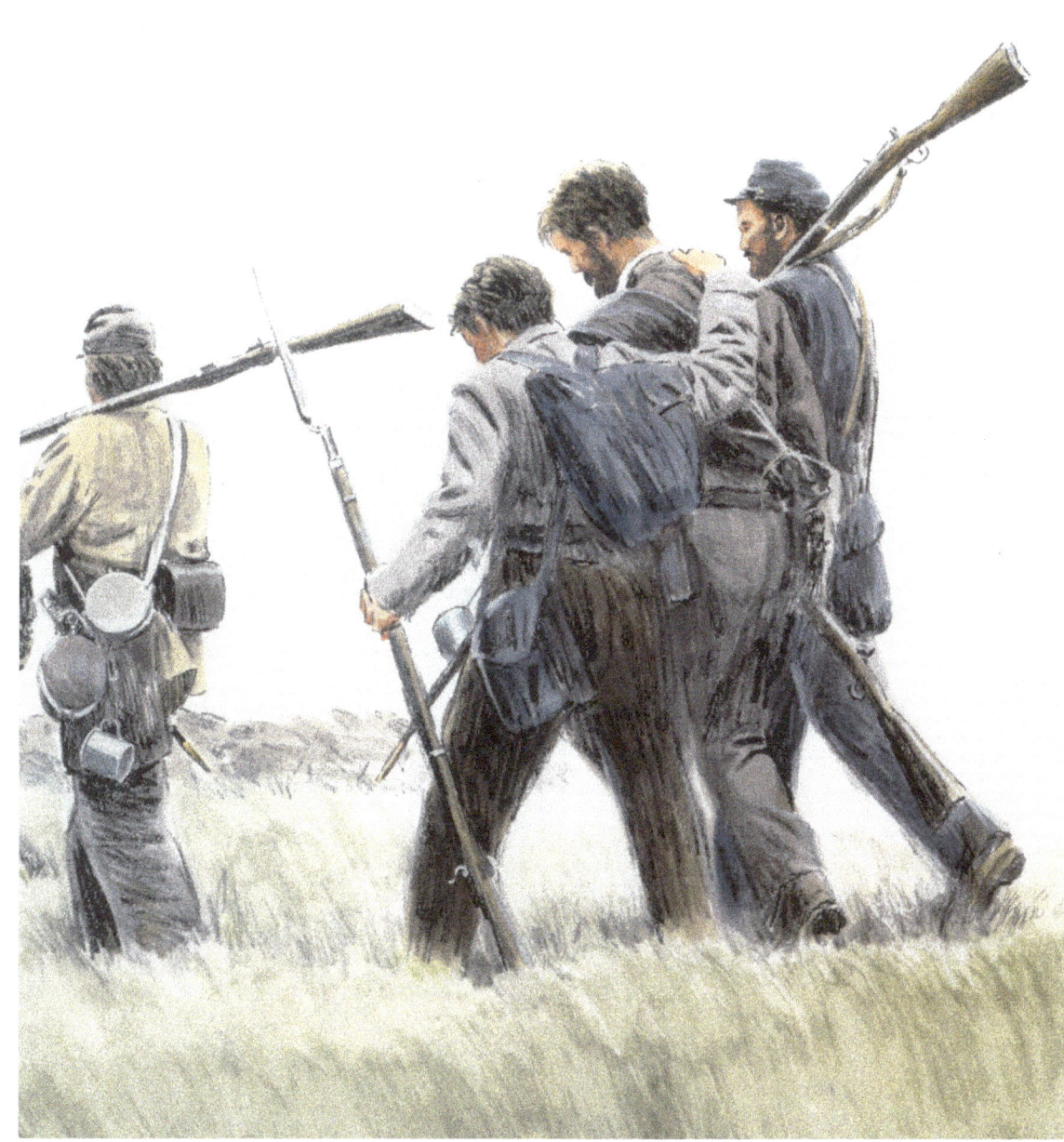

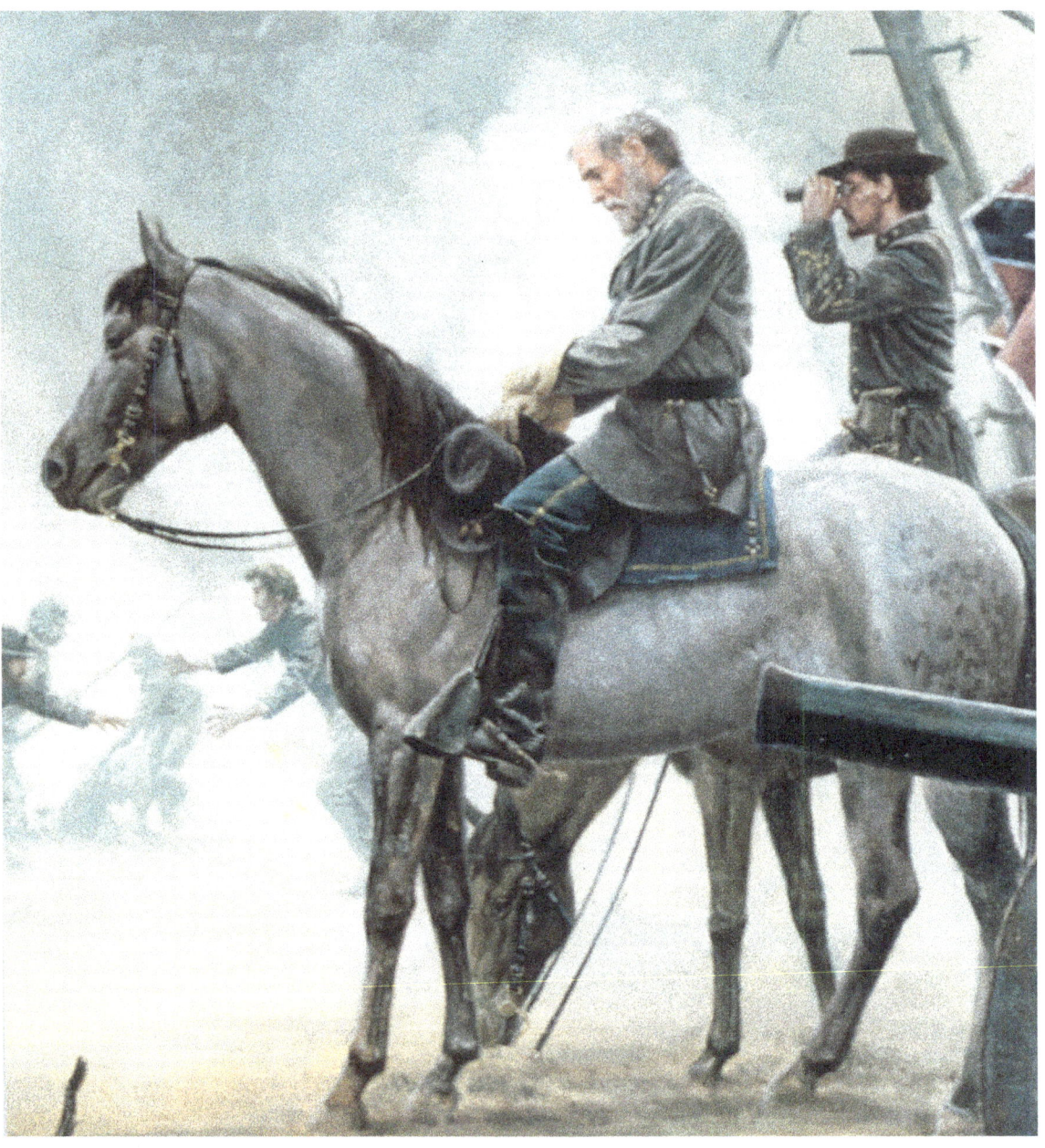

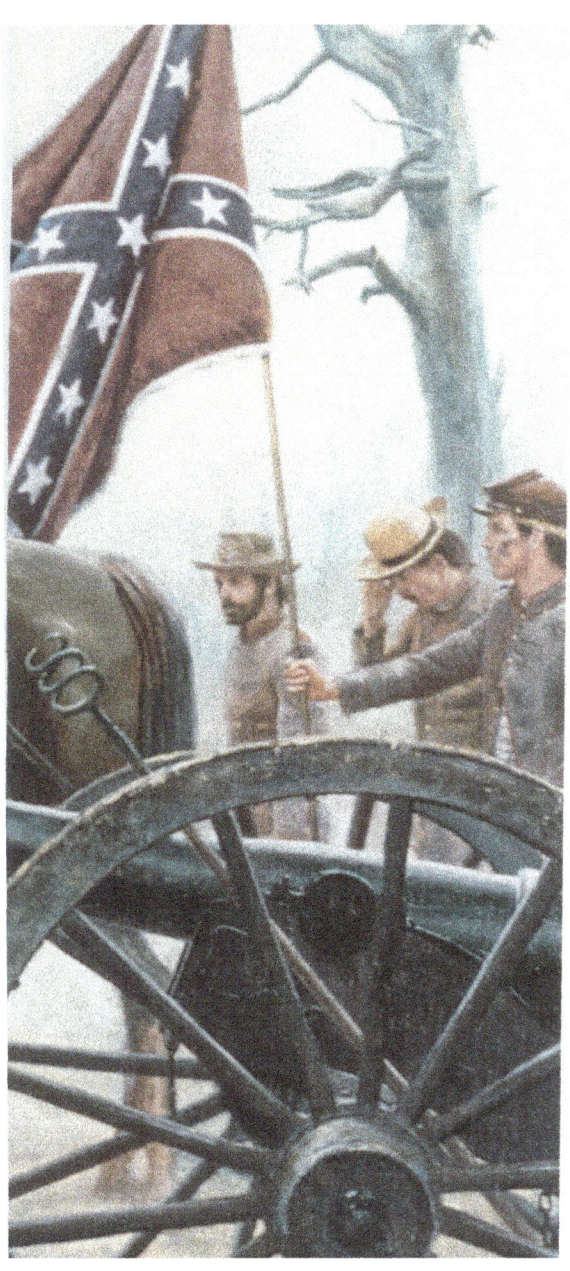

"IT'S ALL MY FAULT"

GEN. ROBERT E. LEE, GETTYSBURG

JULY 3, 1863

1989, oil, 26 x 48

THIS PAINTING WAS A logical sequel for my first Gettysburg painting, *The High Water Mark*. The Confederates, after their repulse, straggled back to their lines, where Robert E. Lee met them. The casualties were enormous, and the pathos and tragedy of that moment are what I have tried to portray in this painting.

Lee and his aide, Lt. Col. Charles Marshall, rode out to the first line of artillery. Here he spoke to them and blamed himself for the defeat.

The artillery piece in the right foreground of the painting is a 10-pound

223

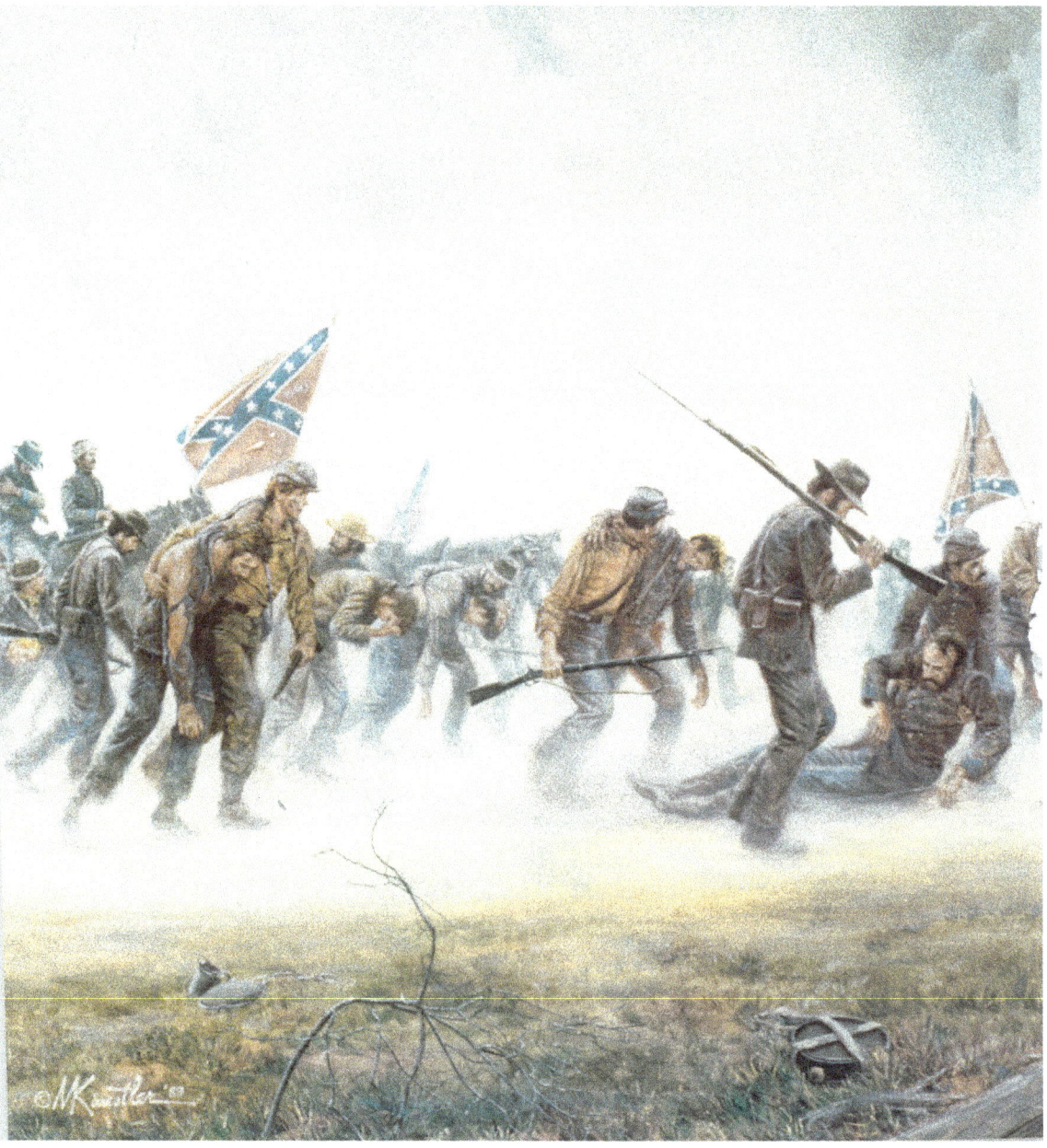

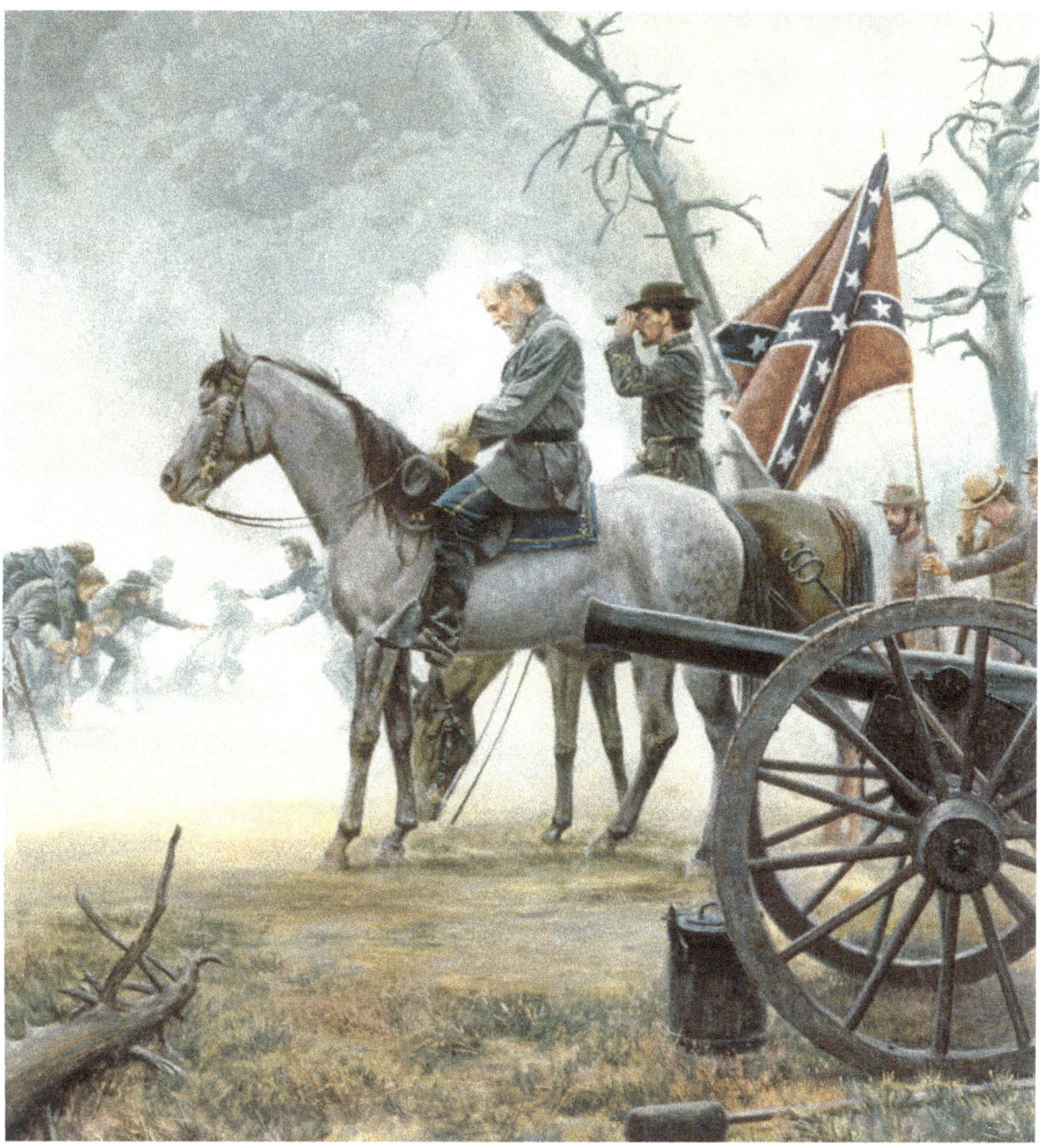

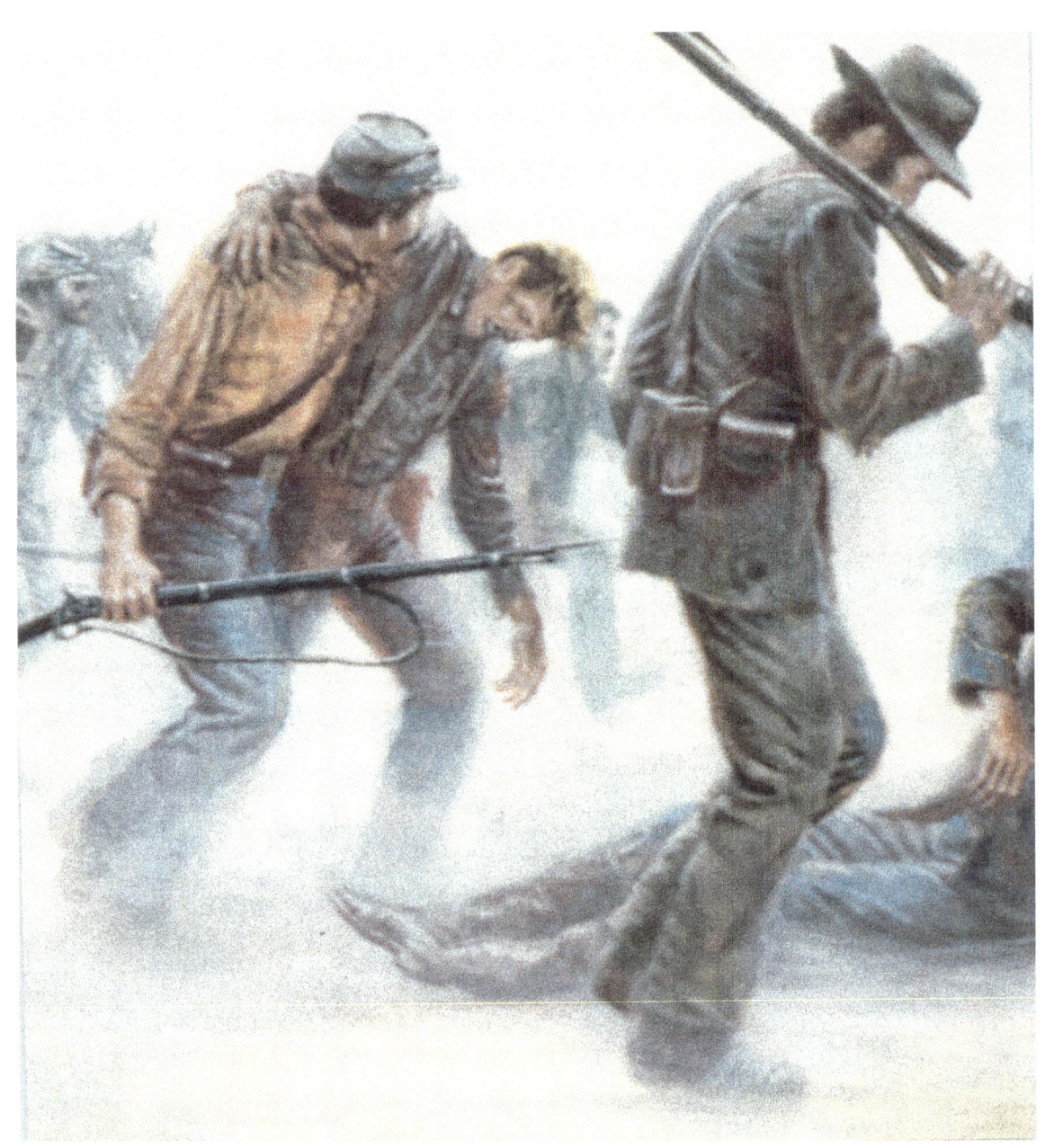

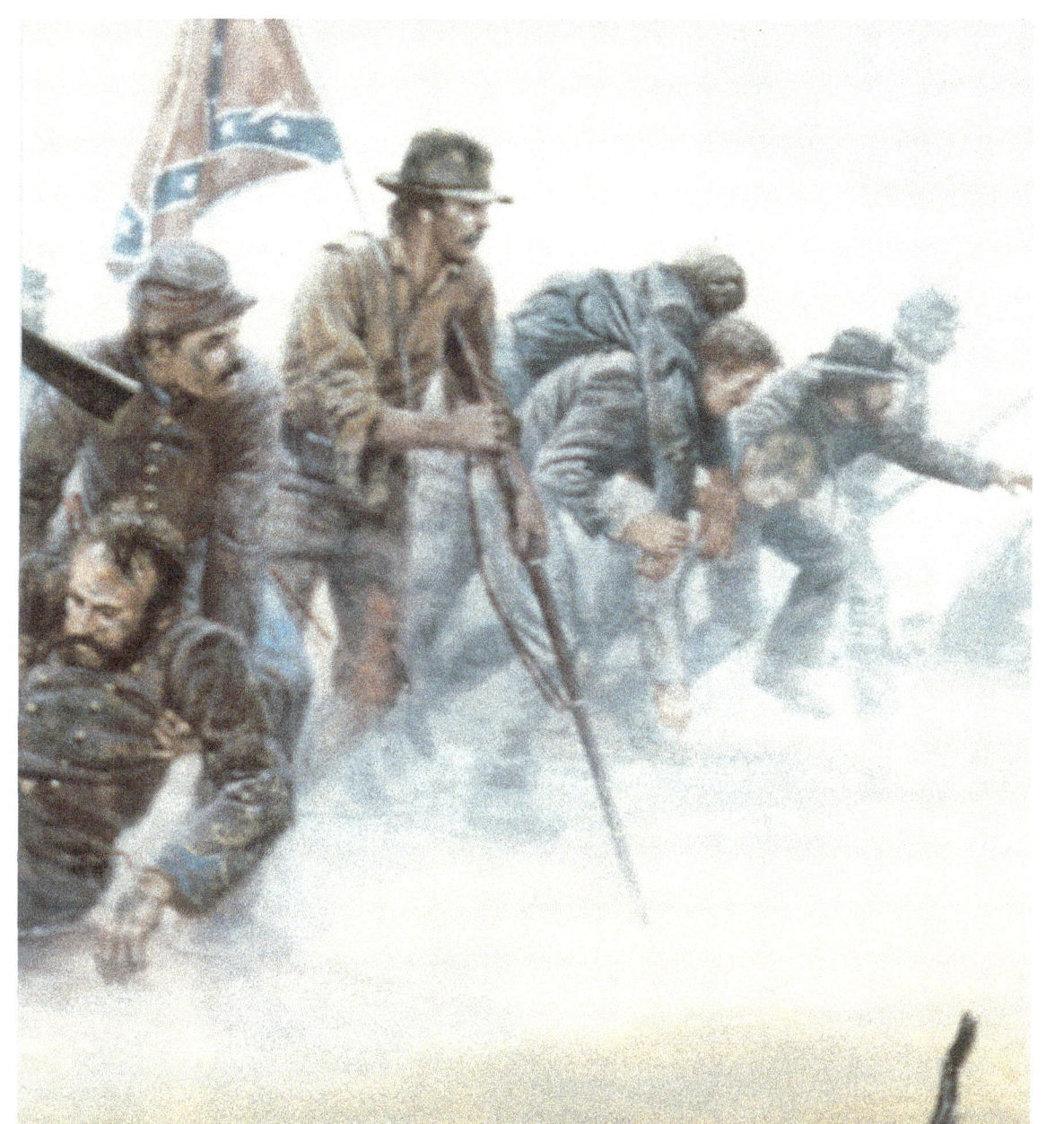

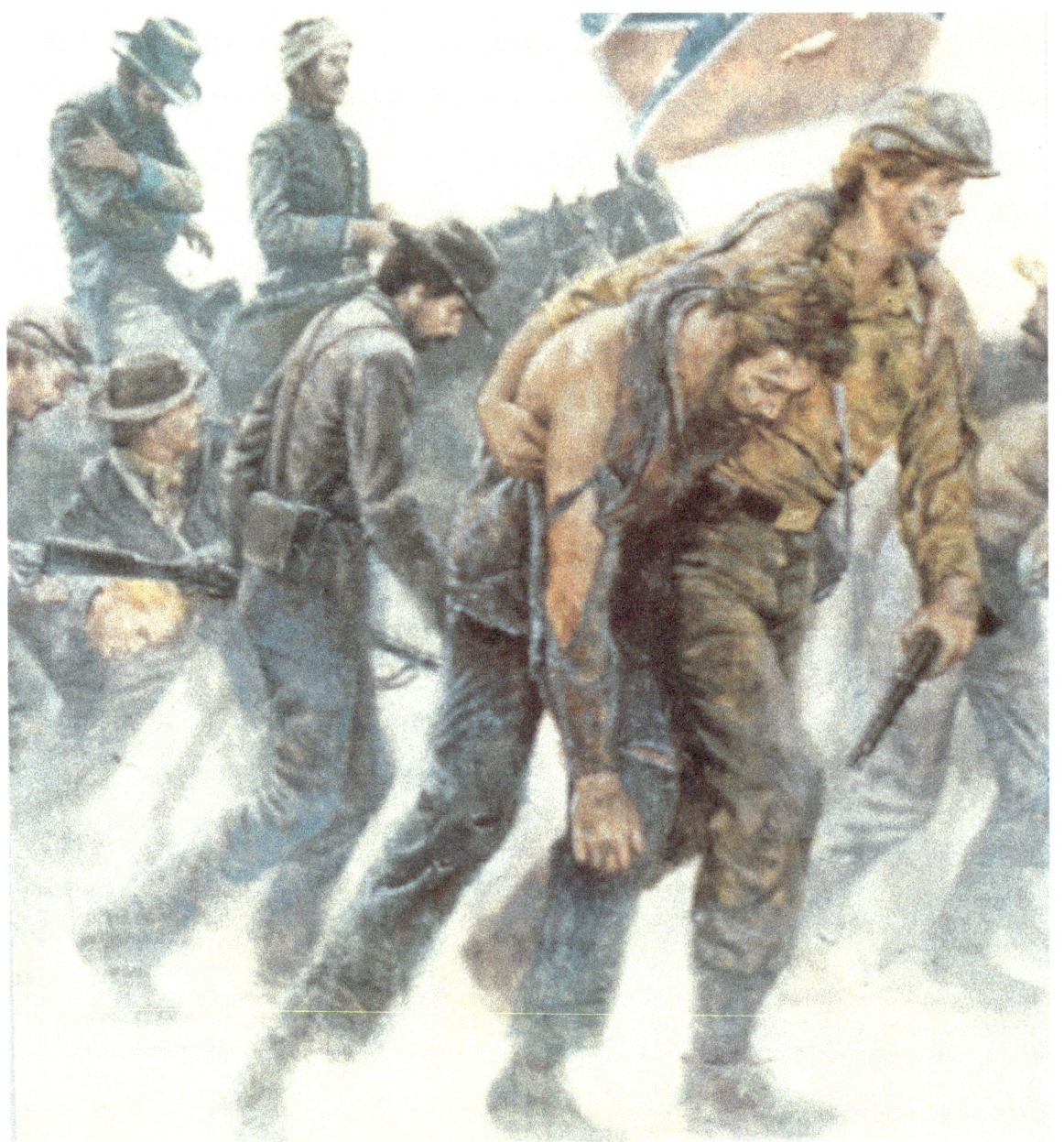

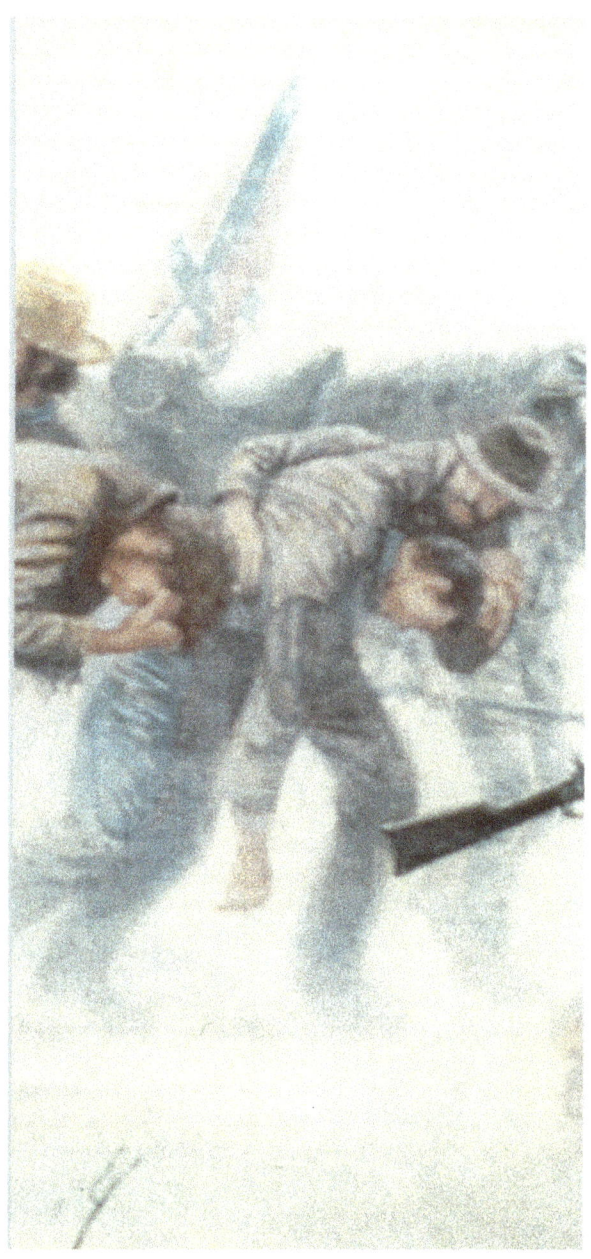

Parrott and can be found today at that location on the battlefield.

I learned that Lee did not have his sword but did wear a sword belt. The rest of his uniform, as well as that of Marshall's, is based on information I found at Gettysburg and in contemporary accounts.

The time was approximately 4:00 p.m. The sunlight is indirect because of an incoming storm. The air is cloudy with smoke from a fire at the Spangler barn, which had been burning all day, and the dust kicked up by the men with horses. The wind was from the west, or right of the painting.

In the background, on the left, are two mounted officers, both wounded. There were maybe six mounted officers in the original assault, and one of the riderless horses is seen farther to the center of the background. A Virginia regiment's flag is prominent among the few battle flags that were not captured.

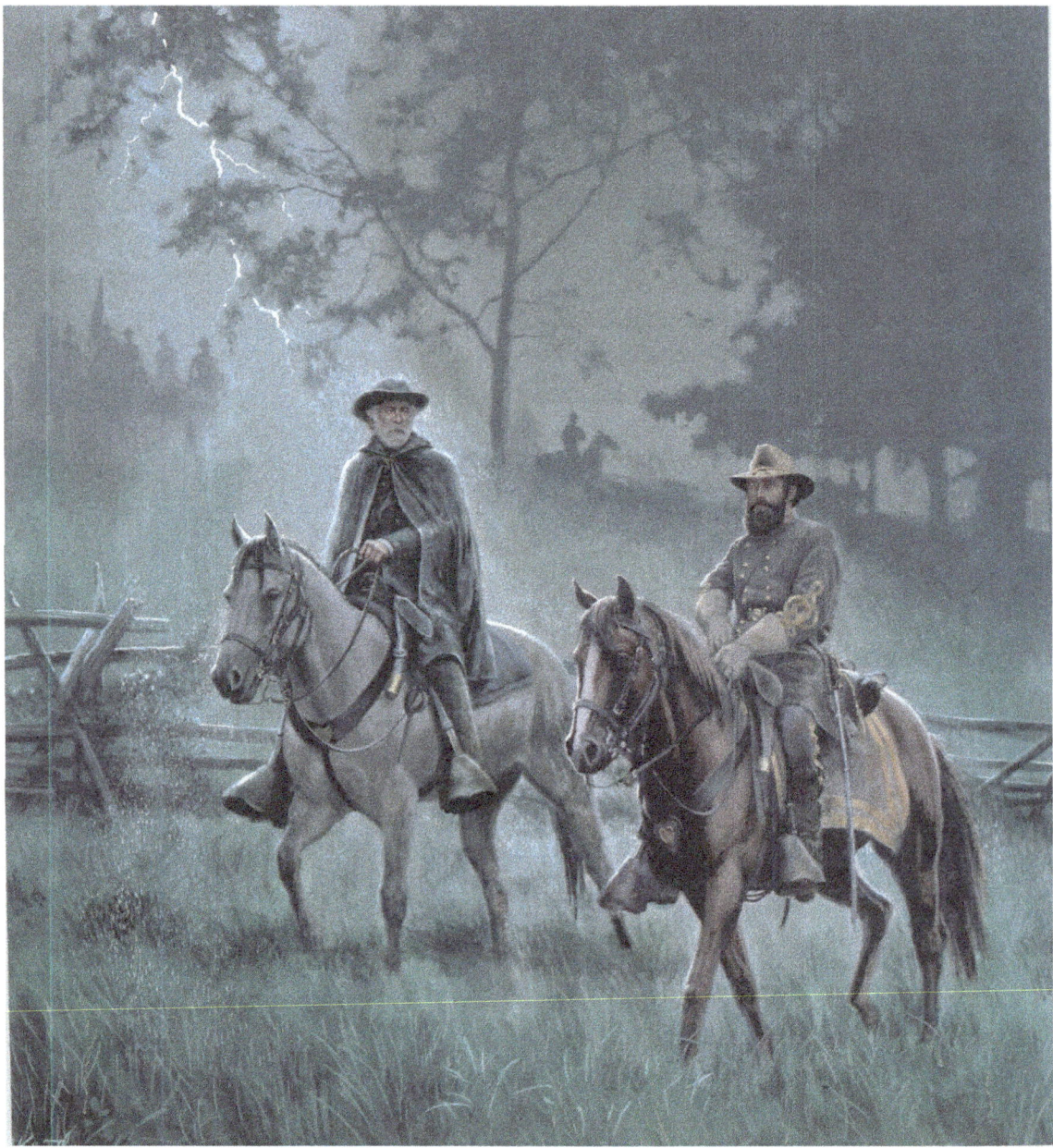

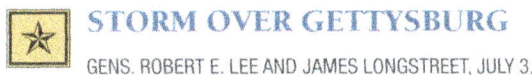

STORM OVER GETTYSBURG

GENS. ROBERT E. LEE AND JAMES LONGSTREET, JULY 3, 1863

1993, gouache, 14½ x 12½

I'VE PAINTED MANY DRAMATIC nighttime events at Gettysburg, but none kindles my imagination more than the brief ride Lee and Longstreet made together on the night of July 3. Hours earlier, the two generals had witnessed the courage and tragedy of Pickett's Charge as it unfolded and devastated the heart of the Confederate army. That night, a ferocious thunderstorm rolled through the area. *Storm over Gettysburg* captures that dramatic moment as the two generals ride together through the storm, discussing the army's next move. Should they stay and fight, hoping somehow to win? Should they wait for a Northern counterattack? Should they retreat?

Meeting later that night with his generals at A. P. Hill's headquarters, Lee announced that the army would return to Virginia as soon as possible, if for no other reason than a lack of ammunition.

In this painting, Lee and Longstreet are backlit by a distant bolt of lightning. Although it's challenging to paint, lightning and its unique appearance are naturally dramatic. The power and drama of the storm underscore the solemnity of the moment.

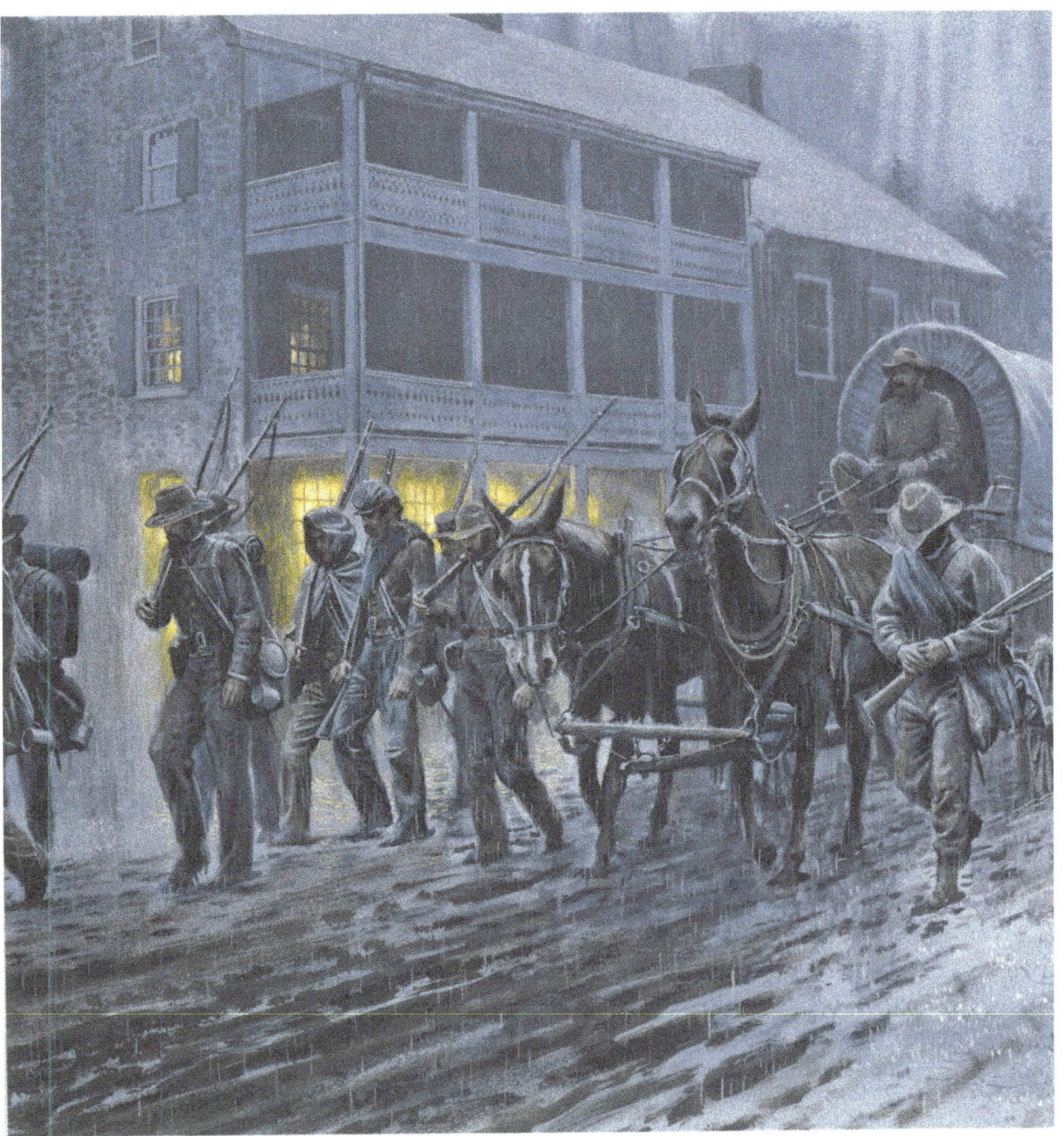

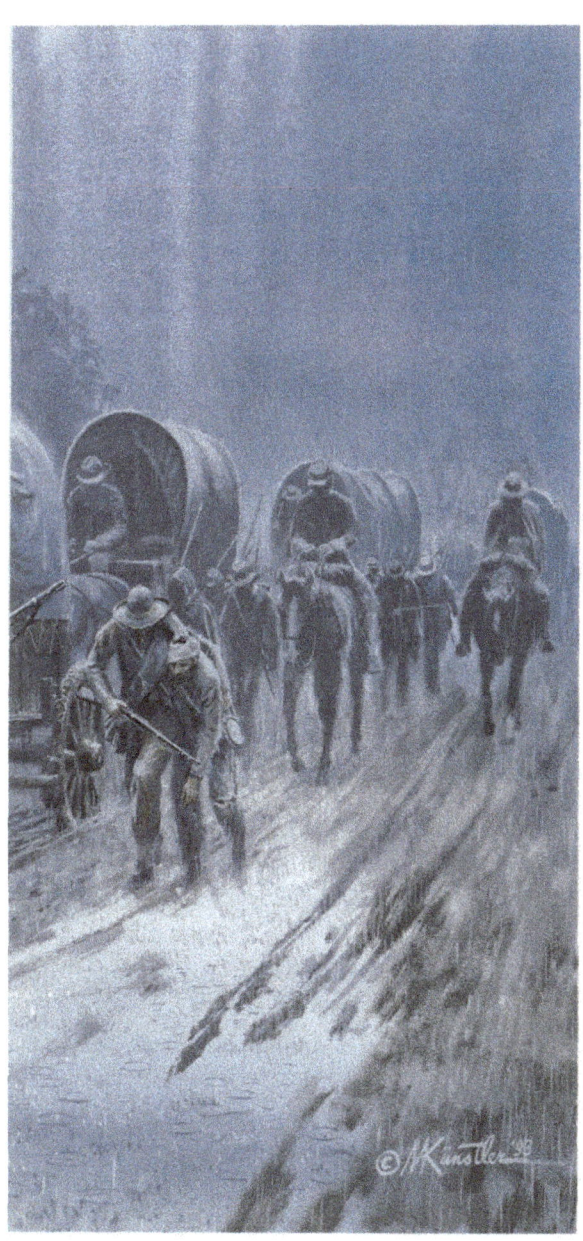

 ## THE LONG ROAD SOUTH

FAIRFIELD, PENNSYLVANIA
JULY 4, 1863

1993, gouache, 11¼ x 17⅞

WHEN THE EXPECTED UNION counterattack did not happen, the next day the Confederates began to evacuate their wounded. The ambulance train, stretching seventeen miles long, jolted and jerked over rain-rutted roads, causing great agony for the thousands of wounded men the Army of Northern Virginia managed to bring back with them. More than four thousand men too badly wounded to move were left behind. Buried were the Confederacy's hopes for victory and the South's quest for independence. Lee's retreat to Virginia marked the biggest turning point of the war.

233

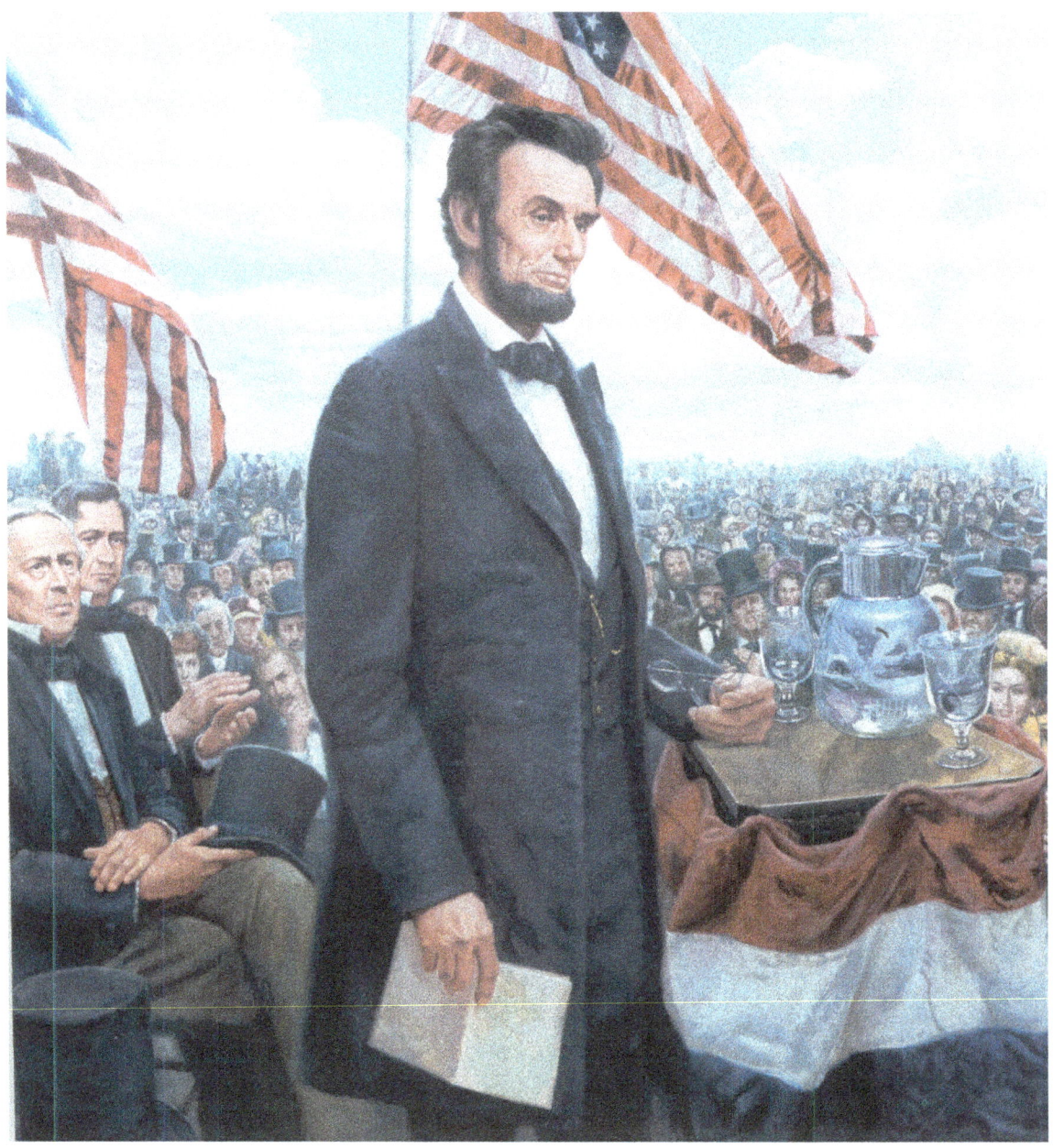

THE GETTYSBURG ADDRESS

NOVEMBER 19, 1863

1987, oil, 30 x 30

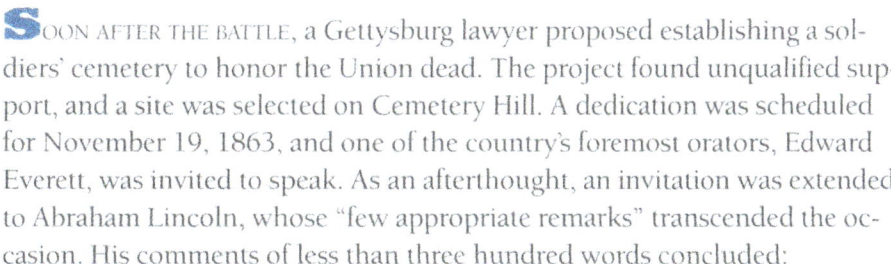

SOON AFTER THE BATTLE, a Gettysburg lawyer proposed establishing a soldiers' cemetery to honor the Union dead. The project found unqualified support, and a site was selected on Cemetery Hill. A dedication was scheduled for November 19, 1863, and one of the country's foremost orators, Edward Everett, was invited to speak. As an afterthought, an invitation was extended to Abraham Lincoln, whose "few appropriate remarks" transcended the occasion. His comments of less than three hundred words concluded:

The world will little note, nor long remember what we say here, but it can never forget what they did here. It is for us the living, rather, to be dedicated here to the unfinished work which they who fought here have thus far so nobly advanced. It is rather for us to be here dedicated to the great task remaining before us—that from these honored dead we take increased devotion to that cause for which they gave the last full measure of devotion—that we here highly resolve that these dead shall not have died in vain—that this nation, under God, shall have a new birth of freedom—and that government of the people, by the people, for the people, shall not perish from the earth.

235

ONE-MAN EXHIBITIONS

1977

Daytona Beach Museum of Arts and Sciences,
 Daytona Beach, FL
Hammer Galleries, New York, NY

1978

Old Orchard Museum, Sagamore Hill National
 Historic Site, Oyster Bay, NY

1979

Hammer Galleries, New York, NY
U.S. Navy Memorial Museum, Washington, DC

1981

Hammer Galleries, New York, NY
Pittsburgh Center for the Arts, Pittsburgh, PA

1982

Hammer Galleries, New York, NY
Hillwood Gallery, C. W. Post Campus, Long
 Island University, Greenvale, NY
U.S. Navy Memorial Museum, Washington, DC

1983

Saks Galleries, Denver, CO

1984

Old Orchard Museum, Sagamore Hill National
 Historic Site, Oyster Bay, NY

1985

Hammer Galleries, New York, NY

1986

Hammer Galleries, New York, NY
Washington County Museum of Fine Arts,
 Hagerstown, MD

1987

Conacher Galleries, San Francisco, CA

1989

Museum of Westward Expansion, Jefferson
 National Expansion Memorial, St. Louis, MO
Hammer Galleries, New York, NY

1991

Dunnegan Gallery of Art, Bolivar, MO

1992

Gettysburg National Military Park, Gettysburg, PA
Hall of Valor Museum, New Market, VA
Hammer Galleries, New York, NY

1993

Gettysburg National Military Park, Gettysburg, PA
Hammer Galleries, New York, NY

1994

Shenandoah University, Winchester, VA

1995

Hammer Galleries, New York, NY
North Carolina Museum of History, Raleigh, NC

1998

Nassau County Museum of Art, Roslyn Harbor, NY
Hammer Galleries, New York, NY

1999

Leon Loard Gallery, Montgomery, AL

2000

Museum of the Confederacy, Richmond, VA
Hammer Galleries, New York, NY

2002

The National Civil War Museum, Harrisburg, PA

2003

Hammer Galleries, New York, NY

2004

Hammer Galleries, New York, NY

2005

Booth Western Art Museum, Cartersville, GA

2006

Nassau County Museum of Art, Roslyn Harbor, NY
Hammer Galleries, New York, NY

ART INDEX

ACKNOWLEDGMENTS

Special thanks:

to Ron Pitkin and Ed Curtis of Cumberland House for their expertise. It has been a pleasure to work with them on this project.

To William C. Davis, renowned author-historian, for his enlightening and wonderfully written foreword.

to Dr. James I. Robertson Jr., the distinguished author-historian, for sharing his wealth of knowledge over the years, as well as being a valued friend.

to Rod Gragg, author-historian, for his advice, expertise, and most important, his friendship over the years.

to Richard Lynch, president of Hammer Galleries in New York City, for more than thirty years of guidance and friendship. Thanks also to Howard Shaw, vice president, and the rest of the staff at Hammer Galleries for all their efforts on my behalf.

to Chris Brooks of American Spirit Publishing, the exclusive publisher of my limited-edition fine-art prints, for his professional guidance and friendship.

to Paula McEvoy and Lissette Portillo of Künstler Enterprises for their dedication in managing the daily operations of a busy studio, as well as their assistance on this volume.

to my daughter, Jane Künstler Broffman, who as project manager spent an extraordinary amount of time and effort in the compilation of this book. Her knowledge and creative input was very much appreciated—I could not have done it without her.

to my wife, Deborah, for her winsome ways, wise counsel, exceptional patience—and for being the love of my life.

—Mort Künstler

www.ingramcontent.com/pod-product-compliance
Lightning Source LLC
Chambersburg PA
CBHW052133170526
45162CB00003B/12